Flyfisher's Guide to

Oregon™

John Huber

Gallatin Gateway, Montana

Published by Wilderness Adventures Press
P.O. Box 627
Gallatin Gateway, MT 59730
800-925-3339
Website: www.wildadv.com
email: books@wildadv.com

10 9 8 7 6 5 4 3 2 1

Printed in the United States of America

Library of Congress Cataloging-in-Publication Data

Huber, John, 1967–
Flyfisher's guide to Oregon / John Huber.
p. cm.
Includes index.
ISBN 1–885106–38–6
1. Fly fishing–Oregon–Guidebooks. 2. Oregon–Guidebooks. I. Title.
SH539.H826 1999
799.1'24'09795––dc21 98–50957
CIP

For my father, Charles, who has taken me onto Oregon's waters my whole life in pursuit of fish.

For my mother, Connie, who has gotten me to this point healthy and happy, and for my three sisters, Cathy, Laura, and Jane, whom I adore.

Table of Contents

Acknowledgments

Where does one begin when it comes to saying thank you? I will start with Wilderness Adventure Press, the publishing company that has given me the opportunity to write this book. I came into the project with a lot more time behind a fly rod than a word processor. I hope I did well—they took a big chance with me.

The amount of support I received from Oregon's fly shops and guides was incredible. Oregon is blessed with some of the finest flyfishers in the world. I would really like to thank Ken Morrish, Bob Gaviglio, Jeff Perrin, Travis Duddles, Chris Daughters, Bernie Babcock, and Milton Fisher. Without these people, there is no way that this book could have been written. Other people who were extremely helpful to me include Denny Rickerts, Judy Carothers, Tom Anderburg, Mark Stensland, Mark Bachmann, Merle Hummer, Bob Quigley, Skip Levesque, Bill Nelson, and Rick Coxen. Each of these people put me through my paces on their favorite waters.

I want to thank Winston rods for the many loaners I used while traveling about Oregon. Also, Jerry Garcia for the music on those long drives and Joseph Campbell for the reading material. There are many anglers I met and fished with on my journeys in Oregon during the past few years who were also helpful to me. I don't remember all their names, but I do remember our conversations about flies and fish and am thankful to have met all of them.

I would also like to thank my closest friends and fishing partners who have taught me that yes, contrary to what I often believe, there are more important things in life than flyfishing. I hope I have left no one out: Eric Lyon, Mike Witthar, Clark Shafer, Scott Schnebly, Greg Thomas, Mike Bordenkircher, Sara Merrill, Brian Gefroh, Steve Hagel, Hanley Dawson, Brooke Williams, and Jeff Schizas.

Finally, I am grateful for the water, the fish, the insects, and the whole perfect cycle that continues despite what happens in our individual worlds. Without fail, flyfishing is always available to anyone willing to look the fool while searching for a moment of grace.

The best anglers' longest, most delicate casts, come from an inner calm—a place achieved, not taught. It has been said before—there is no replacement for time on the water.

Preface

The fact that this book was written is due to the fact that Wilderness Adventure Press recognized a need for a well formatted series of guidebooks specifically for flyfishers that covered all the Northwest states. Greg Thomas and Chuck Johnson presented me with an opportunity to learn as much about the state of Oregon as I reasonably could within a time frame and present it as the *Flyfishers Guide to Oregon.*

I have worked as a guide for many years and grew up romping around Oregon with my family. This included much fishing with my father. When I told my father someone was willing to pay me to go fish and write, he simply responded, "Now you have two jobs where someone is paying you for flyfishing."

I have no complaints really, I am not the greatest flyfisher in the Northwest, but I love to catch fish and writing doesn't seem terribly hard for me. So I agreed to the project, got in the car and went fishing. There are certainly more knowledgeable anglers in Oregon than me, but I guess I had more time. Regardless, I wrote what I feel is an unbiased overview of casting flies in Oregon.

Follow your bliss is an easy call to answer for serious fish-heads. Most of the names in this book are very serious fish-heads who are only traceable in the off-season. They are some of the best flyfishers in Oregon and the ones who provided the information in this book. I made them endure my questions—the same ones they get asked every day, with the promise that I was doing the best book I could for Oregon flyfishers. Some days we sat inside and drank coffee while the snow flew; other days we interviewed while sticking fish on gorgeous blue-sky days. The fact is, you're in good hands in Oregon.

Most of the photos in this book are mine, but the good ones are by Ken Morrish, who also provided the beautiful cover. Nothing though, is as beautiful as being out in Oregon. Rain or shine, the beauty of Oregon is unique and unmatched.

The world of flyfishing is a small one in many ways, yet there is no summit to the sport, no one correct way or ultimate fishery. The more you know and learn the bigger the horizon seems to become in this sport. To a certain extent in flyfishing, we are all amateurs in one facet or another and I hope we all remember this on those crowded days on the river when we are at wits end. Flyfishing will always have teachers and pupils, whether it be two anglers, or angler and fish. With this book I have tried to teach a little about flyfishing, and doing it in Oregon, without saying which rock to stand on. This is a fishing guide, not a net. Go see Oregon, try all these waters I've listed and find a few I couldn't. There is a lifetime of opportunity for flyfishers in Oregon.

John Huber

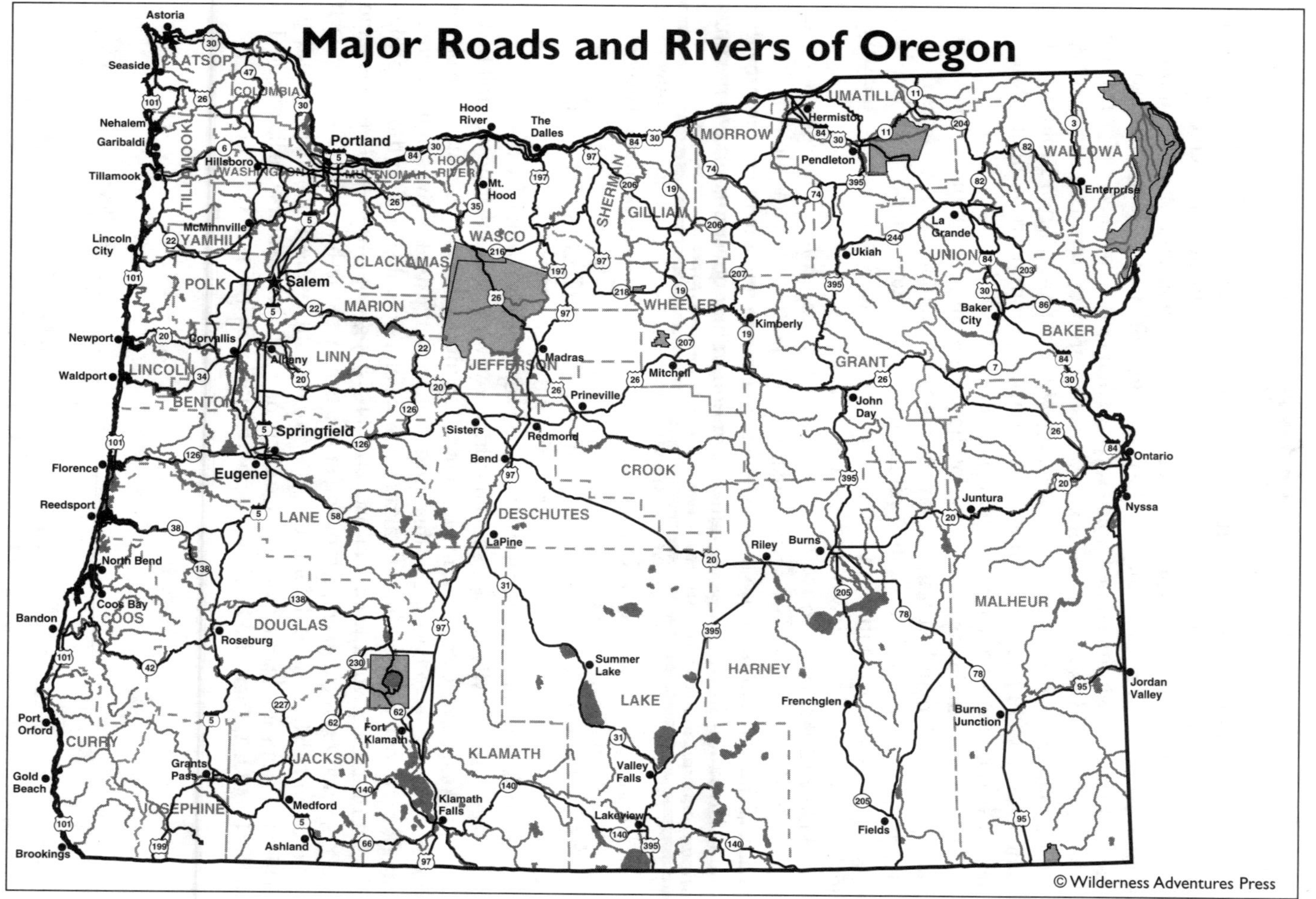
Major Roads and Rivers of Oregon
Astoria
Seaside
Nehalem
Garibaldi
Tillamook
Lincoln City
Newport
Waldport
Florence
Reedsport
North Bend
Coos Bay
Bandon
Port Orford
Gold Beach
Brookings
Portland
Hillsboro
McMinnville
Salem
Albany
Corvallis
Springfield
Eugene
Roseburg
Grants Pass
Medford
Ashland
Fort Klamath
Klamath Falls
Hood River
The Dalles
Mt. Hood
Madras
Prineville
Redmond
Sisters
Bend
LaPine
Summer Lake
Valley Falls
Lakeview
Mitchell
Kimberly
John Day
Riley
Burns
Frenchglen
Fields
Hermiston
Pendleton
Ukiah
La Grande
Enterprise
Baker City
Ontario
Nyssa
Juntura
Burns Junction
Jordan Valley
CLATSOP
COLUMBIA
TILLAMOOK
WASHINGTON
MULTNOMAH
YAMHILL
POLK
LINCOLN
BENTON
MARION
LINN
CLACKAMAS
HOOD RIVER
WASCO
SHERMAN
GILLIAM
MORROW
UMATILLA
UNION
WALLOWA
BAKER
GRANT
WHEELER
JEFFERSON
CROOK
DESCHUTES
LANE
DOUGLAS
COOS
CURRY
JOSEPHINE
JACKSON
KLAMATH
LAKE
HARNEY
MALHEUR
© Wilderness Adventures Press

Oregon Facts

Tenth largest state in the union
96,002 square miles

Elevations: Mt. Hood–11,239; Pacific Ocean–sea level
Counties: 67
Population (1997 est.): 3,243,487

- 7 Indian Reservations
- 1 National Park
- 1 National Historical Park
- 3 National Monuments
- 13 National Forests
- 2 National Recreation Areas
- 21 National Wildlife Refuges
- 36 Wilderness Areas
- 240 State Parks

Nickname: Beaver State
Primary Industries: Aerospace, forestry, agriculture, biotechnology, environmental technology, fisheries, film and video
Capital: Salem
Bird: Western meadowlark
Fish: Chinook salmon
Animal: Beaver
Flower: Oregon grape
Tree: Douglas fir

Tips on Using This Book

The Chambers of Commerce in each of the cities provided the hub city information. Every Chamber I called on was outstanding in providing this information. They should be contacted if you want very specific details. If anyone doubts the friendliness of Oregonians, travel the state alone with no agenda. What a great place.

Wilderness Adventures Press produced the maps with help from me and the people in this book. There are many remote places in Oregon that require detailed road maps. These can be obtained from the Forest Service and in well stocked outdoor and book stores. Use the book maps as an overview for the area when exploring Oregon.

The most important thing I want to stress in using this book is safety on the water. There are many boating opportunities in Oregon, but not everyone is capable of rowing the majority of Oregon's rivers. If you have the slightest doubt about your skills, don't try it. Use a licensed guide so that you can enjoy the floating opportunities without major safety concerns. Floaters with expert skills but who are new to any or all of Oregon's waters should obtain a guidebook for the waters they have chosen to float. Good bookstores and fly shops carry river guides. Before your trip, call local shops and obtain these so that you have time to study them before going on the water.

For anglers who choose to wade or tube in Oregon's waters: practice safety! No fish is worth dying for, and when you can fish with a partner, do so. Always fish with a partner when float tubing.

This guidebook is intended to get an angler off on the right foot on individual waters as well as present the various opportunities awaiting a traveling fly angler. Each section of the state is well worth any fly angler's attention. I divided the state in an unusual format but tried mostly to break it down into geographic sections—keeping the desert separate from the high desert, etc.

Motel cost key: $—less than $30 per night
$$—between $30 and $50 per night
$$$—$50 a night and up

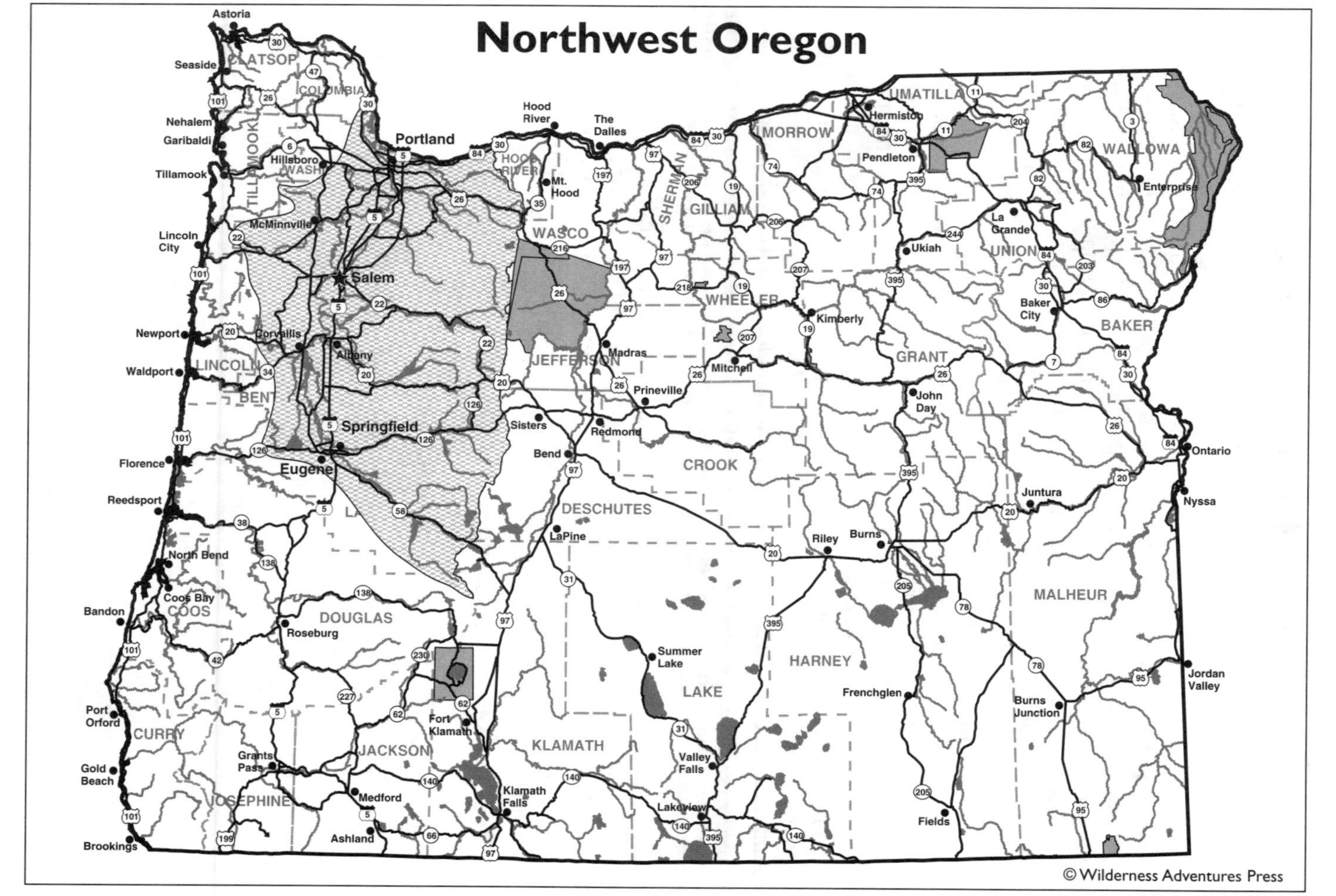
Northwest Oregon
Astoria
Seaside
Nehalem
Garibaldi
Tillamook
Lincoln City
Newport
Waldport
Florence
Reedsport
North Bend
Coos Bay
Bandon
Port Orford
Gold Beach
Brookings
Portland
Hillsboro
McMinnville
Salem
Corvallis
Albany
Springfield
Eugene
Roseburg
Grants Pass
Medford
Ashland
Hood River
The Dalles
Mt. Hood
Madras
Prineville
Redmond
Sisters
Bend
LaPine
Fort Klamath
Klamath Falls
Summer Lake
Valley Falls
Lakeview
Mitchell
Kimberly
John Day
Hermiston
Pendleton
Ukiah
La Grande
Baker City
Enterprise
Ontario
Nyssa
Juntura
Riley
Burns
Frenchglen
Fields
Burns Junction
Jordan Valley
CLATSOP
COLUMBIA
TILLAMOOK
WASH
LINCOLN
BENT
HOOD RIVER
WASCO
SHERMAN
GILLIAM
MORROW
UMATILLA
WALLOWA
UNION
BAKER
WHEELER
JEFFERSON
GRANT
CROOK
DESCHUTES
MALHEUR
HARNEY
LAKE
KLAMATH
DOUGLAS
COOS
CURRY
JACKSON
JOSEPHINE
© Wilderness Adventures Press

Northwest Oregon

Fly anglers in northwest Oregon are at the mercy of Mother Nature, which may keep anglers in check in Oregon's most populous region. Fishing windows are often short if you want warm sunny days. Those kinds of days are found more easily east of the Cascades.

The rains swell northwest Oregon's coastal rivers, enticing steelhead to enter and move upstream. The trout are left to sulk and grow bigger as swollen rivers prevent floaters and fly casters from getting on the water.

Fly anglers in this part of the state learn quickly to take the good with the bad. The nicest days in Oregon are 10 times nicer than the nicest day anywhere else. When curtains of rain finally let the sun shine, we are reminded of what this rain produces. Green is the dominant color, reflecting onto the rivers and lakes and making them appear greener than they really are. The air is aromatic with rich plant life. The light reflecting off a fly-caught fish that has been in these dark waters long enough to give an account of itself after being hooked is both mesmerizing and intoxicating. Bright sunny days on these northwest Oregon rivers and lakes are inspiring, and two of them in a row is practically a flyfisher's heaven.

But for most of the fly angling year, wavers of the long rod put their hoods on and maybe some fingerless gloves, and fish despite the weather. I've done my share of rainy-day fishing—sometimes it has paid off with great fishing, and other times, I've just gotten wet. Either way, it is just good to be fishing no matter what the conditions.

The rain gives fish a chance at survival in northwest Oregon, but always remember that this is the most heavily populated part of the state and is continuing to grow. Make every effort to keep wild fish in the rivers and lakes and tread lightly on the land.

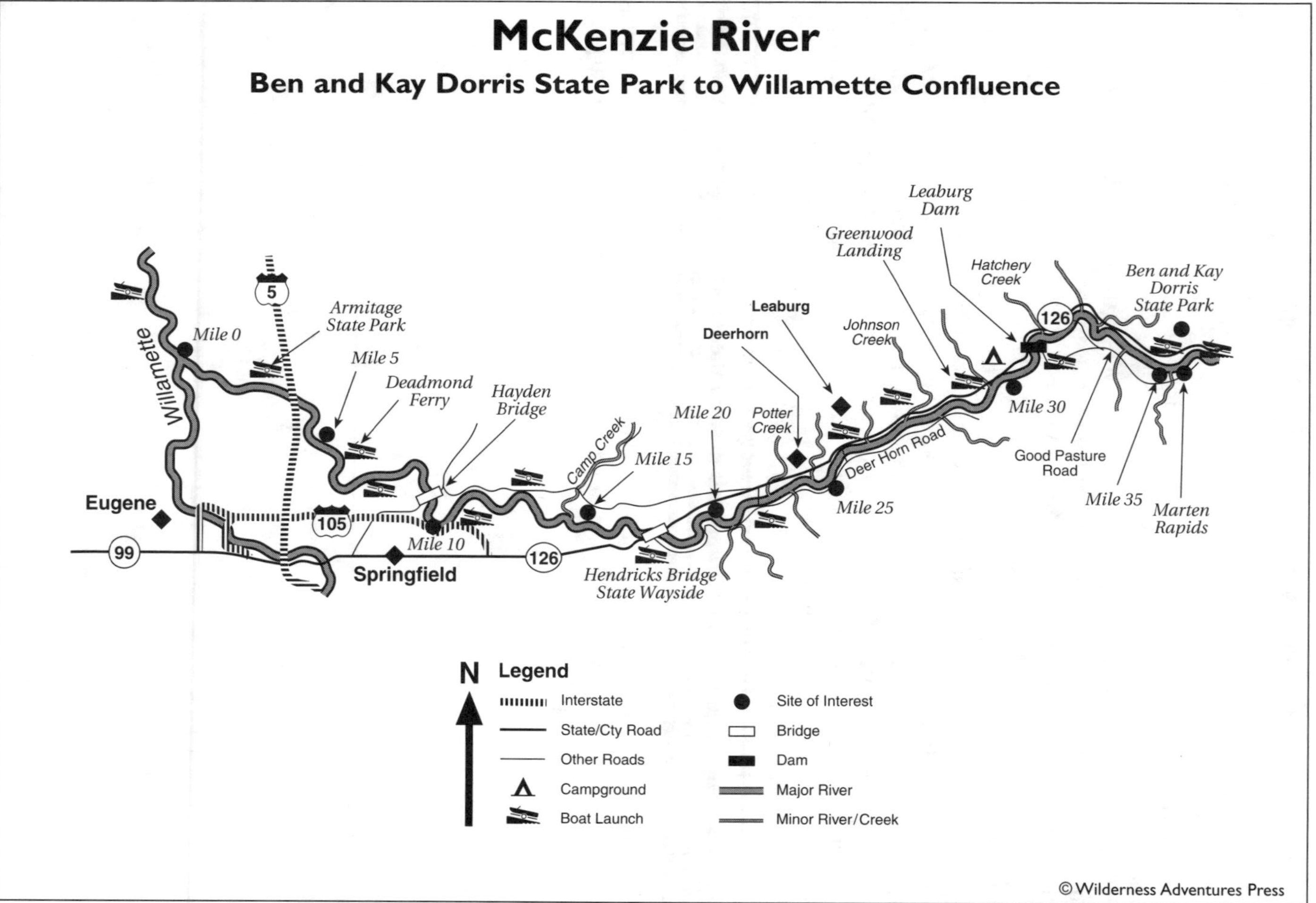
McKenzie River
Ben and Kay Dorris State Park to Willamette Confluence
Leaburg Dam
Greenwood Landing
Hatchery Creek
Ben and Kay Dorris State Park
126
Leaburg
Deerhorn
Johnson Creek
5
Armitage State Park
Mile 0
Willamette
Mile 5
Deadmond Ferry
Hayden Bridge
Mile 20
Potter Creek
Mile 30
Camp Creek
Mile 15
Deer Horn Road
Good Pasture Road
Eugene
105
Mile 25
Mile 35
Marten Rapids
Mile 10
99
Springfield
126
Hendricks Bridge State Wayside
N
Legend
Interstate
State/Cty Road
Other Roads
Campground
Boat Launch
Site of Interest
Bridge
Dam
Major River
Minor River/Creek
©Wilderness Adventures Press

McKENZIE RIVER

There is something special about floating this river in the drift boat that carries its name while casting well-tied dry flies into foam lines that is akin to walking into Yankee Stadium or seeing your first van Gogh painting. It is a special event—one that transforms an angler. The history here is accentuated by the surrounding forests that speak of age and maturity. You get the sense that things have always been this way and that flyfishers have been casting flies here since the Stone Age.

This river is home to redside rainbows, cutthroat, cutt-bows, and steelhead that are pursued by area anglers nearly year-round. The McKenzie has something for just about everyone. Its lower waters, from the town of Leaburg to the mouth, offer uncrowded fishing and are very user friendly. It offers the beginning boater an excellent place for rowing lessons. Experienced McKenzie flyfishers use the lower river because it holds wild trout without the presence of hatchery fish.

From Leaburg upriver, the McKenzie boils with occasional Class III rapids. This is for expert drift boaters only but is a very popular section to float. The river's upper reaches are beautiful, luring both flyfishers and whitewater enthusiasts. Up to 130,000 fish are stocked in this region annually. Although none survive the winter, they do add to catch rates between Blue River and Leaburg. There are quite a few flyfishers in Oregon who believe the upper McKenzie is so beautiful and rich in history that one shouldn't need higher catch rates here to increase the pleasure of floating these waters. Inexperienced boaters should either hire a guide or follow someone who has experience on the McKenzie's upper reaches. This is not the place for beginners.

The McKenzie drift boat earned its stripes on these rapids and riffles and remains the best way to truly appreciate its scenic splendor. The entire river can be floated. Rowing on the lower portion is easy, while the upper reaches require more advanced skills. Wade access is fair on the lower river and very limited on the upper river. Floating the McKenzie during its annual hatches is something all Oregon flyfishers should experience.

The McKenzie's trout season is heralded by the appearance of the March brown mayfly, which can happen as early as February. This hatch lasts into June, and flyfishers can take advantage of it when early season water conditions permit. While heavy rains can put the McKenzie out of shape, it can be back in shape within four or five days.

Other common flies on the river in spring include blue-winged olives, winter stones, little yellow stones, PMDs, golden stones, and plenty of caddis. Chris Daughters, owner of The Caddis Fly in Eugene, says, " The green caddis in the spring is one of the most active bugs on the water. Imitations fished up to a size 10 will bring fish hard to the fly."

There is also an occasional green drake occurrence on the river, although Daughters considers this more of a hatch you run into rather than something a flyfisher would actively seek. When you do come across one, this large insect will bring greedy fish to the surface, offering anglers a chance to cast a big dry fly under hatch conditions to large fish.

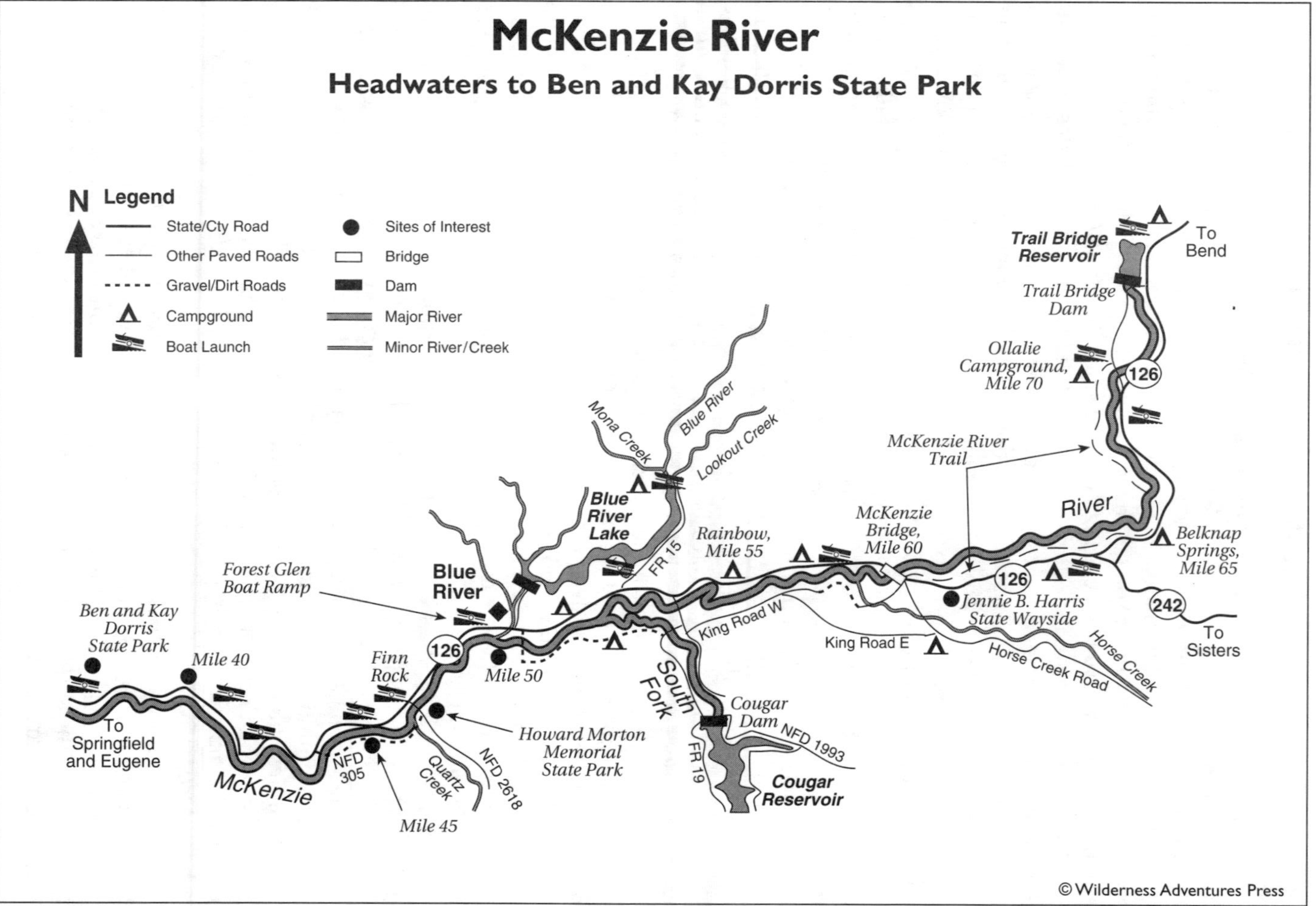
McKenzie River
Headwaters to Ben and Kay Dorris State Park
N
Legend
State/Cty Road
Other Paved Roads
Gravel/Dirt Roads
Campground
Boat Launch
Sites of Interest
Bridge
Dam
Major River
Minor River/Creek
Trail Bridge Reservoir
To Bend
Trail Bridge Dam
Ollalie Campground, Mile 70
126
McKenzie River Trail
River
Belknap Springs, Mile 65
242
To Sisters
Jennie B. Harris State Wayside
Horse Creek
Horse Creek Road
King Road E
King Road W
McKenzie Bridge, Mile 60
Rainbow, Mile 55
Mona Creek
Blue River
Lookout Creek
Blue River Lake
FR 15
Blue River
Forest Glen Boat Ramp
Ben and Kay Dorris State Park
Mile 40
Finn Rock
Mile 50
South Fork
Cougar Dam
NFD 1993
FR 19
Cougar Reservoir
Howard Morton Memorial State Park
NFD 2618
Quartz Creek
NFD 305
Mile 45
To Springfield and Eugene
McKenzie
© Wilderness Adventures Press

Chris Daughters on the upper McKenzie. (Photo by Doc Dumars)

Bigger flies like stimulators are also used as searching patterns while floating the McKenzie. Dropping beadhead flies off of dries or fishing nymphs with indicators or on the swing also produce hookups throughout the year.

Spring also brings steelhead into the river, which are fished in a typical down and across fashion. However, according to Daughters, "A lot of steelhead are caught as a result of trout fishing. We even have a surprising amount of steelhead that are getting caught when we're casting attractor patterns on the surface."

In any event, it is a great bonus to know you can catch 10- to 14-inch fish all day, and maybe even find yourself tied into an 8-pound steelhead before all is said and done. Steelhead continue entering the river into October and remain present in the system all year.

Like most trout streams, there is a brief summer lull on the McKenzie. August heat can sometimes turn the river into an evening fishery, with caddis, PMDs, and little yellow stones being the main focus for evening floaters. This is a great time of year for the wade fisher since flows are very low and more of the river is accessible for wading.

September, October, and nicer days in November bring back decent hatches of blue-winged olives, caddis, and the big October caddis that brings big fish to big flies once again. Autumn is beautiful on the McKenzie when recreational use slows down, and some great fishing can be found at this time of year.

December and January offer limited fishing opportunities. Winter weather and water conditions don't afford anglers many opportunities on the McKenzie. Anglers are better off staying home and perfecting their March brown patterns on the vise.

Recent years have seen an improvement in the McKenzie's fishing. According to Daughters, "Years of clearcutting in the area have been choking the river bottom slowly. The recent floods of the late nineties have scoured the river bottom, increasing aquatic insect populations, which in turn is providing enormous hatches that local anglers haven't seen in years."

It may be only a matter of time before silt chokes the river again, but for now, both fish and flyfisher can take advantage of the increased insect populations.

Standard trout tackle, 4- to 6-weight rods, works well on the McKenzie. A 6-weight may not be necessary for landing fish but does help when casting from a boat, giving an angler better chances at banks and seams with limited backcasts. More experienced casters can get away with lighter tackle. Seven- to 10-foot leaders, tapered to 4X and 5X, cover most McKenzie situations.

If you're a wade angler, access is easiest on the lower waters. Within a 12-mile stretch, an angler can gain access to the lower McKenzie at Armitage State Park, Deadmond Ferry, Harvest Lane, and Hayden Bridge. Above this section, try the Hendricks Wayside.

Several boat ramps provide access from Hwy 26 on the north bank, while Deer Horn Road on the river's south bank offers several accesses. Fly anglers looking for steelhead should try the mile below Leaburg Dam.

For those who choose to fish the lower water by boat, there are very easy floats for novice rowers when water levels are modest. First-time rowers will enjoy Hayden Bridge to Armitage State Park. Another good float for novice rowers is Hendricks Wayside to Hayden Bridge. Deerhorn to Hendricks is an easy float, but a series of islands are present, and at certain times of the year, boaters can use only one channel. Call Chris Daughters at the Caddis Fly if you want to boat this stretch and need directions. Leaburg Dam to Greenwood is a short steelhead float that some anglers will do when good numbers of these sea-run fish are present.

The upper river, from Blue River to Leaburg, has very limited bank access, all of which is off Hwy 126. A few boat ramps and pullouts from the highway are present, but moving up and down from these spots on foot isn't really an option. This area is used mainly by rafters, guides, and many private boaters and is best suited for experienced rowers.

The best upper river opportunities are the stretches above Blue River. Here an angler will find a wild fish fishery, accessible from spots on Hwy 126 or by picking up the McKenzie River Trail at McKenzie Bridge Trail Boat Landing, just upriver from McKenzie Bridge. An angler can hike or bike the trail and find decent pools and runs well worth the effort.

Boating the upper river is popular but also demanding. It is easily rowed in some sections, but several Class III rapids demand the skills of experienced boaters.

Lower McKenzie River. (Photo by Chris Daughters)

Finn Rock to Ben and Kay Dorris State Park is a popular float because there is a take-out a hundred yards above Martens Rapids. These rapids, according to Chris Daughters, can really tear a boat up. I ran Martens Rapids with Merril Hummer, a guide and commercial fly tier from Bend. Even though Hummer is an experienced rafter, we still wore life vests. Some rafters like to start below the rapids and float all the way to the lake at Leaburg Dam.

The upper river offers anglers many boat ramps from which to put in. Above Blue River, only experienced McKenzie floaters should be on the river. According to Daughters, "Not only do you need local knowledge and boating skills for the McKenzie above Blue River but good angling skills as well. Novice casters will not find success in this stretch out of a boat. The casting opportunities go by fast and fly placement makes the difference."

The McKenzie is a special river for many reasons, but the biggest reason is that it is a quality flyfishery on the west side of the Cascade range. This means metropolitan fly anglers can cast to rising trout without traveling great distances or over mountain passes. It also offers flyfishers a chance to cast flies over water surrounded by wonderful scenery and rich history. Fair sized cutthroat, redsides, and steelhead inhabit the river year-round. But the goal on the McKenzie is not only to catch big bruiser fish, it is to catch your fishing partner grinning after a day on the deep green waters of this beautiful river.

Stream Facts: McKenzie River

Seasons

- From the mouth upstream to Leaburg Dam, the river is open the entire year for trout and steelhead. From Leaburg dam upstream to Trail Bridge Dam and the South Fork McKenzie, the season is from April 25 to October 31.

Special Regulations

- From the mouth to Hayden Bridge: Only adipose clipped trout may be taken. Restricted to artificial flies and lures. (Note, there are no hatchery fish in this stretch, so all trout must be released.)
- From Hayden Bridge to Leaburg Dam: Only adipose clipped trout may be taken. Restricted to artificial flies and lures November 1 through April 24.
- From Leaburg Dam to Forest Glen boat ramp: Only adipose clipped trout may be taken.
- From Forest Glen Boat Ramp to Trail Bridge Dam and the South Fork McKenzie: Restricted to artificial flies and lures; catch and release only for trout.

Fish

- Steelhead from 6 to 10 pounds.
- Redside rainbow trout 6 to 20 inches.
- Cutthroat trout 6 to 18 inches.
- Cutt-bows 6 to 18 inches.

Flows

- River Forecast Center, 503-261-9246

River Characteristics

- The McKenzie is a good-sized river. Its upper waters are treelined, and rapids prevent novice boating. As the river nears the Willamette, it begins to lose its turbidity, and riffles and glides become the norm. A variety of hatches keep fly anglers busy and steelhead add nicely to the action on occasion. It is no mistake that McKenzie boats were brought into popular use here—it is definitely the way to fish this river.

Fishing and boating access.

- Access is dependent on one's rowing skills. There are different sections for all abilities. The lower river has plenty of easy rowing and decent wade opportunities. The river above Leaburg Dam is better left to experienced boaters, and bank access is limited. The upper reaches of the river again offer some hike-in and wade access for wild fish. Boat ramps are everywhere on the river, and an angler can mix and match all sorts of different day trips.

Maps

- McKenzie River Map, Magnum Adventures, available at The Caddis Fly

McKENZIE RIVER MAJOR HATCHES

Insect	J	F	M	A	M	J	J	A	S	O	N	D	Time	Flies
Baetis													10–4	Blue-winged Olive Parachute, Sparkle Dun, Blue-winged Olive Hi-Vis Baetis, Adams, Pheasant Tail Nymph #16-22
Winter Stone													10–4	Black Elk Hair Caddis #16-20
March Brown													11–3	Flick March Brown, AK's March Brown, American March Brown #10-16
Brown Stone (Skwala type)													10–4	Gold Stimulator #8-12; Peacock Caddis #10; Spent Stone Brown #10
Golden Stone													Midday	Yellow Stimulators #8-12
Salmonflies													10–4	Stimulators, Turck's Tarantula, Sofa Pillows #4-8
Green Caddis													Afternoon Evening	Green Elk Hair Caddis, Olive Stimulators #8-12
Cinnamon Caddis & others													All day	Elk Hair Caddis, Spent Partridge Caddis, CDC Elk Hair Caddis #8-18
Pale Morning Dun													Morning Afternoon	Sparkle Dun, Quill Body PMD, Thorax PMD, Extended Body PMD #16-20
Big Yellow May													All day	Large Yellow Comparadun #12
Little Yellow Stone													5–10PM	Henry's Fork Yellow Sally #14-18; Yellow Elk Hair Caddis, Yellow Stimulator #16-18

Hatch Chart Prepared by Chris Daughters

McKENZIE RIVER MAJOR HATCHES (cont.)

Insect	J	F	M	A	M	J	J	A	S	O	N	D	Time	Flies
Green Drakes					■	■	■						Afternoon	Parachute, Extended Body, Hairwing Drake #8-12
Mahogany Dun								■	■	■			Afternoon	Parachute, Extended Body, Hairwing Drake #14-18
Gray Drake								■	■	■	■		Afternoon	Parachute, Extended Body, Hairwing Drake #8-12
October Caddis									■	■	■		Afternoon Evening	Orange Madame X, Stimulators, Caddis #6-8
Attractors						■	■	■	■	■	■		Afternoon	Wulffs, Madame X, Humpy's, X-Caddis, Adams, Stimulators, Sparkle Duns #10-16
General Nymphs (early in season)	■	■	■	■	■							■	All Day	Brown & Black Golden Stones, Kaufmann's Stones #6-10; Hare's Ears, Pheasant Tail, Beadheads, Green Rockworms, Cased Caddis #12-16

Hatch Chart Prepared by Chris Daughters

MIDDLE FORK OF THE WILLAMETTE AND TRIBUTARIES

The Middle Fork of the Willamette River and its tributaries offer another flyfishery on the west side of the Cascades. This is a midsize river that fishes much like the McKenzie. Habits of the fish and insects in both rivers tend to be similar. It is accessible by boat much of the year, although most people take advantage of the wade fishing. It also offers a nice winter wade fishery, when flows can be as low as 300 cfs. The river is not stocked between Lookout Point and Hills Creek Reservoir and holds rainbow and cutthroat in the 12- to 13-inch range. Chris Daughters at the Caddis Fly says that fish up to 20 inches are possible but not always in the cards.

There is a fly-only, catch-and-release stretch of water between Lookout Point Reservoir and Hills Creek Reservoir. It is open all year to fishing. Locals float the river when flows are between 800 to 1,500 cfs and bring their McKenzie River fly boxes.

Above Hills Creek Reservoir in the spring, the river offers an opportunity to catch big reservoir fish as the lake backs into the channel. These bigger reservoir fish move into slack water in the river channel and become susceptible to flies. This is also an excellent place to find fish in the fall. Although the river is heavily stocked and recreated above Hills Creek Reservoir in the summer, autumn provides great action because most hatchery fish are gone. Between the native, wild trout remaining in the river and the old growth forest lining the banks, an autumn outing can be a very pleasant experience.

Chris Daughters in Eugene knows the river and surrounding tributaries well. He can help you with fly patterns and offers a guide service for those interested in fishing the west side of the Cascades. You can find Chris at The Caddis Fly, 541-342-7005.

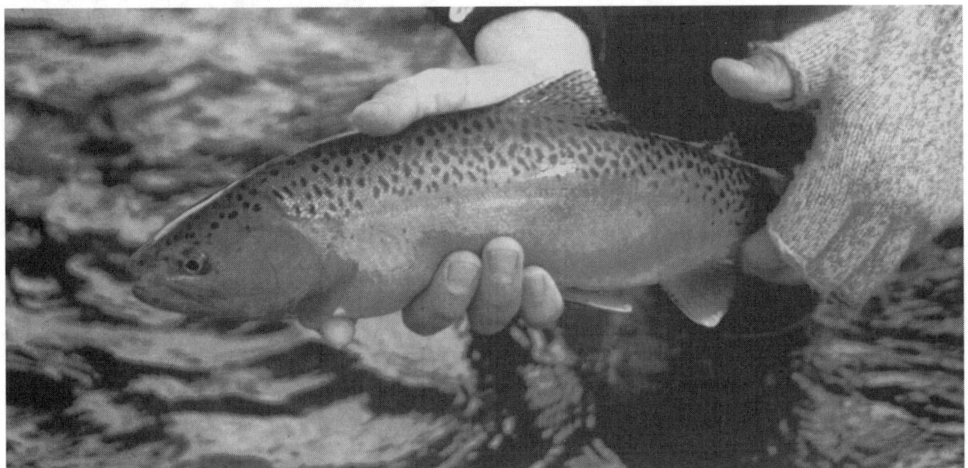

Wild rainbows and a winter fishery on the Willamette system provide nice fly action for year-round anglers.

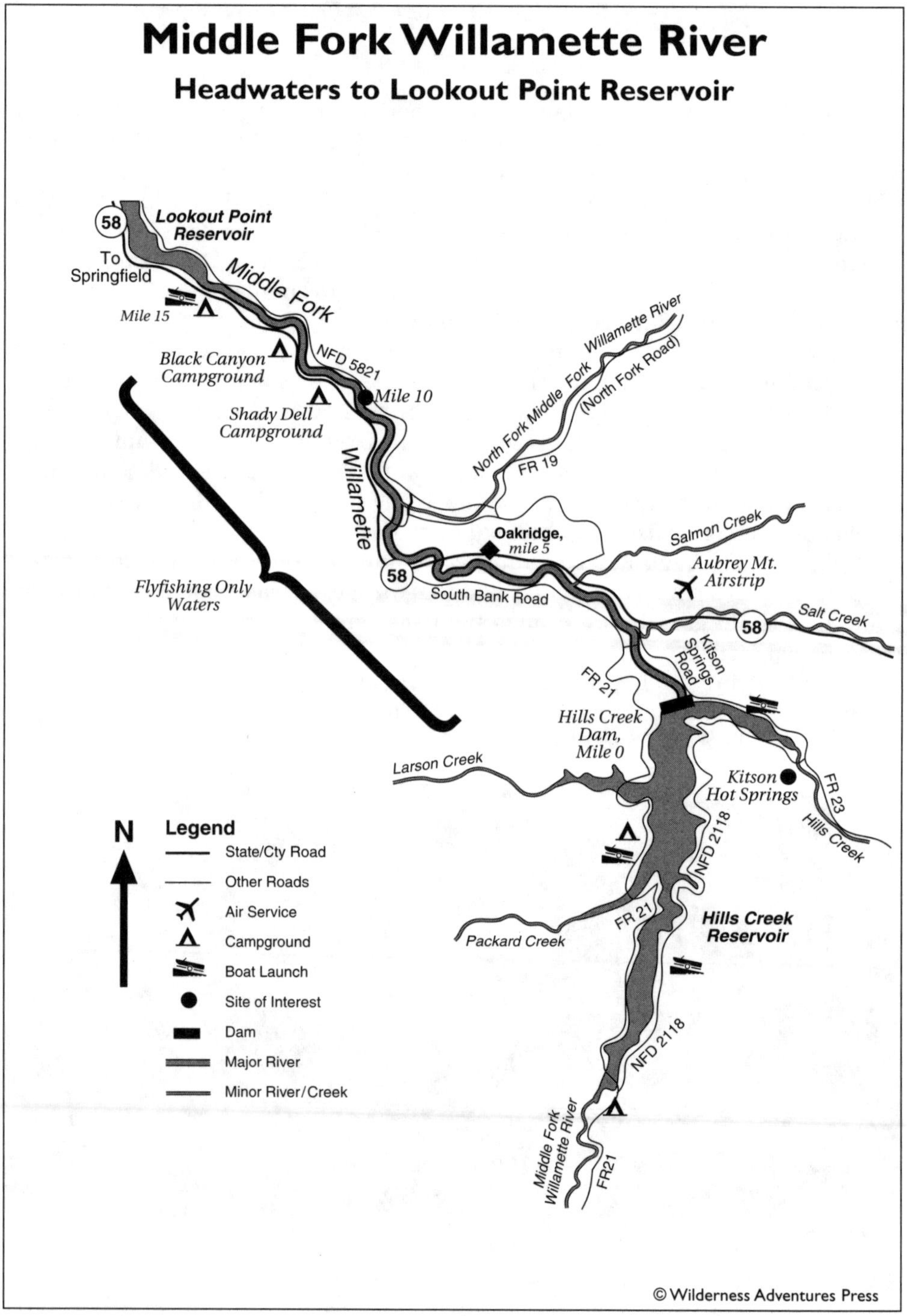
Middle Fork Willamette River
Headwaters to Lookout Point Reservoir
58
Lookout Point Reservoir
To Springfield
Middle Fork
Mile 15
Black Canyon Campground
NFD 5821
Mile 10
Shady Dell Campground
Willamette
North Fork Middle Fork Willamette River
(North Fork Road)
FR 19
Flyfishing Only Waters
Oakridge, mile 5
58
South Bank Road
Salmon Creek
Aubrey Mt. Airstrip
Salt Creek
58
Kitson Springs Road
FR 21
Hills Creek Dam, Mile 0
Larson Creek
Kitson Hot Springs
FR 23
Hills Creek
NFD 2118
N
Legend
State/Cty Road
Other Roads
Air Service
Campground
Boat Launch
Site of Interest
Dam
Major River
Minor River/Creek
FR 21
Hills Creek Reservoir
Packard Creek
NFD 2118
Middle Fork Willamette River
FR21
© Wilderness Adventures Press

MIDDLE FORK WILLAMETTE RIVER MAJOR HATCHES

Insect	J	F	M	A	M	J	J	A	S	O	N	D	Time	Flies
Baetis													10–4	Blue-winged Olive Parachute, Sparkle Dun Blue-winged Olive, Hi-Vis Baetis, Small Adams, PT Nymph #16-22
Winter Stone *Capnia*													10–4	Black Elk Hair Caddis #16-20
Large Dark Stone (like a *Squalla* but brown)													10–4	Gold Stimulator #8-12; Peacock Caddis #10; Spent Stone Brown #10
March Brown													11–3	Flick March Brown, American March Brown, AK's March Brown #10-16
Mahogany Dun													2–5	Sparkle Dun #16-20; Mahogany Brown #16-20
Cinnamon Caddis and and various other													All day	Elk Hair Caddis, CDC Elk Hair, Spent Partridge Caddis #8-18
Little Yellow Stone													5–10 pm	Henry's Fork Yellow Sally #14-18; Yellow Elk Hair Caddis #16-18; Yellow Stimulator #16
October Caddis													Best on overcast days	Large Orange Elk Hair Caddis or Stimulator #4-8

Hatch Chart Prepared by Chris Daughters

MIDDLE FORK WILLAMETTE RIVER MAJOR HATCHES (cont.)

Insect	J	F	M	A	M	J	J	A	S	O	N	D	Time	Flies
Salmonflies													Midday	Stimulators, Sofa Pillows, etc., in #4-8
Golden Stone													Midday	Stimulators, Golden Stones #8-12
Pale Morning Dun													Morning Afternoon	Sparkle Duns, Thorax PMD, Quill Body PMD, Ext Body PMD #16-20
Pale Evening Dun													Afternoon Evening	Sparkle Duns, Thorax PMD, Quill Body PMD, Ext Body PMD #16-20
Big Yellow May													All Day	Large Comparadun Yellow #12
Big Green Caddis													PM	Green Elk Hair Caddis, Olive Stimulators #8-10

Hatch Chart Prepared by Chris Daughters

North Fork of the Middle Fork Willamette

The North Fork offers a fly angler 30 miles of water to wade and fish, as well as tributaries worth exploring. A road follows the river almost its entire length (see Middle Fork Willamette map), and fly-only regulations prevail. From April 25 to October 31, there is a 2-fish limit. After that, the season continues as a catch-and-release fishery.

Treat all the tributaries and trout in the area kindly. Its proximity to Oregon's major population centers means these rivers walk a thin line between pristine fly-fishing environments and sterile, trampled streams. It is especially important to practice a no-trace ethic here, as it is on any stream. The slogan of many years ago, "limit your limit," should still apply everywhere we fish today.

The North Fork is fished with the same patterns found on the Middle Fork and McKenzie, with a little more emphasis on attractor patterns. Most of the smaller rivers and tributaries can be fished with basic dries and nymph patterns and techniques. Fish are generally smaller here, with an occasional fish up to 19 inches being caught. If catching big fish is going to make or break your day, this is not the place for you. The rivers in this area are flyfishing retreats more than trophy trout locations. Big fish here are a small stream flyfisher's bonus. Any time you go out for a small stream experience, there is a chance that a fish may appear that is disproportionate to the river's size. It makes you wonder if all the fish in the river could be as big under ideal conditions, or if these big fish in small waters are an anomaly. Regardless, the mere thought of big fish in small water will keep you going back to these rivers and their tributaries.

Salmon Creek and Salt Creek

Just south of the North Fork, an angler will find Salmon and Salt Creeks. These are both fine freestone fisheries where smaller trout prevail with a few exceptions. Both are easily reached from Oakridge and are tributaries of the Middle Fork of the Willamette (see Middle Fork Willamette map). Basic dry fly and nymphing techniques and patterns will catch fish in these systems.

Salmon Creek is 26 miles long and is accessible from Forest Road 24 off Hwy 58 just east of Oakridge. It is a nice wade fishery for fly anglers looking for willing fish and solitude. Chris Daughters describes it as a midsize stream with the lower 5 miles having stocked fish while the fish are wild above the falls. There are some big pools with fair sized fish in Salmon Creek. Hatches are more important here than on some of the surrounding waters.

Salt Creek is the smaller stream of the two, where small fish are really the only game in town. Teach a friend or child to fish here, and fish size will probably never enter into streamside conversation. Hwy 58 runs parallel to Salt Creek for 27 miles of its 28-mile length. It is fast pocket water where attractor patterns work well. Try dropper flies here as well as in the surrounding creeks. A beadhead suspended 12 to 18 inches under a large dry can sometimes double the action.

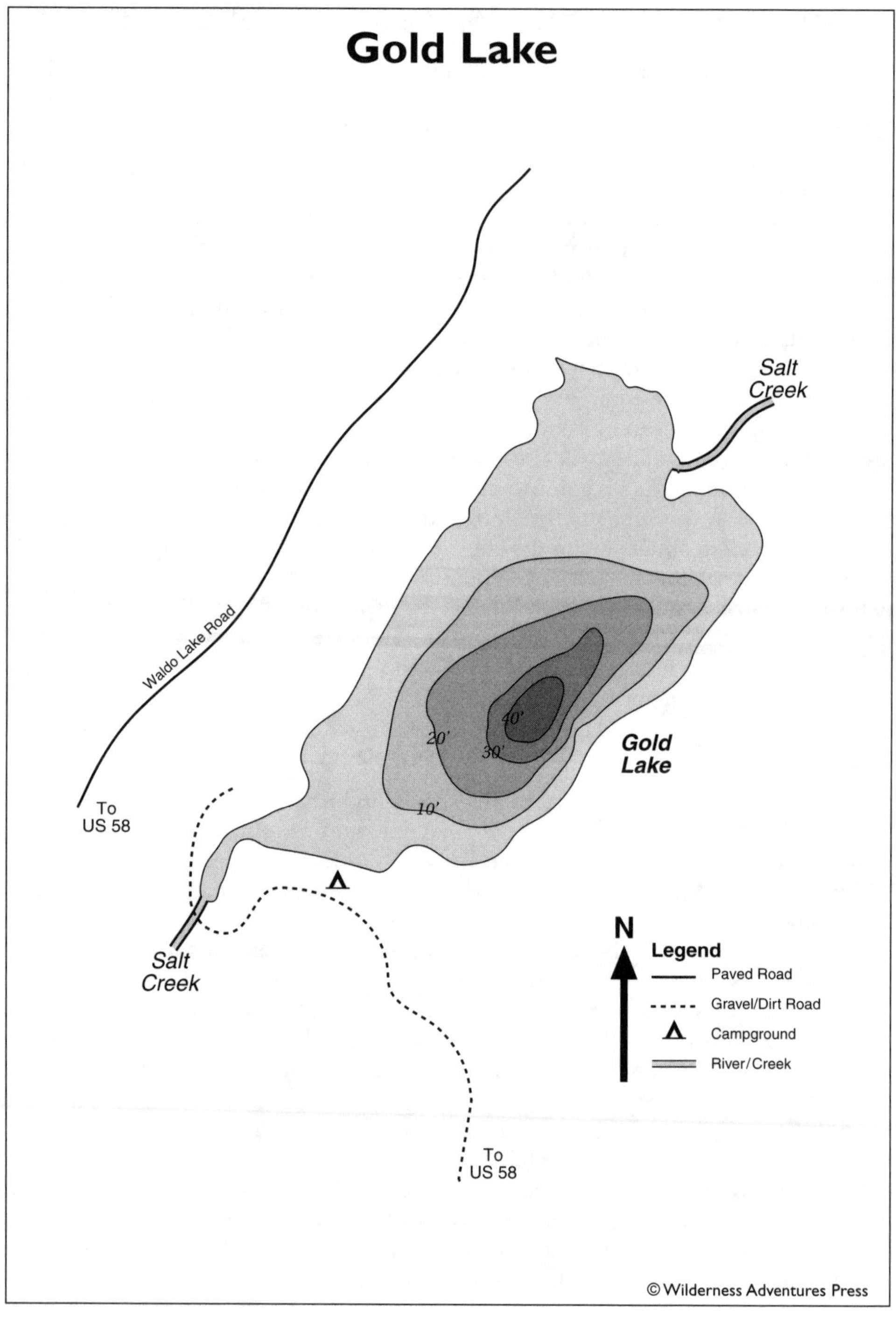
Gold Lake
Waldo Lake Road
To
US 58
Salt
Creek
Gold
Lake
40'
30'
20'
10'
Salt
Creek
To
US 58
N
Legend
Paved Road
Gravel/Dirt Road
Campground
River/Creek
© Wilderness Adventures Press

Gold Lake

Oregon flyfishers have been fishing Gold Lake for twice my lifetime. It is an intimate lake that beckons anglers with fly rods. The lake has been listed as a fly-only lake since the late 1940s. It was originally stocked with rainbow that thrived and grew big in this isolated lake. Before a road was built, anglers walked to the lake and then tried to keep it a secret afterward. It is no secret anymore, but it is no longer the same fishery, either. Introduced brook trout forced rainbow size and populations to drop. There have been efforts to restore the rainbow fishery, and currently there is no limit on the amount of brook trout kept. It is hoped that through these efforts this will continue to be a quality fishery.

Gold lake can be reached from Hwy 58 east of Eugene. Chris Daughters, owner of The Caddis Fly in Eugene, says that the average take in Gold Lake these days consists of rainbow in the 12- to 20-inch class with fish up to 26 inches sometimes being caught. Brook trout are generally in the 6- to 13-inch range.

Chris says the best fishing is in the spring and fall. In the spring, anglers do it the old-fashioned way—they walk to the lake. Snow prevents driving to the lake until late May (usually), and fly anglers who want the first shot at fish after ice-off had better be willing to sweat.

Gold Lake has depths up to 35 feet where fish retreat in midsummer. Fly anglers use type III through VI full-sink lines to reach the fish. Morning and evening fishing become more important at this hot time of year, when fish may move into shallower waters to feed.

Autumn brings fish back out of the depths as they feed aggressively in preparation for the long winter season. The lake is accessible by car this time of year, and small craft, such as tubes or small prams, are used to reach fish. Wade fishing from the banks is not easy or recommended for flyfishers. Flyfishing from a personal craft is the best way to produce trout in Gold Lake.

Leeches are always an excellent pattern to use on Gold Lake. Fish leeches slowly, with an erratic retrieve, and pay attention—fish will sometimes grab the fly lightly as they are swimming toward you. The lack of resistance on a very slow strip can often be as telltale as a hard yank. An angler need only visualize a rainbow coming up behind prey that is moving at one-tenth of the trout's speed. The more you think about it the more maddening it becomes: think of the hundreds or even thousands of fish that have eaten your subsurface offerings and you never even had the slightest clue. Take this one step further: think about the days that you caught no fish because you were daydreaming about huge, fall baetis hatches. How many fish ate and spit out our nymphs on those days? I suppose the only sane way out of this thought pattern is to assume that none have. Still, be aware that a strike isn't always a strike—sometimes a strike is nothing.

Gold Lake is a straightforward fishery, and a variety of patterns will take fish. Pay attention to hatch conditions as they occur, such as damsel and Callibaetis hatches.

Fish Gold Lake with standard fly tackle for trout and remember to bring a sinking line or two when the fish are hanging out in the depths.

Gold Lake is a quality fly-only lake that is easy to reach most of the year. Camping is available, and it is an easy day trip from the Eugene area. Gold Lake has a place in Oregon's flyfishing history, considering how long it has been a fly-only lake. Gold Lake celebrated its 50th year as a fly-only destination in 1998. Please show respect and courtesy to your fellow anglers and treat this resource well.

Lake Facts: Gold Lake

Season

- Last Saturday in May until October 31.

Special Regulations

- Catch and release only for rainbow trout.
- No limit on size or number of brook trout taken.
- Restricted to fly angling only with barbless hooks.
- Open for trout from the boat ramp down Salt Creek 100 yards to markers July 1 to October 31.

Fish

- Rainbows average 12 to 20 inches with some fish up to 26 inches.
- Brook trout from 6 to 13 inches are common.

Lake Size

- 96 acres

Lake Character

- Gold Lake is small and treelined. From its banks, it drops off quickly and has depths to 35 feet. It produces well early and late in the season but can be fished in the middle of summer with quick sinking lines. This lake is perfect for float tubers, and with drive-in access throughout much of the year, flyfishers come back over and over.

Maps

- *Atlas of Oregon Lakes*

GOLD LAKE MAJOR HATCHES

Insect	J	F	M	A	M	J	J	A	S	O	N	D	Time	Flies
Damselflies													10–6	Olive Woolly Buggers #8-10; Damsel Nymphs #8-10
Streamers													All day	Carey Specials #6-8; Yellow Streamers #6-10; Olive, Black, Yellow Woolly Buggers #6-8
Dry Flies (Mayflies, Caddis)													Early AM Evening	Adams #14-18; Quigley Cripple #14-18; Bett's Insect #14-16
Chironomids													All day	Griffith's Gnat #16-18; Black & Red Midge Pupa #14-16
Leeches													All day	Black Woolly Buggers #6-8
Nymphs													All day	Pheasant Tails, Hare's Ears, Prince Nymphs#12-18; Yellow Soft Hackle #12-14

Hatch Chart Prepared by Chris Daughters

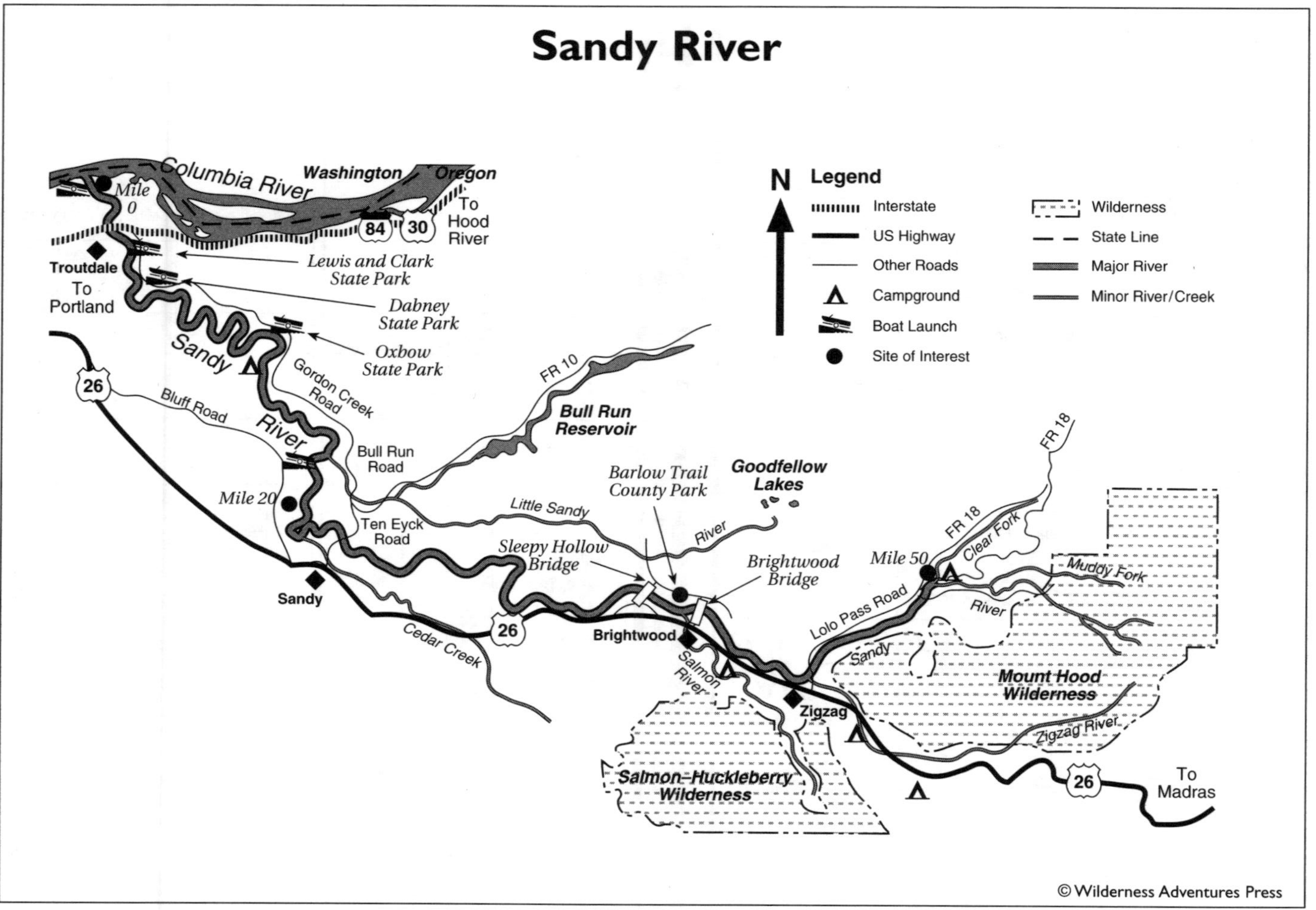
Sandy River
N
Legend
Interstate
US Highway
Other Roads
Campground
Boat Launch
Site of Interest
Wilderness
State Line
Major River
Minor River/Creek
Columbia River
Washington
Oregon
Mile 0
84
30
To Hood River
Troutdale
To Portland
Lewis and Clark State Park
Dabney State Park
Oxbow State Park
26
Sandy
River
Bluff Road
Gordon Creek Road
FR 10
Bull Run Reservoir
Bull Run Road
Mile 20
Ten Eyck Road
Sandy
Little Sandy
River
Cedar Creek
Sleepy Hollow Bridge
Barlow Trail County Park
Goodfellow Lakes
Brightwood Bridge
Brightwood
Salmon River
Salmon-Huckleberry Wilderness
Zigzag
Lolo Pass Road
Mile 50
FR 18
Clear Fork
Muddy Fork
River
Sandy
Mount Hood Wilderness
Zigzag River
To Madras
©Wilderness Adventures Press

SANDY RIVER

One reason that Portland has become one of the finer cities on the West Coast is its proximity to the Sandy River steelhead fishery. How many people on the West Coast can get off work, take the hard-hat or tie off, and begin spey casting to steelhead that inhabit the river year-round? If you have a friend who lives in or near Portland who complains about not getting out with a fly rod enough, I'm sorry, but they're just not trying.

A fertile steelhead river situated near a metropolis should have its banks lined with fishermen, yet the Sandy's banks remain relatively quiet. What is the reason for this paradox? Simply put, the Sandy makes an angler work. Anglers looking to leave work and catch fish after fish should go elsewhere, because the Sandy doesn't yield her fish willingly. Successful Sandy River flyfishers are those who keep moving and putting flies in front of fish consistently.

Mark Stensland, co-owner of The Fly Fishing Shop in Welches, took me out for a beautiful day of fishing on the Sandy. He put me through my paces on the river and is a good resource when the river has you stumped. I was lucky—the weather was gorgeous near Mt. Hood, and the river was in prime shape.

While you might find yourself on a warm summer evening landing a nice steelhead, it's just as likely that you'll find yourself leaning into sleet on a cold, blustery day in one of the other three seasons, wondering if you just felt a strike or if the wind just bounced your rod tip on the water when you weren't paying attention. Steelhead can be caught on this river, but you will need patience and time to be successful.

Like any steelhead fishery, hitting just the right day can yield good numbers of fish. But it's more likely that persistence, a few banged shins, and sweat in your waders while hiking in a rainstorm are what it will take to pick up fish consistently on the Sandy. You can have all this, rain and sweat included, within 45 minutes of home —doesn't sound all that bad to me.

The Sandy River comes charging off Mt. Hood toward Portland, stopping just shy of the city and emptying into the Columbia River. This is a big and rugged river, studded with boulders and rocky cliffs. Getting around on the Sandy is no easy chore. The same features that impede an angler's progress are what entice steelhead into the river. If the river's features made access easy, steelhead wouldn't survive so close to a metropolitan center. Sandy's fish have done well despite the river's proximity to Portland.

Sandy River steelhead are in the system year-round with winter offering the greatest numbers. Of all the fish in the system, winter-run steelhead are the most difficult to fish. Moving under the concealment of high water, these deep-water denizens stick to the bottom, forcing anglers to pull out a variety of homemade and commercial sinktip options.

For those anglers who learn the art of swinging flies into the depths and who don't mind losing a fair number of flies, the reward can be a really big tug. Once you've hooked a wild winter fish, you may find yourself using a few expletives because these fish will often take you for a wild ride.

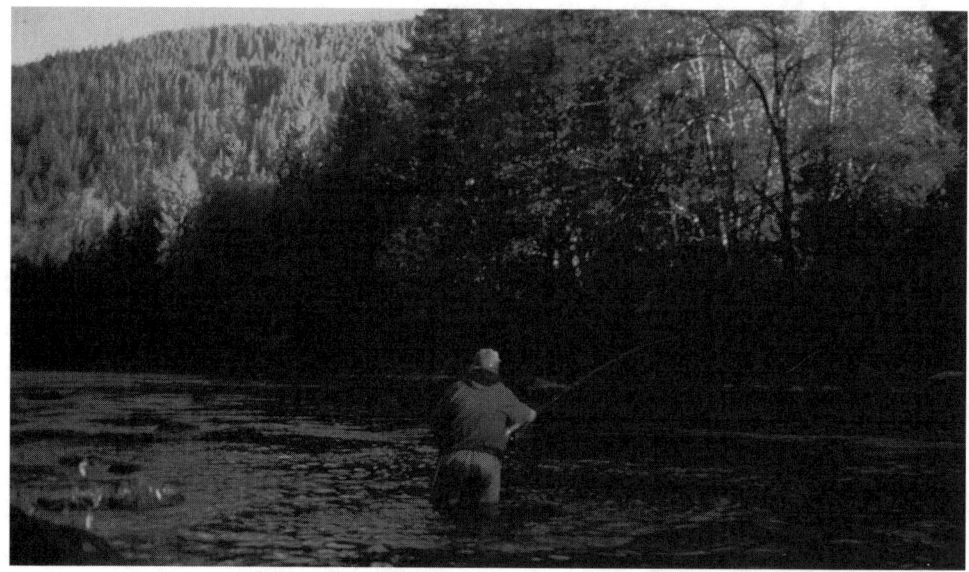

Spey casting on the Sandy is a great way to cover a lot of water according to Mark Stensland.

During the holiday season, hatchery fish show up in great numbers below Marmot Dam. Good numbers of wild steelhead show up in mid-February and continue entering the system through May.

Summer-run steelhead are also an attraction on the Sandy. Sleek, bright, and full of fight, these fish are best taken during low-light periods in summer. Summer runs begin appearing as early as March and increase until they peak in July. Rising waters during these months create safer passage for steelhead as well as other fish. You can find them mixed in with winter-run steelhead, and you should definitely check out shallows and banks during low-light periods in the summer. Fish begin to disperse into the higher reaches and tributaries, like the Salmon and Zigzag Rivers, as early as mid-June.

The Sandy is subject to fluctuation in depth and current speed throughout the year, which means that flyfishers need to have a variety of lines and rods to cover the conditions. You might be able to cast single-handed rods over small pools or you might have to spey cast with a sinktip line over wide, boulder-strewn runs. While standard steelhead gear will work in many situations, you need a variety of gear to get results consistently.

The Sandy is most often fished with a swinging fly. Fly level is dictated by water depths and temperature, which generally keep fish close to the bottom. Several sinktips in a variety of sink rates, from slow to fast, will help get the fly to the fish in a variety of situations. Floating lines also have their place on the Sandy, especially if there are active fish and low flows.

The Sandy's larger tributaries (the Zigzag and Salmon Rivers) have a limited number of places where a swinging fly can be utilized. Generally, these tributaries are fished by experienced anglers who sight-fish. This is commonly done with standard nymphing techniques. Having a friend spot fish movement at flies from higher ground is often helpful if you can't see from your casting position.

The Salmon River runs 31 miles to its confluence with the Sandy, with anadromous fish runs barred at around 13 miles above the mouth by a series of natural waterfalls. Regulations currently prohibit all salmon angling to protect spawning fish. A short hike in can put anglers in a beautiful setting for summer steelhead. The Zigzag joins the Sandy at the town of Zigzag after a short 12-mile run from its headwaters and offers good access from Hwy 26.

For winter fishing, Mark Bachmann of The Fly Fishing Shop in Welches suggests that you include #4 and #2/0 marabou spiders, #4 glo-bugs, #2 steelhead bunnies, #4 eyed shrimp, and #2 agitator. For summer fishing, try #4 woolly buggers, #4 muddler minnow, #4 euphausid, #4 green butt skunk, and #4 eyed shrimp.

Steelhead change their holding lies constantly in response to the Sandy's flow fluctuations. Throughout the year, weather patterns and annual events affect the river and dictate where to fish, so fishing the river often is the key to unlocking its secrets. If you can't get on the river often but still want a chance to hook a fish, get in touch with a guide who lives and works on the Sandy, such as Mark Bachmann or his partner, Mark Stensland, of The Fly Fishing Shop in Welches or try Northwest Flyfishing Outfitters in Gresham.

For those learning the art of steelheading with a fly, the Sandy is an excellent classroom. Do keep in mind that all wild steelhead in this river are subject to catch and release.

Stream Facts: Sandy River

Season

- Mainstem upstream to Brightwood Bridge: Open for steelhead the entire year.
- Upstream from Brightwood Bridge: Open for steelhead May 23 to October 31.

Special Regulations

- Mainstem to Brightwood Bridge: 2 trout per day.
- Closed within 200 feet of chinook spawning areas that are marked by signs in Oxbow Park.
- No angling from a floating device upstream from the powerline crossing located one mile downstream from Oxbow Park.
- Mainstem upstream from Brightwood Bridge: Catch and release only for trout; restricted to artificial flies and lures; no angling from a floating device.

Fish

- Steelhead
- Chinook

Flows

- River Forecast Central, 503-261-9246

River Characteristics

- This is a beautiful river located within an hour's drive of Portland. Small pools and wide, boulder-strewn runs dominate the river.
- County roads cross and parallel the lower portion of the river. Hwy 26 follows the upper river and provides access to its major tributaries.

Maps

- DeLorme *Oregon Atlas and Gazetteer*
- *Sandy River Journal*

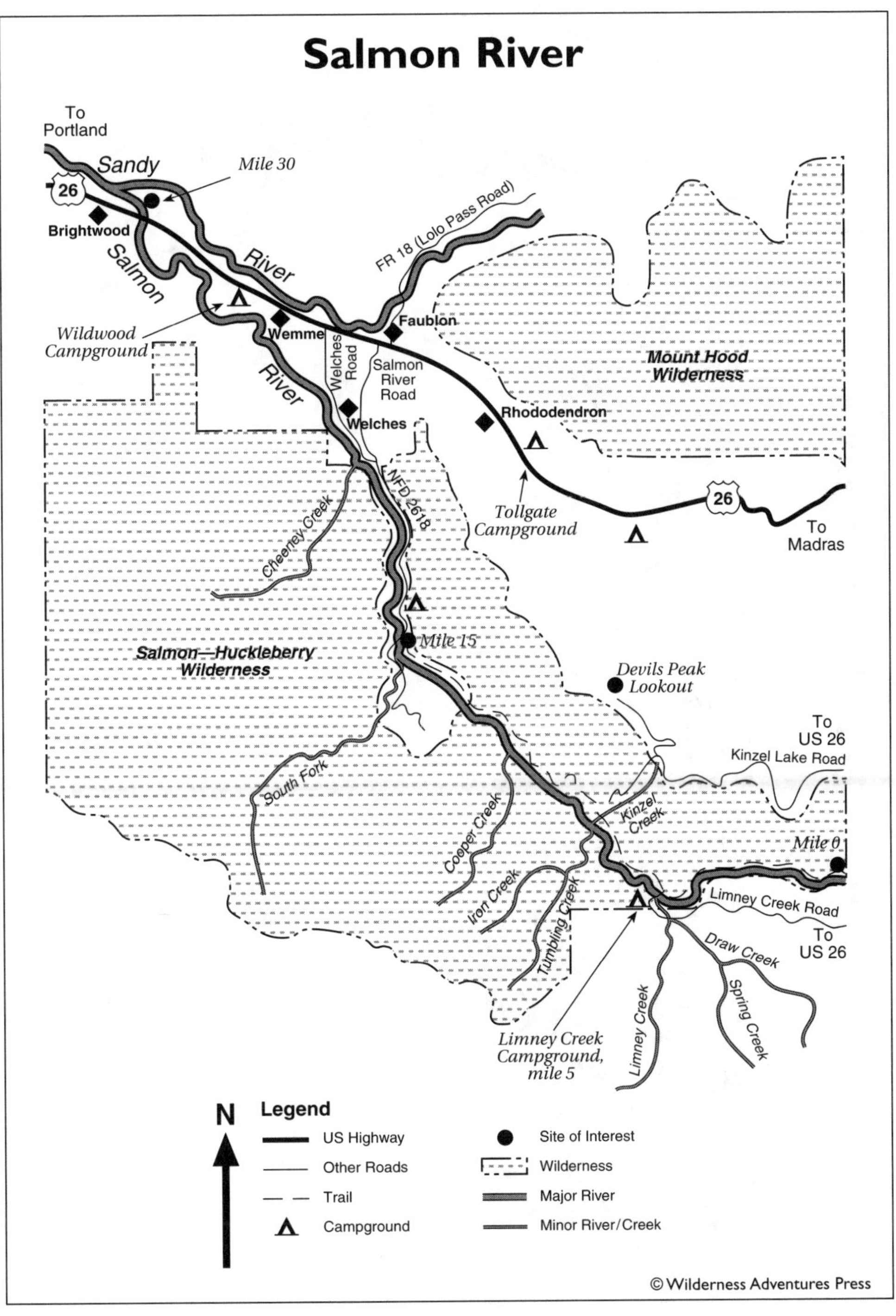
Salmon River
To Portland
Sandy
26
Mile 30
Brightwood
Salmon
River
FR 18 (Lolo Pass Road)
Wildwood Campground
Wemme
Faublon
Welches Road
Salmon River Road
River
Mount Hood Wilderness
Welches
Rhododendron
NFD 2618
Cheeney Creek
Tollgate Campground
26
To Madras
Mile 15
Salmon—Huckleberry Wilderness
Devils Peak Lookout
To US 26
Kinzel Lake Road
South Fork
Cooper Creek
Kinzel Creek
Mile 0
Iron Creek
Tumbling Creek
Limney Creek Road
To US 26
Draw Creek
Spring Creek
Limney Creek
Limney Creek Campground, mile 5
N
Legend
US Highway
Other Roads
Trail
Campground
Site of Interest
Wilderness
Major River
Minor River/Creek
© Wilderness Adventures Press

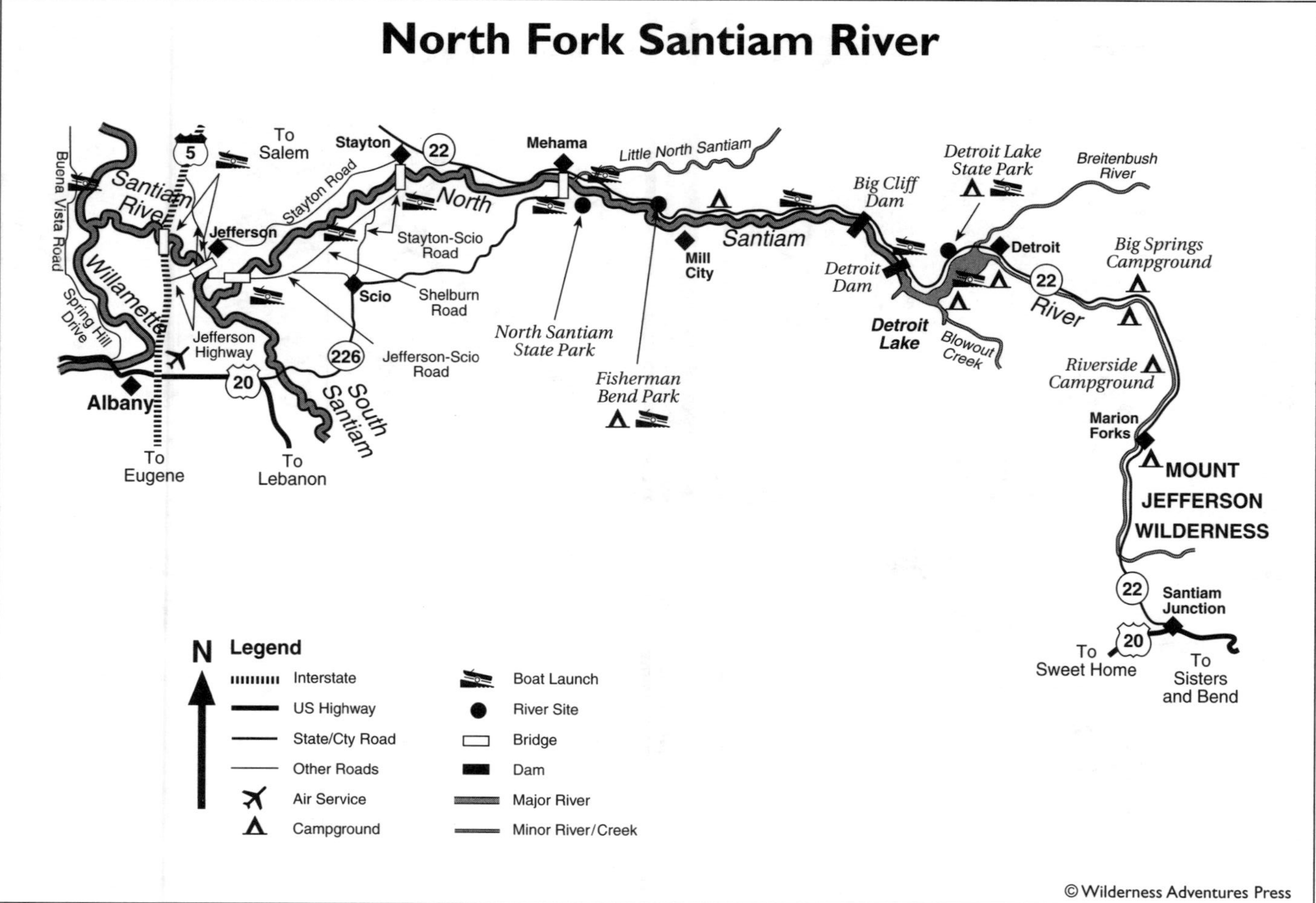
North Fork Santiam River
To Salem
5
Stayton
22
Mehama
Little North Santiam
Buena Vista Road
Santiam River
Stayton Road
North
Jefferson
Stayton-Scio Road
Willamette
Spring Hill Drive
Scio
Shelburn Road
Jefferson Highway
226
Jefferson-Scio Road
20
Albany
South Santiam
To Eugene
To Lebanon
North Santiam State Park
Fisherman Bend Park
Mill City
Santiam
Big Cliff Dam
Detroit Dam
Detroit Lake
Blowout Creek
Detroit Lake State Park
Detroit
Breitenbush River
22
River
Big Springs Campground
Riverside Campground
Marion Forks
MOUNT JEFFERSON WILDERNESS
22
Santiam Junction
20
To Sweet Home
To Sisters and Bend
N
Legend
Interstate
US Highway
State/Cty Road
Other Roads
Air Service
Campground
Boat Launch
River Site
Bridge
Dam
Major River
Minor River/Creek
© Wilderness Adventures Press

North Fork Santiam

The Santiam system hosts 70 percent of Willamette-run steelhead, which is both a blessing and a curse. The blessing is the numbers of fish in the system, and the curse is the numbers of bait and hardware fishers. There are so many that flyfishers are basically out of luck on the South Fork of the Santiam. The majority of fish stack behind Foster Dam, and access to these fish is limited to a hundred-yard stretch of river below the dam, where guns are pulled and fists fly among what is described as Oregon's most out-of-control fishing scene. To add to the mess, the fish were rerun 6 times last year, which probably made the fish as crazy as the anglers. If you really want to fish the South Fork, contact The Scarlet Ibis, 541-754-1544. They provide a private access float down the river, although they are casting mainly for trout in the 6- to 10-inch size. These are often 50- and 100-fish days that anglers new to the sport would really enjoy.

Luckily, fly anglers in Oregon can still appreciate the North Fork Santiam. The North Fork receives about 40 percent of the steelhead in the system. The area in which these are fished is from Fishermen's Bend up to North Santiam State Park, about 7 miles of water. There are special closures on the river above Big Cliff Dam. Consult Oregon Regulations for these closed areas. There is a boat fishery on the North Santiam, but the river is extremely technical and is best done with an outfitter that is familiar with the area. Private boaters need excellent skills and some local knowledge. Wade access on the North Santiam is excellent, with many parks and road sites adjacent to the river.

The Santiam is typically fished when flows are near 650 cfs. There is a steelhead fishery as well as a resident trout population. Steelhead are in the 8-pound range and are fished from May through about mid-September. According to Brian Buggenhagen at The Scarlet Ibis, "We fish steelhead with dry line swinging techniques, with an emphasis on flies with a black profile."

The river is pocketwater by nature with a few classic steelhead runs. Brian says the pocket fishing can be great fun when the fishing is on.

A few of Brian's favorite patterns include silver Hiltons in a size 6 as well as green-butted skunks in the same size. Brian also stresses that these fish should be targeted during low-light periods at sunrise and sunset. Overcast days can produce the best fishing. Brian insists that the harder it rains and the uglier the weather, the better the fishing.

There are trout to be caught on the North Santiam in the 6- to 10-inch range. Again, these fish can be great action for anglers looking to learn basics of the sport. Basic attractor patterns are all that is needed for these fish.

Northwest Hub Cities
Eugene, Oregon

Elevation–426 • Population–126,325

Accommodations

The Timbers Motel, 1015 Pearl Street / 800-653-4167 / $
Best Western New Oregon Motel, 1655 Franklin Boulevard / 800-528-1234 / $$
Campus Inn, 390 East Broadway / 800-888-6313 / $$
Eugene Hilton Hotel, 66 East 6th Avenue / 800-432-5999 / $$$
The Valley River Inn, 1000 Valley River Way / 800-426-0670 / $$$

Restaurants

Hilda's Latin American Restaurant, 400 Blair Boulevard / 541-343-4322
Track Town Pizza, 1809 Franklin Boulevard / 541-484-2799
West Bros. Bar-B-Que, Inc., 844 Olive Street / 541-345-8489
Steelhead Brewery, 199 East 5th Avenue / 541-686-2739
Oregon Electric Station, 27 East 5th Avenue / 541-485-4444

Fly Shops

Caddis Fly, 168 West 6th Avenue / 541-342-7005
Home Waters, 444 West Third Avenue / 541-342-6691
The Scarlet Ibis, 905 Northwest Kings Boulevard (Corvallis) / 541-754-1544

Hospital

Sacred Heart Medical Center, 1255 Hilyard Street / 541-686-7300

Airport

Eugene Municipal Airport, 28855 Lockheed Drive / 541-682-5430
Horizon Airlines / 800-547-9308
Skywest Airlines / 800-453-9417
United Express Airlines / 800-241-6522

Auto Rental

Budget Rent-A-Car, 1380 West 7th Avenue / 541-344-1670 or 800-527-0700
Budget Rent-A-Car, 28801 Douglas Drive / 541-688-1229
Hertz Rent-A-Car, 28801 Douglas Drive, #8 / 541-688-9333
Avis Rent-A-Car, 28801 Douglas Drive / 541-688-9053

Auto Repair

Schweitzer's Automotive, 1120 Arthur Street / 541-342-1664
Oregon Mobile Tune-up, 2520 Lincoln / 541-342-2214

For More Information

Eugene Area Chamber of Commerce
1401 Willamette Street / Box 1107
Eugene Oregon, 97440-1107
541-484-1314

Sandy, Oregon

Elevation–1,020 • Population–5,126

Accommodations

Sandy Best Western Inn, 37465 East Hwy 26 / 503-668-7100
Brookside Bed and Breakfast, 45232 Southeast Paha Loop / 503-668-4766
Resort at the Mountain, 68010 East Fairway (Welches, OR 97067) / 503-622-3101

Campgrounds

Mt. Hood Village (RV), 65000 East Hwy 26 / 800-255-3069

Restaurants

Elusive Trout Pub, 39333 Proctor Boulevard / 503-668-7844
Barlow Trail Inn, 69580 East Hwy 26 (Zigzag, OR 97049) / 503-622-3112
Espresso Deli, 38776 Pioneer Boulevard / 503-668-9477
Joe's Donuts, 39230 Pioneer Boulevard / 503-668-7215

Fly Shops and Sporting Goods

The Fly Fishing Shop, 68248 East Hwy 26 (Welches, OR 97067) / Guide service available / 503-622-4607

Northwest Flyfishing Outfitters, 17302 Northeast Halsey Street (Gresham, OR 97230) / 503-252-1529 or 888-292-1137

Hospital

Legacy Mt. Hood Medical Center, 24800 Southeast Stark (Gresham, OR 97030) / 503-674-1122

Airport

Portland International Airport, 7000 Northeast Airport Way, Portland, OR 97218 / 503-460-4234

Auto Rental

Bee Rent-A-Car, 1975 East Powell Boulevard (Gresham, OR) / 503-665-0101

Enterprise Rent-A-Car, 1475 East Powell Boulevard (Gresham, OR) / 503-665-3300

Gresham Rent-A-Car, 1655 Northeast Burnside Street (Gresham, OR) / 503-667-8284

Also check Portland International Airport for major car rental agencies.

Auto Repair

Suburban Ford, Inc., 37000 Hwy 26 / 503-668-5511
Suburban Chevrolet Geo, Hwy 26 / 503-668-5555
Deane's Auto Repair, 41951 Southeast Hwy 26 / 503-668-4563

For More Information

Sandy Area Chamber of Commerce
P.O. Box 536
Sandy, OR 97055
503-668-4006

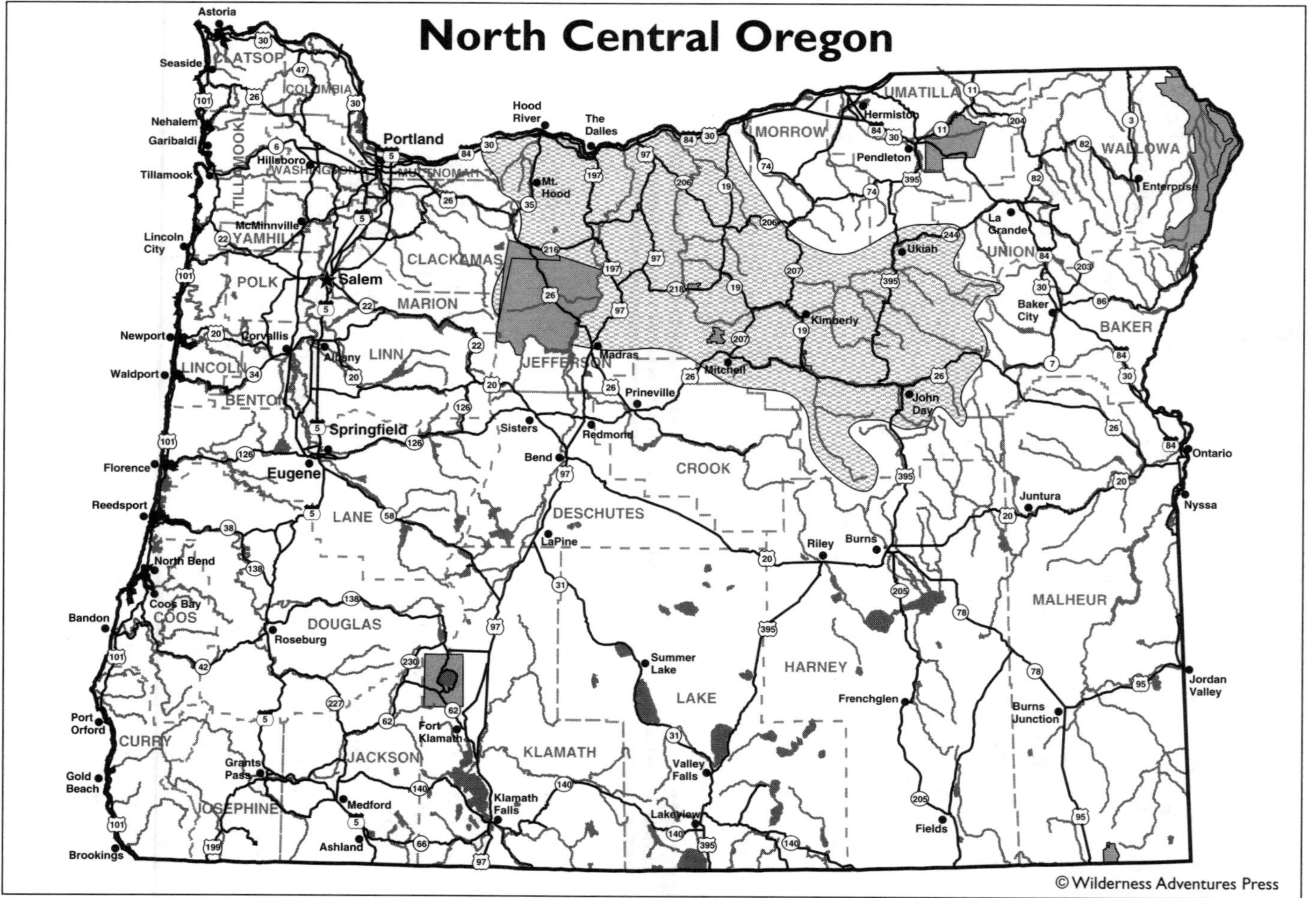
North Central Oregon
Astoria
Seaside
Nehalem
Garibaldi
Tillamook
Lincoln City
Newport
Waldport
Florence
Reedsport
North Bend
Coos Bay
Bandon
Port Orford
Gold Beach
Brookings
Portland
Hillsboro
McMinnville
Salem
Albany
Corvallis
Springfield
Eugene
Roseburg
Grants Pass
Medford
Ashland
Fort Klamath
Klamath Falls
Hood River
The Dalles
Mt. Hood
Madras
Prineville
Redmond
Sisters
Bend
LaPine
Mitchell
Kimberly
Ukiah
John Day
Hermiston
Pendleton
La Grande
Baker City
Enterprise
Ontario
Nyssa
Juntura
Burns
Riley
Frenchglen
Fields
Burns Junction
Jordan Valley
Summer Lake
Valley Falls
Lakeview
CLATSOP
COLUMBIA
TILLAMOOK
WASHINGTON
YAMHILL
POLK
LINCOLN
BENTON
MULTNOMAH
CLACKAMAS
MARION
LINN
LANE
DOUGLAS
COOS
CURRY
JOSEPHINE
JACKSON
KLAMATH
JEFFERSON
DESCHUTES
CROOK
LAKE
HARNEY
MALHEUR
UMATILLA
MORROW
UNION
WALLOWA
BAKER
© Wilderness Adventures Press

North Central Oregon

Oregon is graced with some of this nation's finest fly waters—the Rogue and North Umpqua with their great runs of steelhead, the Williamson and its monster trout, and the McKenzie's boating tradition and deep green surroundings are all well known among U.S. fly rodders.

Yet, nine times out of 10, when you tell someone you're from Oregon and like to cast a fly rod on occasion, the very next thing you'll hear will be about the Deschutes River. You will then nod and begin listening to one story or another about the Deschutes experience.

Is this Oregon's "finest" fly water? On many levels, it certainly is. The combination of wild trout and steelhead in this big desert river is a real treat. Throw in fish with tremendous fight, prolific bug life, more public access than you could fish in six months, sunrises, moonrises, and much, much more, and you can begin to justify this title.

On either side of the Deschutes, there are two systems that have gone separate ways, but both are flyfisheries worth a hard look. On one side, the Hood River serves as a hideout for many metropolitan area flyfishers. It's not a river that offers myriad hookups, but with a rod in hand, it does a good job of soothing the soul.

The other side of the Deschutes is the river's much-changed twin, the John Day. Once it was much like the Deschutes but has now become a warmwater fishery and one of the greatest smallmouth flyfisheries from coast to coast.

North central Oregon offers a wilderness flyfishing experience. While its remote canyons can make you feel physically small, when a trout, steelhead, or bass pull hard on your line, I promise your soul will swell with every enormous leap and thrash of these wild fish.

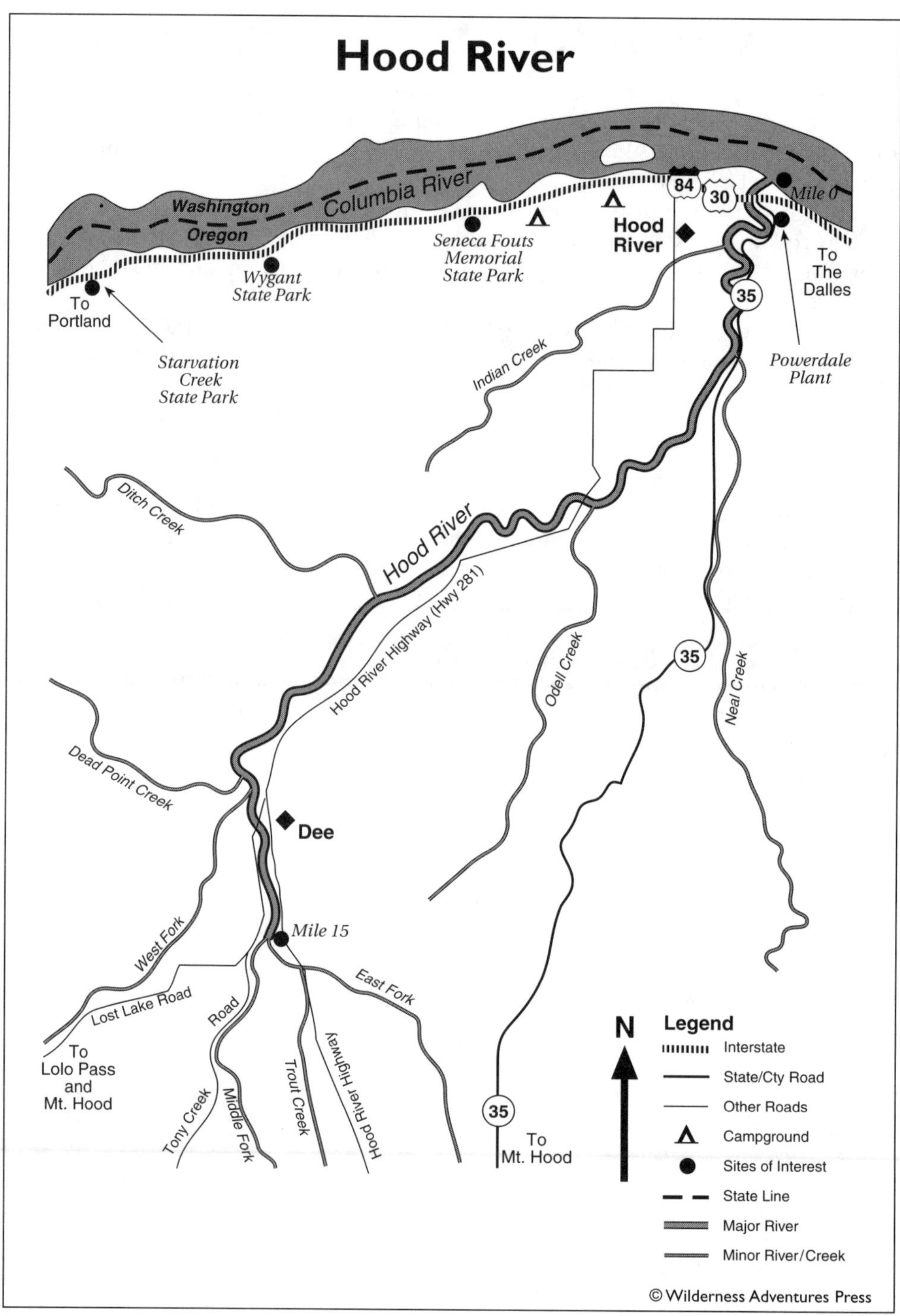
Hood River
Washington
Oregon
Columbia River
84
30
Mile 0
Hood River
Seneca Fouts Memorial State Park
Wygant State Park
To Portland
Starvation Creek State Park
To The Dalles
35
Powerdale Plant
Indian Creek
Ditch Creek
Hood River
Hood River Highway (Hwy 281)
Odell Creek
Neal Creek
Dead Point Creek
Dee
West Fork
Mile 15
East Fork
Lost Lake Road
Road
To Lolo Pass and Mt. Hood
Tony Creek
Middle Fork
Trout Creek
Hood River Highway
To Mt. Hood
N
Legend
Interstate
State/Cty Road
Other Roads
Campground
Sites of Interest
State Line
Major River
Minor River/Creek
© Wilderness Adventures Press

Hood River

The Hood River tumbles down from Mt. Hood on a relatively short run to the Columbia. It holds several runs of fish, and its cool waters offer a brief respite to ocean fish heading farther up the Columbia River system. Its two forks twist through rock and forest. The East Fork runs 10 miles, and the West Fork runs 15 miles to where they meet to form the main stem, which then runs a quick 13 miles to the Columbia where it gathers its fish.

Steelhead and chinook use the Hood's glacial waters for reproduction and a rest stop. The Hood holds one or both of these migratory fish 12 months of the year and is open to fishing the whole year. A fair trout population calls the Hood home, and there is a season in place on the river.

Fish are caught year-round, with steelhead catch rates spiking in June for summer runs and late February and March for winter runs. River levels fluctuate greatly during the year, since rainfall and snowmelt easily affect the Hood. When the river drops below 2,000 cfs, it begins to fish well with fly tackle. Water temperatures dictate what levels to fish your flies. For example, in the summer, as water temperatures rise, steelhead are more willing to move through the water for a fly, whereas cold winter flows will keep fish close to the bottom, where they can hold and save energy.

Fishing for steelhead in summer is generally done with floating lines and the occasional sinktip. The lower river offers good opportunities to present flies on the swing. Some of the holding runs are small, so creative mending and a discreet profile can help your chances. Some of Travis Duddles' (owner of Gorge Fly Shop in Hood River) favorite flies for summer-run fish are green-butted skunks, purple perils, freight trains, and blue charms. He will fish these in sizes 6 through 2/0.

Winter steelhead are pursued with the heaviest sinktips in the 10-foot range or floating lines with a long leader and weight. The need for depth is important this time of year and having a fast sinking line will help you search the water more effectively. Duddles likes to fish polar shrimp, popsicles, articulated leeches, and glo-bugs when fishing for winter steelhead.

Fishing to both runs of fish can be done using down and across methods or dry line indicator tactics. Most fishing seems to get done on the swing, but flies fished with indicators will take fish.

The basic setup on the Hood River for steelhead is an 8-weight rod at least 9 feet in length. Match rods with floating lines and sinktips, depending on the time of year you are fishing. A 10-foot leader tapered to 10 or 12 pounds is necessary for most Hood River fish.

Hood's access is relatively good. The mouth can be fished from the town of Hood River, while a footpath heads upriver at the Powerdale plant, located just above town on Hwy 35. The trail follows the river well upstream. There are a couple of miles of fishable river in this stretch. The only other access to the main stem of the Hood is a little farther up the highway at the viewpoint on Hwy 35 just past the Powerdale plant. Here you will find a trail dropping into the Hood River Gorge that will give you

With little effort and a few extra hours, fly anglers can find classic steelhead runs in the Hood River system.

some limited access up and down the river. The lower water on the main Hood is best fished in the bottom 4 miles. At mile 4, there is small dam that diverts water into an immense pipe that feeds the Powerdale powerhouse. The viewpoint access will put you a few miles below this small impoundment.

Hood River's forks offer several angling opportunities. The West Fork used to have a fly-only stretch, but this has been removed recently and the area is subject to continuous rule changes. It draws steelhead all the way up to a natural punchbowl that is passable for fish. The West Fork's small narrow canyons and dense forest make some of the river inaccessible, but a little sweat can put you into some pristine waters. The West Fork has a fair trout population that can be fun with light fly gear, especially for a beginner. The heavily forested nature of this area will definitely teach some creative casting skills. Lost Lake Road and Lolo Pass Road offer access to the West Fork.

The East Fork is stocked with rainbows of catchable size. Fishing for trout is a summertime activity here. Very basic flies and trout tackle are all that one needs, and this is a great place for people to hone flyfishing skills. Take a few beadhead nymphs and some parachute dry flies, and you're set. The East Fork is followed by Hwy 35 and Hwy 281 from Hood River to the town of Dee.

It's a lot easier for fish to move through the forks of the Hood River than it is for anglers.

The Hood River system may not be a world-class fishery, but it does offer area fly anglers a relatively consistent fishery close to home. Few people call the Hood River a blue-ribbon fishery, but for Portland area fly anglers looking for a line-throwing fix, it is worth checking out occasionally. If you need more direction or a good guide, talk to Travis Duddles at his Gorge Fly Shop in Hood River.

As of this writing, Oregon regulations list the river as open, but the rules have been changing every few months. With luck, the river will remain open, at least on a catch-and-release basis, so that area anglers have a close place in which to escape with fly rod in hand. Check current regulations or call Duddles for recent changes.

Stream Facts: Hood River

Season

- Open for trout May 23 to October 31.
- Open for chinook salmon, coho salmon, and steelhead entire year.

Special Regulations

- Closed from wall of the PP&L plant located at Powerdale downstream 200 feet. Check locally for any changes to special regulations for the Hood River.

Fish

- Steelhead
- Chinook and marginal coho salmon
- Rainbow trout

River Flows

- Best when under 2,000 cfs
- River Forecast Center, 503-261-9246

River Character

- Hood River provides good habitat for steelhead with small runs twirling through rock and forest.
- Access is fairly good on the main stem at the mouth and from a trail at the Powerdale plant. There is also a trail from Hwy 35 into the Hood River Gorge.
- The Forks provide options to catch smaller fish and can be reached by access roads off Hwy 281.

Maps

- DeLorme *Oregon Atlas and Gazetteer*

JOHN DAY RIVER

Oregon is blessed with one of the finest smallmouth fisheries in the nation. The John Day River is the second longest free-flowing river in the continental United States, with 200 miles of undammed river flowing north to the Columbia.

Arid landscapes and desert canyon greet anglers coming to cast flies on this river, and aggressive smallmouth are there to greet the flies. Fly anglers who have been weaned on trout and steelhead are often given bass religion on the John Day. Smallmouth are big fun on a fly rod.

The John Day was once a prolific steelhead river, and the fishery was used as such. Draw-down from irrigation, coupled with summer's blazing heat in this part of Oregon, has raised the river's temperature beyond its historical average. Steelheading on the John Day is now done only by a limited number of anglers who are well in tune with today's small steelhead runs.

Steelhead anglers no longer flock to John Day, and many anglers feel that Oregon didn't need to trade a prolific steelhead system for a warmwater fishery. However, the introduction of smallmouth in the 1970s has produced a fishery well worth checking out.

John Day's smallmouth bass can be caught anywhere from half a pound up to 5 pounds, with middle range fish making up the majority of the catch. From the community of Kimberly downstream to the mouth, the river is productive. A few guides in Oregon love to float clients down the river's remote canyon stretches during prime boating and fishing months. For those not boating, there is also a long stretch of easy wade access from Kimberly downriver about 25 miles to Service Creek.

During late spring and early summer, fishing is fast and furious. Anglers brag of 50-fish days while floating, and that's with a nap in the afternoon. Flyfishers can be on the water as early as April and fish into the month of October. The drift boat season is normally from April to June. After June the water gets too low for drift boats, although smaller, light craft can get through the canyons with some rowing effort. A minimum of 1,000 cfs is needed for drift-boating. Maximum flow for decent fishing is no more than 3,000 cfs. The John Day has some big water as well as stretches that you will have to row through. It is for experienced boaters only.

Midday heat makes the river a morning and evening affair. A nap may be in order so that you can get up early and stay up late. For hardy anglers who don't mind the sun, there are plenty of fish willing to grab a fly for lunch. The rare cloudy day in summer can produce not only big numbers of fish but outstanding catches of big fish as well. Low-light periods move the biggest of John Day's fish to flies—all the more reason to concentrate your efforts in the morning and evening.

Smallmouth are commonly fished with 5- and 6-weight setups. A stout rod will allow you to set the hook aggressively, although many bass will hook themselves as they try to kill the fly. A 6-weight will also help turn over big bass flies like poppers and buggers. If you are able to cast big flies with lighter tackle, do it. The typical 12-inch smallmouth on a 4-weight is a lot of fun. A fish over 5 pounds can

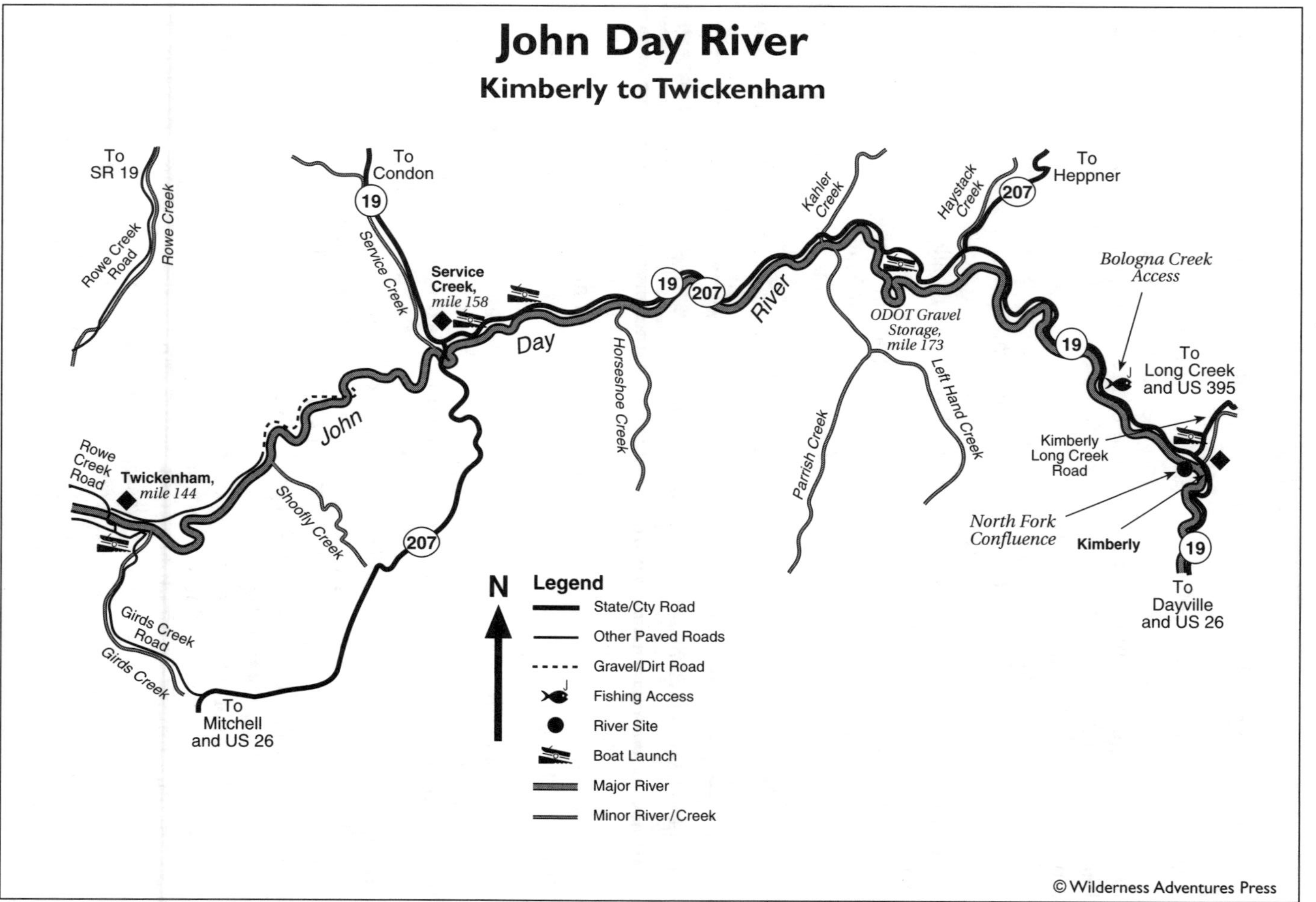
John Day River
Kimberly to Twickenham
To SR 19
Rowe Creek Road
Rowe Creek
To Condon
19
Service Creek
Service Creek, mile 158
Day
19
207
River
Kahler Creek
Haystack Creek
207
To Heppner
Bologna Creek Access
ODOT Gravel Storage, mile 173
Horseshoe Creek
Parrish Creek
Left Hand Creek
19
To Long Creek and US 395
Kimberly Long Creek Road
North Fork Confluence
Kimberly
19
To Dayville and US 26
John
Rowe Creek Road
Twickenham, mile 144
Shoofly Creek
207
Girds Creek Road
Girds Creek
To Mitchell and US 26
N
Legend
State/Cty Road
Other Paved Roads
Gravel/Dirt Road
Fishing Access
River Site
Boat Launch
Major River
Minor River/Creek
© Wilderness Adventures Press

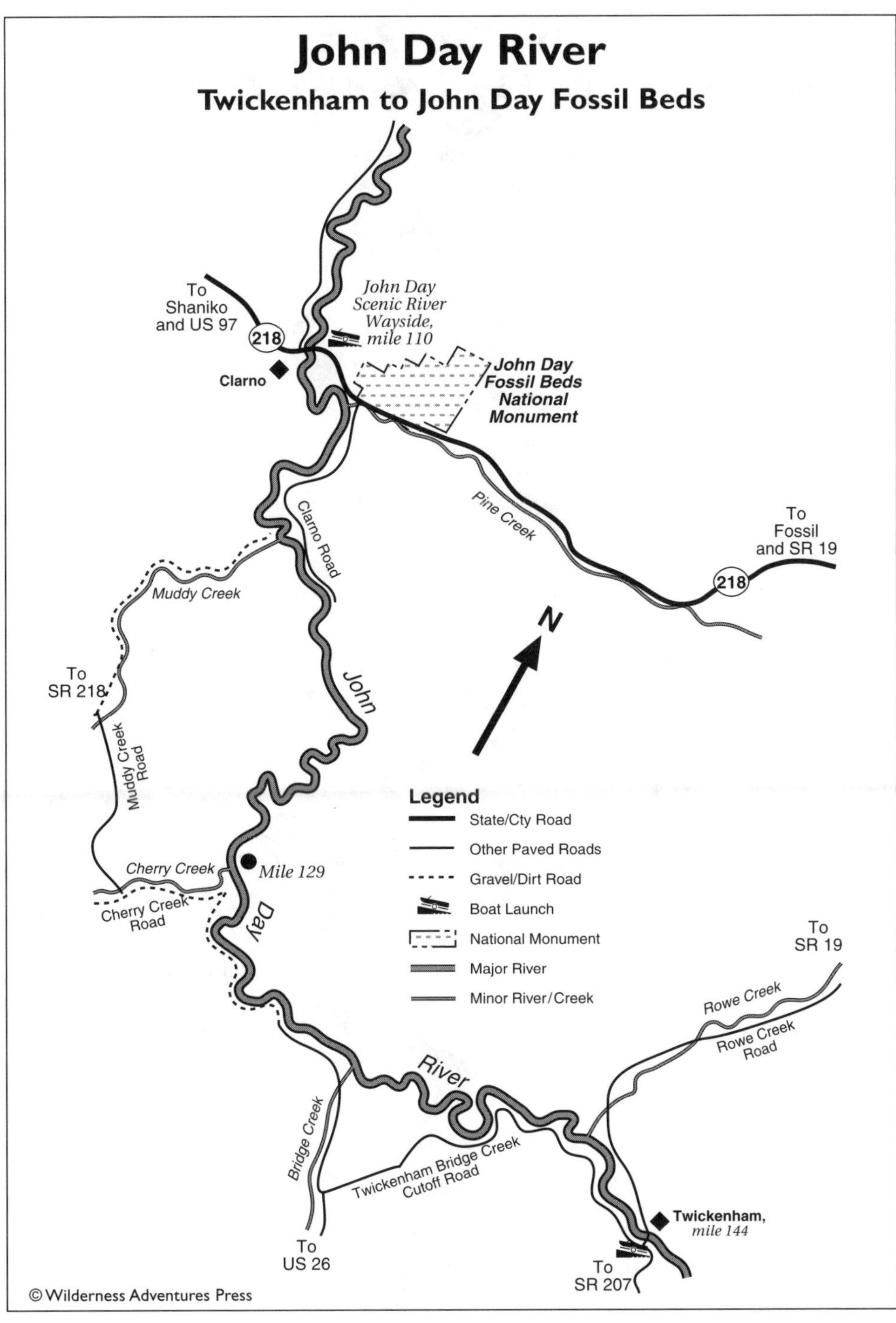

John Day River
Twickenham to John Day Fossil Beds
To Shaniko and US 97
218
John Day Scenic River Wayside, mile 110
Clarno
John Day Fossil Beds National Monument
Clarno Road
Pine Creek
To Fossil and SR 19
218
Muddy Creek
To SR 218
N
John
Muddy Creek Road
Legend
State/Cty Road
Other Paved Roads
Gravel/Dirt Road
Boat Launch
National Monument
Major River
Minor River/Creek
Cherry Creek
Mile 129
Cherry Creek Road
Day
To SR 19
Rowe Creek
Rowe Creek Road
River
Bridge Creek
Twickenham Bridge Creek Cutoff Road
Twickenham, mile 144
To US 26
To SR 207

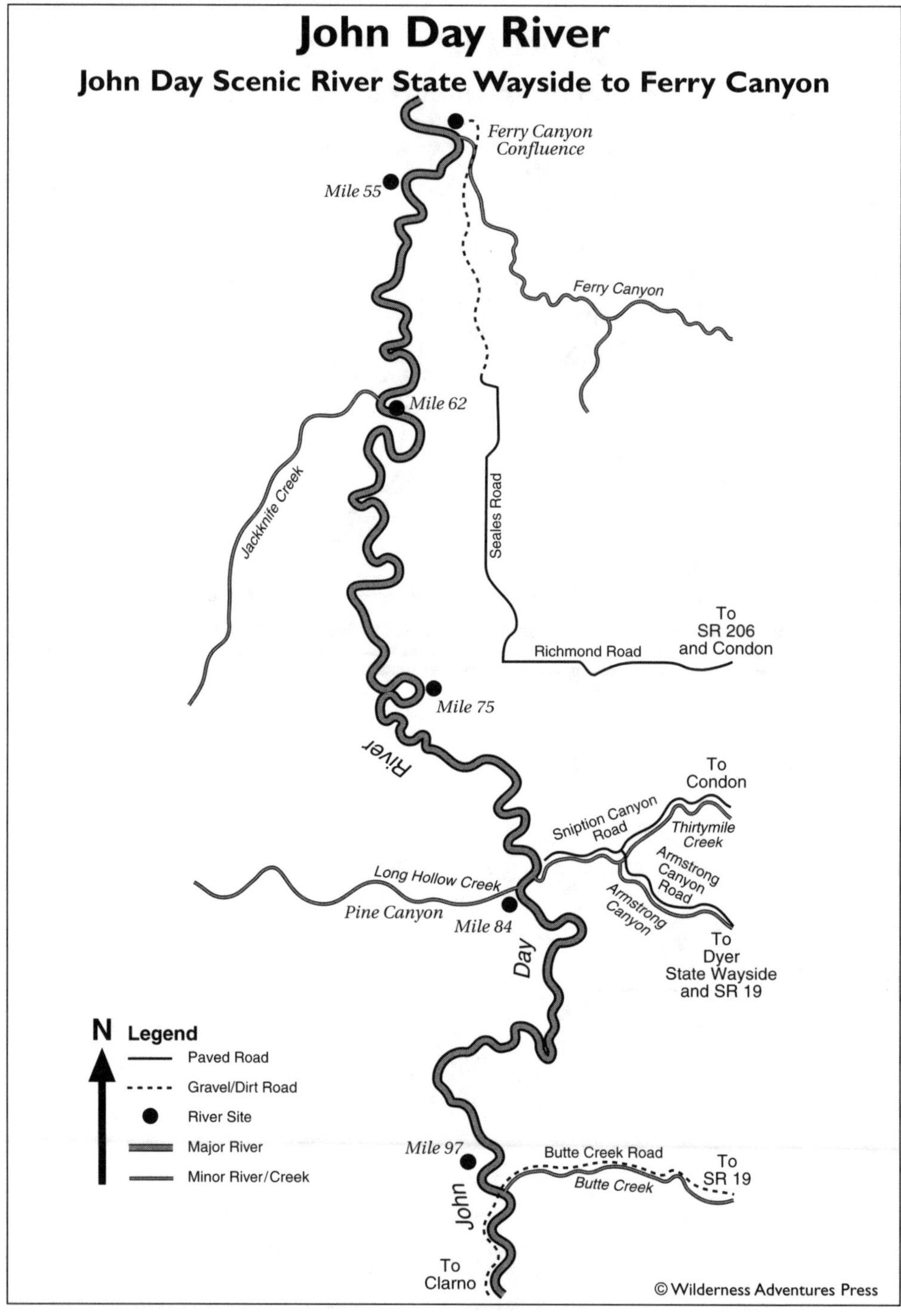
John Day River
John Day Scenic River State Wayside to Ferry Canyon
Ferry Canyon Confluence
Mile 55
Ferry Canyon
Mile 62
Jackknife Creek
Seales Road
To SR 206 and Condon
Richmond Road
Mile 75
River
To Condon
Sniption Canyon Road
Thirtymile Creek
Armstrong Canyon Road
Long Hollow Creek
Armstrong Canyon
Pine Canyon
Mile 84
Day
To Dyer State Wayside and SR 19
N
Legend
Paved Road
Gravel/Dirt Road
River Site
Major River
Minor River/Creek
Mile 97
Butte Creek Road
To SR 19
Butte Creek
John
To Clarno
© Wilderness Adventures Press

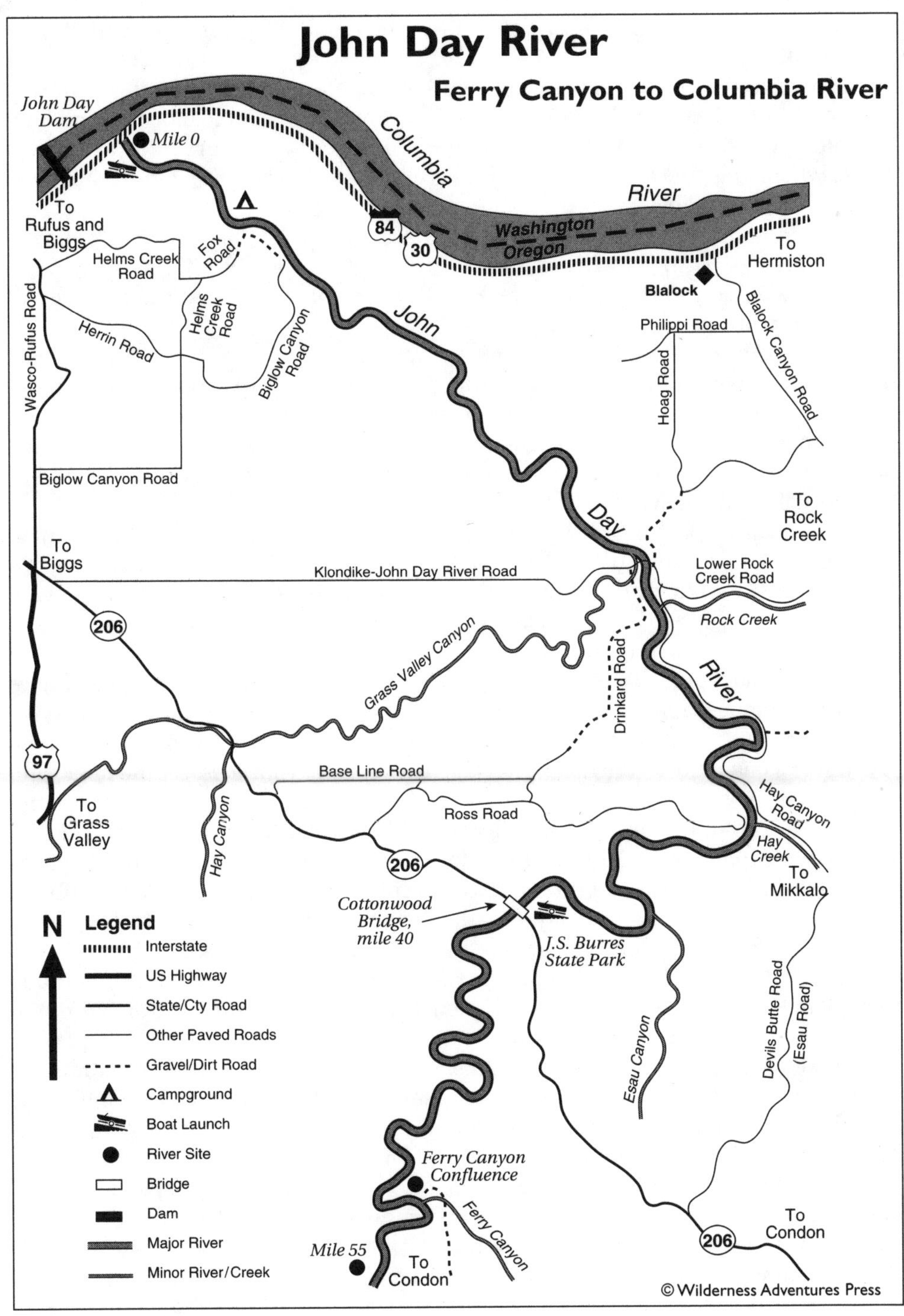
John Day River
Ferry Canyon to Columbia River
John Day Dam
Mile 0
Columbia
River
Washington
Oregon
84
30
To Rufus and Biggs
Helms Creek Road
Fox Road
Helms Creek Road
Herrin Road
Biglow Canyon Road
Wasco-Rufus Road
Biglow Canyon Road
To Hermiston
Blalock
Philippi Road
Hoag Road
Blalock Canyon Road
John
Day
River
To Rock Creek
To Biggs
Klondike-John Day River Road
Lower Rock Creek Road
Rock Creek
206
Grass Valley Canyon
Drinkard Road
97
Base Line Road
To Grass Valley
Hay Canyon
Ross Road
Hay Canyon Road
Hay Creek
To Mikkalo
206
Cottonwood Bridge, mile 40
J.S. Burres State Park
Esau Canyon
Devils Butte Road (Esau Road)
N
Legend
Interstate
US Highway
State/Cty Road
Other Paved Roads
Gravel/Dirt Road
Campground
Boat Launch
River Site
Bridge
Dam
Major River
Minor River/Creek
Ferry Canyon Confluence
Ferry Canyon
Mile 55
To Condon
206
To Condon
© Wilderness Adventures Press

be landed with a 4-weight, although a 6-pound smallmouth may test the brand name on the rod.

Travis Duddles, owner of the Gorge Fly Shop, does several multiday float trips on the John Day each season. He tells me, "We like to start early in the morning and float flies along banks and rocky outcrops, anywhere there is structure. It is a numbers game, where anglers catch lots of 10- to 14-inch fish, and are treated to the occasional 3- to 5-pounder."

It is a common practice on the river to start with surface flies, such as poppers. When a big bass comes rocketing to the surface and explodes on a popper in the middle of a quiet drift right at the crack of dawn, you may find that the third cup of coffee that morning was a bad idea.

Duddles' favorite flies for the John Day are foam poppers in colors like chartreuse, yellow, white, and black. Buy or tie poppers with lots of rubberlegs, the more action the better. If taking fish off the top gets difficult, a switch to natural patterns, such as big Dave's hoppers, can sometimes draw strikes. If surface activity just isn't happening, don't hesitate to go subsurface. Standard streamers like buggers and zonkers will hook plenty of fish.

To entice strikes from smallmouth, work poppers erratically on the surface making plenty of racket. Subsurface flies should be allowed to sink but try to stay in contact with the fly while this is happening—bass often smash flies as they fall toward the bottom. Strip streamers with a lot of action, keeping the rod tip right at the water. Try to imitate an injured baitfish or fleeing crawdad.

Rigid leaders, tapered to 10 or 12 pounds are needed for these fish. What you've learned about the leader-shy habits of trout and the accompanying delicacy needed to fish them should be left at home when you come here. The best way to approach bass is with the same attitude the fish have—aggressive. Work your flies, set the hook, and fight these fish with as much vigor as they exhibit when hooked, and you'll excel here.

The river from Kimberly to Service Creek is followed closely by Hwy 19 and provides a ton of road access. Land abutting the river is a mix of public and private property, but wade access is not a problem. Wet-wading on John Day is also no problem on a typical spring or summer day. Breathable lightweight waders can be helpful on cooler days or to avoid sunburn on hot ones. Below Service Creek the river enters a scenic desert canyon. This is a remote stretch with no road access, offering solitude to anglers looking for a wilderness experience. Be aware that on all stretches of the John Day rattlesnakes are a concern.

Multiday floats are a great way to experience this river, and permits are not required as of 1998. A float trip from Service Creek to Twickenham can be done in one day, but if you want to work the water carefully, plan to take two days. Floating from Twickenham to Clarno Rapids can take up to four days. Another popular float is Clarno Rapids to Cottonwood Bridge, which takes at least five days even with good current. There is also a little bank access at the town of Clarno.

The John Day River is a one-of-a-kind flyfishery in Oregon. The quality of smallmouth fishing coupled with its unique geological setting, make it a place all fly

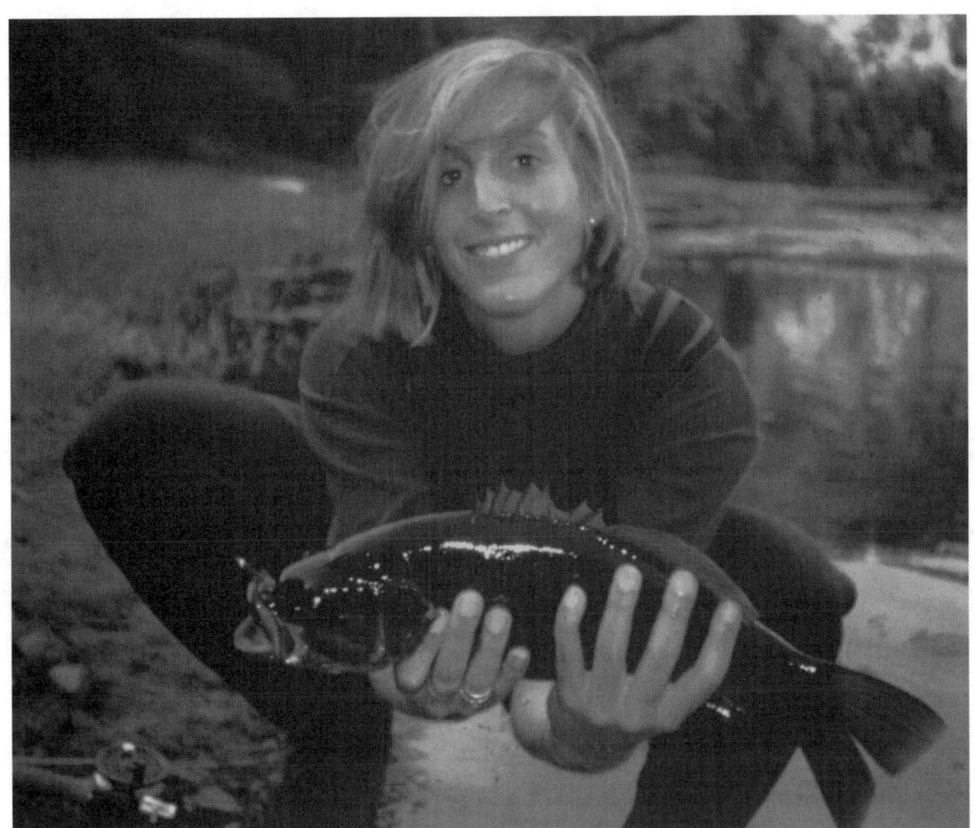

Vanessa McLean with a John Day River smallmouth bass.
(Photo by Chris Daughters)

anglers should visit. Boating opportunities through its deep canyons offer solitude with little fishing pressure. Consider a multiday trip with an outfitter—this will allow you to concentrate on fishing rather than preparing food or finding shade. If you only have a day or two, this river offers the best walk and wade opportunity for smallmouth bass in Oregon.

Stream Facts: John Day River

Seasons

- Open the entire year for smallmouth from Tumwater Falls up to the North Fork confluence at Kimberly.

Special Regulations

- Five bass per day may be kept but no more than 3 over 15 inches in length. Consult current Oregon Fishing Regulations for steelhead rules.

Fish

- Smallmouth bass, some up to 5 pounds.
- Steelhead are sometimes in the system.

Flows

- 3,000 to150 cfs

River Characteristics

- During the prime smallmouth months, John Day can be one of the hottest fisheries in the state—both the temperature and the fishing. Hot sun and desert conditions make this a warmwater fishery. There is plenty of structure, such as rocky outcrops and weedbeds, where bass love to wait in ambush. Both boat and wade access are readily available.
- Walk and wade stretches are between Service Creek and Kimberly from pullouts on Hwy 19.

Maps

- BLM
- Drifters and Historical Guide to the John Day River

Area Fly Shops

- Gorge Fly Shop, 201 Oak Street, Hood River, OR / 541-386-6977

Lower Deschutes River

My friend, Mike Bordenkircher, and I had waded into the Deschutes near Maupin one overcast day. I was thankful for the slight drizzle falling from the gray fall skies because it provided a constant blue-winged olive emergence. I cast tiny cripple patterns over the noses of several decent sized redsides. About every 15 minutes I was hooked into one of these powerful trout.

A hundred and fifty yards ahead of me I could see Mike lobbing a heavily weighted nymph into a current seam along a good-sized eddy. He would swing his fly through, lifting it as it came below him. About every 15 minutes Mike was hooked into a redside, much like what I was catching, with a few that were even bigger.

I like catching big fish, but the dry fly opportunity that day was more than I could pass up. I wondered why Mike was not taking advantage of this late fall occurrence as well. After all, there weren't going to be many more dry fly opportunities for us during the long Oregon winter. I continued to fish despite my urge to get Mike on the surface.

An hour went by and the hatch grew stronger. Fish were taking my fly every 5 or 10 minutes by then, and occasionally I was releasing fat 18-inchers after terrific battles. Upstream, Mike continued to fish his heavy nymph. I could stand it no longer—perhaps Mike didn't think the big fish were up or maybe his dry fly stock was depleted. I decided to give him an earful.

Rather than shout over the big water of the lower Deschutes, I waded back to the bank, reeling as I went. I secured my fly to the rod, cranked the line tight, and headed upriver.

When I got within 20 yards of Mike, I shouted "Hey, how about this hatch? Do you need any..." As the word "flies" was exiting my mouth, I bit my bottom lip hard enough to draw blood, as 10 pounds of silver steelhead cartwheeled in the air not 10 feet from my head. I looked in shock from the fish to Mike and saw he was looking back at me, with a smile far too big for his face. His reel screamed, and he laughed as he began running toward me in pursuit of a fish seemingly headed back to the ocean.

Mike and I slapped hands 10 minutes later after he released the steelhead, his smile never shrinking. After the appropriate congratulations on my behalf, he headed back upriver. Ten steps from where he left me, he turned back and asked, "What were you yelling when I hooked that fish?"

"Nothing important," I replied, never lifting my eyes from my fly box as I searched for a big stonefly nymph.

Such is the nature of the Deschutes River—a big river capable of producing big days and big fish. The Deschutes usually runs clear from Pelton Dam at Lake Billy Chinook to its mouth at the Columbia River. It powers through a deep desert gorge most of the way and provides awesome habitat for its unique redside trout population as well as good runs of steelhead. The river holds both species year-round. Steelhead are the main focus between July and December.

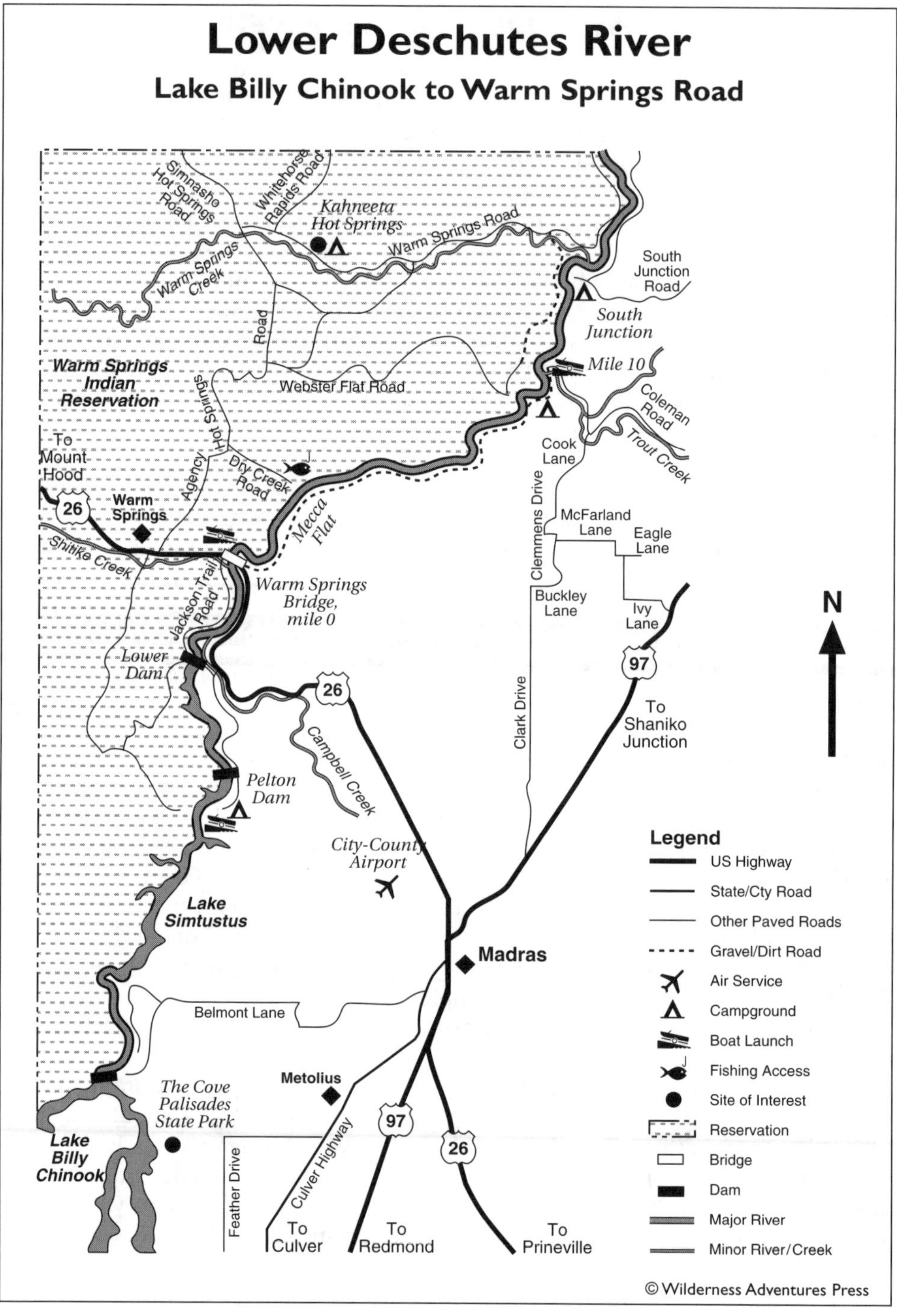

Lower Deschutes River
Lake Billy Chinook to Warm Springs Road
Simnasho Hot Springs Road
Whitehorse Rapids Road
Kahneeta Hot Springs
Warm Springs Road
Warm Springs Creek
South Junction Road
South Junction
Road
Warm Springs Indian Reservation
Hot Springs
Webster Flat Road
Mile 10
Coleman Road
Trout Creek
Cook Lane
To Mount Hood
Agency
Dry Creek Road
26
Warm Springs
Mecca Flat
Clemmens Drive
McFarland Lane
Eagle Lane
Shitike Creek
Jackson Trail Road
Warm Springs Bridge, mile 0
Buckley Lane
Ivy Lane
N
Lower Dam
97
26
To Shaniko Junction
Campbell Creek
Clark Drive
Pelton Dam
City-County Airport
Lake Simtustus
Madras
Belmont Lane
Metolius
The Cove Palisades State Park
Lake Billy Chinook
Feather Drive
Culver Highway
97
26
To Culver
To Redmond
To Prineville
Legend
US Highway
State/Cty Road
Other Paved Roads
Gravel/Dirt Road
Air Service
Campground
Boat Launch
Fishing Access
Site of Interest
Reservation
Bridge
Dam
Major River
Minor River/Creek

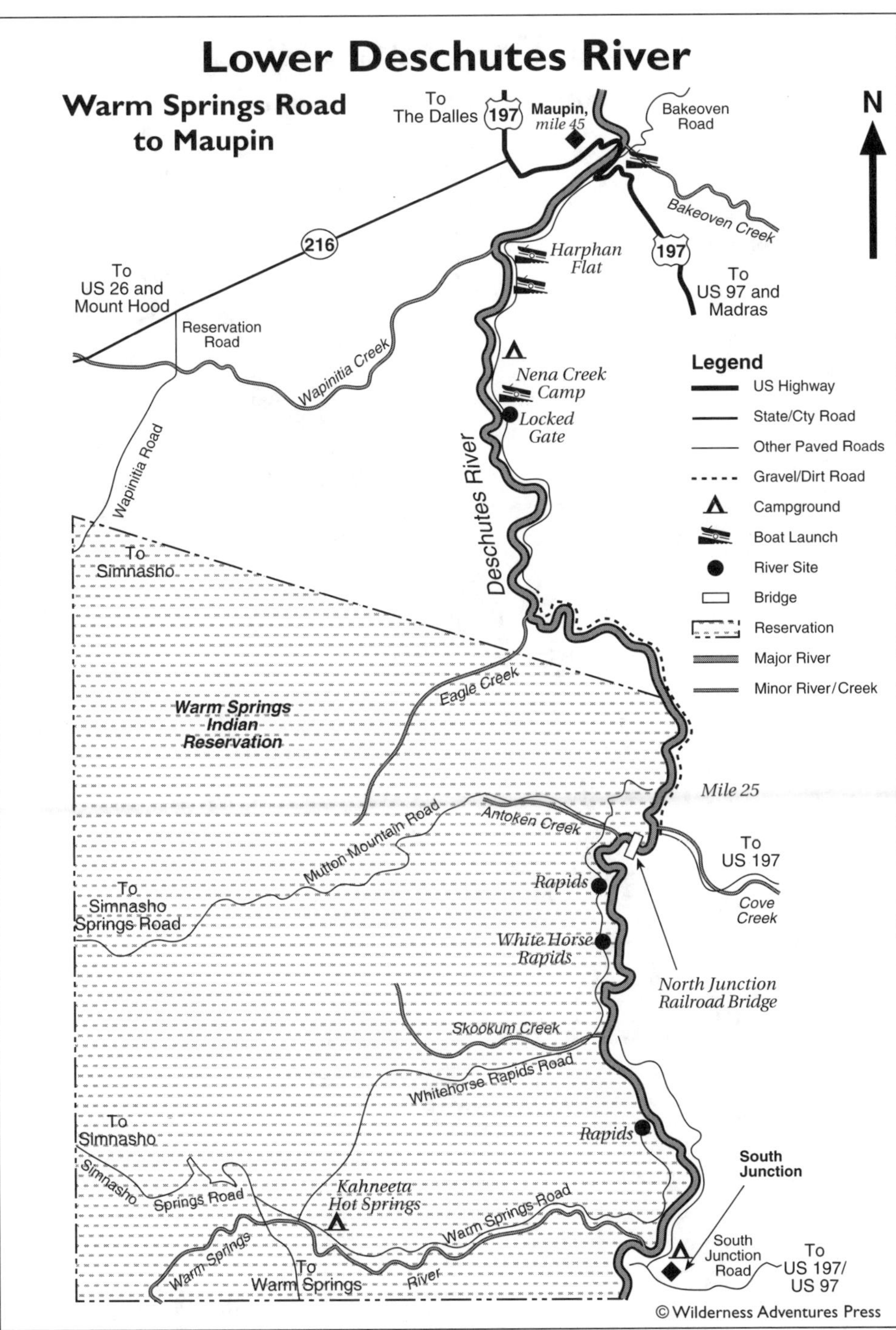
Lower Deschutes River
Warm Springs Road to Maupin
N
To The Dalles
197
Maupin, mile 45
Bakeoven Road
Bakeoven Creek
216
Harphan Flat
197
To US 97 and Madras
To US 26 and Mount Hood
Reservation Road
Wapinitia Creek
Nena Creek Camp
Locked Gate
Wapinitia Road
Deschutes River
Legend
US Highway
State/Cty Road
Other Paved Roads
Gravel/Dirt Road
Campground
Boat Launch
River Site
Bridge
Reservation
Major River
Minor River/Creek
To Simnasho
Eagle Creek
Warm Springs Indian Reservation
Mile 25
Mutton Mountain Road
Antoken Creek
To US 197
Rapids
Cove Creek
To Simnasho Springs Road
White Horse Rapids
North Junction Railroad Bridge
Skookum Creek
Whitehorse Rapids Road
To Simnasho
Rapids
South Junction
Simnasho Springs Road
Kahneeta Hot Springs
Warm Springs Road
South Junction Road
To US 197/ US 97
Warm Springs River
To Warm Springs
© Wilderness Adventures Press

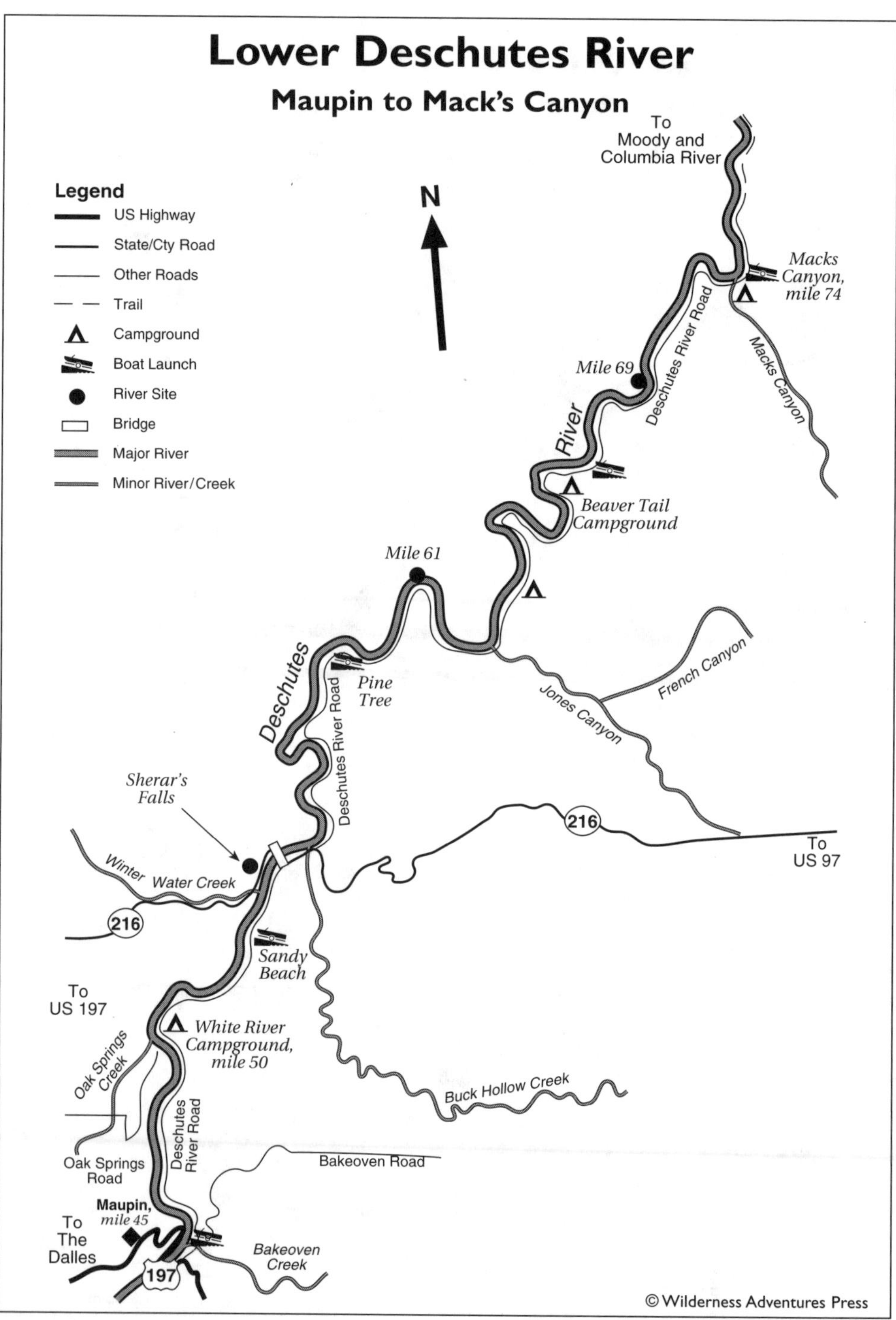
Lower Deschutes River
Maupin to Mack's Canyon
Legend
US Highway
State/Cty Road
Other Roads
Trail
Campground
Boat Launch
River Site
Bridge
Major River
Minor River/Creek
N
To
Moody and
Columbia River
Macks
Canyon,
mile 74
Deschutes River Road
Macks Canyon
Mile 69
River
Beaver Tail
Campground
Mile 61
Deschutes
Pine
Tree
French Canyon
Jones Canyon
Deschutes River Road
Sherar's
Falls
216
To
US 97
Winter Water Creek
216
Sandy
Beach
To
US 197
White River
Campground,
mile 50
Oak Springs
Creek
Buck Hollow Creek
Deschutes
River Road
Bakeoven Road
Oak Springs
Road
Maupin,
mile 45
To
The
Dalles
197
Bakeoven
Creek
© Wilderness Adventures Press

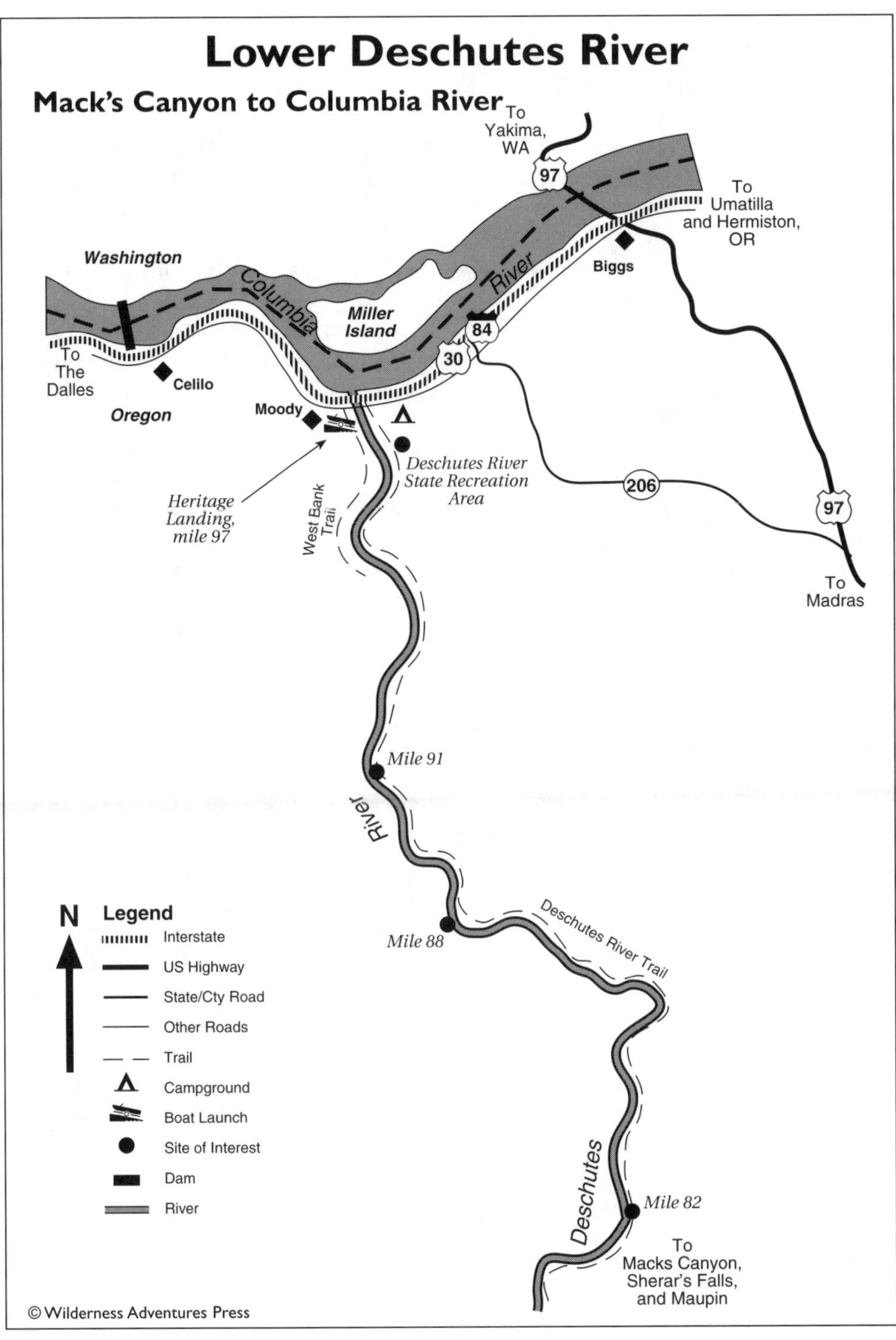
Lower Deschutes River
Mack's Canyon to Columbia River
To Yakima, WA
97
To Umatilla and Hermiston, OR
Washington
Columbia River
Miller Island
Biggs
84
30
To The Dalles
Celilo
Oregon
Moody
Deschutes River State Recreation Area
Heritage Landing, mile 97
West Bank Trail
206
97
To Madras
Mile 91
River
Mile 88
Deschutes River Trail
Deschutes
Mile 82
To Macks Canyon, Sherar's Falls, and Maupin
N
Legend
Interstate
US Highway
State/Cty Road
Other Roads
Trail
Campground
Boat Launch
Site of Interest
Dam
River

The Deschutes is heavily used in the summer months by both rafters and anglers, yet always offers respite from crowds for anglers willing to fish the river's off hours and less used sections. If you're looking for solitude, late fall and early winter are the times to fish the Deschutes.

The native Deschutes trout act much like ordinary rainbows but are tougher fish due to the river's rugged conditions. An angler who doesn't anticipate the redside's brute strength will learn some lessons here. An 18-inch redside that is able to find the main current of this big river is as good as gone. These fish feed readily from the surface on the river's myriad insects and can be taken consistently with nymphs and streamers under the surface.

Fly anglers targeting redside rainbow rather than steelhead must learn to read the Deschutes. This river is large enough and strong enough that trout anglers are relegated to fishing the banks. From the bank an angler is only limited by his length of cast and wading ability.

Good anglers regularly break a big river down visually into a few smaller rivers. This tends to keep the focus on smaller seams and buckets, thereby keeping an angler over a likely spot longer, allowing the spot to be fished more effectively. When looking at hundreds of yards of prime water, an angler may be apt to move on to ever-greener pastures, and on the Deschutes, the grass looks greener almost everywhere. Fly anglers are better off concentrating on the smaller picture. Pick a particular water type and method of fishing and then stick to it. This may produce better on the Deschutes than constantly moving and changing technique.

Deschutes redside are made strong by the heavy currents and changes in water level. Although the river runs through a desert environment, abundant insect life makes it possible for fish to live and grow big here. Big fish need more calories to survive, so the rich abundance of insects benefits both fish and angler.

The "hatch heard around the world" these days seems to be the Deschutes salmonfly hatch. It doesn't matter where you live, when people start talking about places they have fished, the Deschutes salmonfly will enter into the conversation. Late May and early June typically provide this unparalleled salmonfly opportunity. Big, beaded stonefly patterns are a favorite, and Kaufmann's stoneflies in brown and black, tied with rubberlegs, are deadly. Sofa pillows, stimulators, and bullethead stoneflies are great dry fly patterns that will take fish off the top. They are also effective fished subsurface as a drowned stonefly. This can be a deadly way to fish the bottoms of heavy riffles and behind whitewater. Try it in the summer with hoppers as well. The best stonefly action takes place from the town of Maupin upriver to Pelton Dam.

The Deschutes has good populations of smaller stoneflies, as well as a large variety of mayflies. Blue-winged olives can show up in good numbers any day of the year here. Caddis and midges are prevalent, and terrestrials make up a good part of the trout's diet in summer. If you've seen an insect on other Oregon streams, there is a good chance it also lives on the Deschutes. Serious Deschutes troutheads come to the river with an arsenal of flies, including several life stages for all the aforementioned insects.

A beautiful summer steelhead on the lower Deschutes River.
(Photo by Ken Morrish)

Leader length varies according to conditions. Wind can rip through the canyon, making long leaders out of the question. Oftentimes, hand tying short leaders that taper quickly can be the key to turning a fly over. When howling canyon winds blow hard enough to rip flies off your patch and pelt you with real insects, knot-tying skills are a must. Don't be too alarmed—there are also times when the river will act like a polite little spring creek offering calm winds and glassy runs, full of tiny mayflies and big rising fish. When this happens a leader tapered beyond 12 feet, with some extra 6X to maintain play through imperceptible microcurrents is needed to make a fish take—don't take shortcuts with leaders here!

The amount and variety of life found on the Deschutes create many types of conditions and a need for different techniques. This, in turn, forces a flyfisher to be well prepared when coming to meet the river's redside rainbows.

With a good supply of flies and gear, an angler is ready for the Deschutes. Standard dry fly techniques will catch fish but be prepared for some rodeo casting as well. The ability to cast flies under overhanging branches is important, especially during the salmonfly hatch. Big fish stare intently up into the streamside vegetation, waiting for these large insects to fall into the river. Casting a large dry fly well up under branches without hanging the fly may make the difference between a five-star

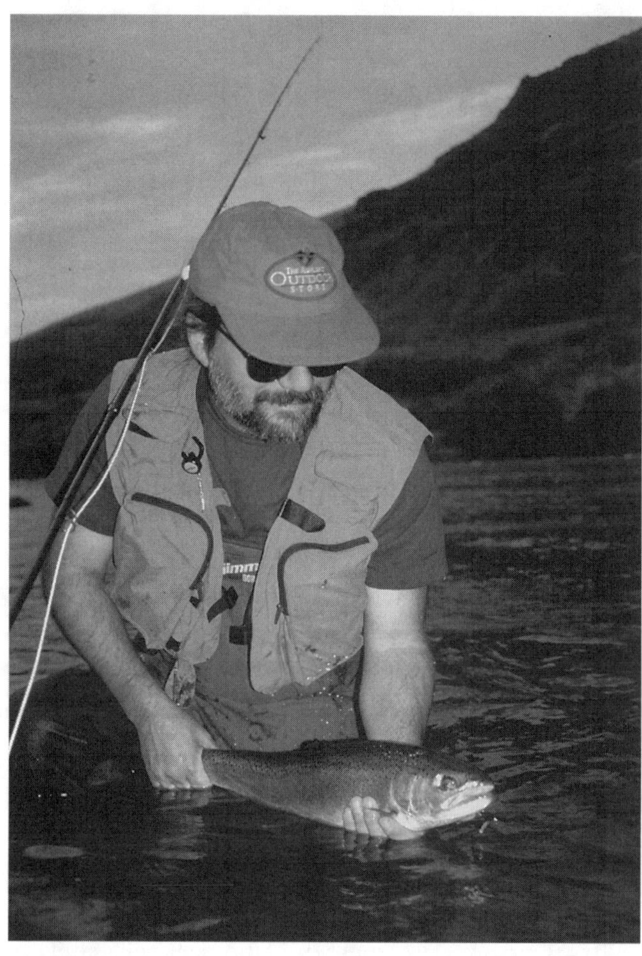

The Deschutes River produces nice steelhead. (Photo by Ken Morrish)

day and a frustrating one. Wind also creates problems, forcing anglers to use good technique in order to drive flies into a stiff breeze. Ofttimes, distance can be an issue when boulders and riffles, located well off the bank, offer an opportunity and limited back cast room will challenge your every attempt to reach those spots. It is necessary to be a proficient angler to excel on the Deschutes in a variety of conditions, and what you don't know already, the river will beat out of you in the long run.

Nymphing techniques on the river are also relatively standard, but they also offer the same casting challenges presented to dry-fly fishers. It becomes even more important to cast well once you start dealing with weighted nymphs and multifly setups. Swinging a variety of flies with a down-and-across presentation moves plenty of fish, as do dead-drift, indicator techniques.

Back eddies are a favorite target for Deschutes nymphing. Allowing flies to mill around in the depths of a large eddy, especially on slower days, can be very productive. Riffles, boulder filled troughs, and under streamside vegetation are also good places to concentrate nymphing efforts. It is impossible to get away from the fact that most of the river and water types hold fish almost all the time. Pick your favorite technique and water type, then work hard at it before switching or moving on.

Fly rodding for Deschutes River trout is a great experience for seasoned and novice anglers alike. Although tough at times, the river is prolific enough to grant all anglers good shots at quality trout. It also offers every trout angler something few other prolific trout streams in the nation do—the opportunity to tie into a bright, angry steelhead while fishing for trophy trout.

Steelhead are found in the Deschutes from its mouth to Pelton Dam year-round. There is a good population of die-hard steelheaders who frequent the Deschutes. Many outfitters guide for steelhead and know most of the favorite slots that steelhead frequent on their way upriver. Most of the fishing is done with dry lines and sinktips in a down-and-across fashion. Favorite steelhead fly patterns include the Mack's canyon, freight train, purple peril, and the signal light, to name a few.

It is not uncommon to see steelhead roll on the surface in the Deschutes. Upon seeing this, many anglers start with bombers and other skated flies trying to get the steelhead to roll up on a dry. The best steelhead fishing occurs during the low-light periods of day. Many anglers will begin fishing just before daybreak until the sun hits the water and again when the canyon's shadows have reclaimed the river. In between these times, many anglers fish for trout.

Water temperature, time of day, and water depth determine whether to use a floating line or a sinktip. Floating lines are most common in the summer. Anglers often switch to sinktips in the middle of the day. The Deschutes is a productive dry line steelhead fishery, but it is often necessary to be able to go deeper. Try fishing the top first, and then go back through the same water with consistently heavier sinktips. This is a good way to learn where fish hold and when, but this can only be done on the most uncrowded days.

Steelhead flyfishers commonly work their way down a run, not lingering long in any one place. Thus, it is acceptable to step in well upstream of someone who is in the bottom of a run but never below an angler swinging a fly.

Trout fishermen must also be aware of what other anglers are doing. Working upriver with indicators or dry flies for trout can interfere with a steelhead angler's progress. There are many more trout than steelhead in the Deschutes, and the right of way should go to the steelhead angler if they were there first. When in doubt on any river, just do the nice thing and ask. I've never been in a dispute with any angler who has exchanged a cordial hello and asked what my fishing plan was and vice versa.

The river's best steelhead fishing begins in July and lasts as long as December. As the season progresses, the river's higher reaches will produce more and more grabs as fish move upriver. August, September, and October are peak months in the lower river from the mouth to Mack's Canyon. From Mack's Canyon to Maupin, the run is fished from August through the first part of November, and from Maupin to Pelton Dam, the fishing can last until December. This late in the season, more and more sinktips are used to find fish.

Steelhead in the Deschutes average between 4 and 8 pounds. The fish aren't very big, but they do have a reputation for being hard fighters. These fish seem to have an attitude the moment they reach the Deschutes, and if you happen to hook one, stay on your toes.

Typical gear for fishing Deschutes River steelhead includes rods from 9 feet up to spey lengths. Seven- and 8-weights are used on the river to aid in mending and casting when desert winds are blowing and to help fight aggressive fish in strong currents. Once practiced by only a few anglers, spey casting has become more popular recently. Fly anglers are learning that flyfishing is rich in two-handed rod history. It is a great tool for covering huge pieces of water without throwing your arm out and hooking bushes on every other back cast. The two-handed rod's merits far outweigh the time, effort, and cost of picking up this traditional form of steelheading. Each year in Oregon, more and more spey casting is being done. Several guides and shops can give you lessons, and there are a few videos on the market if you want to learn on your own. Travis Duddles says all his guides carry at least one in the boat and teach clients how to use them on a regular basis.

The lower Deschutes covers a lot of miles from Pelton Dam to the Columbia River. Access is varied all along the river—hike-in wading, park and wade, and drift boats are all employed. Boating is only for anglers who have good skills and experience behind oars. Be aware that a Boater Pass for any floating device is required on the river. Licensing agents in the area have boater passes or can tell you where to get one.

Fishing out of a boat is illegal, so all fishermen must wade while fishing anywhere on the river between the mouth and the dam. Wading on the Deschutes is often tricky, and much precaution is advised. A wading staff is worth its weight in gold on the river, and studded boots really help grip the rocky bottom. The current is very strong in some places, and if you're not wet wading, use a wader belt. Don't take too many chances when wading the Deschutes—you'll almost always end up wet, and the river does take lives. When floating from spot to spot, boaters should always wear life preservers on this often technical river.

The river can be broken into sections according to access. The lower 24 miles of river, from the mouth to Mack's Canyon, has no road access, but a trail follows the east side of this stretch the whole way. Some anglers will mountain bike in on this side of the river, although not all the trail is in good enough shape for bikes. The river's lower section is popular with steelhead fishermen, especially in August, but it also holds plenty of trout. From Interstate 84 take the Celilo exit, then take Hwy 206 east to the mouth. From the east, take the Biggs exit from Interstate 84 and use Hwy 97 and then Hwy 206 west to the mouth. Always watch for rattlesnakes and poison oak when hiking the Deschutes River canyon.

The trail leading down from Mack's Canyon is easily reached via the Hwy 216 crossing. An angler can drive along this 20-mile stretch of river downstream from the

The Deschutes' abundance of insects benefits both fish and anglers. (Photo by Ken Morrish)

Hwy 216 crossing, below Sherar's Falls to Mack's Canyon, and get on the river from numerous pullouts.

From the Hwy 216 crossing, an angler can also take the Deschutes River Road south to Maupin, which provides another 8 miles of access. From Maupin an angler can continue up the east bank on a rough road heading upstream. To find this road, look for a road leaving Hwy197. It is the first right coming from the west, heading east over the bridge at Maupin. Look for speed bumps on the road after the turn. This road provides access to another 7 or 8 miles of river until you reach Locked Gate. From the locked gate an angler can hike upriver at least 13 more miles to North Junction.

The next drive-in point is at South Junction where an angler can find a little over a mile of bank access. The road into South Junction is from the intersection of Hwy 97 and Hwy 197. At this point, an angler can get on South Junction Road and follow it to the river.

The next east bank access is from Trout Creek up to Mecca Flat. A trail follows the river 10 miles between these two points. There are two ways to reach the Trout Creek access. From Madras, take Hwy 97 north to Clark Drive, turn left and follow Clark Drive until it turns right and becomes Buckley Lane. Turn left on Clemmens Drive and continue north through the unincorporated community of Gateway until Clemmens makes a right turn and becomes Cook Lane. Cooks Lane ends at Coleman Road, which follows Trout Creek to the Deschutes River access. Coming from the north on Hwy 97, make a right turn at Ivy Lane. Follow Ivy Lane to Emerson Drive and take a right until you reach Eagle Lane. Take a left and follow the road until it becomes McFarland Lane, which meets Clemmens Lane, then turn right on Clemmens through the unincorporated community of Gateway. Follow the directions given above from this point on.

The Deschutes' west bank offers anglers less access, but there are a few spots. The mouth of the river has a trail that follows the west bank about 2 miles, at which point it meets with railroad tracks that are private property and used by trains. Anglers are advised not to use them.

The next west side access is at the Oak Springs Hatchery. Take Oak Springs Road, which is located north of Maupin from Hwy 197/216. The only other access on the west bank is from the Warm Springs Indian Reservation at Dry Creek Campground. From Warm Springs, go north on Agency Hot Springs Road until it meets with Dry Creek Road, then turn right and follow the road to the river. Reservation permits are five dollars a day. Permits are available through retailers in the town of Warm Springs.

Floating the Deschutes is a wonderful and productive way to fish the whole river. There are long stretches that can be made into single or multiday trips. The Deschutes has a lot of big water with Class III and IV rapids being common. Sherar's Falls is impassable. Floaters should always have a floater's guide that thoroughly explains all the rapids on the river.

Because the Deschutes offers plenty of whitewater, rafters use the river extensively in the summer. Guides and flyfishers also float the river in drift boats, although fishing from a boat is not allowed. Anglers use boats for easier access to banks that aren't often fished by those who park and wade. Also note that on the upper river, anglers who choose to fish using boats are limited to fishing the river's east bank where the river abuts the Warm Springs Reservation. From Dry Creek down, there is a 5-mile stretch that may be fished with a reservation permit.

Because the Deschutes is so popular with boaters, the state has been forced to limit guide usage as well as jetboating to certain days of the week in the summer. Book early, at least a month in advance if you want a guided trip in the summer or fall. Anglers using boats on the Deschutes should be wary of jetboats on the lower river. If you hear one coming, wait for it to pass. Floaters have the right of way, but the many blind rapids and the high speeds of downstream jetboats are a recipe for disaster.

Some of the most popular flyfishing floats include:

- Warm Spring Bridge to Trout Creek (a nice day float)
- Trout Creek to Maupin (a three-day float with several Class III rapids)
- Below Sherar's Falls to Mack's Canyon (at least five boat ramps to drift between—float times vary according to which ramp is chosen as a take-out))
- Mack's Canyon to the Columbia River (no roads, two- or three-day float, at least two each of Class III and IV rapids)

A canyon on the lower Deschutes River offers incredible scenery as well as its fabled fishery. (Photo by Ken Morrish)

No matter how you fish the Deschutes, this big river requires time, effort, and preparation. Amenities along the river are few and far between, so it is best to bring food, water, and shelter in order to avoid a long and winding drive to get food or accommodations. If you do not want to camp, it is wise to make reservations in advance since there will be a demand for what little accommodations are available.

If you have limited time available for a flyfishing trip, hiring a guide for this river might allow you to spend more time fishing and less time planning, packing, launching your boat, deciding which and how many flies to take, and all the rest of the things that a Deschutes guide can do more easily. By the time you outfit yourself for a weekend on the Deschutes, you might as well have hired a guide anyway. Guides are in high demand on the Deschutes, so make arrangements well in advance if you want to experience the river's prime season.

Please treat the Deschutes River and the surrounding environment with great care. This is a heavily used resource and anything that we can do to protect the area adds up in a big way. This is one of Oregon's legendary waters, and its national reputation grows with each hatching bug and leaping steelhead. Do anything you can to make sure this Oregon treasure stays a blue ribbon fishery.

Stream Facts: Deschutes River

Season

- From the mouth to the northern boundary of the Warm Springs Reservation: open to trout the entire year; open for steelhead the entire year.
- From the northern boundary of Warm Springs Reservation to Pelton Dam: open for trout April 25 to October 31; open for steelhead April 25 to December 31.

Special Regulations

- From the mouth to the northern boundary of Warm Springs Reservation: 2 trout per day, 10-inch minimum and 13-inch maximum length; restricted to artificial flies and lures; no angling from a floating device that supports the angler.
- From the northern boundary of the Warm Springs Reservation to Pelton Dam: 2 trout per day, 10-inch minimum and 13-inch maximum length; restricted to artificial flies and lures; no angling from a floating device that supports the angler.
- Closed from Pelton Regulating Dam downstream 600 feet to ODFW markers.
- The Warm Springs Reservation borders the Deschutes River for 31 miles from 4 miles below North Junction Railroad Bridge (Two Springs Ranch) to Pelton Dam. Anglers are restricted to the eastern half of the river where it borders the reservation. For exceptions, call the reservation at 541-553-3233.

Trout

- Deschutes redsides, some over 20 inches.
- Steelhead from 4 to 8 pounds with a few larger.
- Brown trout are present in the upper river but are not numerous.

River Flows

- Best fishing flows are below 8,500 cfs. The maximum fishable flow considered by some anglers is 5,500 cfs, but serious Deschutes anglers can produce fish when it's higher. For current flow information, call 503-464-7474.

River Characteristics

- The Deschutes is a desert river flowing through deep, rugged canyons and has some of the biggest trout water a fly angler will ever fish. Hatches are prolific and the river holds huge numbers of fish. The steelhead fishery is also well known and very popular among serious steelhead flyfishers. Access is plentiful and camping along the river is available. The Dalles, Maupin, and Warm Springs are the only places to get supplies. Boating is a common practice but is only for experienced whitewater boaters. First-time boaters should always prearrange to follow someone through the rapids or should study floater's guides and scout the river well. This is whitewater boating!!!!!

Maps

- DeLorme *Oregon Atlas and Gazetteer*

LOWER DESCHUTES RIVER MAJOR HATCHES

Insect	J	F	M	A	M	J	J	A	S	O	N	D	Time	Flies
Little Yellow Sally					■	■	■						Afternoon Evening	Yellow Stimulator, Hare's Ear Nymph #16-18
Little Black Stone		■	■										PM	Black Elk Hair Caddis, Blackback Hare's Ear Nymph, Black Stimulator, Parachute Adams #16-18
Golden Stone					■	■							Afternoon Evening	Yellow Stimulator, Kaufmann's Yellow Stonefly Nymph #8
Salmonfly					■	■							Afternoon Evening	Bullethead Stonefly, Orange Turck's Tarantula, Orange Stimulator, Kaufmann Stonefly Nymph, Royal Stimulator, Beadhead Rubberlegged Stonefly, Sofa Pillow #6
Tan Caddis					■	■							Afternoon Evening	Tan Elk Hair Caddis, Goddard Caddis #16
Gray Caddis		■	■										Afternoon Evening	Parachute Adams (Spinner), Goddard Caddis, Gray Elk Hair Caddis, Hemingway Caddis #16
October Caddis									■	■			Afternoon Evening	Orange Stimulator, Royal Stimulator, Orange Soft Hackle #6-8
Pale Morning Dun					■	■							Morning Afternoon	PMD Thorax, PMD Cripple, PMD Parachute, PMD Spent-wing #16-18
Blue-winged Olive	■	■	■	■	■	■	■	■	■	■	■	■	Morning Afternoon Evening	Blue-winged Olive Parachute, Sparkle Dun, Parachute Adams, Comparadun, Gulper Special #16-20

LOWER DESCHUTES RIVER MAJOR HATCHES (cont.)

Insect	J	F	M	A	M	J	J	A	S	O	N	D	Time	Flies
Pale Evening Dun			X	X	X	X	X						Afternoon Evening	PMD Thorax, Sparkle Dun, Rusty Spinner #14
Trico							X	X	X	X			Morning	Stalcup Fan-wing CDC Trico, Zing-wing Spent Trico, Cut-wing Trico #20-24
Brown Drake					X	X	X						Evening	Extended Body Drake, Hair-wing Drake, Brown Drake Cripple #10-12
March Brown			X	X	X								PM	Quill Body March Brown, Adams, AK's March Brown #12-14
Green Drake					X	X	X						PM	Hairwing Drake, Extended Body Green Drake, Epoxyback Green Drake Nymph, Green Drake Cripple #10-12
Midges	X	X	X	X	X	X	X	X	X	X	X	X	Morning Evening	Sly's Midge, Red & Black Midge Pupa, Griffith's Gnat, Disco Midge #14-20
Grasshoppers							X	X	X				PM	Dave's Hopper, Parachute Hopper, Yellow Turck's Tarantula #8-12
Ants/Beetles						X	X	X	X	X			Morning Afternoon Evening	Parachute Ant, Harrop's Beetle, Hi-Vis Beetle #12-16

North Central Hub Cities

Maupin, Oregon

Elevation–1,200 • Population–465

Accommodations

C and J Lodge Bed and Breakfast, 304 Bakeoven Road (P.O. Box 130) / 541-395-2404 / $$$
Deschutes Motel, 616 Mill Street, Hwy 197 / 541-395-2626 / $$
The Oasis Resort, Hwy 197 South / 541-395-2611 / $$

Campgrounds

Maupin City Park, on the Deschutes / RV and camping / 541-395-2252

Restaurants

Deschutes River Inn, 509 Deschutes Avenue / 541-395-2468
Drift In Bar-BQ, C and J Lodge / 541-395-2474
Henry's Deli-Mart, North end of Deschutes River Bridge / 541-395-2278
Kanyon River Cafe, 505 Deschutes Avenue / 541-395-2401
The Oasis Resort Cafe, Hwy 197 South / 541-395-2611
Rainbow Tavern, 5th and Deschutes / 541-395-2497

Fly Shops and Sporting Goods

Deschutes Canyon Fly Shop, 599 South Hwy 197 / 541-395-2565
Henry's Shuttle Service, North end of the Deschutes River Bridge / 541-395-2278
Maupin Hardware Service and Supply, 403 Deschutes Avenue / 541-395-2217
The Oasis Resort Shuttles and Licenses, Hwy197 South / 541-395-2611

Hospitals

Mountain View Hospital, 470 Northeast A Street, Madras, OR / 541-475-3882

Airport

Madras Jefferson County Airport, 2028 Northwest Airport Way / 541-475-6947

Auto Rental

Miller Ford Nissan, 681 Northeast Hwy 97 / 541-475-7204

Auto Service

Barnett Service, Deschutes Avenue / 541-395-2543
Richmond's Service, 511 Deschutes Avenue / 541-395-2638

For More Information

Greater Maupin Area Chamber of Commerce
P.O. Box 220
Maupin, OR 97037
541-395-2599

Hood River, Oregon

Elevation–151 • Population–5,065

ACCOMMODATIONS

Best Western Hood River Inn / 541-386-2200
Brown Bed & Breakfast, 3000 Reed Road / 541-386-1545
Fir Mountain Ranch, 4051 Fir Mountain Road / 541-354-2753
Inn at Cooper Spur Lodging, 10755 Cooper Spur Road / 541-352-6692
Meredith Gorge Motel, 4300 Westcliff Drive / 541-386-1515

CAMPGROUNDS

Sunset Motel RV Park & Laundromat, 2300 Cascade Avenue / 541-386-6098
Lost Lake Resort & Campgrounds, P.O. Box 90 / 541-386-6366

RESTAURANTS

Andrew's Pizza & Bakery, 107 Oak Street / 541-386-1448
Fisher's Inn Restaurant & Lounge, 1301 Belmont Avenue / 541-386-5557
Kampai Steak & Seafood, 101 4th Street / 541-386-2230
Mesquitery Restaurant & Bar, 1219 12th Street / 541-386-2002
Montero's Authentic Mexican Restaurant, 1810 Cascade Avenue / 541-386-8788
Santacroce's Italian Restaurant, 4780 Highway 35 / 541-354-2511

FLY SHOPS AND SPORTING GOODS

Gorge Fly Shop, 416 Oak Street / 541-386-6977
WalMart, 2700 Wasco Street / 541-387-2300

HOSPITAL

Hood River Memorial Hospital, 13th & May Streets / 541-386-3911
Skyline Hospital, 211 Skyline Drive / 541-386-5348

AIRPORT

Flightline Services, 3608 Airport Drive / 541-386-1133

AUTO RENTAL

Cliff Smith Motors Inc., 3100 Cascade Avenue / 541-386-3311
Knoll Motor Company Inc., 1105 12th Street / 541-386-3011

AUTO REPAIR

AAA Towing / 541-386-5233
Car Care Center, 2043 12th Street / 541-386-2428
River's Edge Auto Repair, 125 Country Club Road / 541-386-6774
Les Schwab Tire Center, 3140 Cascade Avenue / 541-386-1123

An angler and his dog work through some of the best water on the Hood River, close to the mouth.

For More Information

Hood River Chamber of Commerce
Port Marina Park
Hood River, OR 97031
541-386-2000

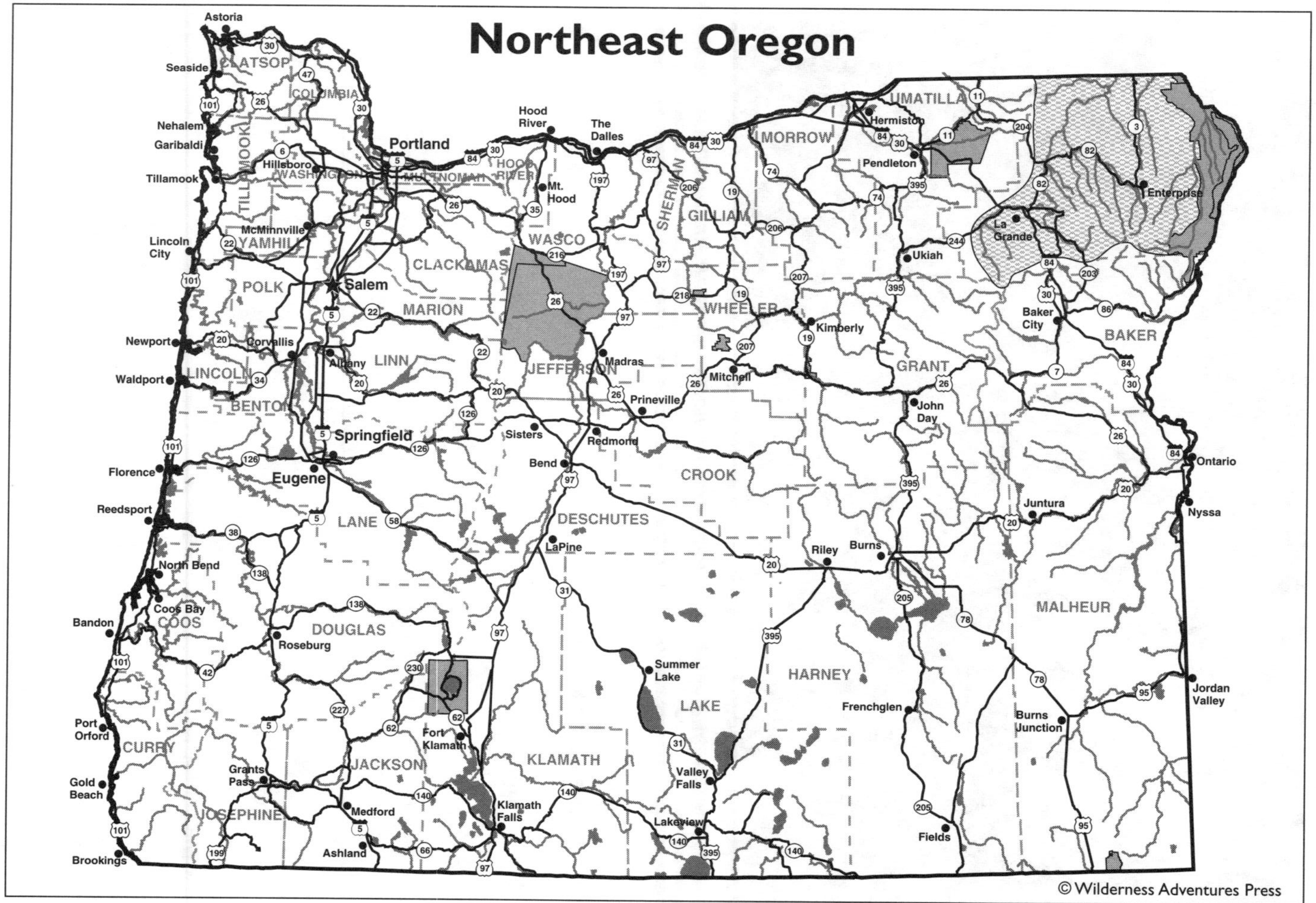
Northeast Oregon
© Wilderness Adventures Press
Astoria
Seaside
Nehalem
Garibaldi
Tillamook
Lincoln City
Newport
Waldport
Florence
Reedsport
North Bend
Coos Bay
Bandon
Port Orford
Gold Beach
Brookings
Portland
Hillsboro
McMinnville
Salem
Corvallis
Albany
Eugene
Springfield
Roseburg
Grants Pass
Medford
Ashland
Hood River
The Dalles
Mt. Hood
Madras
Redmond
Prineville
Sisters
Bend
LaPine
Summer Lake
Valley Falls
Lakeview
Klamath Falls
Fort Klamath
Hermiston
Pendleton
Ukiah
La Grande
Enterprise
Baker City
Ontario
Nyssa
Juntura
John Day
Kimberly
Mitchell
Burns
Riley
Frenchglen
Fields
Burns Junction
Jordan Valley
CLATSOP
COLUMBIA
TILLAMOOK
WASHINGTON
YAMHILL
POLK
LINCOLN
BENTON
LINN
MARION
CLACKAMAS
MULTNOMAH
HOOD RIVER
WASCO
SHERMAN
GILLIAM
MORROW
UMATILLA
WHEELER
JEFFERSON
CROOK
DESCHUTES
LANE
DOUGLAS
COOS
CURRY
JOSEPHINE
JACKSON
KLAMATH
LAKE
HARNEY
GRANT
BAKER
MALHEUR

Northeast Oregon

Friends with whom I have fished have taught me the virtues of steelhead in the fall and two-handed fly rods. One day on the banks of the Grande Ronde River, John Arnold lent me a rod, and Richie Thurston gave me a casting lesson. They are to blame for hooking me on the big swing. There is something very meditative about working down a steelhead run. This feeling seems to increase the deeper one travels into wilderness to find sea-run rainbows. Northeast Oregon's waters are a great place to get lost in the down-and-across world of steelhead flyfishing.

Northeast Oregon is a place that haunts my memory. As a child my family backpacked into the Wallowa Mountains. I was the youngest of four and could barely carry myself up the trails much less any gear. I rambled along behind my father, who carried my belongings and filled my ears with the story of Chief Joseph and the Nez Perce Indians. I grew up with a sense of guilt that my forefathers had evicted the people of this area. Once in the Wallowas, it is easy to understand the strong attachment that native people had for this land. In a certain sense, I think these thoughts kept me from returning to the Wallowas as a young adult. Eventually, the time came to venture back and, like other places I've been to, I was drawn to northeast Oregon by fish and the fly rod.

Now I'm glad that flyfishing took me back to this part of the state. The stories my father told me still ring in my ears when I see the Wallowas. I know now that I can't right past wrongs, but I can appreciate why the Nez Perce called these places home and celebrate the rivers as symbols of constant change.

Lost in the meditative grip of flyfishing for steelhead, it seems somehow important that fish and fly rodders meet one another here, if for no other reason than to keep ritual part of this land. New water constantly pours over ancient rocks in the Wallowas, thus time both moves forward and stands still, all at once, in these Oregon waters.

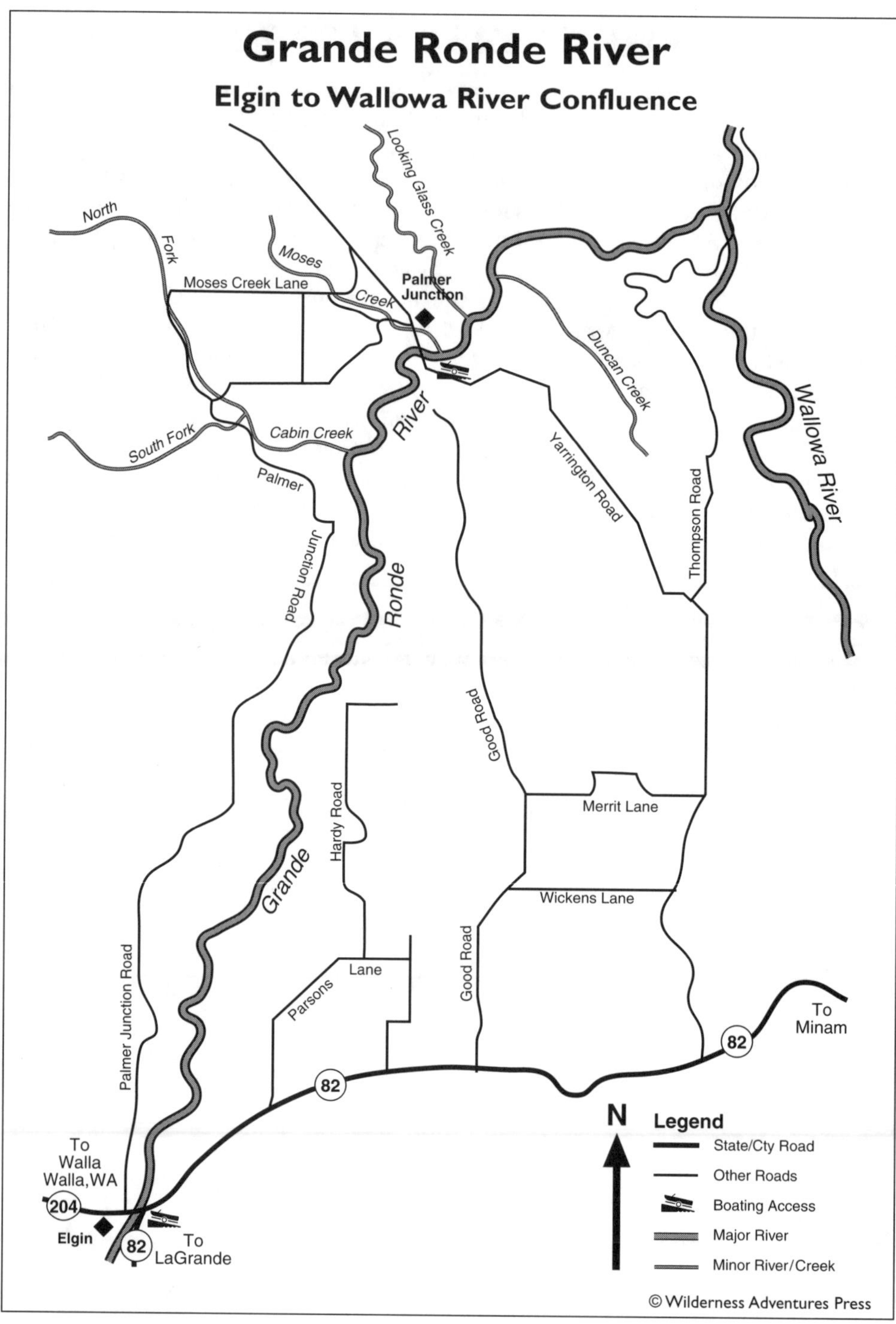

Grande Ronde River
Elgin to Wallowa River Confluence
Looking Glass Creek
North Fork
Moses Creek
Moses Creek Lane
Palmer Junction
Duncan Creek
Wallowa River
South Fork
Cabin Creek
River
Palmer Junction Road
Yarrington Road
Thompson Road
Ronde
Grande
Good Road
Hardy Road
Merrit Lane
Wickens Lane
Parsons Lane
Palmer Junction Road
To Minam
82
To Walla Walla, WA
204
Elgin
82
To LaGrande
N
Legend
State/Cty Road
Other Roads
Boating Access
Major River
Minor River/Creek
© Wilderness Adventures Press

GRANDE RONDE RIVER

The Grande Ronde River runs out of the Blue Mountains and goes on a 200-mile journey through Oregon and Washington to join the Snake River. Trout, smallmouth bass, and steelhead are all present in the river. Most of the fishing takes place from the confluence with the Wallowa River to the mouth. Some of the river is only accessible by boat, but there are good stretches where park and wade fishing is no problem.

The Ronde is a fair size river and can be boated in the fall by craft like small rafts and pontoons when levels are lower. Autumn here is primarily a steelhead fishery. Rob Lamb, owner of The Joseph Fly Shop, says of the Ronde, "We start fishing the lower reaches of the river by September and concentrate on the upper reaches as the season progresses. Standard down and across techniques are employed to catch these fish in the fall."

Lamb says some anglers use strike indicator techniques for steelhead but most people like to swing flies. This river's size and water types are perfect for a tight line grab when swinging flies. It has been my experience on the Ronde that many anglers are decidedly against indicator fishing, especially near the mouth.

Floating lines as well as sinktips are employed when steelhead fishing. Spey fishing has become popular on the river, and Lamb says he always has a few spey rods

Mike Witthar fights a nice fall steelhead on the Grande Ronde.

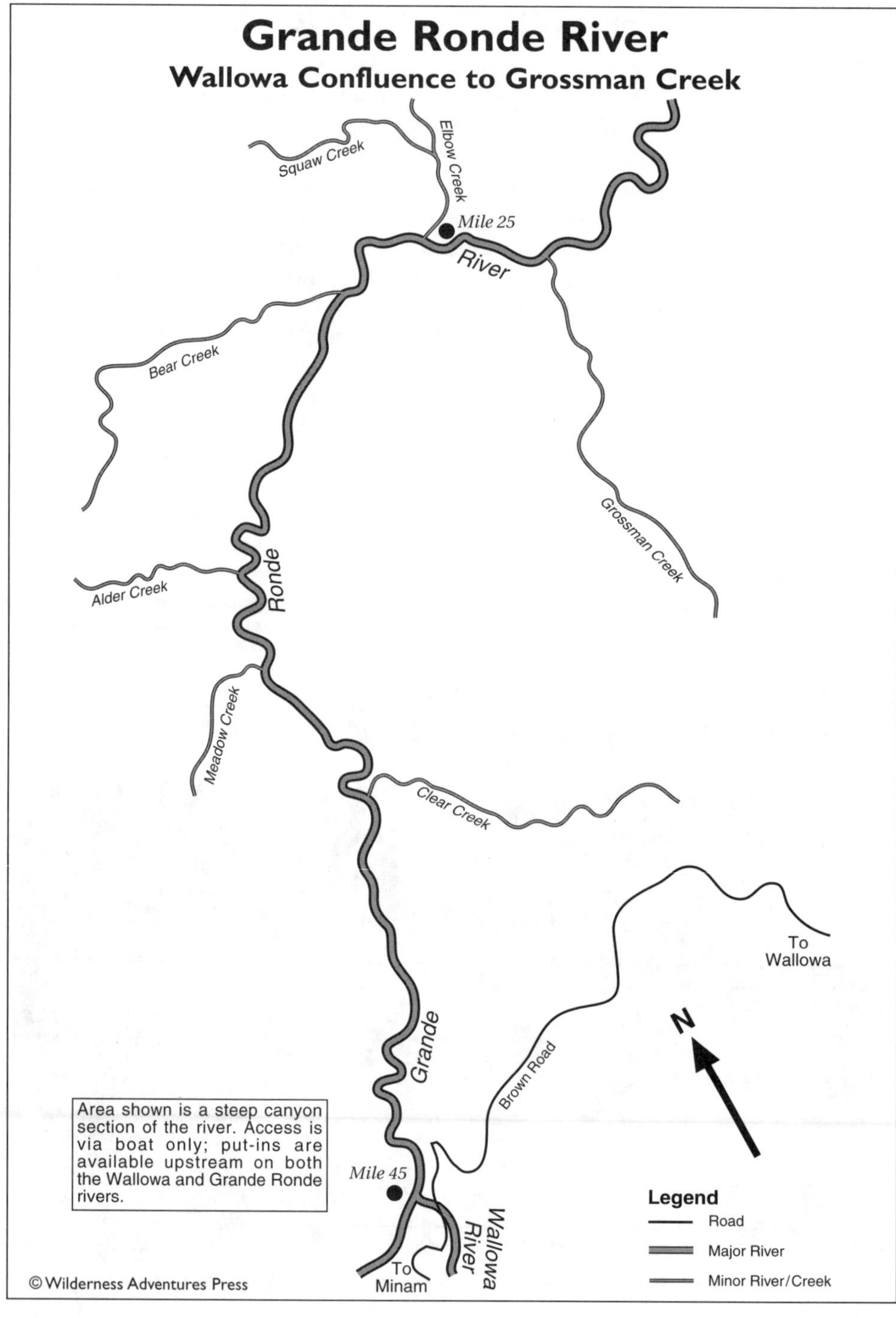
Grande Ronde River
Wallowa Confluence to Grossman Creek
Squaw Creek
Elbow Creek
Mile 25
River
Bear Creek
Grossman Creek
Ronde
Alder Creek
Meadow Creek
Clear Creek
To Wallowa
N
Brown Road
Grande
Area shown is a steep canyon section of the river. Access is via boat only; put-ins are available upstream on both the Wallowa and Grande Ronde rivers.
Mile 45
Wallowa River
To Minam
Legend
Road
Major River
Minor River/Creek
© Wilderness Adventures Press

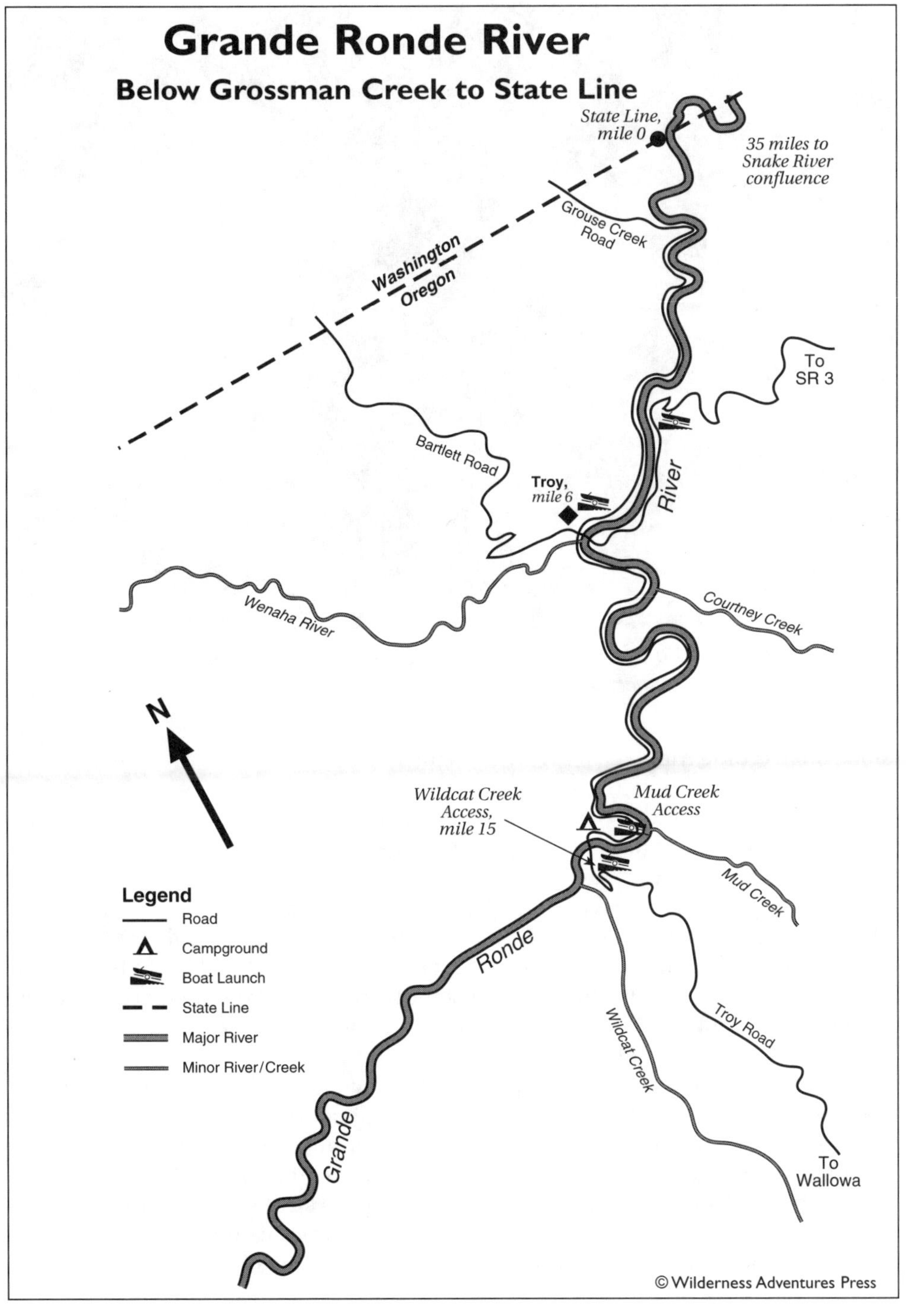
Grande Ronde River
Below Grossman Creek to State Line
State Line,
mile 0
35 miles to
Snake River
confluence
Grouse Creek
Road
Washington
Oregon
To
SR 3
Bartlett Road
Troy,
mile 6
River
Wenaha River
Courtney Creek
N
Wildcat Creek
Access,
mile 15
Mud Creek
Access
Mud Creek
Legend
Road
Campground
Boat Launch
State Line
Major River
Minor River/Creek
Ronde
Troy Road
Wildcat Creek
Grande
To
Wallowa
© Wilderness Adventures Press

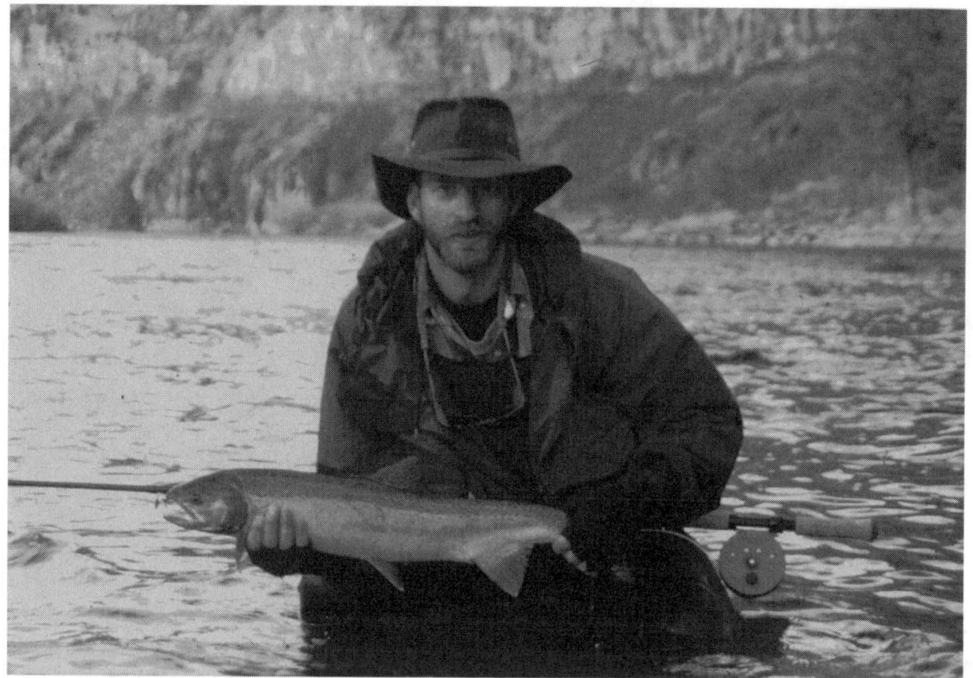

Grande Ronde steelhead will give an account of themselves even against the leverage of a spey rod.

along on his guide trips. He teaches how to fish these long rods and likes the amount of water one can cover with spey techniques.

The Grande Ronde's lowest waters are accessible from Washington state. Because this section is heavily used, anglers need to be aware of steelhead etiquette before casting a line down low.

There is plenty of access from the Oregon border to about 10 miles past the town of Troy. This section does see significant pressure in late summer and early fall. Don't expect to fish alone on the Ronde's road sections until late fall. Above this, there are no roads, and access is only by boat. Flyfishers who choose to float are advised to use smaller craft. Lamb tells me, "We see a lot of paint on the rocks every year from driftboats trying to get through at low levels."

Rafts and pontoon boats are better choices than a driftboat when water is low. Because this float takes a minimum of three days, boats big enough to hold gear yet small enough to navigate low water are ideal. A popular float is the three-day trip from Minam on the Wallowa River, to Wildcat Creek on the Grande Ronde.

Because of its size and accessibility, this is an ideal steelhead river. However, getting to the Grande Ronde takes commitment. Drive times can be long, tedious, and road conditions can be tricky in spring and fall. The area surrounding the Wallowa

A fly angler is rarely fishing alone in northeast Oregon.

Mountains is very pristine, and the Grande Ronde is no exception. Make every effort to keep this environment beautiful.

John Arnold, an accomplished fly tier and guide, has been fishing the Ronde for many years. His favorite flies for this river include green-butted skunks, purple perils, and black bunny leeches, to name a few. Arnold says many steelhead patterns will work but be sure to have some steelhead dries as well. Try muddlers, greased liners, and steelhead dragonflies. Arnold suggests 9 feet of leader, tapered to 8 pounds. Grande Ronde's steelhead average between 3 and 6 pounds. They are typically hard fighting fish in spite of the great distance they have traveled to reach this upper water.

Most fisheries in Oregon require that wild fish must be released unharmed, and it is no different here. Please observe proper steelhead flyfishing etiquette on the Grande Ronde. Be courteous and timely through runs, never step in below a fellow flyfisher, and when in doubt, ask.

The Ronde has excellent smallmouth bass and rainbow trout populations as well as steelhead. Mac Huff, owner of the Wallowa Outdoor Store, tells me that flyfishing for trout is worth doing almost the entire trout season on the Grande Ronde. "Things are slower by the end of October, but in the summer months, trout can be taken with hoppers and caddis patterns. The caddis, under the right circumstances, will bring up the biggest fish in the river."

There is also decent golden stonefly action in the early season as well as some evening mayfly appearances that will bring up fish. The river's biggest trout will go 16 or 17 inches, according to Mac. Most guided trout trips on the river consist of one- and two-day float trips. Plan on throwing hopper patterns in the summer if hatch conditions are poor.

A decent smallmouth fishery exists on the river's lower reaches, but not many anglers take advantage of it. Huff says the fishery is similar to John Day's smallmouth fishery but is overshadowed by trout and steelhead.

Stream Facts: Grande Ronde River

Seasons

- Open for steelhead September 1 to April 15.
- Open for trout the last Saturday in May to October 31.
- Open for smallmouth during trout and steelhead season.

Special Regulations

- Only adipose clipped trout and steelhead may be taken. All wild fish must be released.
- All bull trout must be released.

Fish

- Steelhead
- Rainbow trout
- Smallmouth bass
- Bull trout

River Characteristics

- This is a nice-sized river to fish, with twists and turns through a variety of countryside, and offering good fishing in a variety of water types. This is serious steelhead country. Anglers who fish here have been doing it for a long time—don't get caught up in a race for the best pools with your fellow angler, don't sit on pools, and be courteous to all fellow anglers. Depending on skill rather than staking claim to a certain spot is certainly a key to being a good fly angler.

Fishing and Boating Access

- The Grande Ronde can be floated from the mouth of the Wallowa River to its confluence with the Snake River. The lower river is very accessible by car, so floating through these stretches on busy days is not suggested. The river's roadless areas offer plenty of boating opportunity.

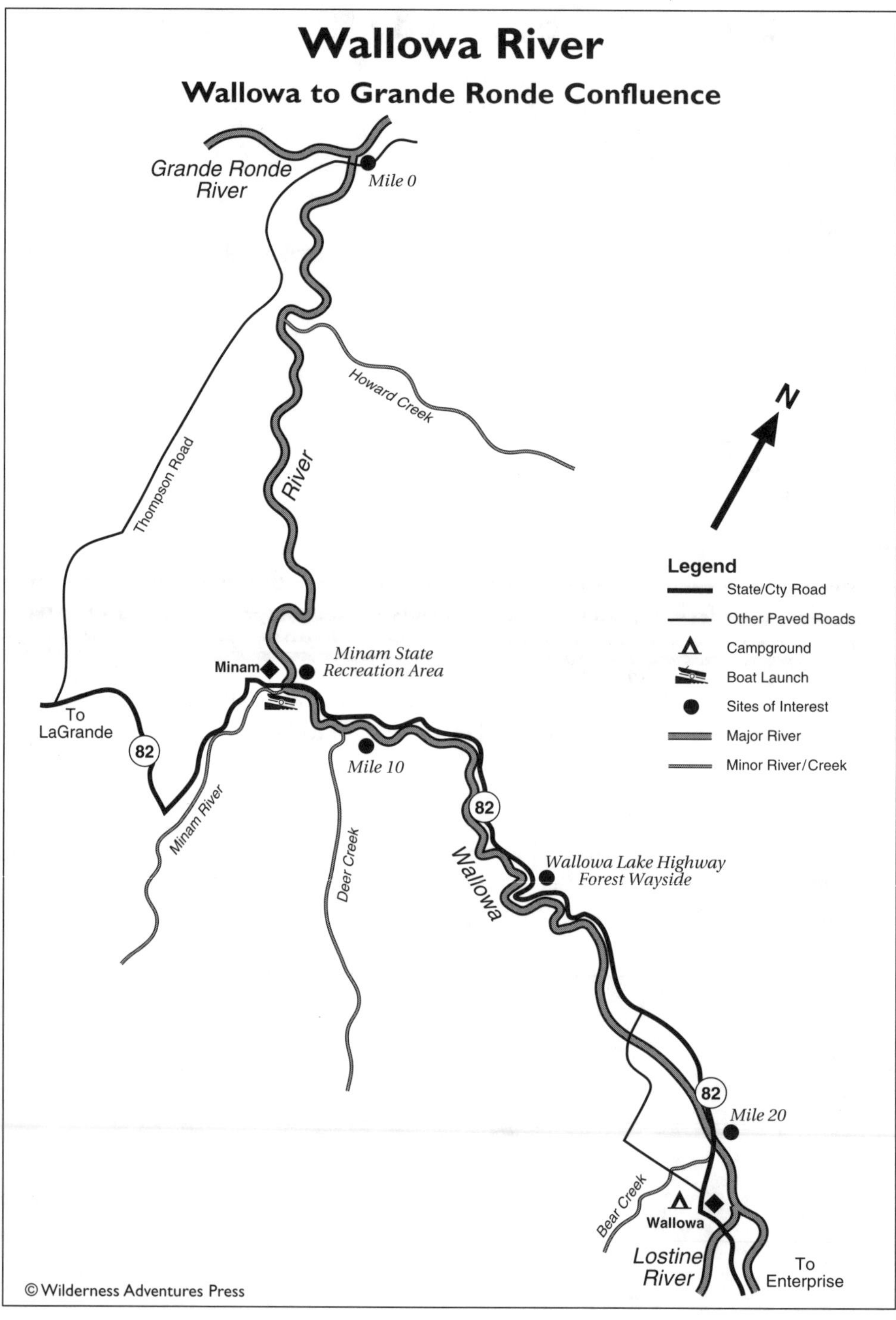
Wallowa River
Wallowa to Grande Ronde Confluence
Grande Ronde River
Mile 0
Howard Creek
N
River
Thompson Road
Legend
State/Cty Road
Other Paved Roads
Campground
Boat Launch
Sites of Interest
Major River
Minor River/Creek
Minam
Minam State Recreation Area
To LaGrande
82
Mile 10
82
Minam River
Deer Creek
Wallowa
Wallowa Lake Highway Forest Wayside
82
Mile 20
Bear Creek
Wallowa
Lostine River
To Enterprise
© Wilderness Adventures Press

WALLOWA RIVER

The Wallowa River is born in the Wallowa Mountains within the Eagle Cap Wilderness area. It flows into Wallowa Lake, one of the few points where trailheads can be found leading into the Eagle Cap Wilderness and the high mountain lake fishing found there. As the river comes out of Wallowa Lake, it heads toward its confluence with the Grande Ronde and is paralleled closely by Hwy 82.

Because the highway isn't heavily traveled, it doesn't intrude on a fly angler's experience. Rob Lamb, owner of the Joseph Fly Shop, says, "We do guide trips on the river all day in the summer, and most of my clients say that they can hardly tell the highway is there." Of course, the Wallowa River's nice fly water will also distract them from the highway. Fish in the river run up to 16 inches, and there are good enough numbers to keep anglers busy. Lamb tells me, "Good rods can have 30- and 40-fish days in the summer, and that's sometimes on a half-day trip."

Beginners will also appreciate this river and the willingness of its trout to take flies. Insect and hopper numbers are both good, and Lamb's favorite flies include the beadhead Prince nymph, stimulators, and Goddard caddis.

Mac Huff, owner of The Wallowa Outdoor Store, also guides the Wallowa during the summer. According to him, "The Wallowa is just an extension of the Ronde. Whatever hatches happen on the Ronde will be happening on the Wallowa River two weeks to a month later."

The Wallowa River holds some fair-sized trout and plenty of access.

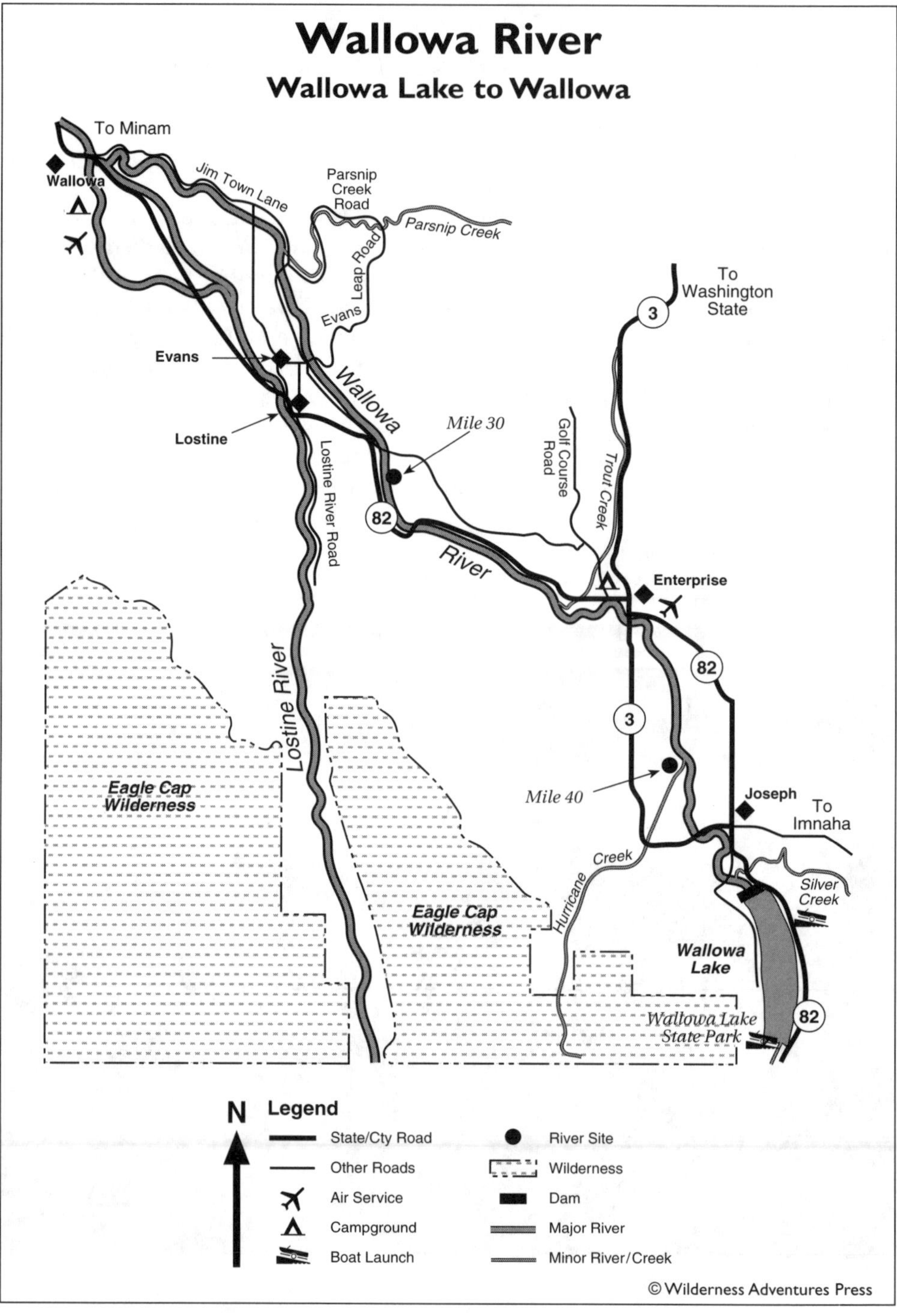

Wallowa River
Wallowa Lake to Wallowa
To Minam
Wallowa
Jim Town Lane
Parsnip Creek Road
Parsnip Creek
Leap Road
Evans
To Washington State
3
Evans
Lostine
Wallowa
Mile 30
Golf Course Road
Trout Creek
Lostine River Road
82
River
Enterprise
82
Lostine River
3
Mile 40
Joseph
To Imnaha
Eagle Cap Wilderness
Creek
Hurricane
Silver Creek
Eagle Cap Wilderness
Wallowa Lake
Wallowa Lake State Park
82
N
Legend
State/Cty Road
Other Roads
Air Service
Campground
Boat Launch
River Site
Wilderness
Dam
Major River
Minor River/Creek
© Wilderness Adventures Press

The lowest reaches of the river are only accessible by floating, which means a floater is committed all the way to Wildcat Creek on the Grande Ronde—a minimum three-day float when fishing. The river's most popular stretch is accessible from Hwy 82, where there are plenty of pullouts to park and wade, beginning at Minam and continuing at least 8 miles upstream. Find an entry point and then walk and wade the river up or down. The river's upper end is privately owned, and permission can be obtained by calling Mac at the Wallowa Outdoor Store.

On a warm summer day, the Wallowa River can provide fly rod entertainment for anglers of all levels. A very nice trip can be planned for this river by combining it with hike-in opportunities to the area's high mountain lakes.

For guided trips or up-to-the-minute information on the Wallowa, call Rob Lamb at the Joseph Fly Shop, or Mac Huff at the Wallowa Outdoor Store.

Stream Facts: Wallowa River

Seasons

- Mouth to Trout Creek: Open for steelhead from September 1 to April 15.
- Open for trout the last Saturday in May to October 31.

Special Regulations

- All wild steelhead must be released.
- All wild trout must be released below Rock Creek.
- All bull trout must be released.

Fish

- Steelhead
- Rainbow trout
- Bull trout
- Brook trout

Flows

- Best flows for floating and fishing are between 1,500–3,000 cfs.
- River Forecast Central, 503-271-9246.

River Characteristics

- This is a user-friendly river and can certainly be an entertaining place to cast a fly rod. Good fish numbers help ensure that anglers of all skill levels will have fun. Both floating the river in inflatables and wading the river are easy to do from the highway.

Fishing and Boating Access

- Guides often float the river, although wading from the road is an easier option for an angler who wants to hit the river for a day or a few hours. Using a guide service will really show the colors of this northeast Oregon trout stream. The river is accessed via Hwy 82 from Minam to Enterprise. From Minam downriver, access is by floating only and may take several days.

Maps

- DeLorme *Oregon Atlas and Gazetteer*

IMNAHA RIVER

The Imnaha is a small, steelhead stream that hosts wild and hatchery fish. According to Rob Lamb of the Joseph Fly Shop, approximately 30 percent of the fish are wild.

Access to this river is limited, with most of it requiring a hike or a four-wheel drive. Although there is a road paralleling the majority of the river, private property dominates most of the riverbank. Access on the lower water involves a drive on a twisting dirt road, located well above the river and eventually winding back to the water. From the town of Imnaha, an angler will find this road by driving downstream on the river's east bank.

There is some private property in the area, so be watching for posted property. Treat this whole area with care to assure continued public access. The final few miles to its confluence with the Snake are limited to hike-in access only. From this trail an angler can hike into some nice steelhead runs.

Standard steelhead techniques will take fish here, but remember that patience is necessary, not only for hooking up to sea-run rainbows but just getting on this river. Allow plenty of time for traveling to Imnaha. It is sufficiently remote that a multiday stay is just about necessary in order to find and catch steelhead.

The Imnaha in the fall has a lot to offer the adventurous fly angler.

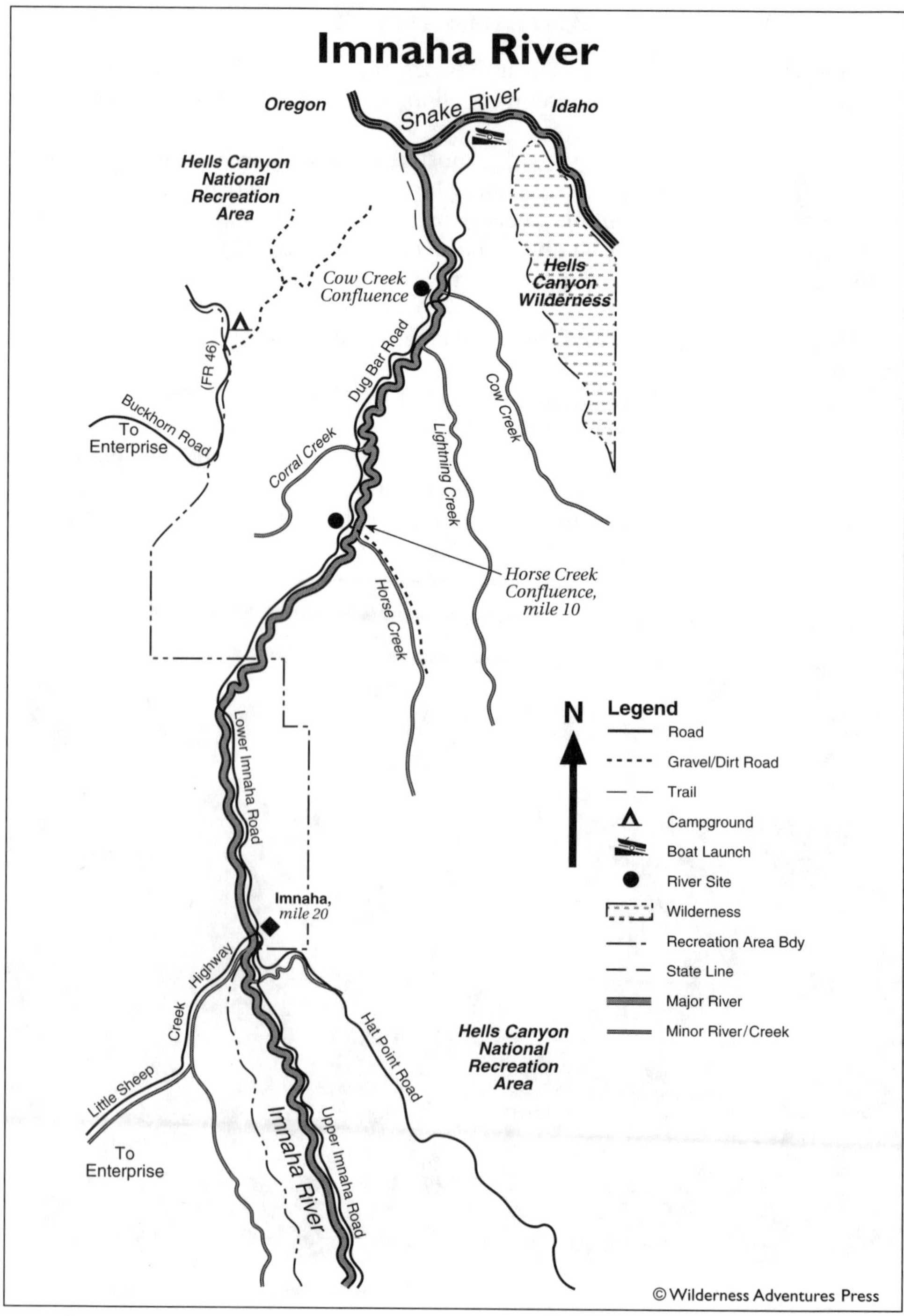
Imnaha River
Oregon
Snake River
Idaho
Hells Canyon National Recreation Area
Hells Canyon Wilderness
Cow Creek Confluence
(FR 46)
Dug Bar Road
Cow Creek
Buckhorn Road
To Enterprise
Corral Creek
Lightning Creek
Horse Creek Confluence, mile 10
Horse Creek
Lower Imnaha Road
Legend
Road
Gravel/Dirt Road
Trail
Campground
Boat Launch
River Site
Wilderness
Recreation Area Bdy
State Line
Major River
Minor River/Creek
Imnaha, mile 20
Little Sheep Creek Highway
Hat Point Road
Hells Canyon National Recreation Area
To Enterprise
Imnaha River
Upper Imnaha Road
© Wilderness Adventures Press

The upper reaches of the Imnaha have some trout water in designated areas.

The river's upper reaches hold a decent trout fishery, according to Mac Huff. However, much of the riverbank above the town of Imnaha is private property. Rather than walking through private fields to get to these areas, look for the well-posted public access areas. Once you get far enough upriver, you will reach National Forest land, and access is no longer a problem. Although most of the fish in the upper stretch are in the 8- to 10-inch range, they are wild, providing a nice opportunity to fish light tackle on water with little pressure. There is a trout population downstream as well. Huff says that he likes to cast big dries to these fish in the summer. Try stimulators, Wulffs and hoppers in bigger sizes.

Enjoy the Imnaha if you go, and please treat the area well. Obey all posted property signs and enjoy the natural richness this part of Oregon offers. Call the Joseph Fly Shop or Wallowa Outdoor Store for guided trips.

Stream Facts: Imnaha River

Seasons

- Open for steelhead September 1 to April 15 below Big Sheep Creek (just below the town of Imnaha).
- Open for trout the last Saturday in May to October 31 below Big Sheep Creek (just below the town of Imnaha).

Special Regulations

- Only adipose clipped trout and steelhead may be kept below Big Sheep Creek. All wild fish must be released.
- All bull trout must be released.

Fish

- Steelhead
- Rainbow trout
- Bull trout

Flows

- Best fishing is when flows are under 1500 cfs. Flows can go as low as 100–200 cfs.

River Characteristics

- The Imnaha is a small river, protected by its remoteness, and having very little public access unless you are willing to make a hike or a long drive. Its pools are smaller than typical steelhead waters but are interesting to fish. This river will not tolerate misuse—it is small and dependent on good stewardship for both the land and the fish.

Fishing Access

- The best access for steelhead is from Cow Creek down the trail to the mouth. From Cow Creek upriver there is road access for about 7 miles. Above the town of Imnaha, there is marked access for trout and Forest Service access begins farther upriver.

Maps

- Wallowa-Whitman National Forest maps
- Eagle Cap Wilderness map (for high mountain lakes in Wallowas)

Outfitters

- Joseph Fly Shoppe, 541-432-4343
- Wallowa Outdoor Store, 541-426-3493

Northeast Hub City

Enterprise, Oregon

Elevation–3,757 • Population–2020

Accommodations

Best Western Rama Inn and Suites, 1200 Highland Avenue / 541-426-2000 / $$$
Ponderosa Motel, 102 East Greenwood / 541-426-3186 / $$
Wilderness Inn Motel, 301 West North Street / 800-365-1205 / $$
Country Inn, 402 West North Street / 541-426-4986 / $

Restaurants

Terminal Gravity Brewery and Restaurant, 803 School Street / 541-426-0158
Wildflour Bakery, 803 School Street / 541-426-2086
Cloud 9 Donut Co., 105 Southeast 1st Street / 541-426-3790
Toma's Restaurant, 301 South River / 541-426-4873
The Embers Brew House, 204 North Main / Joseph, OR / 541-432-2739
Vali's Alpine Delicatessen, 59811 Wallowa Lake Hwy / Joseph, OR / 541-432-5691

Fly Shops

The Wallowa Outdoor Store, 110 South River Road / 541-426-3493
Joseph Fly Shoppe, 203 North Main Street / Joseph, OR / 541-432-4343

Hospital

Wallowa Memorial Hospital, 401 Northeast 1st Street / 541-426-3111

Airport

Enterprise Airport, 905 East Greenwood Street / 541-426-3562
Union County Airport, 60175 Pierce Road, La Grande / 541-963-6615

Auto Rental

Summit Ford-Mercury, 300 West Main Street / 541-426-4574

Auto Service

Les Schwab Tire Center, Northwest 1st Street / 541-426-3139
Moffit Brothers Transportation, 918 Lostine River Road / Lostine OR / 541-569-2284
Tom's Auto and Hardware, 506 North 7th Street / Wallowa OR / 541-886-8811

For More Information

Wallowa County Chamber of Commerce
P.O. Box 427
107 Southwest 1st Street
Enterprise OR 97828
800-585-4121

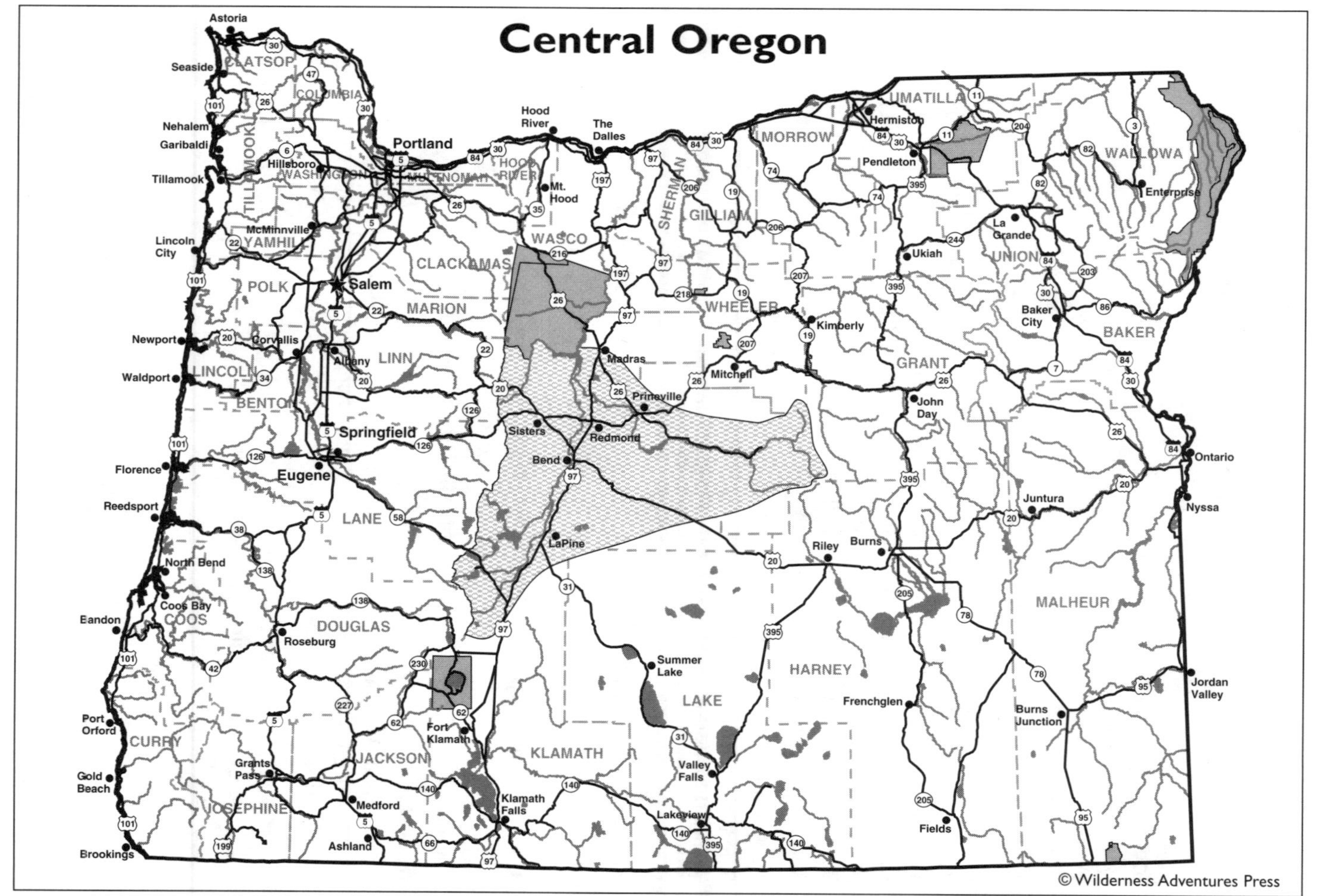
Central Oregon
© Wilderness Adventures Press
Astoria
Seaside
Nehalem
Garibaldi
Tillamook
Lincoln City
Newport
Waldport
Florence
Reedsport
North Bend
Coos Bay
Eandon
Port Orford
Gold Beach
Brookings
Hillsboro
McMinnville
Portland
Salem
Corvallis
Albany
Eugene
Springfield
Roseburg
Grants Pass
Medford
Ashland
Hood River
The Dalles
Mt. Hood
Madras
Prineville
Redmond
Sisters
Bend
LaPine
Fort Klamath
Klamath Falls
Summer Lake
Valley Falls
Lakeview
Mitchell
Kimberly
John Day
Ukiah
Pendleton
Hermiston
La Grande
Enterprise
Baker City
Ontario
Nyssa
Juntura
Burns
Riley
Frenchglen
Fields
Burns Junction
Jordan Valley
CLATSOP
COLUMBIA
TILLAMOOK
WASHINGTON
YAMHILL
POLK
LINCOLN
BENTON
LINN
MARION
CLACKAMAS
MULTNOMAH
HOOD RIVER
WASCO
SHERMAN
GILLIAM
MORROW
UMATILLA
UNION
WALLOWA
BAKER
GRANT
WHEELER
LANE
DOUGLAS
COOS
CURRY
JOSEPHINE
JACKSON
KLAMATH
LAKE
HARNEY
MALHEUR

CENTRAL OREGON

Central Oregon contains a veritable flyfishing smorgasbord that other areas can only dream about. The Cascade Lakes Highway, south of Bend, provides access to many of the waters mentioned in this chapter and many that aren't. The lakes and streams on this scenic highway are a flyfisher's dream. Spending a day casting flies in this surreal setting, the result of the area's volcanic past, is inspiring. The quality of these waters and their proximity to one another is virtually unparalleled anywhere in the nation.

North of Bend, central Oregon's desert canyons and sun-filled forests provide refuge and access to the angler willing to sweat. The area's temperature extremes and physical nature speak to the fly angler of survival and grandeur. Steep canyon walls whisper to us of the secret hiding places of wild trout. The urge to see what's around the next bend can take an angler farther than was originally intended.

Central Oregon has water with big fish, water with countless fish, and water with unique fish. Rivers and lakes provide numerous opportunities and many different kinds of trophies. Landlocked Atlantic salmon have taken hold in the area and are great fun on a fly rod. Deschutes River redside rainbows continue to survive in rugged parts of central Oregon that resist intrusion, and every time you hook one of these wild fish, they prove just how wild they are. Bull trout have probably eaten as many hatchery fish as the average limit-monger, reminding us that Mother Nature sometimes wins despite our best intentions. Throw in browns, rainbows, brook trout, and a few other species that make good fly targets, and you've got one hell of a nice place to fish.

In the middle of all this fishing sits the small city of Bend, whose microbreweries and eateries can tempt even the most avid camping flyfishers away from their tents. In spring and fall, Bend's amenities offer an angler hot showers, warm beds, and respite from early- and late-season snows. Almost all the waters in this chapter are close enough to Bend that you can grab a pint and a movie and still be on the water when the mist rises in the morning. If this still isn't close enough, central Oregon's smaller towns and resorts provide golfing, rafting, skiing, horseback riding, mountain biking, and more. A flyfisher with a family would do well to check out the fishing in this part of the state.

In many cases, flyfishing in central Oregon will make anglers want to change their zip code. But even if you can't load up the moving van, you can still pack your bag and check out this area. Rest assured that somewhere in the high desert right now, some big fish are growing bigger, and you could be a dead-drift away from hooking up. Central Oregon is no secret to most people, but it still holds some secrets for those brandishing the long rod.

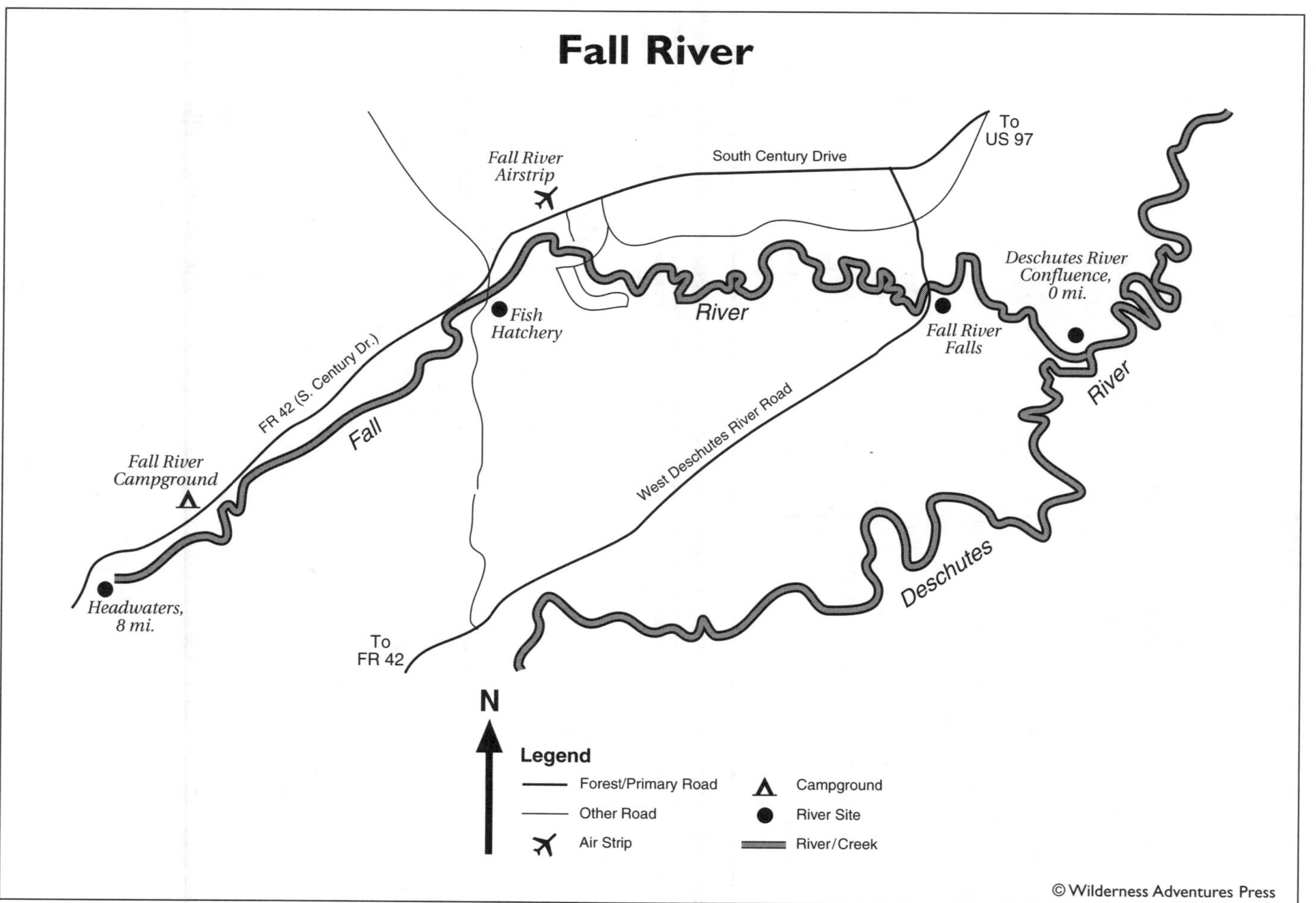
Fall River
Fall River Airstrip
South Century Drive
To US 97
Deschutes River Confluence, 0 mi.
Fish Hatchery
River
Fall River Falls
FR 42 (S. Century Dr.)
River
Fall
West Deschutes River Road
Fall River Campground
Deschutes
Headwaters, 8 mi.
To FR 42
N
Legend
Forest/Primary Road
Other Road
Air Strip
Campground
River Site
River/Creek
© Wilderness Adventures Press

Fall River

Tiny mayflies ride down a current seam, floating along a reed-lined bank, arriving one after another into the lane of a 16-inch rainbow. You can see his head tilt up and take every third one, almost. All you have to do is cast your size 18 baetis comparadun about 8 inches above his nose. Watch it drift for an 8-inch eternity. Then as you see him rise, so high that you swear he's looking at you, gently lift your rod tip until it comes firm, and then hold on.

It's a sight that will make saltwater flyfishers want to catch smaller fish and can get bass pros to put down their flippin sticks to see if they can set a hook as delicately. Fall River offers this flyfishing challenge to the well-tuned angler and a lesson to everyone else.

Fall River is born beautiful. The entire river emerges from the woods not far from Sunriver Resort in central Oregon. When I say, "emerges," I mean it quite literally. The river just rises out of the ground and heads north through a pine forest to join the Deschutes 7 miles later. This river offers all anglers a chance to test their skills. Fall River will bring out the best and worst of your angling ability. Good flyfishers will have an enjoyable time here, and novices will be forced to learn the skills that more experienced anglers are employing.

Fall River is a designated "flyfishing-only" water for its entire 7-mile length. This is a rarity in Oregon and a treat. Please note that in "fly-only" waters in Oregon, the use of external split shot is illegal—you must weight the fly. (In waters that allow flies and lures only, the use of external weight is all right.) Although Fall River may have quite a few anglers on any given day, at least they are flyrodders. You won't find any Styrofoam worm containers littering the pristine banks of this Oregon trout stream.

Fall River has a good population of rainbows, both hatchery and wild, which dominate its middle and upper sections. These hatchery fish are not your common, trashed-looking hatchery fish—they are often indistinguishable from wild rainbows. The lower water, below Fall River Falls, provides a wild brown trout fishery. There are also wild redside rainbows that come out of the Deschutes River. Hatches include a variety of insects—mayflies, caddis, midges, and terrestrials are all on the trout's menu here. The river is generally easy to wade but always deeper than it looks. Rarely does an angler have the opportunity to fish in water as clear as the Fall's.

It is relatively easy to access Fall River. Generally, where you find the most fishermen is where you will find the most fish. Obviously, water near the hatchery is a good place to start, and the headwaters are also popular. A keen eye and some patience will put you over well-hidden fish in the less populated sections of river. These fish become easier to find when there is a big hatch in progress. It may be best to wait for these moments if you feel like exploring.

Fall River is a spring creek by definition but also qualifies as a spring creek by flyfishing standards that aren't found in the dictionary. By this I mean it's placid, meandering, and cold. The river has great dry fly hatches that rise out of crystalline, waist-deep waters in great enough numbers to force an angler to match the hatch

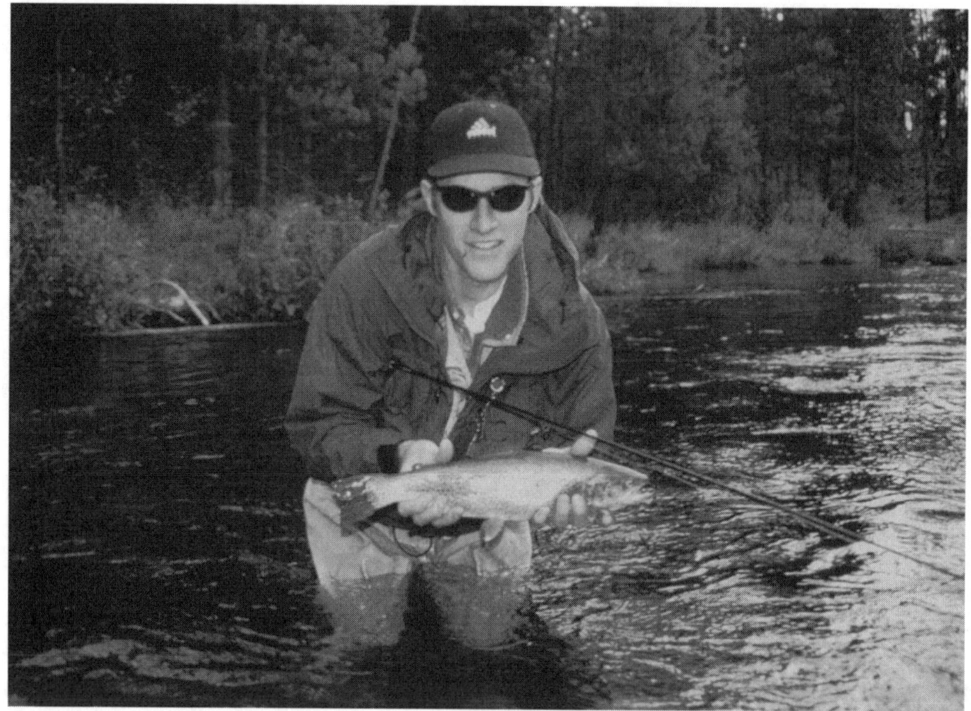

Eric Lyon took this Fall River fish on his 7-foot, 3-weight, but not before it almost took him.

and have a good arsenal of flies. Perhaps the most important and most frustrating quality of a spring creek is that, in most situations, there can be 2 or 10 different current lines between you and your fly.

This last problem is unique to this type of river. Freestone rivers and tailwaters offer similar situations but on a grander scale. On Fall River things happen close in and in slow motion. A few things to keep in mind on Fall River are long leaders, casts that allow some play in the line, and excellent mending skills both in the air and on the water.

A standard 12-foot leader tapering to 5X or 6X is a good place to start on the Fall. Use 4X for most nymphing situations. Have plenty of tippet for days when 12 feet is not enough. Fall River is as clear as water gets in any fishing situation. Tippet diameter here can make the difference between catching and not catching fish. If you find yourself fishing to risers using reliable patterns with good drifts but getting no takers, then stop and take the time to go to a lighter tippet. Going slowly is the key to fishing spring creeks. Wade slowly, take time casting, and tie good knots! Don't let a big, rising fish stress you into hurrying through your skills. Shortcuts will ruin you here. Be very purposeful and you'll do fine.

When you cast on a spring creek like Fall River, do it with the right gear. Three- and 4-weight rods are perfect here. Heavier rods produce heavier hands, and bad casting here scares fish. The no external split shot rule on the Fall also makes heavier rods unnecessary when nymphing this river. Knowing a variety of casting techniques will serve the fly angler well here. Slack line casts are very effective on this river as they allow more play in the line, thus giving an angler good drag-free drifts to rising fish. Slack line, when fishing subsurface, will also take tension off the fly, allowing the fly to sink more quickly through the water. Parachute casts, reach casts, and the like are more than helpful on Fall River—they are necessary.

My guiding experience has convinced me that what is done with the line on water is far more important than any one skill an angler can have. Good line-on-the-water skills can turn an OK cast into an awesome drift. Knowing how to mend up, down, and across a stream while keeping the fly drag-free will often separate a good angler from a great angler. It is always fun to throw a long line, but all the casting skill in the world isn't going to produce perfect drifts every time, yet decent casting with excellent mending skills can come close. Manipulating your line to keep a tiny dry fly dead-drifting while your line lies across several, ever changing current lines is the kind of skill that can be learned on this river. It will make other rivers you have fished before seem suddenly easier when you return to fish them again.

Whether you are a fly tier or not, have plenty of flies in your box and include a variety of life stages for insects found on the hatch chart. As with most spring creek fish, Fall River fish learn to avoid the easily replicated dun and often lock onto an emerging insect to avoid an angler's offering.

Be prepared to learn some skills and entomology the hard way on Fall River. Remain patient, look for hatches and the right opportunities on this river, and then challenge yourself. What you can learn by fishing gin-clear water like this will make you a better angler and make less clear, more turbulent waters much easier to fish.

To learn casting and mending techniques that are required to succeed on spring creeks, don't hesitate to use a guide service. Look at this fee as tuition for a one-day school and let the guide know that you want a teacher. Don't put your catch rate ahead of learning some essential flyfishing skills when fishing with a professional guide. Bob Gaviglio, owner of Sunriver Fly Shop, and Jeff Perin of The Fly Fisher's Place are excellent guides should you decide to hire one.

Stream Facts: Fall River

Seasons

- Downstream from the falls: Open to angling the last Saturday of April to September 30.
- Upstream from the falls: open to angling the entire year.

Special Regulations

- Downstream from the falls: 2 trout per day; catch and release only for all nonfinclipped rainbow trout; restricted to artificial flies with barbless hooks.
- Upstream from the falls: 2 trout per day; restricted to artificial flies with barbless hooks.

Fish

- Above the falls, you will find rainbows, both hatchery and wild, between 8 and 18 inches.
- Below the falls, brown trout dominate, with nice-sized, wild redside rainbows mixed in. Fish are also 8 to 18 inches.

River Characteristics

- The Fall River is a pristine spring creek. Complete with gin-clear, cool water, it weaves through a pine forest. Most of the river is a casting length across. Banks have good trails, and the river is relatively easy to wade, but watch for a few deep spots. Osprey and otter are a common sight and will compete with you for fish.

Access

- The river flows for less than 10 miles from its headwaters to its confluence with the Deschutes and has walk and wade access at the headwaters, the Fall River Campground, several pullouts from Fall River Road, and the hatchery. Below the falls, access is via Forest Road 4360 off Hwy 42.

Maps

- Deschutes National Forest
- DeLorme *Oregon Atlas and Gazetteer*

FALL RIVER MAJOR HATCHES

Insect	J	F	M	A	M	J	J	A	S	O	N	D	Time	Flies
Midges *Chironomidae*	■	■	■	■	■	■	■	■	■	■	■	■	A, E	Griffith's Gnat, Palamino Midge, CDC Hatching Midge, Century Drive Midge, Suspender Pupa, Para Midge #18-26
Blue-winged Olive *Baetis* sp.		■	■	■	■				■	■	■		A (Duns) SF: M & D	Beadhead Pheasant Tail, RS2, Captive Dun, Comparadun, Thorax, H1V12 Parachute, D Biot Spinner #16-24
Pale Morning Duns *Ephemerella* sp.					■	■	■	■	■				A (Duns) SF: M	Flashback Pheasant Tail, Captive Dun, Sparkle Dun, PMD Parachute, Biot Spinner (light olive and brown) #16-20
Mahogany Dun *Paraleptophlebia* sp.								■	■	■			A, E (Duns)	Poxyback Nymph, Floating Nymph, CDC Biot Comparadun, Parachute Adams #16
Terrestrials (Ants/Beetles/Hoppers)					■	■	■	■	■	■			M to E	Foam Ant, Crowe Beetle, Parahopper, Madame X
Yellow Sally Stonefly						■	■	■	■				M, A	Yellow Sally #14-18
Spotted Sedge, *Hydropsyche* Little Sister Sedge, *CheumatopsycheAl*				■	■	■	■	■	■	■			A, E	Yellow Serendipity, Green Serendipity, Sparkle Pupa, CDC Caddis, X-Caddis #14-18
Speckled Peter Caddis *Helicopsyche*					■	■	■	■					A, E	Yellow Soft Hackle, Sparkle Pupa, X-Caddis, Elk Hair Caddis #14-18
Little Western Weedy Water Sedge, *Amiocentrus*					■	■	■	■	■				A, E	Cased Caddis, Green Soft Hackle, Sparkle Pupa, Henryville, X-Caddis #16-20

HATCH TIME CODE: M = morning; A = afternoon; E = evening; D = dark; SF = spinner fall; / = continuation through periods.

Hatch Chart Prepared by Jeff Perin and Bob Gaviglio

East Lake

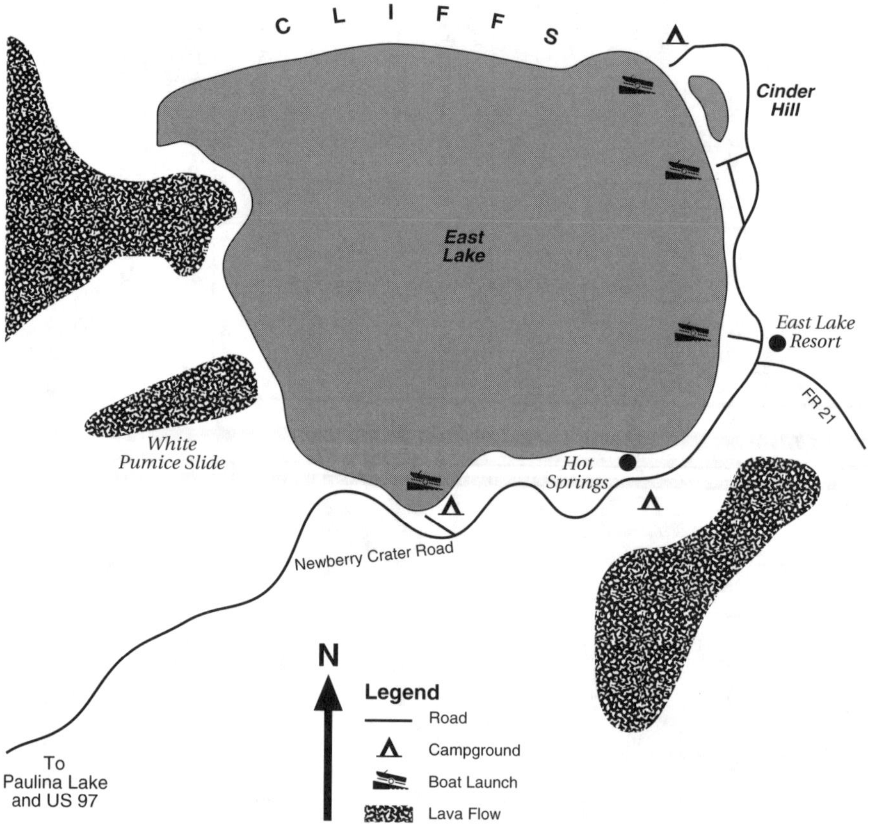

CLIFFS

Cinder Hill

East Lake

East Lake Resort

FR 21

White Pumice Slide

Hot Springs

Newberry Crater Road

To Paulina Lake and US 97

N

Legend

Road

Campground

Boat Launch

Lava Flow

WARNING!

Fish in this lake are tainted by mercury; children 6 years old and younger, women of childbearing age, and women either pregnant or nursing should eat no more than 8 oz. of these fish every 6 weeks. All others should eat no more than 8 oz. every 10 days. No brown trout over 16 inches should ever be eaten.

EAST LAKE

Big brown trout and alpine lakes are not usually synonymous in flyfishing, but East Lake is an exception. It sits right next to its companion, Paulina Lake, within the Newberry Crater about 35 miles from Bend, Oregon. Fishing on top of this volcano can be explosive, figuratively speaking.

Both bodies of water are good fisheries, but East Lake has become an awesome flyfishery for two reasons: first is size—although it is a large, deep lake by flyfishing standards, it is much smaller than neighboring Paulina Lake (also an excellent fly lake); second is the presence of mercury in East that naturally seeps in through the lake bottom. Although mercury has no effect on fish as far as the sporting aspect goes, eating these fish is not healthy and, subsequently, keeps the lake a catch-and-release sport fishery by default rather than by law. As of 1998 Oregon lists nine fisheries where everyone should avoid taking and eating fish. East Lake is on this short list. The Oregon Health Division is very serious about this, as anglers should be, also. Guidelines for eating fish are found in Oregon's fishing regulations every year.

Essentially, what we have is a catch-and-release fishery, made so by Mother Nature. Like most catch-and-release fisheries, the result is bigger fish and more of them. East Lake holds good populations of browns, rainbows, landlocked Atlantic salmon, Kokanee, and an occasional brook trout. Paulina Lake does as well but without the natural catch and release occurrence.

All these species are available to flyfishers, although Kokanee are often found in slightly deeper water than the rest. Most flyfishers pass up Kokanee in favor of browns and rainbows, but in East Lake a flyfisher should take advantage of this fishery. Kokanee are larger here than in other waters around Oregon and can often be found schooling in shallower waters. When browns and rainbows aren't biting, try going a little deeper for these landlocked fish. A bright, 18-inch Kokanee can be a ton of fun on a fly rod, and generally, where there is one there are many.

East Lake is a deeper body of water than what most fly anglers choose, but brown and rainbow populations here tend to stay relatively close to the surface. Large shoal areas close to the shoreline offer these fish plenty of shallow water in which to find a meal. These circumstances provide the ideal setting for fly anglers.

Generally, fish cruising around looking for a meal do this in the top 4 to 6 feet of water throughout most of the prime season. Despite East Lake's great depths, a floating line and an intermediate sinking line are all one needs most of the time.

Like most central Oregon stillwater fisheries, East Lake's prime seasons are spring and fall. As soon as ice starts melting and the road opens, East Lake is ready to be fished. This can vary year to year depending on snowpack. Always call one of the Sunriver or Bend area fly shops for up-to-date information on lake accessibility. Most of these shops also offer stillwater guide services on East Lake.

East Lake's spring season starts slightly later than surrounding waters due to its high altitude. It is usually accessible by May, and fish can be found cruising in shallow waters looking to plump up again after a long winter under the ice. This is prime time on East Lake. Float tubes and shore wading will give you access to fish. Most general subsurface patterns will draw strikes on East Lake.

Streamers fished as baitfish can be killers here. Bob Gaviglio, owner of Sunriver Fly Shop, says he often tucks his fly rod under his arm and uses a two-handed strip to entice the lake's biggest fish that are looking for minnows to fill their bellies.

On the other end of the spectrum, a nymph suspended or retrieved very slowly in the shallows will also take big fish looking for an easy meal. In either case, start near the surface and count down your line until you find the most productive depth. Then try to keep the fly in that region until the fishing slows down. If the fishing turns off, don't panic. In spring, big lake fish are not going to stop feeding, but they might change to the next most abundant food source in the afternoon or evening. So, the thing to do is find which food they switched to or where they have moved, or both. This may or may not be at the depth you found them during the morning hours. This may mean changing flies and techniques to imitate different food.

Hotter summer months may push fish down slightly during midday, but these months may also offer some fantastic dry fly opportunities during morning and evening hours. On less windy afternoons, look for callibaetis mayflies to draw fish to the surface. This aquatic insect will show up in spring and continue through midsummer. When fish are on the surface, basic patterns, such as a royal Wulff fished with the occasional twitch, are often all one needs to draw strikes. Callibaetis can make fishing both easy and difficult. Bob Gaviglio assures me that when things get tough during summer afternoons on East Lake, it is because fish are locking on to callibaetis emergers. If you think this is happening, try stripping callibaetis imitations, such as soft hackles and ostrich nymphs, subsurface. This can turn a slow day into an event. Also be aware that dragonfly nymphs are active this time of year and, along with damselflies, become an important food source for the lake's fish.

Autumn on East Lake again draws fish into shallows. Browns looking to fatten up or looking for spawning opportunities will be checking into the shallows on a regular basis. Fishing to these monster fish is a great challenge. Rainbows also cruise the shallows looking for chub, the resident baitfish and biggest mouthful in the lake. Your best chances for the lake's biggest fish are in the shallowest waters during low-light periods of spring and fall.

There are hot springs in the lake just south of East Lake Resort. This shoreline, all the way to the white pumice slide that is very obvious on the west shore, is a great place to begin looking for fish in shallows. The hot springs area in spring can be fantastic. Also, the north shore cliff area is a draw for fish looking to remain close to the safety of deep water while cruising the shoreline.

East Lake fish are not overly selective when found. More often than not, basic buggers and nymphs used in the Cascade lakes area will work here. Check with local shops for their favorites. Find the depth, match the right stripping technique with the right fly, and you're in business. Generally, large flies fished with long, quick strips

A central Oregon trout poses for the camera.

will imitate the lake's baitfish. Leeches fished on long, slow strips will take fish, and nymphs fished with short, erratic strips will get the lake's most finicky fish to eat. Short, stout leaders from 5-foot 1X to 4X will handle sinking line situations, and a 9- to 12-foot 4X and 5X leader will take care of the dry fly opportunities.

Don't let East Lake's size intimidate you—work the shorelines and be ready for some great fish. Year in and year out, East Lake offers consistent fishing. It is East Lake's size that makes it a great fishery. Drought years have less effect here than the rest of central Oregon's shallower reservoirs and lakes, making East Lake a favorite and consistent place to cast flies at big browns and rainbows.

Lake Facts: East Lake

Season

- Open to angling the last Saturday of April through October 31.

Special Regulations

- Health advisory due to mercury contamination—children 6 years old and younger should not eat fish from this lake. Children older than 6 years, women of childbearing age, and women who are pregnant or nursing should eat no more than 8 ounces of these fish every 6 weeks. Other men and women should eat no more than 8 ounces every 10 days. No brown trout over 16 inches or longer should be eaten. I suggest no one eat any of these fish. There are too many other places to go, very close by, if you want fish for dinner.

Fish

- Brown trout to 20 pounds, rainbows to 10 pounds, some brook trout and Atlantic salmon. Kokanee up to 18 inches are not uncommon.

Lake Size and Depth

- Over 1,000 acres most years, with depths to 175 feet.

Lake Characteristics

- The lake sits in the Newberry Crater with Paulina Lake, well over 6,000 feet in elevation. Shallower water near the banks hold fish. It is quite a large lake by flyfishing standards and holds great populations of fish year in and year out. Its elevation keeps the season short and the water cold. Boats or neoprenes will keep you fishing longer.

Boat Ramps

- Five ramps are easily accessed on the south and east banks. This is the shallower side of the lake. There is a resort with some basic supplies in the summer and three campgrounds at the boat ramps.

Maps

- Oregon Atlas of Lakes
- DeLorme *Oregon Atlas and Gazetteer*

EAST LAKE AND PAULINA LAKE MAJOR HATCHES

Insect	J	F	M	A	M	J	J	A	S	O	N	D	Time	Flies
Chubs													All day	Matukas, Minnowbuggers, South Twin Specials, Cascade Specials, Body Fur Streamers #6-10
Dragonflies and Nymphs													All day	Standard Dragon Nymph, Carey Specials #6
Damselflies													Midday	Standard Marabou Damsels, Richard's Stillwater Nymph #10-12
Scuds/Leeches													All day	Olive & Tan Scuds #12-16; Richard's Seal Buggers #8 (4X hook)
Callibaetis Mayflies													After-noon Evening	Adults: Two Feather, Thorax or Comparadun Callibaetis #14-18 (smaller as season progresses) Emergers: CDC Callibaetis, Sparkle Emerger, Hare's Ear #14-18 (smaller as season progresses)
Midges													All day	Griffith's Gnats, Midge Pupas, Suspended Pupas #12-14

Hatch Chart Prepared by Bob Gaviglio

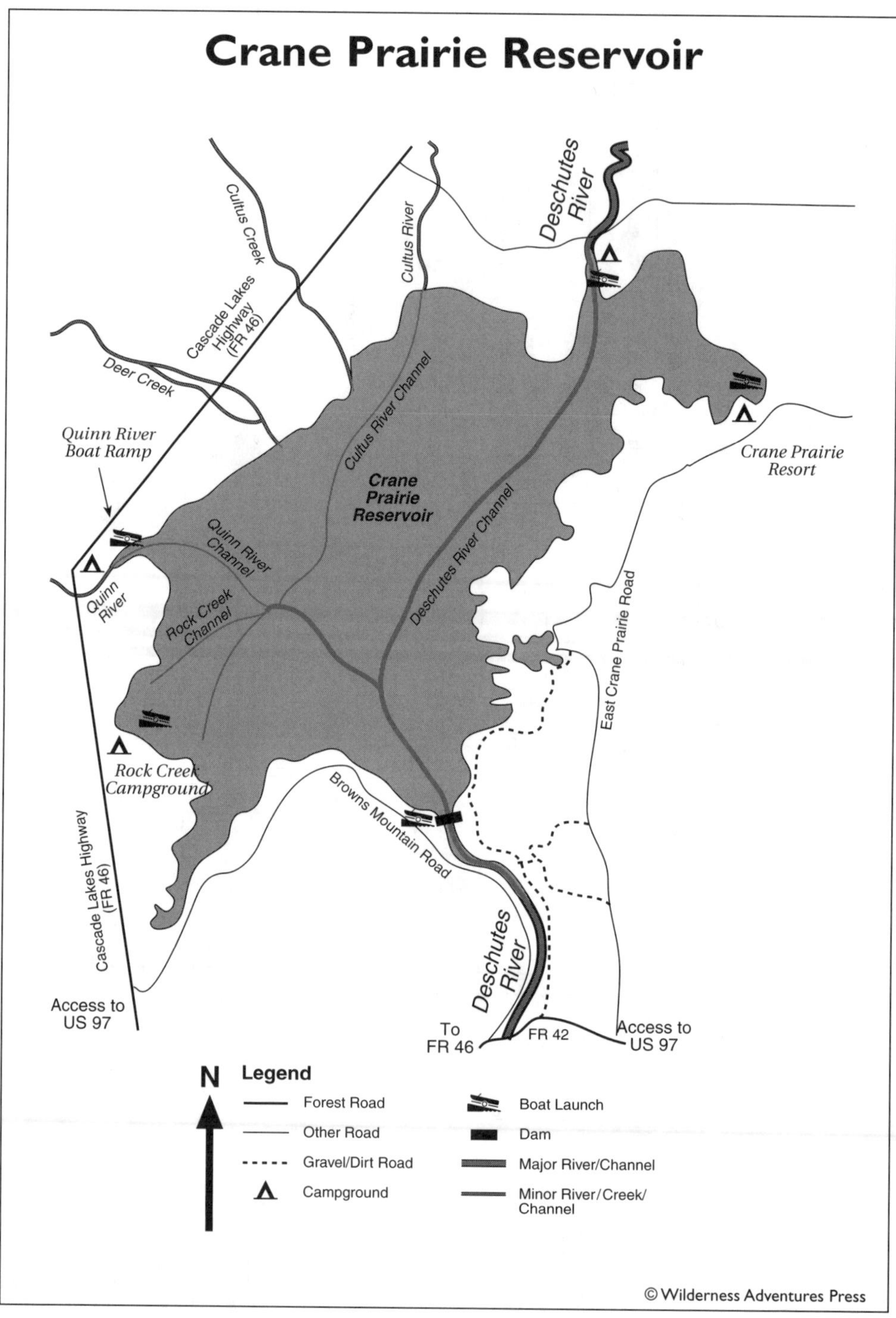
Crane Prairie Reservoir
Deschutes River
Cultus Creek
Cultus River
Cascade Lakes Highway (FR 46)
Deer Creek
Quinn River Boat Ramp
Cultus River Channel
Crane Prairie Reservoir
Deschutes River Channel
Crane Prairie Resort
Quinn River Channel
Quinn River
Rock Creek Channel
East Crane Prairie Road
Rock Creek Campground
Browns Mountain Road
Cascade Lakes Highway (FR 46)
Deschutes River
Access to US 97
To FR 46
FR 42
Access to US 97
N
Legend
Forest Road
Other Road
Gravel/Dirt Road
Campground
Boat Launch
Dam
Major River/Channel
Minor River/Creek/Channel
© Wilderness Adventures Press

CRANE PRAIRIE RESERVOIR

If you grew up trout fishing in Oregon, most likely the first place you attached such words as incredible and monster fish to was Crane Prairie. One look at this central Oregon reservoir and everything you've ever heard about Crane is confirmed. You don't need to wet a line to know that huge trout must lurk in this eerie waterscape. In the early 1900s, Crane Prairie Reservoir was formed by a dam on its northwest end. Trees in the soon-to-be-flooded area were left standing, and many remain standing today. Forests that were once home to big bull elk, mule deer, and bear have become the favorite haunts of big buck rainbow trout.

Crane Prairie Reservoir is just south of Bend, nestled in with one great fishery after another off the Cascade Lakes Highway. I asked Bob Gaviglio, owner of Sunriver Fly Shop, what distinguishes Crane Prairie from central Oregon's other stillwater fisheries. Bob's reply was short and sweet: "It's a highly fly-fishable lake, full of trophy trout! Numerous patterns are effective and the shear size and fight of the fish make it a fabulously unique fishery."

Crane Prairie is a very shallow reservoir, only averaging about 8 feet deep. The old river channels that are carved into the bottom of Crane get to about 20 feet deep at the most. These channels are fish highways much of the time and are important places for flyfishers. Many of the channels are obvious, such as the Quinn Channel off the Quinn River boat ramp, where dead, standing timber lines the river's old path. Some are less obvious and can be found with a map and a guess, by using a depth finder, or just by observing other anglers on the water. Fish love to visit underwater springs, found in and around the channels, for a cool-down and some oxygen. These are the places that locals know and where the biggest fish are found.

Crane's channels are very important, but fish do use the entire reservoir, drawn into the shallows to feed on myriad insects that inhabit Crane's water. The well-lit shallows combined with the old tree stands and a rich, mucky bottom create bug life unparalleled by any stillwater in the state. It is this immense insect population that makes fishing at Crane so popular—not the bugs per se, but the trout that feed on them. These trout grow big and they grow fast—4 to 5 pounds of fighting rainbow is oftentimes the norm rather than the exception on Crane Prairie. Couple this trout diet with the amount of structure in the reservoir and it makes for one great trophy trout formula.

Success on Crane Prairie is a matter of knowing where to fish and when. Whether fishing the shallows or the channels, most of the reservoir can be fished with the same gear. An intermediate sinking line and a floating line are usually enough unless you know that fish are hugging the channel bottom, in which case a slightly quicker sink rate could save a little time getting down to the fish. If you don't want to invest in too many lines, stick with your intermediate line. In the last few years, some flyfishers have been using the newer, stillwater lines by Scientific Anglers. These lines are clear, giving a flyfisher a slight advantage when fishing pressure is at its peak in the summer.

Whichever lines you fish here, they are best fished on a 6-weight rod. Fish size as well as the reservoir's obvious structure result in many broken-off fish. It is not uncommon on Crane to have a monster fish gingerly pick up your fly and head into the submerged timbers. By the time you're feeling the resistance, the fish already has you wrapped around countless snags. If you're able to detect a strike before it's too late, a 6-weight outfit might help keep fish away from structure during the fight. Note that I said it might help—some fish in Crane Prairie are going to have their way with you regardless of your experience and skill with a fly rod.

Many flyfishers approach Crane Prairie with float tubes, while others use drift boats. Both get the job done and have great benefits. Float tubes allow an angler to work slowly and precisely over known lies of fish. Boats offer comfort and speed when searching for Crane's trophies, but neither is as suited to the style of fishing on Crane Prairie as the single-person pontoon boats that have appeared on the flyfishing market in recent years. These craft keep an angler upright and comfortable, while allowing the ability to fin slowly through the water or scoot along the surface using oars. Oftentimes, Crane is too big to fish a lot of water in a float tube and too technically demanding to fish out of a boat, making the single-person pontoon an excellent alternative. Whatever gear you have, even if it's a 4-weight and wading boots, go try your luck at Crane. It is a fantastic place to cast at exciting fish and remains a mecca for serious Oregon fly anglers.

Like surrounding waters, Crane Prairie's fishing commences in spring. Although fish activity can get off to a slower start than other central Oregon stillwaters, Crane in the spring still presents an opportunity for some memorable fish and some rare solitude on the reservoir.

Spring is a time for experimenting with many reservoir patterns. Leeches fished very slowly can produce jarring tugs. This is the kind of pull that will make you want to fish stillwaters exclusively for the rest of your life. Small nymphs, such as Prince nymphs and zug bugs, will entice trout. Streamers, scuds, midge patterns, damselfly and dragonfly nymphs will all catch the occasional fish in the spring. It goes without saying, but I will anyway: Spring weather is temperamental, so be prepared for anything. The fact that weather may keep you close to shore and the shelter of timbered areas is fine. These are excellent places to find big fish cruising in the spring. You can find better places than Crane Prairie for spring fishing around central Oregon, but few are better fisheries.

June brings flyfishermen and hardware fishers to Crane Prairie like supermodels draw stares. Everyone looks but not everyone touches. Fishing begins to heat up as the warming waters turn the fish and bug life on. Things begin to get a little more complex as fish lock on to the most plentiful food sources. This is not to say they won't eat opportunistically, but a flyfisher tied into the right pattern can produce tenfold to adjacent anglers.

This is no time to rest on your laurels at Crane Prairie. Fish are going to be eating in the summer months, and their food choices and sources are many. Fly anglers must become observant as fish change their eating habits all day long. One minute, fish may be locked on to a damsel nymph migration and, in no time at all, switch to a callibaetis emergence.

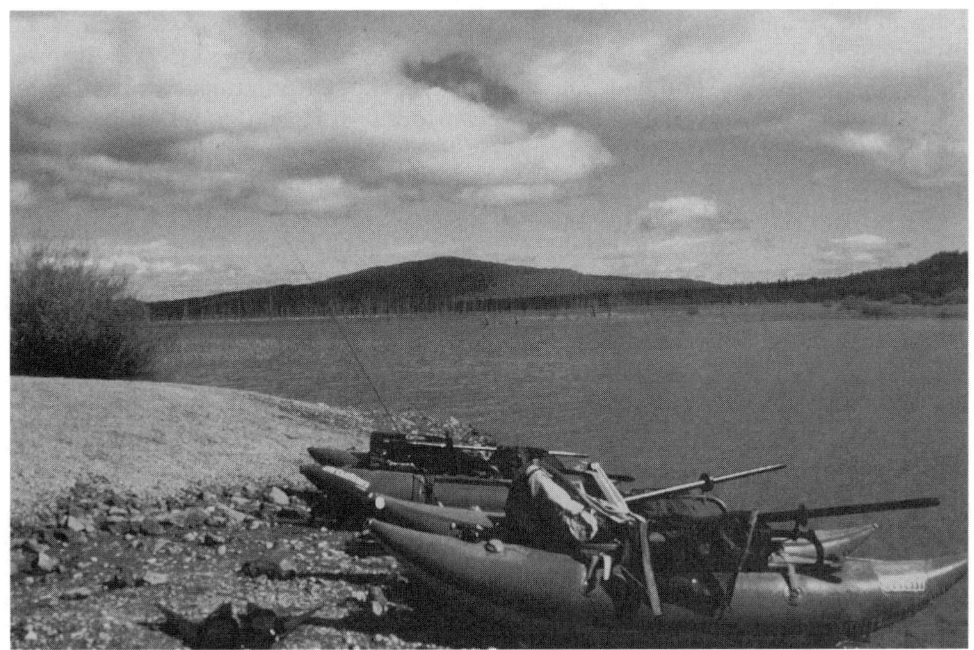

Pontoon boats are a great way to get around on Crane Prairie Reservoir.

June, July, and August offer some of the best action as well as greater numbers of anglers. The flyfishers who produce in these months are the well-versed locals and the observant anglers. By watching the fish, the insects, and nearby anglers you can quickly deduce what is working and what isn't. Frequent fly changes and the willingness to switch from a fly that was hot half an hour ago to an as-yet-untried pattern and technique can produce all day action, as opposed to an occasional hot streak during the day.

Rising water temperatures and fishing pressure during summer months will tend to concentrate fish in Crane's channels. Hot weather may also slow the fishing down and put fish over submerged springs within the channels. The main channels are the Deschutes River, the Quinn River, and the Cultus River. The Cultus is the coldest of the three and is a good place to cast your offerings on the hottest days. This channel is also a big draw to brook trout, which love cold water. The depths and edges of all these channels are a good place to concentrate your efforts. Look for fish to move out from the channels and into shallower areas during low-light periods of the day.

Like most other stillwater fisheries, Crane's morning and evening rises can be fantastic and short-lived. Fish will rise on midges and caddisflies. This is a good time to get out soft-hackled patterns and cast to boils in the water. Summer also produces hot and heavy midday rises to both callibaetis mayflies and damselflies. Callibaetis on most stillwaters in central Oregon typically start out as large insects. They are about a size 14 in June and typically get smaller as the season progresses.

What can I say about damselflies? If you encounter a big hatch and an equally big rise (or should I say mop-up) by Crane Prairie's swimming footballs and you have some decent damsel patterns, you might as well sit down and light a cigar when it's all over because that's as good as it gets anywhere.

In the past few years, Crane has seen a slight decline in damselfly and callibaetis activity and a rise in the amount of sticklebacks. The stickleback is a small baitfish about an inch to an inch and a half long. This has made streamer fishing in Crane a much more commonly used technique. Check with Gaviglio for some great stickleback imitations. Fish these streamers erratically and quickly. Most fish that have not been released back into Crane have at least a few of these baitfish in their bellies.

When autumn arrives on Crane Prairie Reservoir, the cooler temperatures in this high desert of central Oregon can be a blessing. Autumn's chill air cools the water, and trout respond. When fish get that first sense of winter, an angler can almost feel the urgency in their strike. Big fish are looking to get bigger in order to sustain themselves during winter's sparse offerings. Consistent hatches begin to diminish, while feeding frenzies become harder to find but more intense when found. Searching patterns that were used in spring once again regain their merit and draw strikes. Fall is a good time to check out local patterns that can be found in Bend, Sisters, and Sunriver fly shops. Look for storm fronts, whether coming or going, to turn activity on, but be careful of them as well. Central Oregon's high desert gets cold as winter bores down, but fishing will stay productive right up to the end of the season, which is always the end of October. Look for fish in all areas and depths as fall begins to turn to winter.

Crane Prairie Reservoir is a quick drive from Bend, which offers a variety of hotel accommodations and microbreweries. Many improved and unimproved campgrounds also surround the reservoir. It is also a very short drive to both Davis and Hosmer Lakes if you want to camp with a bunch of flyfishers and talk shop. These campgrounds tend to be quieter and less improved than those surrounding Crane.

To reach the south end of Crane Prairie Reservoir, take US 97 south from Bend and turn right onto Vandevert Road for a short way, then left onto South Century Drive, which is also Forest Road 42. Continue on South Century Drive to the south end of the reservoir, where you can turn right to reach a boat access. Forest Road 42 continues to its junction and end at Forest Road 46, where you can turn right (north) to reach campgrounds and access on the lake's west side. To reach the north end of the lake from Sunriver, follow Forest Road 40 to the north end, where you can turn left on Forest Road 46. You can also take the Cascade Lakes Highway out of Bend, heading toward Mt. Bachelor, to reach the reservoir's west side via Forest Road 46.

It is well known in Oregon and other states that Crane is one of Oregon's premier flyfisheries. Quantity and size of fish in Crane can vary from year to year depending on water levels, but Oregon Fish and Wildlife has done a good job protecting the fishery in dire years, thus keeping Crane Prairie an awesome place to cast a fly.

Lake Facts: Crane Prairie Reservoir

Season

- Open to angling the last Saturday of April to October 31.

Special Regulations

- Closed 1 hour after sunset until 1 hour before sunrise.

Fish

- Wild rainbow trout and up to 200,000 stocked rainbows. Brook trout show up in decent numbers and there is a population of largemouth bass.

Reservoir Size and Depth

- The lake is 4,157 acres, which changes from year to year and throughout the seasons. The water only averages around 8 feet in depth. Channels are only 20 feet at their deepest point.

Reservoir Characteristics

- You haven't seen Crane Prairie until you've seen morning mist mingle with the forests of standing snags. It looks eerie and even primordial, although the only monsters lurking in Crane are its fish. The reservoir is surrounded by pine forests and frequented by many osprey and the occasional bald eagle.

Boat Ramps

- The best ramps are at Rock Creek, Quinn River, and Crane Prairie Resort. Float tubes and other hand-carried craft can be launched at any of the campgrounds or road accesses.

Maps

- *Oregon Atlas of Lakes*

CRANE PRAIRIE RESERVOIR MAJOR HATCHES

Insect	J	F	M	A	M	J	J	A	S	O	N	D	Time	Flies
Baitfish: Sticklebacks, Chub				■	■	■	■	■	■	■			All day	Matukas, Minnowbuggers, South Twin Specials, Cascade Specials, Body for Streams #6-10
Dragonflies					■	■	■	■	■				All day	Standard Dragon Nymphs, Carey Specials #6
Damselflies						■	■	■					10:30–3:30	Standard Marabou Damsels, Richard's Stillwater Nymph #10-12
Scuds				■	■	■	■	■	■	■			All day	Olive & Tan Scuds #12-16
Leeches				■	■	■	■	■	■	■			All day	Rickard's Seal Buggers #8
Callibaetis Mayflies					■	■	■	■	■	■			10:30–5:00	Adults: Two Feather Thorax, Comparadun Callibaetis #14-18 Emergers: CDC Callibaetis, Sparkle Emerger, Hare's Ears #14-18
Caddis					■	■	■	■	■				Morning Evening	Soft Hackles, Sparkle Pupas, Tied Down Caddis, Carey Specials #10-16
Boatman and Backswimmers				■	■	■	■	■	■	■			All day	Prince Nymphs, Zug Bugs #10-12
Midges				■	■	■	■	■	■	■			All day	Griffith's Gnats, Midge Pupas, Suspended Pupas #12-14
Snails				■	■	■	■	■	■	■			All day	Borger Snail #10-12

Hatch Chart Prepared by Bob Gaviglio

Upper Deschutes River

When most people hear the word "Deschutes," what comes to mind is a giant, green river weaving down a tall desert canyon. This is the Deschutes most often seen in pictures of drift boats and smiling anglers posing with steelhead and redside rainbows. The Deschutes of this chapter is the same river but nothing like the lower bigger water downstream. Because of the Deschutes' length and its great size differences, this chapter will only deal with the upper and middle Deschutes. The lower Deschutes is covered in the North Central Region chapter starting on page 45. In this book, the upper river encompasses the headwaters to the city of Bend and consists of three distinct sections: Little Lava Lake to Crane Prairie Reservoir, Crane Prairie to Wickiup Reservoir, and Wickiup Reservoir to Bend. Oregon Fish and Wildlife is careful to protect the spawning fish that use the upper reaches, so be aware of special seasons on these waters.

Little Lava Lake to Crane Prairie

The Deschutes begins its journey to the Columbia River at Little Lava Lake. From this point it flows about 7 miles to Crane Prairie Reservoir. It is considered a freestone stream at this point but can often act like a spring creek. Little Lava Lake is formed from percolating snowmelt and has no inlet, so essentially, the headwaters are a spring creek.

Fish in the upper Deschutes are smaller than most neighboring waters, although bigger brook trout are often migrating up from Crane Prairie. There are good hatches of caddis and golden stones on this section, and blue-winged olives and green drakes appear here, also. Terrestrials are always a good bet on this small water as well.

The upper Deschutes is easily waded and can be fished with basic dry fly techniques. Short line nymphing is also employed on this section of river as many of the bigger fish will hold under deeply-cut banks during the day.

Brook trout are joined in this section by resident rainbows. Luckily for them and us, rainbows may only be fished on a catch-and-release basis and only with single barbless flies and lures. The river can be accessed along the Cascade Lakes Highway for much of its 7-mile length and can be intercepted at the Hwy 40 crossing. An angler can also hike up from the mouth at Cow Meadow Campground.

The headwaters can be an enjoyable place to spend a summer day. It's a good place to teach a friend to fish or spend a day trying to find the big fish that are harder to come by. The Deschutes headwaters are beautiful enough to exchange for an occasional day on the more popular big fish waters. Tread lightly and don't forget your camera.

Seasons
- Open to angling June 1 to September 30.

Special Regulations
- Catch and release only for rainbow trout.
- Restricted to artificial flies and lures.
- No limit on size or number of brook trout.

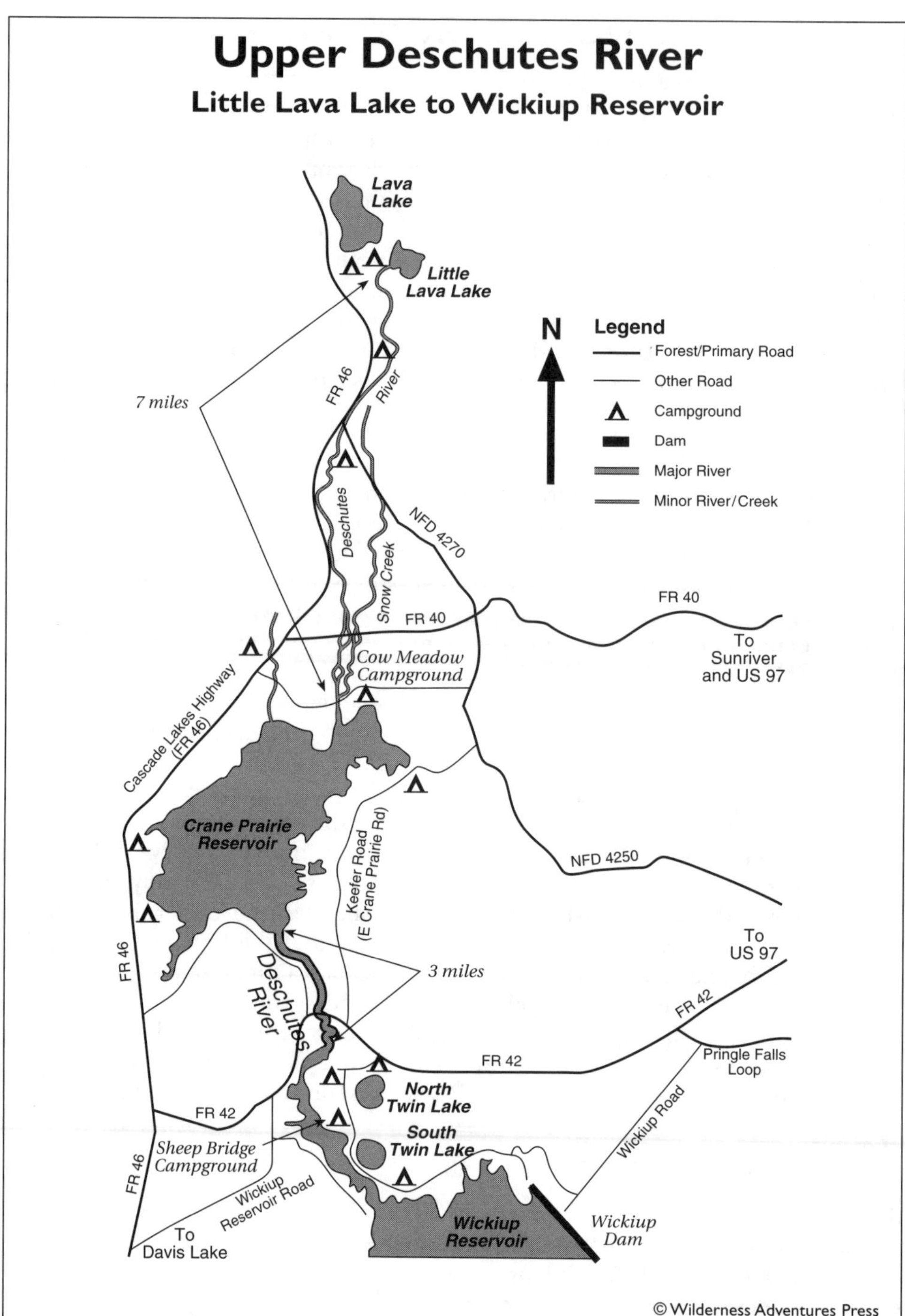

Upper Deschutes River
Little Lava Lake to Wickiup Reservoir
Lava Lake
Little Lava Lake
N
Legend
Forest/Primary Road
Other Road
Campground
Dam
Major River
Minor River/Creek
7 miles
FR 46
River
Deschutes
Snow Creek
NFD 4270
FR 40
FR 40
To Sunriver and US 97
Cow Meadow Campground
Cascade Lakes Highway (FR 46)
Crane Prairie Reservoir
Keefer Road (E Crane Prairie Rd)
NFD 4250
FR 46
To US 97
3 miles
Deschutes River
FR 42
FR 42
Pringle Falls Loop
North Twin Lake
South Twin Lake
FR 42
Sheep Bridge Campground
FR 46
Wickiup Road
Wickiup Reservoir Road
To Davis Lake
Wickiup Reservoir
Wickiup Dam
© Wilderness Adventures Press

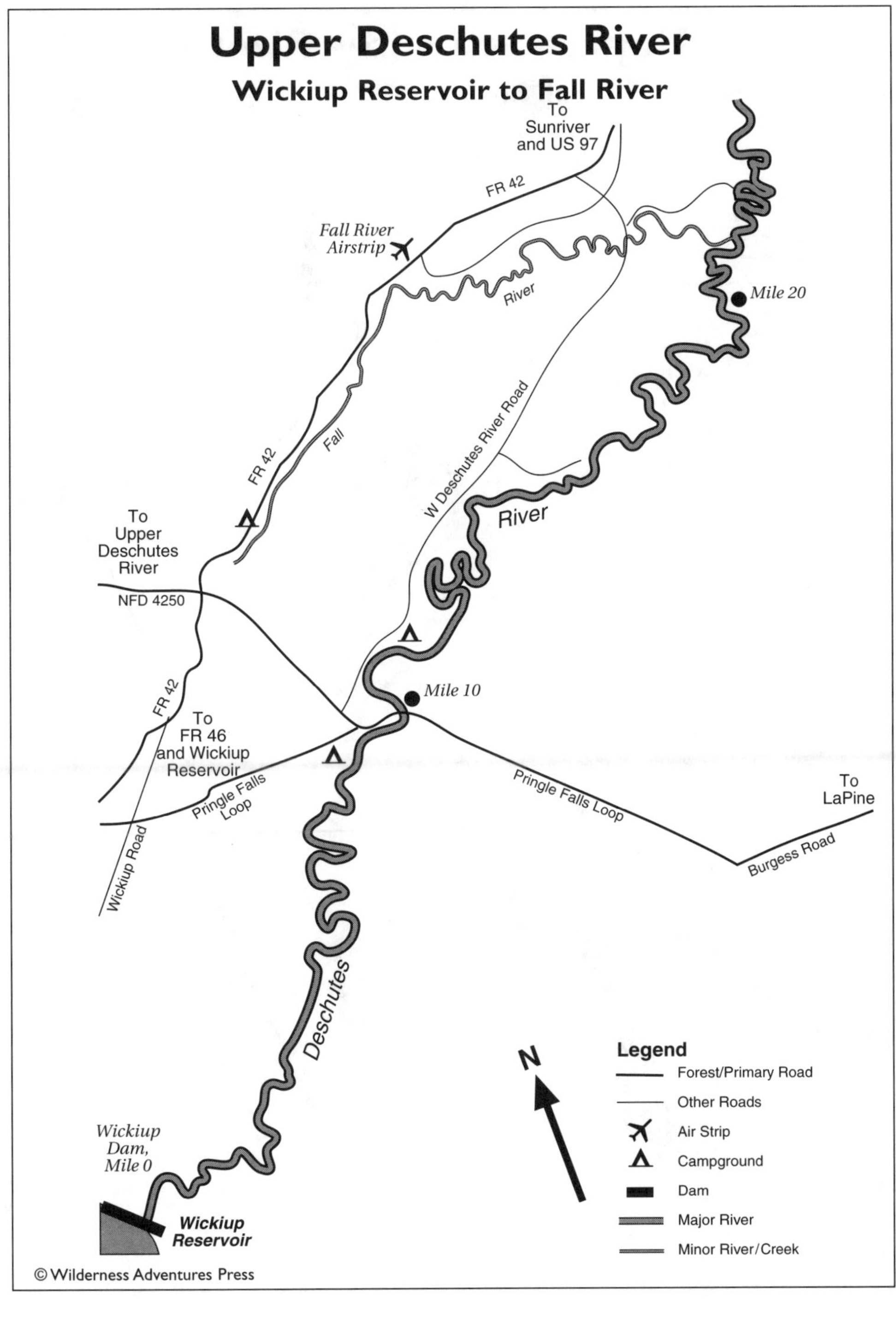

Upper Deschutes River
Wickiup Reservoir to Fall River
To
Sunriver
and US 97
FR 42
Fall River
Airstrip
River
Mile 20
Fall
FR 42
W Deschutes River Road
To
Upper
Deschutes
River
River
NFD 4250
Mile 10
FR 42
To
FR 46
and Wickiup
Reservoir
Pringle Falls
Loop
Pringle Falls Loop
To
LaPine
Burgess Road
Wickiup Road
Deschutes
N
Legend
Forest/Primary Road
Other Roads
Air Strip
Campground
Dam
Major River
Minor River/Creek
Wickiup
Dam,
Mile 0
Wickiup
Reservoir

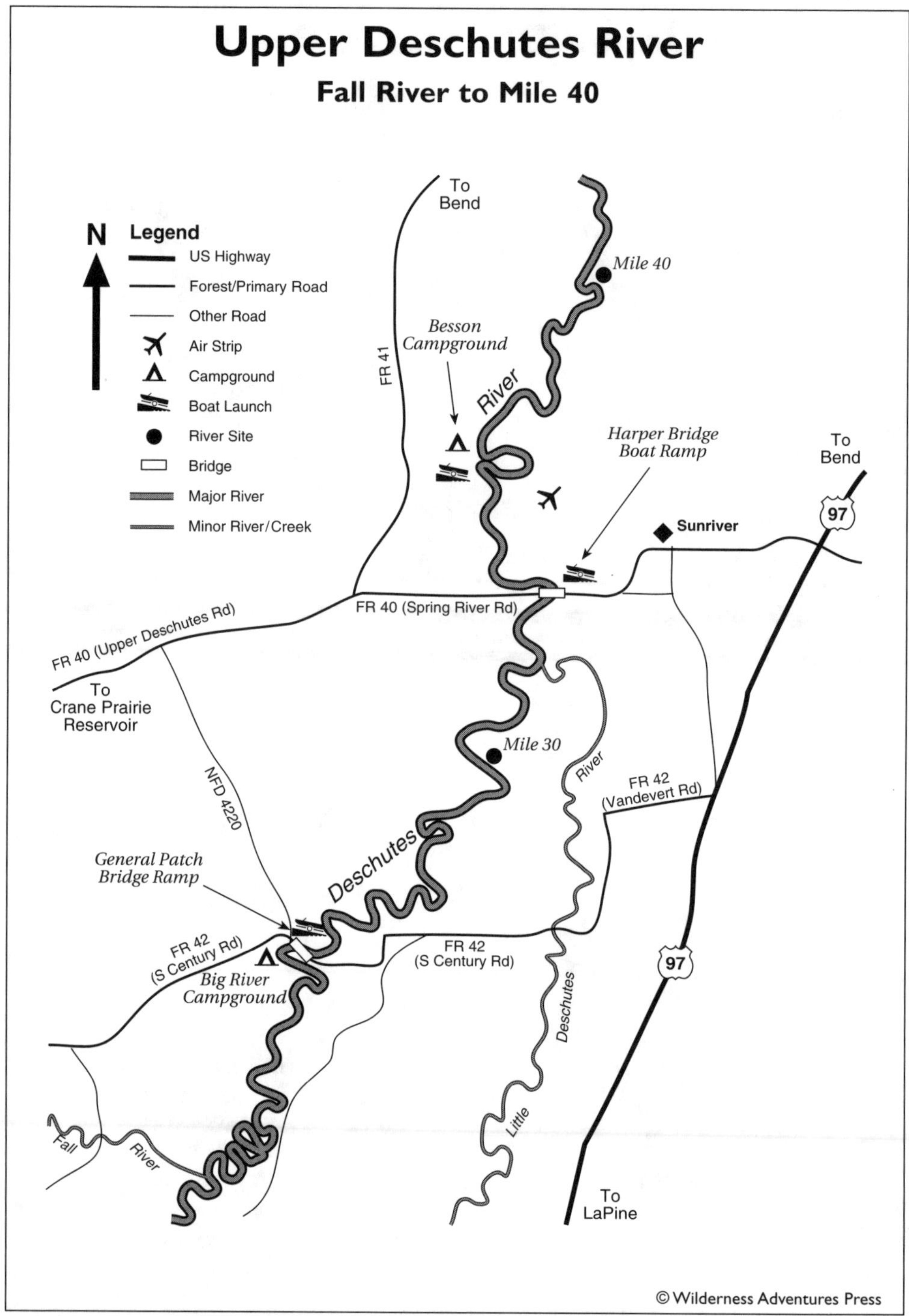
Upper Deschutes River
Fall River to Mile 40
N
Legend
US Highway
Forest/Primary Road
Other Road
Air Strip
Campground
Boat Launch
River Site
Bridge
Major River
Minor River/Creek
To Bend
Mile 40
Besson Campground
FR 41
River
Harper Bridge Boat Ramp
To Bend
97
Sunriver
FR 40 (Spring River Rd)
FR 40 (Upper Deschutes Rd)
To Crane Prairie Reservoir
Mile 30
River
FR 42 (Vandevert Rd)
NFD 4220
Deschutes
General Patch Bridge Ramp
FR 42 (S Century Rd)
FR 42 (S Century Rd)
Big River Campground
97
Deschutes
Little
Fall
River
To LaPine
© Wilderness Adventures Press

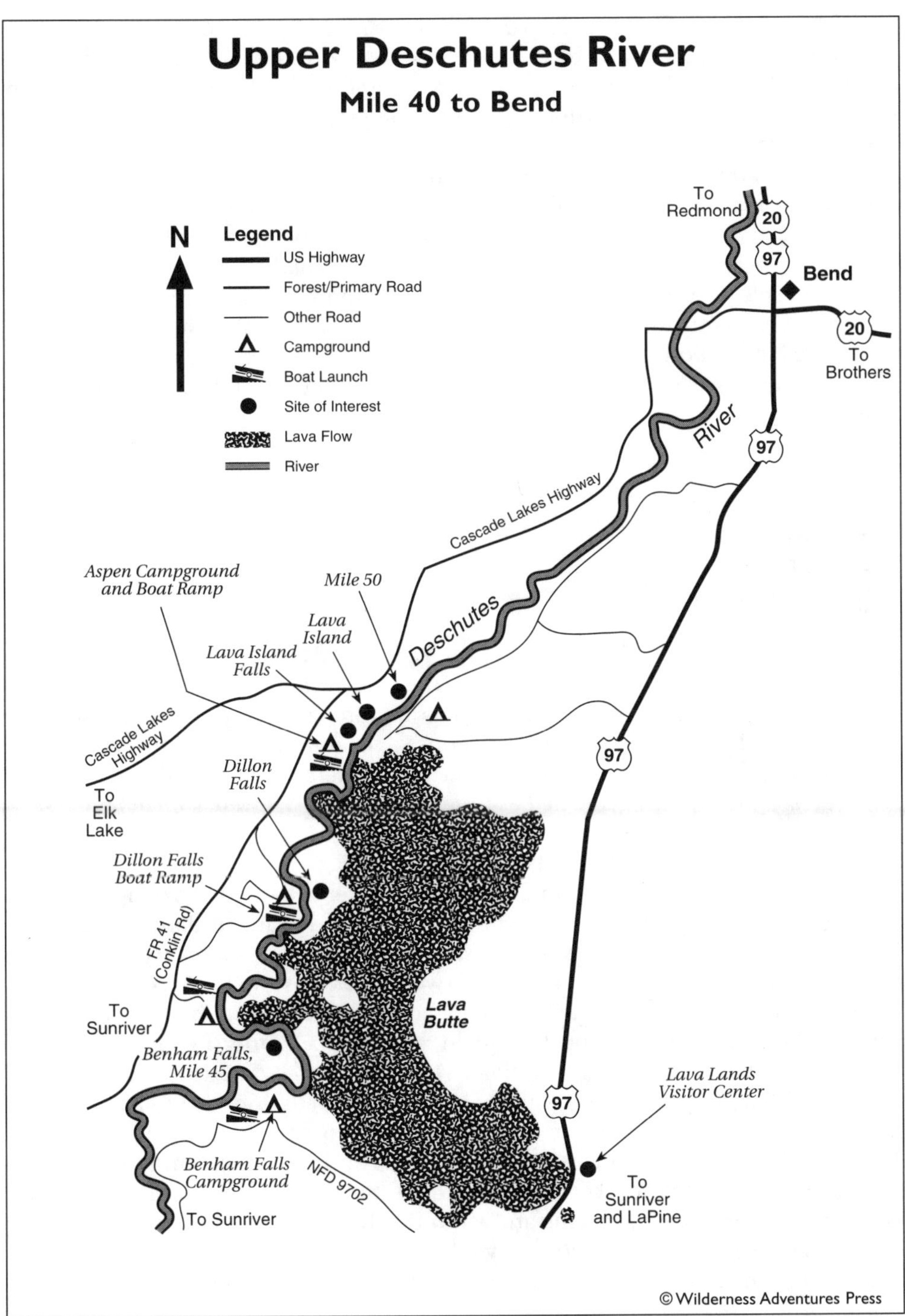
Upper Deschutes River
Mile 40 to Bend
N
Legend
US Highway
Forest/Primary Road
Other Road
Campground
Boat Launch
Site of Interest
Lava Flow
River
To Redmond
20
97
Bend
20
To Brothers
River
97
Cascade Lakes Highway
Deschutes
Aspen Campground and Boat Ramp
Mile 50
Lava Island
Lava Island Falls
Cascade Lakes Highway
To Elk Lake
97
Dillon Falls
Dillon Falls Boat Ramp
FR 41 (Conklin Rd)
To Sunriver
Lava Butte
Benham Falls, Mile 45
97
Lava Lands Visitor Center
Benham Falls Campground
NFD 9702
To Sunriver
To Sunriver and LaPine
© Wilderness Adventures Press

Crane Prairie Reservoir to Wickiup Reservoir

This section offers large brown and smaller brook trout that lurk beneath undercut banks and around whatever structure they can find. This is not a fishery that gets used constantly but is worth running a line through when you want to try something a little different.

Short sinktips and streamers on stout leaders, thrown under the cutbanks, is the best way to approach this water. It is a short section, accessed from Hwy 42, where an angler can walk up or down the river. It may also be accessed from the Sheep Bridge Campground, which can be reached from a marked access road between North and South Twin Lakes. This area becomes a more popular stretch in late summer as fly anglers try to find big browns before the late August closure.

There is a rainbow population in this section with catch-and-release regulations. This is a short 3-mile stretch of water that is worth looking into when the urge to search hits you.

Season

- Open to angling June 1 to August 31.

Special Regulations

- 2 brown trout per day.
- Catch and release only for rainbow trout.

Wickiup Reservoir to Bend

Bob Gaviglio calls this stretch central Oregon's sleeper fishery: "This is a stretch of river you can drive or bike in the evenings and find your very own secret spot. It's entirely possible that you will be the only one to fish that spot the entire season."

The fact is that the fishing is so good on other waters all around this stretch of the Deschutes, it just doesn't get fished as much as it would if it were somewhere else. A few locals and guides use it, but your average fisherman out of Portland is going to blow right by it heading to Crane Prairie or Davis Lake.

Small boats can be floated on this section of river, although bank angling is just as productive. The river can be swift, and floating it can be dangerous. Below Sunriver Resort especially, consult a fly shop or guide before shoving off. There are falls that can't be floated and a lot of big water. Perhaps the best sections are the reaches closer to Bend where car, bike, and foot access is easiest. Take Cascade Lakes Highway out of Bend heading toward Mt. Bachelor. At the Inn of the Seventh Mountain, turn onto gravel road 41. Road 41 will give access to side roads heading to various falls and camping areas where you can park, walk, and start looking for that first secret spot. Crossing the river is not possible in most spots during summer flows. To access the other side of the river, take Hwy 97 south from Bend and turn into the Lava Lands Visitor Center. Follow the road to the left to reach the Benham Falls camping area. From here, walking and mountain bike access is excellent.

Benham Falls is about 8 miles upriver from Bend and is the cutoff point for a regulation change. Upstream, the river has a 5-fish limit but is catch and release on all

Eric Lyon caught this nice rainbow while fishing the upper Deschutes River.

non-finclipped rainbow trout. Two browns may be kept above the falls. Below Benham Falls, the same brown trout rules apply but all rainbows must be released. This lower water is also restricted to artificial flies and lures.

There are some good fish and good fishing opportunities between Wickiup Reservoir and Bend. One of these days, as you're flying down to Fall River or Crane Prairie for the evening rise, consider hitting the brakes—you just might find a pleasant surprise.

Season

- From Benham Falls upstream to Wickiup: Open for trout the last Saturday of April to September 30.
- From Benham falls downstream to Bend: Open to angling for trout the entire year.

Special Regulations

- From Benham Falls upstream to Wickiup Reservoir: 5 trout per day that can include two brown trout. Catch and release only for non-finclipped rainbow trout.
- From Benham Falls downstream to Bend: 2 trout per day, which can include 1 bull trout that must be at least 24 inches in length.
- Restricted to artificial flies and lures.

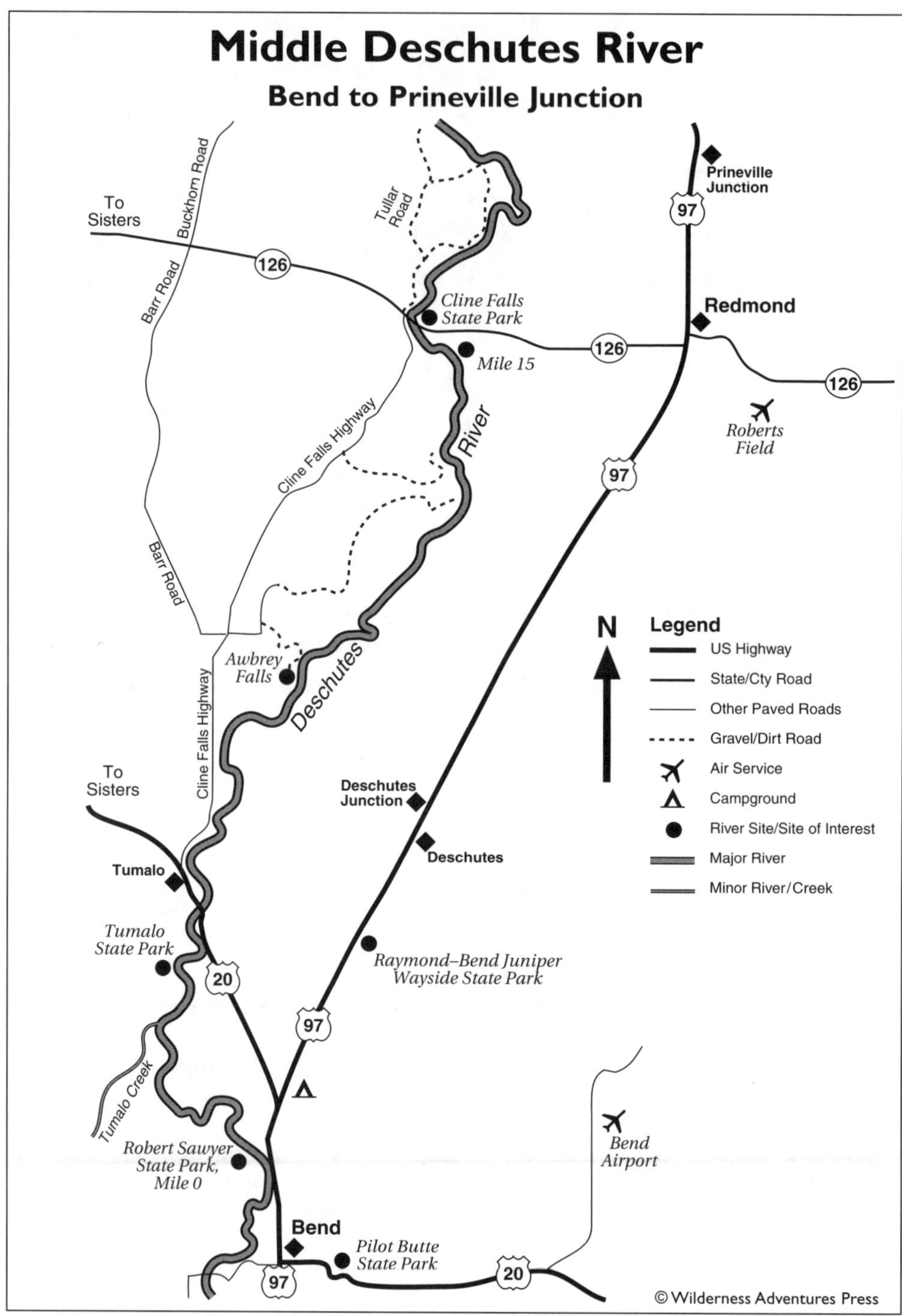
Middle Deschutes River
Bend to Prineville Junction
To Sisters
Buckhorn Road
Barr Road
126
Tullar Road
Prineville Junction
97
Redmond
Cline Falls State Park
Mile 15
126
126
Roberts Field
River
Cline Falls Highway
97
Barr Road
N
Legend
US Highway
State/Cty Road
Other Paved Roads
Gravel/Dirt Road
Air Service
Campground
River Site/Site of Interest
Major River
Minor River/Creek
Aubrey Falls
Deschutes
Cline Falls Highway
To Sisters
Deschutes Junction
Deschutes
Tumalo
Tumalo State Park
20
Raymond–Bend Juniper Wayside State Park
97
Tumalo Creek
Bend Airport
Robert Sawyer State Park, Mile 0
Bend
Pilot Butte State Park
97
20
© Wilderness Adventures Press

MIDDLE DESCHUTES RIVER

Bend to Lake Billy Chinook

As the Deschutes leaves Bend, it begins to take on some of the characteristics associated with the famous lower river. Winding north the river leaves the pine forests and enters a sage and juniper desert, complete with deep canyons, hot sun, and the occasional rattlesnake.

Much of this middle section is accessible only by sheer will and muscle power. In many areas, steep canyons with outright cliffs drop straight to the water's edge. There are remote trails that offer some access into these canyons, and a few spots where you wish there were even a remote trail.

The good news is that the river is crossed by a few roads and is bordered by a couple of public parks. Generally, the banks in the park areas offer decent access, however, outside the park's boundaries, you will be faced with a scramble over boulders and through brush in order to get to some tricky wading. Added to these access problems, water is often too high to fish and can turn color quickly.

So why bother with this section of river? I must have forgotten to mention the most important characteristic this stretch shares with the more famous lower river—the fish. Unlike any rainbow I've ever seen, the Deschutes redside found in the

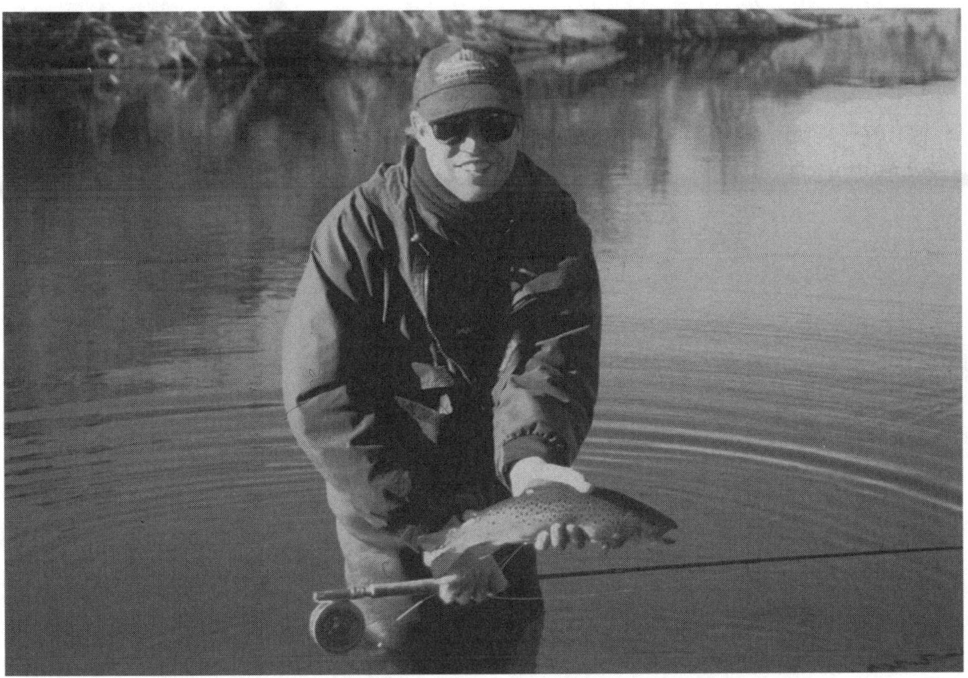

Flatwater on parts of the middle Deschutes provides great midge opportunities for winter trout.

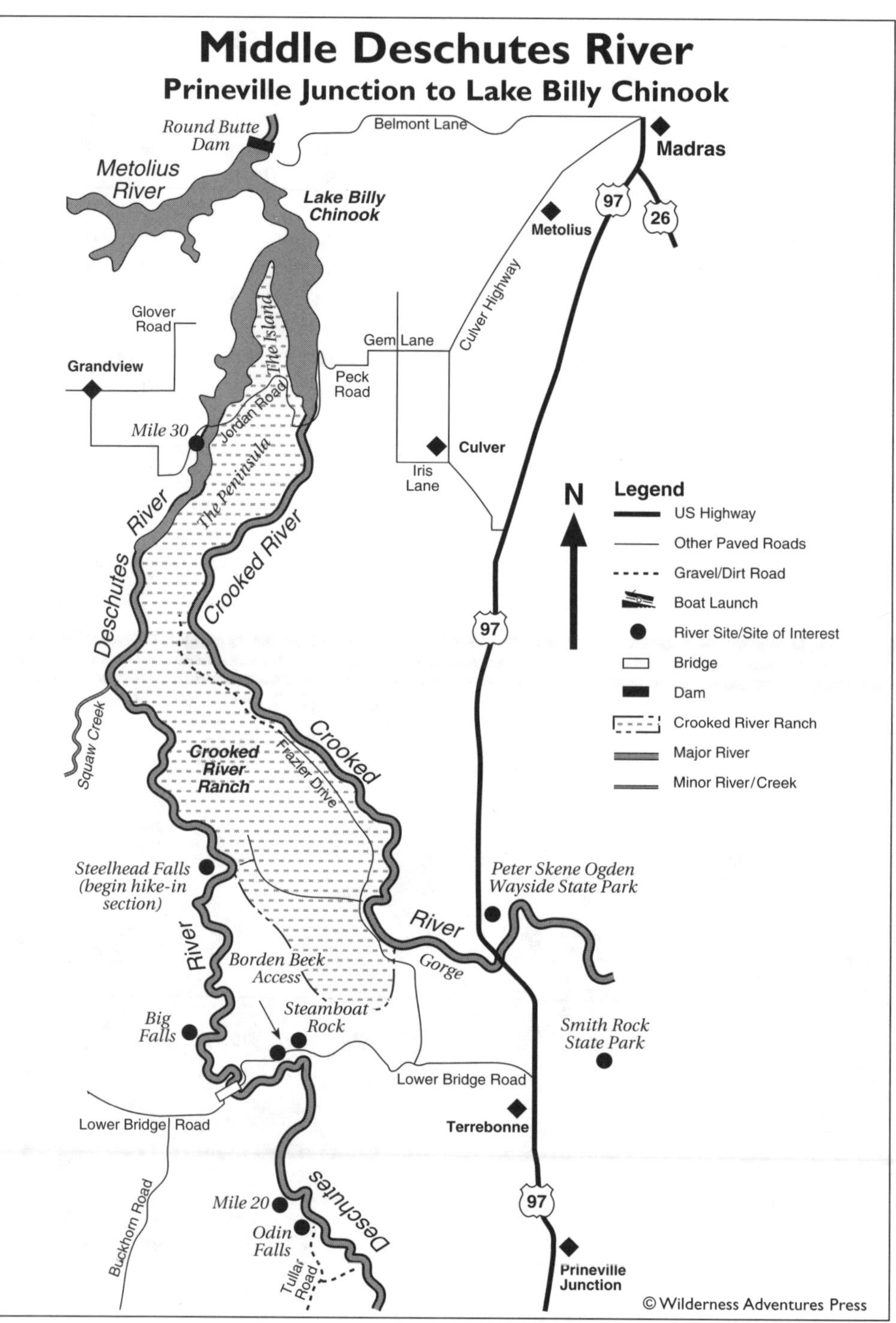

Middle Deschutes River
Prineville Junction to Lake Billy Chinook
Round Butte Dam
Belmont Lane
Madras
Metolius River
Lake Billy Chinook
97
26
Metolius
Culver Highway
Glover Road
The Island
Gem Lane
Grandview
Jordan Road
Peck Road
Mile 30
The Peninsula
Culver
Iris Lane
N
Legend
US Highway
Other Paved Roads
Gravel/Dirt Road
Boat Launch
River Site/Site of Interest
Bridge
Dam
Crooked River Ranch
Major River
Minor River/Creek
River
Deschutes
Crooked River
97
Squaw Creek
Crooked
Crooked River Ranch
Frazier Drive
Steelhead Falls (begin hike-in section)
Peter Skene Ogden Wayside State Park
River
River
Gorge
Borden Beck Access
Steamboat Rock
Big Falls
Smith Rock State Park
Lower Bridge Road
Terrebonne
Lower Bridge Road
Buckhorn Road
Deschutes
Mile 20
97
Odin Falls
Tullar Road
Prineville Junction
© Wilderness Adventures Press

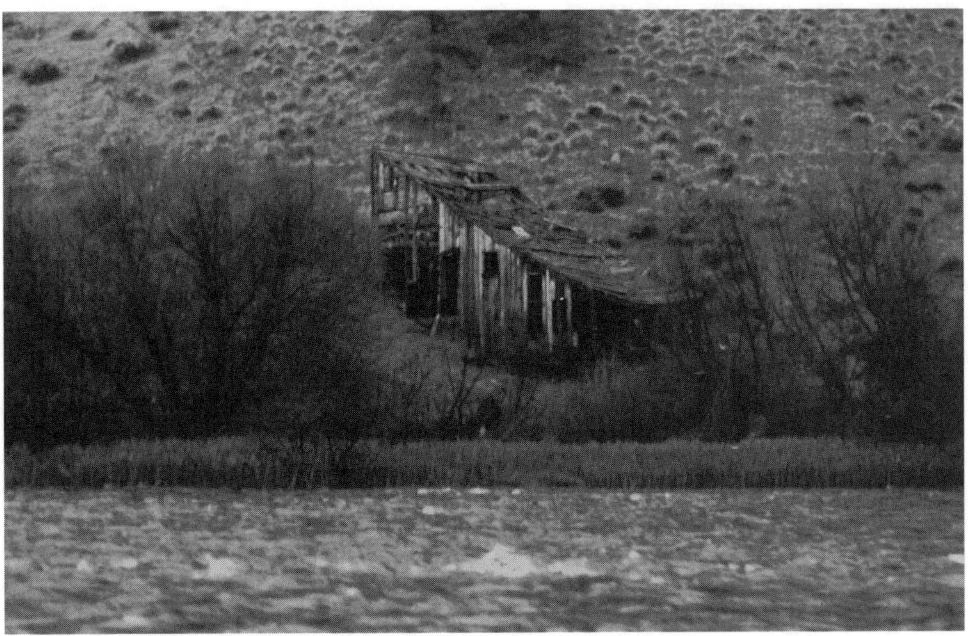

The middle Deschutes near Terrebonne offers wide-open riffles and shallow water opportunities.

middle section is lavender—more purple than red. You can see the wildness of this fish in its markings. These fish live a tough life, but surviving these conditions makes them strong and mean. They can put up a chilling fight. These fish should never see the disgrace of a stringer or frying pan. I would eat dog chow before I'd whack one of these fish. Throw in the occasional brown trout, and it becomes a little clearer why the middle Deschutes has some appeal despite its rugged nature.

The middle river is open the entire year to flies and lures only. It really only fishes well with flies during draw-down periods when irrigators drop water levels. The river replenishes itself with springs and begins to offer slightly easier access and good shots at fish, generally from May through October. If you're traveling a great distance to fish this area, be sure to call ahead for conditions, especially in the winter months. Jeff and Renee Perin, owners of The Fly Fisher's Place in the town of Sisters, are the ones to call for current conditions.

Downriver from Bend, the river is intercepted by Tumalo State Park, Cline Falls State Park, Tetherow Bridge, Odin Falls, Borden Beck Access, Lower Bridge Road, and a hike-in section at Steelhead Falls within the Crooked River Ranch. There is private property in all of these areas, so be sure to ask for permission before trespassing. All

The middle Deschutes can be difficult to wade with its deep holes and heavy streamside vegetation, but big fish lurk here.

these points can be intersected from Hwy 97 between Terrebonne and Bend or from small highways in the Sisters area.

Most of the river can be fished with 4-, 5- and 6-weight rods. Dry fly opportunities are good in the summer months, especially during the first and last light of day. Like most desert fishing, big fish like to stay out of sight when the sun is on the water. Attractor patterns are a great way to search the river—concentrate on stoneflies and big parachute patterns. There are many hatches in this section and often many at once. Baetis, March browns, PMDs, PEDs, mahogany duns, green drakes, golden stones, yellow sallies, salmonflies, caddis, and midges are all flies you'll want to have in your box for this section of river.

Nymphing and streamer fishing will work through the middle Deschutes, but plan on losing many flies to the lava bottom. This bottom also makes wading a bit tricky. A wading staff in here is not a bad idea.

The middle Deschutes River is a rough environment with some tough trout. Always carry water, watch for snakes, and just be careful in general around here. Respect this desert environment and it can offer up some magical moments. I have had some of my favorite fishing days here, but more often then not I've seen the river's temperamental side. Don't judge this section until you've put some sweat into fishing it.

Stream Facts: Middle Deschutes River

Seasons

- Open to angling trout the entire year.

Special Regulations

- 2 trout per day that may include 1 bull trout that must be at least 24 inches in length.
- Restricted to artificial flies and lures.

Fish

- Rainbow trout
- Brown trout
- Bull trout

Flows

- Irrigation drawdowns beginning in April and May bring this section into shape for angling.

Character

- This rugged and scenic section can offer some incredible days for those willing to work a little. Wading can be tricky and currents fast. The payoff is a chance at some of Oregon's hardest fighting and most colorful redside rainbows.

Maps

- Deschutes National Forest

MIDDLE DESCHUTES RIVER MAJOR HATCHES

Insect	J	F	M	A	M	J	J	A	S	O	N	D	Time	Flies
Blue-winged Olive Baetis sp.													M, A: Dun M, D: SF	A.P. Nymph, Captive Dun, RS2, Knock Down Dun, Sparkle and Comparadun, Parachute, BWO Thorax, CDC Spinner, Yellow Comparadun #16-22
March Brown													A: Dun D: SF	Hare's Ear Soft Hackle, March Brown, Comparadun #12-14
Pale Morning Dun													A	PMDs, Beadhead P.T., Captive Dun, Knock Down Dun, Comparadun, Thorax PMD, Olive & Rust Spinner #16-18
Pale Evening Dun													E	Yellow Soft Hackle, Comparadun, Light Cahill #12-16
Salmonfly													A	Sofa Pillow, Kaufmann's Stonefly Nymph #4-8
Golden Stone													M, A	Stimulator, Clark's Stone #6-10
Little Black Stone													A	Fast Eddie, Black Stimulator #12-16
Yellow Sally													M, A	Yellow Sally #14-16
HATCH TIME CODE: M = morning; A = afternoon; E = evening; D = dark; SF = spinner fall; / = continuation through periods.														

Hatch Chart Prepared by Jeff Perin

MIDDLE DESCHUTES RIVER MAJOR HATCHES (cont.)

Insect	J	F	M	A	M	J	J	A	S	O	N	D	Time	Flies
Caddis, *Glossosoma*													A, E	Soft Hackle, Sparkle Pupa, CDC Caddis #16-18
Speckled Peter Caddis *Helicopsyche*													A, E	Yellow Soft Hackle, Sparkle Pupa, X-Caddis, Elk Hair Caddis #14-18
Grannom, *Brachycentrus*													A, E	Cased Caddis, Sparkle Pupa, X-Caddis, Elk Hair Caddis #14-16
Green Sedge, *Rhyacophlia*													A, E	Green Rock Worm, Green Soft Hackle, CDC Caddis, Elk Hair Caddis #12-14
Spotted Sedge, *Hydropsyche* Little Sister Sedge, *Cheumatopsyche*													A, E	Serendipity, Sparkle Pupa, X-Caddis, CDC Caddis, Elk Hair Caddis, Parachute Caddis #12-16
Fall Caddis, various sp.													A, E	Cased Caddis, October Caddis Pupa, Stimulator #6-10
Little Western Weedy Water Sedge, *Amiocentrus*													E	Cased Caddis, Green Soft Hackle, Henryville, X-Caddis #16-20
HATCH TIME CODE: M = morning; A = afternoon; E = evening; D = dark; SF = spinner fall; / = continuation through periods.														

Hatch Chart Prepared by Jeff Perin

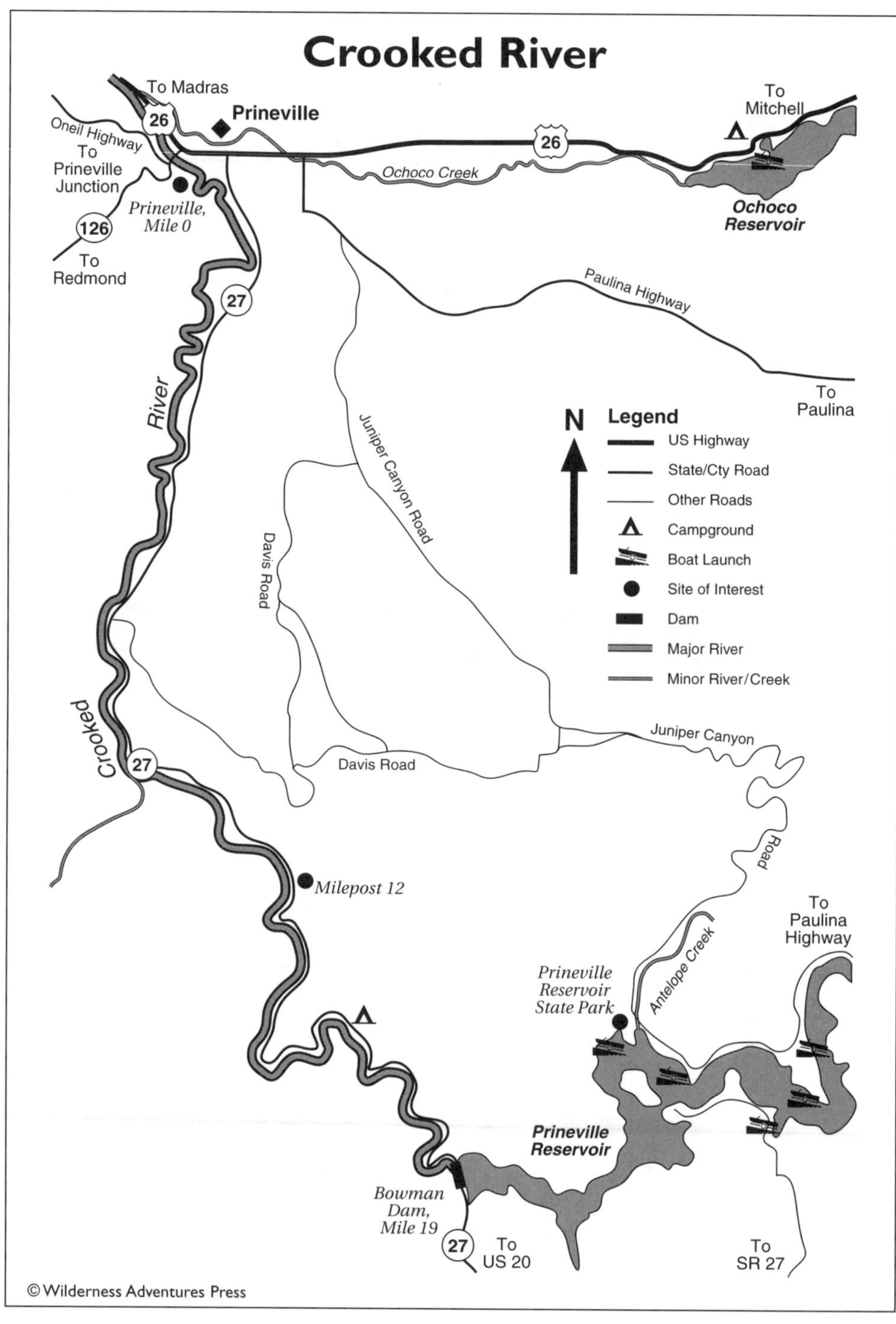
Crooked River
To Madras
26
Prineville
To Mitchell
Oneil Highway
To Prineville Junction
26
Ochoco Creek
Prineville, Mile 0
Ochoco Reservoir
126
To Redmond
27
Paulina Highway
River
To Paulina
Legend
N
US Highway
State/Cty Road
Other Roads
Campground
Boat Launch
Site of Interest
Dam
Major River
Minor River/Creek
Juniper Canyon Road
Davis Road
Juniper Canyon
Crooked
27
Davis Road
Road
Milepost 12
To Paulina Highway
Antelope Creek
Prineville Reservoir State Park
Prineville Reservoir
Bowman Dam, Mile 19
27
To US 20
To SR 27
© Wilderness Adventures Press

CROOKED RIVER

Mike Bordenkircher laughingly and lovingly refers to the Crooked River as "the best 9-inch trout fishery in the state." To hear a great flyfisherman say this and then see pictures of the fish that used to come from the Crooked is enough to break any fly angler's heart. Unfortunately, the pictures I've seen have always been photos of dead fish on a stringer. Limits of 19- to 26-inch fish were commonplace 20 years ago. A lot of finger pointing gets done when you try to find out what happened. All is not lost: What was once a big fish fishery has turned into a numbers fishery. How does 8,000 fish per mile sound? If hookups are what you're looking for, then the Crooked will serve them up.

This is another desert canyon fishery and tailwater. The dam's bottom release keeps water temperatures down in summer heat but it gives a permanent tint to the water. The off-color water doesn't affect fishing but does make wading difficult if you're not familiar with the river. Use a wading staff to avoid bruised shins when fishing up and down the Crooked.

Most of the fishing on the Crooked River takes place from milepost 12 on Hwy 27, which leaves the town of Prineville from the south, up to Bowman Dam.

There are some big fish in here but finding them can be tough. In order for larger fish to have a chance at your fly, you may have to hook the quicker, smaller fish in an area first. Whether you hook a trophy trout or not, the Crooked's merit is obvious. I can think of no better place to educate a beginning flyfisher or hone a novice's skills. There is plenty of dry fly action on the river throughout the day. Basic upstream, over-their-head presentations are all one needs. Currents are forgiving enough to practice line-mending skills with the occasional midriver boulder to add some challenge.

This river is also loaded with scuds, which tend to be the fly of choice with local flyfishers. This makes for a great strike indicator opportunity while dead-drifting nymphs. Scuds here are big—size 12 to 16 is the norm—mostly in olive and orange colors.

The presence of mayflies and caddis provide a chance to perfect the vanishing art of down-and-across nymphing. Pick a riffle or glide and then present the fly by casting across, allowing the fly to sink. As the line swings down below you, mend the line up and straighten the line, keeping the rod tip down. This will raise the fly from the bottom, imitating an emerging insect making a break for the surface. This technique will draw strikes from the river's bigger fish and is an important technique to know on any moving water when fishing is tough or slow.

Caddisflies and PMDs dominate the Crooked River's early season. Summer brings a variety of bugs, such as baetis and stoneflies, with caddis taking the evening stage. Autumn on the Crooked is full of activity, with big October caddis around, along with mahogany duns, midges, and intense blue-winged olive hatches.

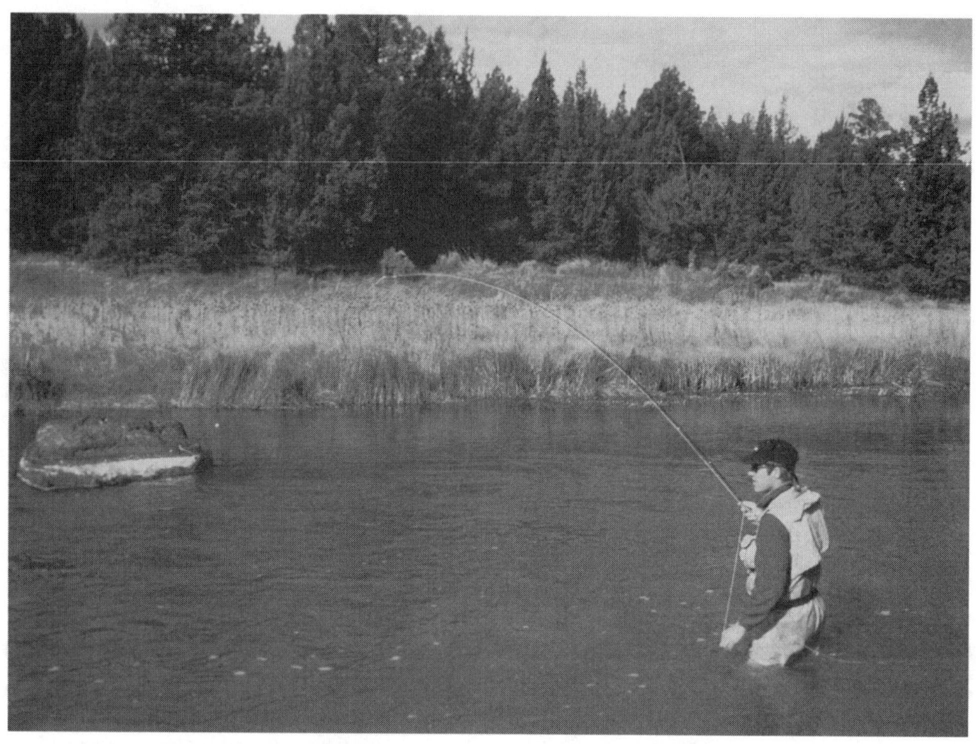

The Crooked River is loaded with fish and beautiful water that novice flyfishers will find very enjoyable.

The Crooked River is a gorgeous place to fish with plenty of easy access and fishing. Take your kids or significant other—chances are you'll have more fun just watching the action. When you get tired of watching or teaching, go after the river's more sizable fish. If you see my friend, Mike, be sure to ask him if he's broken 9 inches yet that day.

Stream Facts: Crooked River

Season

- Open to angling the entire year.

Special Regulations

- Catch and release for trout.
- Restricted to artificial flies and lures January 1 to the last Saturday in April and November 1 to December 31.
- Closed for 150 feet downstream from Bowman Dam.

Fish

- Rainbow trout.

River Characteristics

- The Crooked River is pretty much crooked, always a bit off-color, and, during draw-down months, can be waded very easily. It twists through a breathtaking desert canyon. The area can get really hot at times, but canyon walls offer the relief of shade. A beautiful place to fish for anglers of all ages and skill levels.

Flows

- Fishing is excellent when flows are between 150 to 400 cfs. Levels fluctuate throughout the year as the reservoir is drained based on need and levels. Always call ahead for current cfs.

Access

- About 8 miles of fishable water from Bowman Dam, which forms Prineville Reservoir, to milepost 12 on Hwy 27. Beyond this, there is a lot of private property.
- The river has no boat ramps and is too shallow to float most of the time, anyway. Hwy 27 follows the river very closely all the way from the town of Prineville. There are plenty of pulloff points and day use areas once you've gotten beyond the private property south of town all the way to the dam.

Maps

- DeLorme *Oregon Atlas and Gazetteer*

CROOKED RIVER MAJOR HATCHES

Insect	J	F	M	A	M	J	J	A	S	O	N	D	Time	Flies
Midges	■	■	■	■	■	■	■	■	■	■	■	■	A, E	Palamino, Griffith's Gnat, CDC Midge, Suspender Pupa, Brassie, Serendipity Paramidge#18-26
Blue-winged Olive Baetis sp.		■	■	■	■				■	■			A: Duns M, D: SF	Flashback Pheasant Tail, Captive Dun, RS2, Comparadun, Sparkle Dun, H-V12 Parachute, Biot Spinner #16-24
Mahogany Dun *Paraleptophlebia* sp.								■	■	■			A	Beadhead P.T., Featherdusters, Parachute Adams, Comparadun #14-16
Scuds	■	■	■	■	■	■	■	■	■	■	■	■	M, A, D	Olive, Tan, and Orange Scuds #10-18
Grannom/Mother's Day Caddis, *Brachycentrus*				■	■								A, E	Cased Caddis, Sparkle Pupa, X-Caddis, Henryville #14-16
Green Sedge *Rhyacophila*					■	■	■	■	■				A, E	Green Rock Worm, Soft Hackle, CDC Caddis Elk Hair Caddis #14-16
Spotted Sedge and Little Sister Sedge, *Hydropsyche Cheumatopsyche*					■	■	■	■	■				A, E	Serendipity, Sparkle Pupa, X-Caddis, CDC Caddis, Elk Hair Caddis #12-18
October Caddis *Dicosmoecus*									■	■			E	Cased Caddis, October Caddis Pupa, Stimulator #6-12

HATCH TIME CODE: M = morning; A = afternoon; E = evening; D = dark; SF = spinner fall; / = continuation through periods.

Hatch Chart Prepared by Jeff Perin

METOLIUS RIVER

The Metolius is a perennial bug factory, with insect hatches that blanket the water. In years past it was hard to fish the Metolius when campgrounds filled up and fishermen waited to catch the plentiful stocked fish. This is one of the most beautiful springborn rivers you will ever see. The thought of any stocked fish in it is horrifying, but until recently that was commonplace. As of 1995 the practice of stocking has been discontinued, and catch-and-release regulations for all fish have been adopted. Coming years should produce a very nice wild trout fishery.

The river appears out of the earth a mile upriver from Camp Sherman. I can't describe the color of the Metolius, because it's like no other river. It runs through towering stands of pine trees but even in their shadows the river is bright. This clarity will trick you—you'll be over the tops of your waders more times than you'll ever want to admit.

Heading north and then east, it eventually has its style cramped, as do the Deschutes and Crooked Rivers, by Lake Billy Chinook. The Metolius retains its clarity, levels, and temperature throughout the year, making it a good place to cast a fly when other central Oregon waters have gone off-color. Its water temperature is always cool, and neoprene waders are recommended. The Metolius is open to angling all year with the exception of some of the uppermost water above Allingham Bridge. The river is always closed within a hundred feet of Camp Sherman Bridge. Standing on the bridge, you can see that more than one big fish knows this.

Access is plentiful, but wading can be difficult. The Metolius offers rainbows and good bull trout opportunities to flyfishers.

Jeff Perin, owner of The Fly Fisher's Place in Sisters, has been fishing the Metolius long enough to see changes in management over the years. "The river has definitely seen positive improvements. The quality of fishing continues to get better, and eventually, I expect to see greater numbers of fish than there have been in a long time."

The most amazing thing about the Metolius River is its aquatic insect life. Hatches are present all year on the river. Even if there weren't a fish to be found in the river, it would still be worth any fish-head's time to see the amount of insects that can appear on the water. I must admit there have been several times I've seen hatches like this and swore there were no fish in the river. Perin insists that you will find fish nosing in discreet back eddies and such. He also admits that sometimes the fish just won't come up. As the wild population takes hold in coming years, the odds of finding rising fish will increase.

Perin also describes Metolius fish as migratory—not moving hundreds of miles but moving to different parts of the river, seemingly to meet different hatches. It is certainly possible that a wild fish can become genetically inclined to find hatches.

Well-placed dry flies can get these fish to eat, but a good selection of flies is important. Metolius fish will lock on to an insect, and often, only an exact imitation is going to fool fish in this translucent water. A long leader tapered to 5X is a good

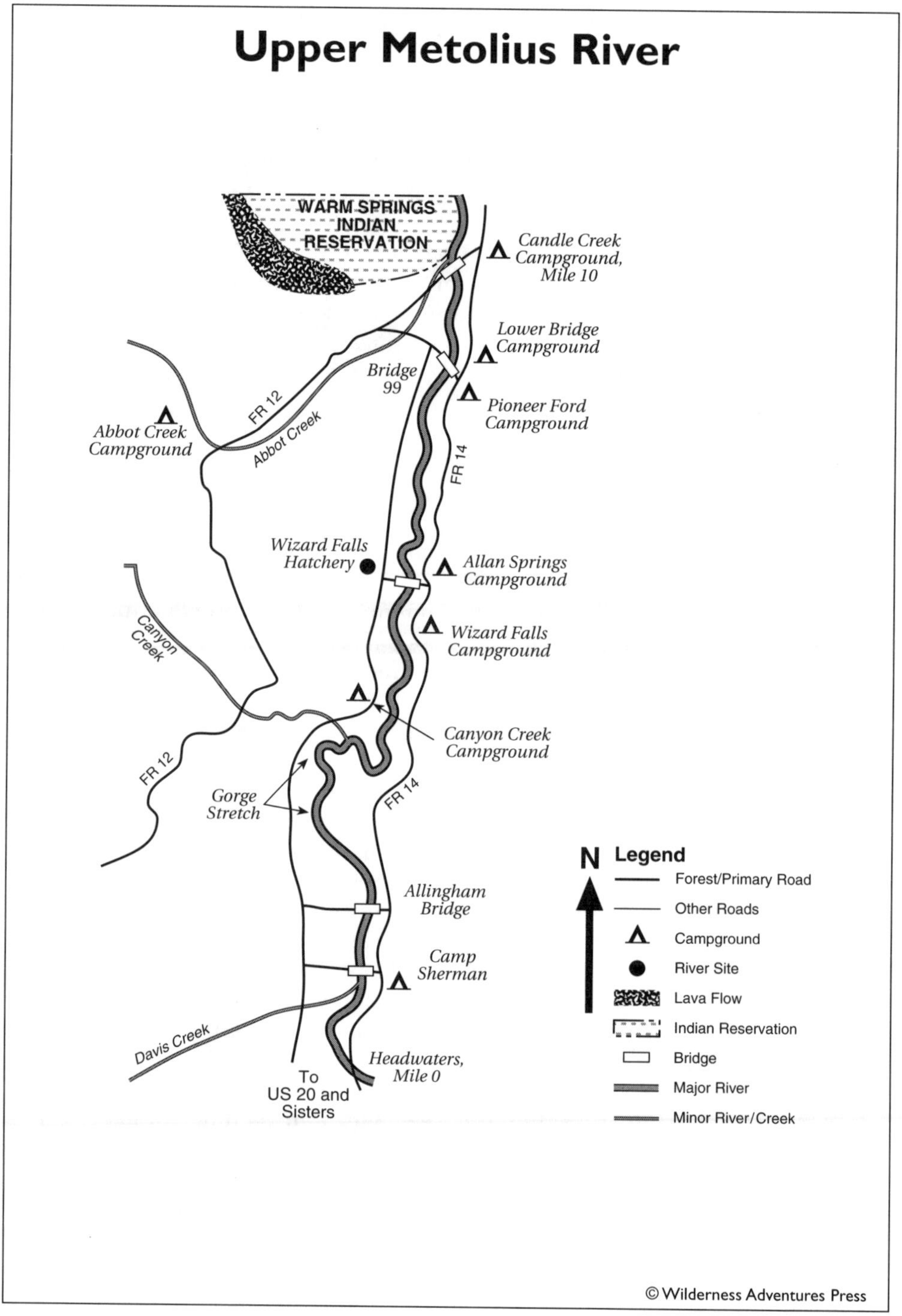

Upper Metolius River

Warm Springs Indian Reservation
Candle Creek Campground, Mile 10
Lower Bridge Campground
Bridge 99
Pioneer Ford Campground
FR 12
Abbot Creek
Abbot Creek Campground
FR 14
Wizard Falls Hatchery
Allan Springs Campground
Wizard Falls Campground
Canyon Creek
Canyon Creek Campground
FR 12
Gorge Stretch
FR 14
Allingham Bridge
Camp Sherman
Davis Creek
Headwaters, Mile 0
To US 20 and Sisters

N
Legend
Forest/Primary Road
Other Roads
Campground
River Site
Lava Flow
Indian Reservation
Bridge
Major River
Minor River/Creek

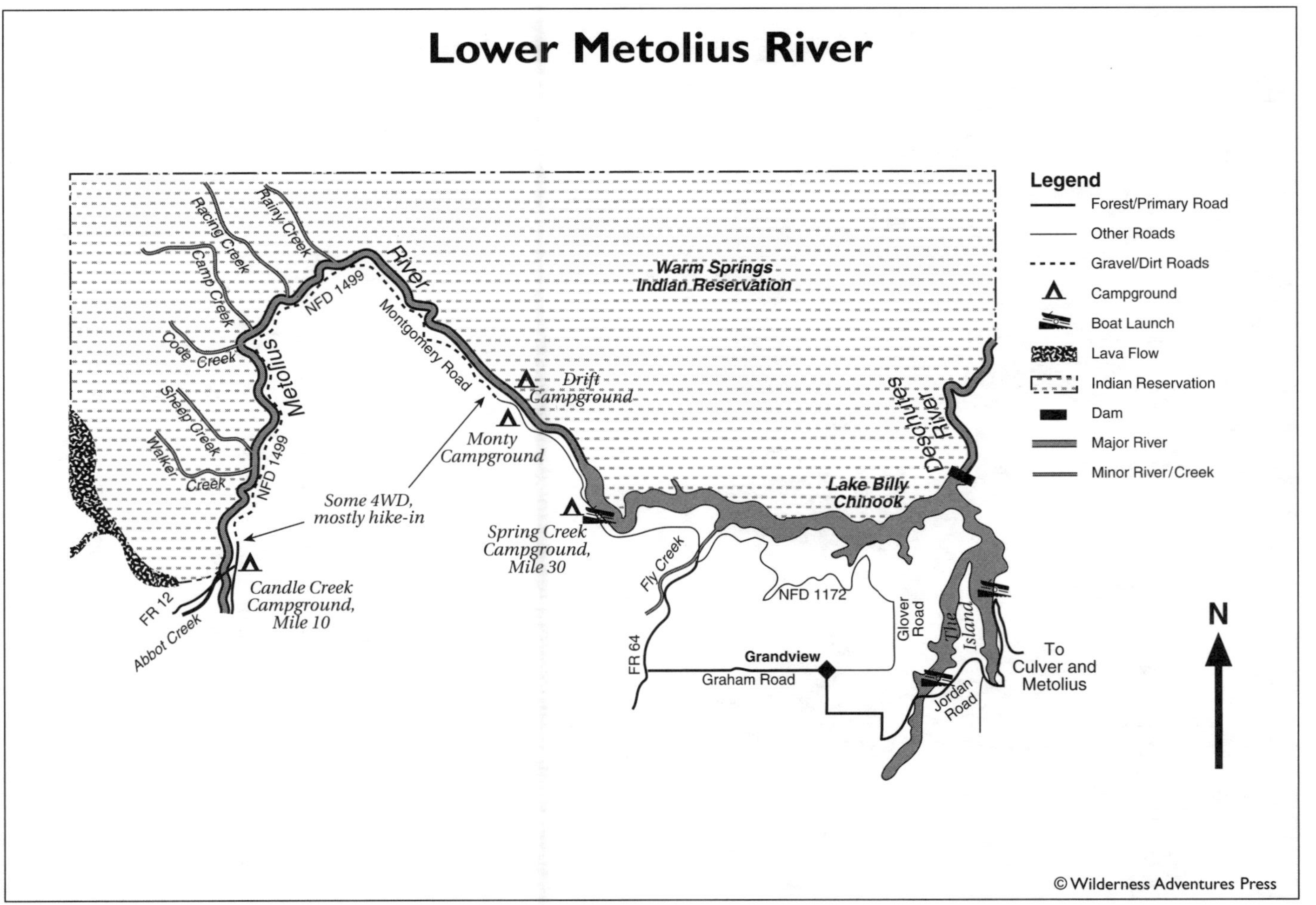
Lower Metolius River
Legend
Forest/Primary Road
Other Roads
Gravel/Dirt Roads
Campground
Boat Launch
Lava Flow
Indian Reservation
Dam
Major River
Minor River/Creek
Warm Springs Indian Reservation
Rainy Creek
Racing Creek
Camp Creek
Code Creek
Sheep Creek
Walker Creek
Metolius
River
NFD 1499
NFD 1499
Montgomery Road
Drift Campground
Monty Campground
Some 4WD, mostly hike-in
Candle Creek Campground, Mile 10
FR 12
Abbot Creek
Spring Creek Campground, Mile 30
Fly Creek
FR 64
NFD 1172
Glover Road
Grandview
Graham Road
Lake Billy Chinook
Deschutes River
The Island
Jordan Road
To Culver and Metolius
N
© Wilderness Adventures Press

The crystal clear waters of the Metolius add to the challenge for any angler. Here, Mike Bordenkircher casts to spring risers.

place to start when fish are on the surface, however, be ready and willing to go lighter. Plan on finding rainbows in the 10- to 20-inch range.

High-sticking heavy nymphs through very deep slots in the reaches between Gorge Campground and the Wizard Falls Hatchery is another fishing method that gets used frequently on the Metolius. Trout will hunker down in the depths when insect activity is down.

It is illegal to use external lead on the Metolius or anywhere in Oregon that is designated fly-only water. On the Metolius this is from Bridge 99 to the headwaters. This gives fly tiers a big edge over everyone else. A good tier can customize nymphs to specific depths on different sections of the river, even specific runs and holes. If you can do this sitting at a picnic table, you're really a leg up on anglers stuck with store-bought flies. General guidelines for tying Metolius nymph patterns are as follows: add a little more weight than you would for most situations; then add just a little bit more.

Cast upstream and let the fly sink, then try to stay in touch with it as the line drifts by you. It can't hurt to give some life to the fly by occasionally lifting the rod tip after your line tightens. Some people like to use a strike indicator when employing nymphing methods. Other people, like my friend and fellow author, "Dredge Thomas," swear that indicators are unholy. Their preferred technique is to always nymph a tight line and wait for the yank. Both methods will move rainbows as well as bull trout, although bull trout are more susceptible to streamers.

Bull trout are best pursued with at least a 6-weight rod. Even 7-weights aren't overkill considering the heavy flies and lines needed to cast them proficiently. Sinktips (but not metal-core tips in the fly-only water) with stout leaders attached to large streamers imitating sculpins, rainbows, and Kokanee can all be used. Swinging these flies into holes, under ledges, and around woody debris will produce violent takes from these predatory trout. Using smaller bright flies, fished much like nymphs, is also an effective means to entice bulls. Bull trout will run between 2 and 15 pounds. They average 4 to 6 pounds and are a great game fish. The Metolius presents a rare opportunity to catch this fish in a system that can take the pressure of catch-and-release flyfishing.

To reach the Metolius, use US Hwy 20 west from Sisters or east from the Corvallis-Eugene area. Turn onto Forest Road 14 following the signs to Camp Sherman. The river is paralleled on its east side by the road and has plenty of campgrounds, complete with day-use areas. There are also many pullouts with some hike-in opportunities. From Bridge 99 downriver, travel the road at your own risk. Hiking or mountain biking are probably better choices. The river down here can be hiked for days, but it is big enough that it can't be forded.

Good management choices have been made on the Metolius, and the resource seems to be responding well. The river should regain much of its reputation as a blue-ribbon spring creek in coming years.

Stream Facts: Metolius River

Seasons

- Open to angling the entire year.
- Closed upstream from Allingham Bridge January 1 to the last Saturday in April.
- Closed entire year within 100 feet of Camp Sherman Bridge.

Special Regulations

- Catch and release for all fish.
- Restricted to artificial flies and lures downstream from Bridge 99.
- Restricted to artificial flies only upstream from Bridge 99.
- No angling from a floating device.

Fish

- Wild rainbow trout from 8 to 20 inches.
- Bull trout 12 to 30 inches

River Characteristics

- A spring creek with stunning clarity all year. The river runs through a towering pine forest and several tight canyons, becoming a river of respectable size as it nears Lake Billy Chinook. Hatches are frequent, but the fishing is not always easy.

Access

- There are about 12 miles of road and hike-in access from the headwaters to Bridge 99. Below that there is another 20 miles of hike-in, bike-in, or serious 4-wheel access.
- Access is park-and-wade, with several hike-in opportunities along its entire length. There are a few pieces of private property on the river. The House on the Metolius, within the gorge section of the river below Gorge Campground, is the most notable.

Maps

- Deschutes National Forest

METOLIUS RIVER MAJOR HATCHES

Insect	J	F	M	A	M	J	J	A	S	O	N	D	Time	Flies
Blue-winged Olive Baetis sp.													A, M: Dun M, D: SF	A.P. Nymph, Captive Dun, RS2, Knock Down Dun, Sparkle and Comparadun, Parachute, BWO Thorax, CDC Spinner #16-22
Little Yellow May *Cinygmula* sp.													A	Knock Down Dun, Yellow Comparadun #14-16
Green Drake, *Drunella* sp.													A	Paradrake, Green Drake, Wulff, Bunse's Natural Dun #8-12
Pale Morning Dun *Ephemerella* sp.													A: Dun D: SF	Beadhead P.T., Captive Dun, Knock Down Dun, Comparadun, Thorax PMD, Olive & Rust Spinner #16-18
Golden Stone													M, A	Stimulator, Clark's Stone #8-10
Salmonfly													A	Sofa Pillow #4-6
Yellow Sally													M, A	Yellow Sally #14-16
Little Olive Stone													A, D	Hemingway, Henryville, Renegade #14-18
Caddis, *Glossosoma*													A, E	Soft Hackle, Sparkle Pupa, CDC Caddis #16-18

HATCH TIME CODE: M = morning; A = afternoon; E = evening; D = dark; SF = spinner fall; / = continuation through periods.

Hatch Chart Prepared by Jeff Perin

METOLIUS RIVER MAJOR HATCHES (cont.)

Insect	J	F	M	A	M	J	J	A	S	O	N	D	Time	Flies
Speckled Peter Caddis *Helicopsyche*													A, E	Yellow Soft Hackle, Sparkle Pupa, X-Caddis, Elk Hair Caddis #14-16
Grannom, *Brachycentrus*													A, E	Cased Caddis, Sparkle Pupa, X-Caddis, Elk Hair Caddis #14-16
Green Sedge, *Rhyacophlia*													A, E	Green Rock Worm, Green Soft Hackle, CDC Caddis, Elk Hair Caddis #12-14
Spotted Sedge, *Hydropsyche* Little Sister Sedge, *Cheumatopsyche*													A, E	Serendipity, Sparkle Pupa, X-Caddis, CDC Caddis, Elk Hair Caddis, Parachute Caddis #12-16
Fall Caddis, various sp.													A, E	Cased Caddis, October Caddis Pupa, Stimulator #8-12
Little Western Weedy Water Sedge, *Amiocentrus*													E	Cased Caddis, Green Soft Hackle, Henryville, X-Caddis #16-20
HATCH TIME CODE: M = morning; A = afternoon; E = evening; D = dark; SF = spinner fall; / = continuation through periods.														

Hatch Chart Prepared by Jeff Perin

Hosmer Lake

If it's possible for a lake to imitate a spring creek, Hosmer fits this bill. This is not an easy place to catch fish, but it does offer fly anglers a great opportunity to fish over less-common targets. Landlocked Atlantic salmon and brook trout both grow big and smart in the shallow depths of Hosmer.

Located about 35 miles south of Bend off the Cascade Lakes Highway, Hosmer is one of Oregon's most scenic fly waters. It is restricted to flyfishing only and teaches tough lessons on stillwater fishing. I compare it to a spring creek because many of the fish are easy to see, which means you get a clear view of one denial after another. You'll tighten the grip on your cork as you watch both 20-inch Atlantics and brook trout investigating your fly. Sometimes it's easier on the ego to troll or cast and strip. At least this way you can get some action and won't see the refusals.

Hosmer's fish are very used to seeing people. It is an extremely popular place to fish and has its crowded moments at certain times of the year. Constant attention make the fish selective and the fly angling slightly more challenging than other nearby stillwaters.

At times humbling, Hosmer is still worth fishing if only to observe a good caster with Mt. Bachelor and The Three Sisters as the backdrop. Always bring your camera to Hosmer. A photo of a trophy size Atlantic salmon with snow-capped Mt. Bachelor in the background is a much better trophy then any mount would ever be.

The lake is essentially two main bodies of water with a channel that runs between them. This channel offers fantastic fishing and also the most difficult. Its main bodies are lined with aquatic plants that provide both food and shelter to the lake's denizens. The whole lake provides great evening rises, and when things are quiet, a well-tied nymph imitation can provide decent action.

Bob Gaviglio of Sunriver Fly Shop likes the times when things seem slow. "Sometimes, John, when things are slow, I'll tie on woolly buggers tied specifically for Cascade lakes. I'll put the rod tip in the water and retrieve the fly as fast as I can. Even if I have to go to a two-handed strip."

When you find fish that are used to analyzing hundreds of imitations a year, the best policy may be to never let them get a good look. Fish have to make decisions all the time and have limited time to make them. By stripping the fly very quickly, you can work on a fish's most basic instincts—eat now or keep looking! This is what you're telling the fish when you blitz the fly by him.

Hosmer is well suited, in terms of size, for all kinds of human-powered craft and is best fished while floating. Single-person prams are very popular among Hosmer's most avid fly anglers. The lake is relatively sheltered and can fish well when other nearby stillwaters, such as Crane Prairie Reservoir and Davis Lake, are too wind-blown to approach in small craft.

Most anglers fish 4-, 5-, and 6-weight fly rods on Hosmer with floating lines and occasionally an intermediate sink to match. Hosmer is a great place to use the new,

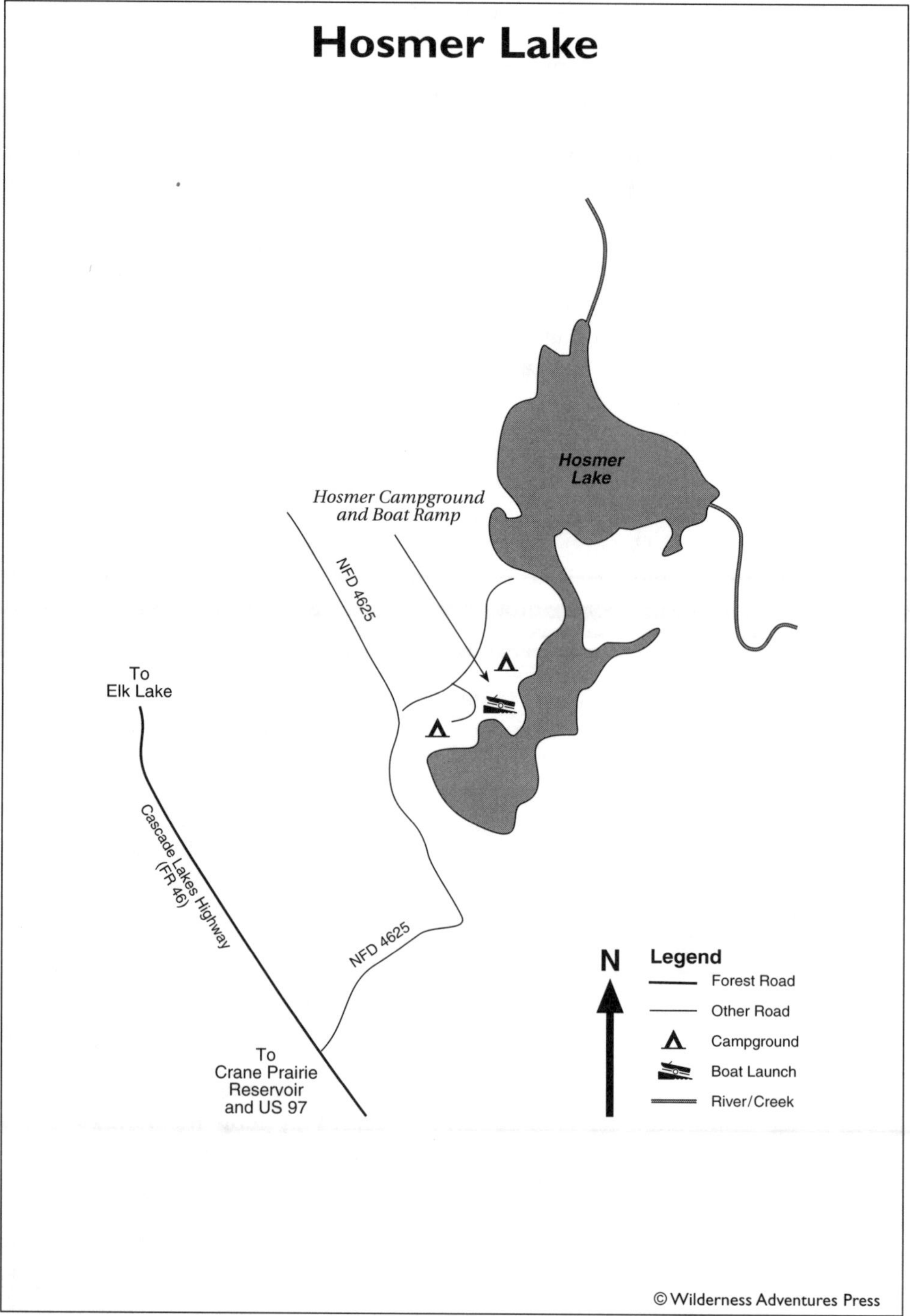
Hosmer Lake
Hosmer Lake
Hosmer Campground and Boat Ramp
NFD 4625
To Elk Lake
Cascade Lakes Highway (FR 46)
NFD 4625
To Crane Prairie Reservoir and US 97
N
Legend
Forest Road
Other Road
Campground
Boat Launch
River/Creek
© Wilderness Adventures Press

Bob Gaviglio has a lot to smile about sitting in the middle of Hosmer Lake. Bob owns the Sunriver Fly Shop.

clear sinking lines found in most fly shops. Seven to 12-foot leaders, tapered from 5X through 3X, are the norm here.

Hosmer's aquatic life is rich with scuds, leeches, callibaetis, caddis, midges and damselflies. You will want your very best representations of these when trying to fool Hosmer fish. This is not the best place to learn stillwater flyfishing skills, but it is a great place to test them.

Lake Facts: Hosmer Lake

Season
- Open to angling all year, although not accessible all year.

Special Regulations
- Catch and release only for Atlantic salmon
- Restricted to artificial flies
- No fishing from motor-propelled craft while motor is operating. Electric motors only.

Fish
- Atlantic salmon to 20 inches
- Brook trout to 20 inches

Lake Size and Depth
- 198 acres
- Averages 10 feet deep.

Lake Characteristics
- One of the most popular fly lakes in Oregon, not only for the fish but also the scenery. Surrounded by trees and marsh, the lake draws plenty of wildlife. There are two campgrounds and a small boat ramp on the lake.
- A good place to test your skills on some big, wily fish. Hosmer can frustrate and elate an angler in a short period of time.
- Always take your camera to Hosmer.

Access
- One small boat ramp. The lake is easily accessed off the Cascade Lakes Highway.

Maps
- *Atlas of Oregon Lakes*

HOSMER LAKE MAJOR HATCHES

Insect	J	F	M	A	M	J	J	A	S	O	N	D	Time	Flies
Callibaetis													After-noon Evening	Adults: Two Feather, Thorax, Comparadun Callibaetis #14-18 Emergers: CDC Callibaetis, Sparkle Emerger, Hare's Ear #14-18
Scuds													All day	Olive & Tan Scuds #12-16
Leeches													All day	Rickard's Seal Buggers #8 (4X hook)
Midges													All day	Griffith's Gnats, Midge Pupas, Suspended Pupas #12-14
Caddis													Morning Evening	Soft Hackles, Sparkle Pupas, Tied Down Caddis, Carey Specials #10-16
Damselflies													PM	Standard Marabou Damsels, Richard's Stillwater Nymph #10-12
Dragonflies													All day	Standard Dragon Nymphs, Carey Specials #6
Backswimmers and Boatmen													All day	Prince Nymphs, Zug Bugs #10-12
Batifish													All day	Yellow, White, Orange Woolly Buggers #6-10

Hatch Chart Prepared by Bob Gaviglio

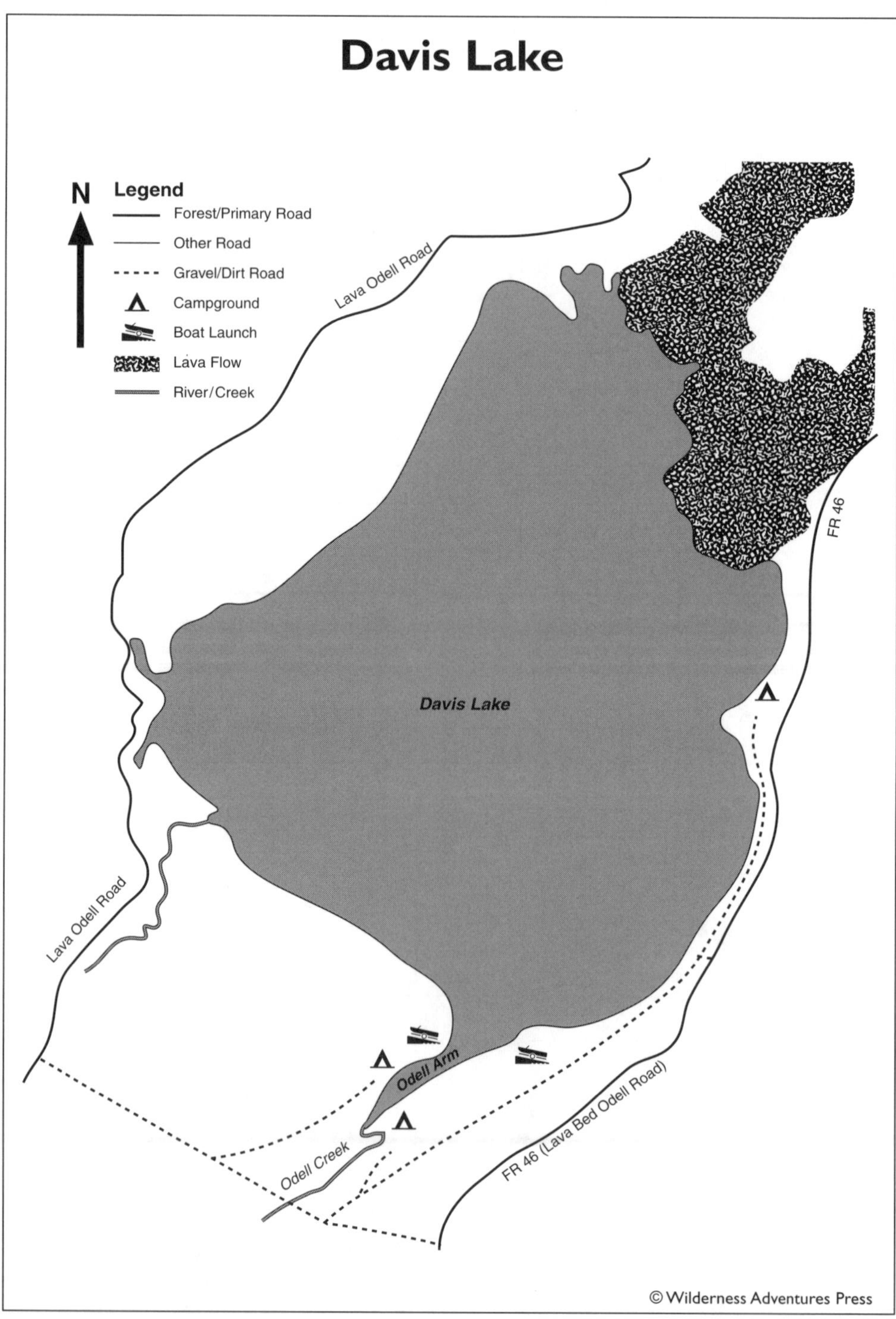
Davis Lake
N
Legend
Forest/Primary Road
Other Road
Gravel/Dirt Road
Campground
Boat Launch
Lava Flow
River/Creek
Lava Odell Road
FR 46
Davis Lake
Lava Odell Road
Odell Arm
Odell Creek
FR 46 (Lava Bed Odell Road)
© Wilderness Adventures Press

Davis Lake

I've thought about changing my zip code more than once after a day of fishing at Davis Lake, part of the incredible chain of Cascade lakes south of Bend. On any given year it is also the best. When drought years are replaced by several consecutive good water years, Davis produces some of the biggest rainbows in the state. Rainbows are accompanied in this large but shallow fishery by Atlantic salmon that not only grow big, but also rise well on many occasions. If hooking 24-inch rainbows isn't enough for you, try taking an Atlantic off the surface. Not only do they rise, but they love to jump when hooked.

Davis is a float-tuber's dream come true. Although the lake is big, fish are not hard to find, and basic stillwater techniques will get you hookups.

Bob Gaviglio says, "When Oregon strings together three or four good snowpack years, there is no question among serious lake and reservoir fly anglers that Davis Lake is the most exciting stillwater flyfishery in the state." There are some who would argue with this observation, but being as objective as I can, I will have to agree with Gaviglio.

Davis Lake is much more than a great flyfishery, it is a wonderful place to just be a flyfisher. The fly-only regulations that have been established for Davis draw a great group of anglers together.

Eric Lyon, an avid Oregon flyfisher and friend, once said to me, "Even when I fish the nearby waters like Crane Prairie and Fall River, I still come to Davis and camp. It's the equivalent to camping in a good fly shop. People don't hesitate to stroll around sharing patterns and stories of the day's fishing."

Davis was created naturally by a wall of lava that blocked the path of Odell Creek. Odell's waters fill the shallow lake and then eventually seep through the lava to neighboring Wickiup Reservoir. The lake's shallow nature is what makes Davis such great fly water. Light penetrating the shallower water helps aquatic vegetation grow more readily than a deeper body of water. This plant growth provides food and shelter to myriad aquatic insects, leeches, and baitfish that feed Davis' larger denizens. Don't curse too loudly when you get a hook full of weeds in here, they are a major part of the food chain that brings us to Davis in the first place.

Springtime fishing provides instant action on Davis as open water energizes fish and insects. Fish spend the day cruising in search of warmer water and food. This often puts them at the lake's north end where lava rock warms the water slightly by absorbing rays from the sun. They may also be found near the south end, in and around the Odell Creek arm of the lake. It is not uncommon to find fantastic morning and evening rises in this part of the lake when the wind isn't blowing. Atlantic salmon and rainbows cruise in pods taking midges and the occasional callibaetis mayfly off the surface.

Summer brings even more callibaetis activity, along with damselflies, which can provide some epic days. Leeches and baitfish imitations are a staple this time of year, and a variety of nymphs and streamers can be used to hook fish. An intermediate sinking line and a floating line will cover the variety of situations you encounter at

The Odell Arm of Davis Lake is a great place to find large Atlantic salmon cruising the surface on calm evenings.

Davis. A 6-weight rod and a reel with good drag can make a huge difference here. This heavy setup should give an angler enough leverage to see fish up close. Good knots and strong tippets are also recommended. Losing one of these fish due to inadequate gear and inattention to detail will haunt you. I am also sure the fish don't want to be decorated, either.

Autumn can provide some of the year's best fishing, provided the weather lets you on the water. Luckily, Fall River and Crane Prairie are near enough to fall back on if need be. Short autumn days may not produce great numbers of fish, but the lake may also show you some of its biggest fish. Big streamers are the ticket this time of year.

On a recent fall trip to Davis Lake, Ray Irvin, head guide at The Fly Box in Bend, gave me some of the biggest flies I've ever cast at stillwater fish. I took the flies and his word that they would work—let's just say it was an eye-opener. Never make assumptions and generalizations when you're fishing unfamiliar waters. Area fly shops and guides can show you a simple technique or pattern that might make all the difference between success and failure or between landing a fish of a lifetime versus a hatchery dog. Sunriver, Bend, and Sisters all have professionals who can show you a hot fly or simply how to cast in the wind—use their services and advice.

Davis is one of my personal favorites in Oregon, and even though there is a 2-fish limit here, make your limit less than that, or better yet, let everything go so that others can feel what a 25-inch fish feels like 25 feet into the backing.

Lake Facts: Davis Lake

Season
- Open to angling all year, although not always accessible and freezes over in winter.

Special Regulations
- Davis Lake and Odell Arm of Davis up to ODFW markers at Davis Lake Campground: no limit on size or number of warmwater game fish; restricted to artificial flies only with barbless hooks; closed from 1 hour after sunset until 1 hour before sunrise.

Fish
- Rainbow trout up to 25 inches after good water years.
- Atlantic salmon up to 24 inches.

Lake Size and Depth
- The lake is 3,906 acres; levels drop as summer progresses.
- 12 to 20 feet deep where most fishing takes place.

Lake Characteristics
- Davis is a pretty good-sized body of water but relatively shallow. Most fishing takes place near the lava dam and the Odell channel. Banks are tree-lined and campgrounds mostly unimproved. Fish size can vary depending on good or bad snowpack years, but recently Davis has produced some giants.

Boat Ramps
- There is a ramp at the Davis Lake Campground.

Maps
- *Atlas of Oregon Lakes*

DAVIS LAKE MAJOR HATCHES

Insect	J	F	M	A	M	J	J	A	S	O	N	D	Time	Flies
Chubs			■	■	■	■	■	■	■	■	■		All day	Matukas, Minnowbuggers, South Twin Specials, Cascade Specials, Body Fur Streamers #6-10
Dragonflies and Nymphs					■	■	■	■	■				All day	Standard Dragon Nymph, Carey Specials #6
Damselflies						■	■						Midday	Standard Marabou Damsels, Rickard's Stillwater Nymph #10-12
Scuds/Leeches			■	■	■	■	■	■	■	■	■		All day	Olive & Tan Scuds #12-16; Richard's Seal Buggers #8 (4X hook)
Callibaetis Mayflies					■	■	■	■	■				After-noon Evening	Adults: Two Feather, Thorax or Comparadun Callibaetis #14-18 (smaller as season progresses) Emergers: CDC Callibaetis, Sparkle Emerger, Hare's Ear #14-18 (smaller as season progresses)
Boatmen and Backswimmers			■	■	■	■	■	■	■	■	■		All day	Prince Nymphs, Zug Bugs #10-12
Midges			■	■	■	■	■	■	■	■	■		All day	Griffith's Gnats, Midge Pupas, Suspended Pupas #12-14

Hatch Chart Prepared by Bob Gaviglio

ANTELOPE FLAT RESERVOIR

Antelope Flat Reservoir is a good-sized body of water with a reputation for growing big trout quickly. Like most desert waters, the reservoir's shallows provide plenty of food for fattening trout. Fish average in the 12- to 15-inch range, but there are also plenty of fish up to 18 inches when water conditions are good. Bad water years and reservoir draw-downs, which are also traits of desert waters, can cause fish kills. The reservoir recovers fast after fish kills and currently fishes very well.

The reservoir holds a huge midge population as well as callibaetis and damselflies. When in doubt, flyfishing author Greg Thomas swears that a size 6 beadhead leech is deadly. Stripping flies from the shoreline is very effective on Antelope Flat. When the wind is up, the bank offers a safe alternative to tubing.

The reservoir has some red clay banks that tint the water when conditions are windy, but don't let the lack of clarity stop you. The reservoir will still fish well under muddy conditions. Antelope Flat is a great early season fishery—try the reservoir's north end in the spring. Fishing shallow water will be effective, especially during low-light periods.

To reach Antelope Flats Reservoir, take the Paulina Hwy from Prineville about 25 miles. Turn on Pine Creek Road. There are camping facilities at the reservoir.

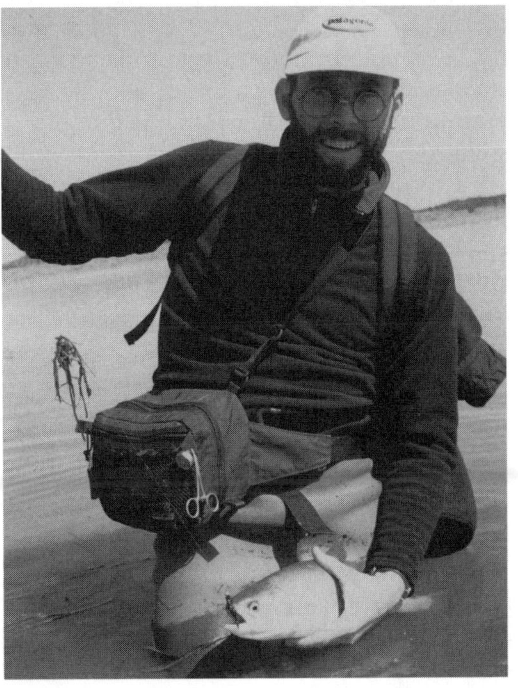

T.R. McCrystal holds a nice fish from Antelope Flat Reservoir.

GRINDSTONE LAKES

Growing up and fishing in Oregon during the 1970s and 1980s, I quickly learned that Grindstone Lakes set the standard for fee fisheries. Due to the location, only the most die-hard fly anglers make the trek to the middle of Oregon. As Matt Ramsey, who works at the Scarlet Ibis in Corvallis, puts it, "The lakes have seen change. When word was first getting out about Grindstone, guys were going over there and catching enormous fish. What you couldn't tell by the pictures was that they were only catching a few of those big fish a day and had to work hard for them."

Fish populations slowly increased, and, as can be expected, trout size dropped. At present, Grindstone is fishing better than ever. Fly anglers with good skills and knowledge of the lakes can have 30- to 50-fish days, with many fish over 20 inches.

Grindstone consists of four lakes: Grindstone proper, which holds good numbers of fish in the 12- to 16-inch range; Williams Lake (the largest at 55 acres) is where the ranch house is located and holds fish up to 22 inches; Buker and Norcross Lakes are the last two and hold fish over 20 inches.

Callibaetis, damselflies, chironomids, and caddis are all present in good numbers in all the lakes. Leeches, scuds, dragonflies, water boatmen, and snails are also favorite foods of Grindstone rainbows. When reservations are made at Grindstone, a list of gear and fly needs is provided, as well as a strict set of rules and guidelines for the lakes.

The most important rule to keep in mind at these lakes is rod weights. Rods smaller than 5-weight are not allowed. Grindstone's alkaline desert lakes make it hard to revive fish after prolonged fights. It is necessary to use strong tippets and stout rods to ensure fish survival.

Grindstone is limited to 10 anglers per day. Rod fees are currently $220 dollars per rod, per day. This may seem steep, but the price includes access, meals, lodging, and guides. Lodging is rustic and some gear will be needed—information that is provided upon booking. To make reservations for Grindstone, call The Scarlet Ibis in Corvallis at 503-754-1544, Country Sport in Portland at 503-221-4545, or Bill Beardsley at 541-330-5508.

Barnes Butte Lake

Barnes Butte Lake is another pay fishery only 3 miles from Prineville. It contains stocked rainbows in the 3-pound range, largemouth bass up to 8 pounds, and bluegill that will grow to 2 pounds. Two pounds of bluegill is a lot of fun on a fly rod. The warmwater species were stocked in 1952. Rainbows were added in 1990 and have been stocked each year since.

The lake is managed as a fishery from March 15 through October 15. It is fly only and catch and release for rainbows. Trophy bluegill can be taken for mounting purposes if desired. There is a $100 dollar rod fee per day, but no more than six anglers are allowed on the lake at a time, unless it is one group. Reservations are required to fish here.

Barnes Butte Lake is 35 feet at its deepest spot and about 40 acres in size. Float tubes, pontoon boats, or car-top boats are allowed, but no gas engines may be used. Scuds and snails are prime food for the fish as are other fish. A stocked rainbow must be irresistible to an 8-pound largemouth.

To get on Barnes Butte Lake, contact Roger Hudspeth at 541-447-4400. He will take your reservation and be able to give you day-to-day fishing reports and tips for catching the lake's biggest bluegill.

Central Hub Cities

Bend, Oregon

Elevation–3,628 • Population–33,740

Accommodations

City Center Motel, 509 Northwest Franklin / 541-388-8228 / Some pets / $
Chalet Motel, 510 Southeast Third Street / 541-382-6124 / Some pets / $
Best Western Inn and Suites of Bend, 721 Northeast Third Street / 541-382-1515 / Some pets / $$
The Sleep Inn, 600 Northeast Bellevue / 541-330-0050 / Some pets / $$
Bend Riverside Motel, 1565 Northwest Hill Street / 800-284-2363 or 541-389-2363 / Some pets / $$$
Pine Ridge Inn, 1200 Southwest Century Drive / 800-600-4095 or 541-389-6137 / No pets / $$$
Bend Cascade Hostel, 19 Southwest Century Drive / 800-299-3813 or 541-389-3813 / No pets / $

Campground

Bend Kampground (RV Park), 63615 North Hwy 97 / 800-713-5333 (reservations only) or 541-382-7738 / $

Restaurants

Jake's Truck Stop, 61260 South Hwy 97 / 541-382-0118
Legends Publick House, 125 Northwest Oregon Avenue / 541-382-5654 / $
Bend Brewing Company, 1019 Brooks Street / 541-383-1599 / $
McKenzie's Restaurant and Bar, 1033 Northwest Bond Street / 541-388-3891 / $$
Deschutes Brewery and Public House, 1044 Northwest Bond Street / 541-382-9242 / $$
Scanlon's, 61615 Mt. Bachelor Drive / 541-382-8769 / $$

Fly Shops and Sporting Goods

Sunriver Fly Shop, 1 Center Drive (Sunriver Industrial Park), Sunriver 97707 / 541-593-8814
The Fly Box, 1293 Northeast 3rd Street, Bend / 541-388-3330
Deschutes River Outfitters, 61115 South Hwy 97, Bend / 541-388-8191
G.I. Joe's, 63455 North Hwy 97, Mountain View Mall / 541-388-3771

Hospitals

St. Charles Medical Center, 2500 Northeast Neff Road / 541-382-4321

Airport

Redmond Municipal Airport, 2520 Southeast Jessie Butler Circle (16 miles north of Bend) / 541-548-6059; Horizon Airlines / 800-547-9308; United Express / 800-241-6522

AUTO RENTAL

Avis, 2522 Southwest Airport Way / 800-331-1212 or 541-923-3730

AUTO SERVICE

Les Schwab Tire Center, 105 Northeast Franklin Avenue / 541-382-3551
Gardner Auto Center, 902 Southeast Textron Drive / 541-382-7911
Happy Danes Auto Repair, 233 Southeast Second Street / 541-382-8555

FOR MORE INFORMATION

Bend Area Chamber of Commerce
63085 North Hwy 97
Bend, OR 97701
541-382-3221

Sisters, Oregon

Elevation–3,100 • Population–820

Accommodations

Sisters Motor Lodge, 600 West Cascade / 541-549-2551 No Pets / $
Comfort Inn at Sisters, 525 Hwy 20 West (west end of Sisters) / 541-549-7829 / Some pets / $$
Best Western Ponderosa Lodge, 505 Hwy 20 West / 541-549-1234 / Some pets / $$$

Campgrounds

Sisters KOA, 67667 West Hwy 20 (3½ miles east of Sisters) / 541-549-3021 / Pets accepted / $
Mountain Shadow RV Park, 525 Hwy 20 West / 541-549-7275 / Pets accepted

Restaurants

Ali's Town Square Deli, 100 East Cascade Avenue / $
Coyote Creek Cafe, 20 West Three Wind Shopping Center / 541-549-9514 / $
The Gallery Restaurant, Downtown Sisters / 541-549-2631 / $-$$
Hotel Sisters Restaurant, 190 East Cascade Avenue / 541-549-7427 / $-$$
Sisters Brewing Company, 160 East Cascade Avenue / 541-549-0518 / $-$$

Fly Shops and Sporting Goods

The Fly Fisher's Place, 151 West Main Avenue / 541-549-3474
John Judy's Fly Fishing, 248 Camp Sherman Road, Camp Sherman / 541-595-2073

Hospitals

Bend Memorial Clinic (Sisters), 241 East Cascade Avenue / 541-549-0303

Airport

Redmond Municipal Airport, 2520 Southeast Jessie Butler Circle (16 miles north of Bend) / 541-548-6059; Horizon Airlines / 800-547-9308; United Express / 800-241-6522

Auto Rental

Avis, 2522 Southwest Airport Way / 800-331-1212

Auto Service

Les Schwab Tire Center, 377 Sisters Park Drive / 541-549-1560
Mountain Muffler, 207 West Sisters Park Drive / 541-549-1134

For More Information

Sisters Area Chamber of Commerce
222 West Hood
Sisters, OR 97559
541-549-0251

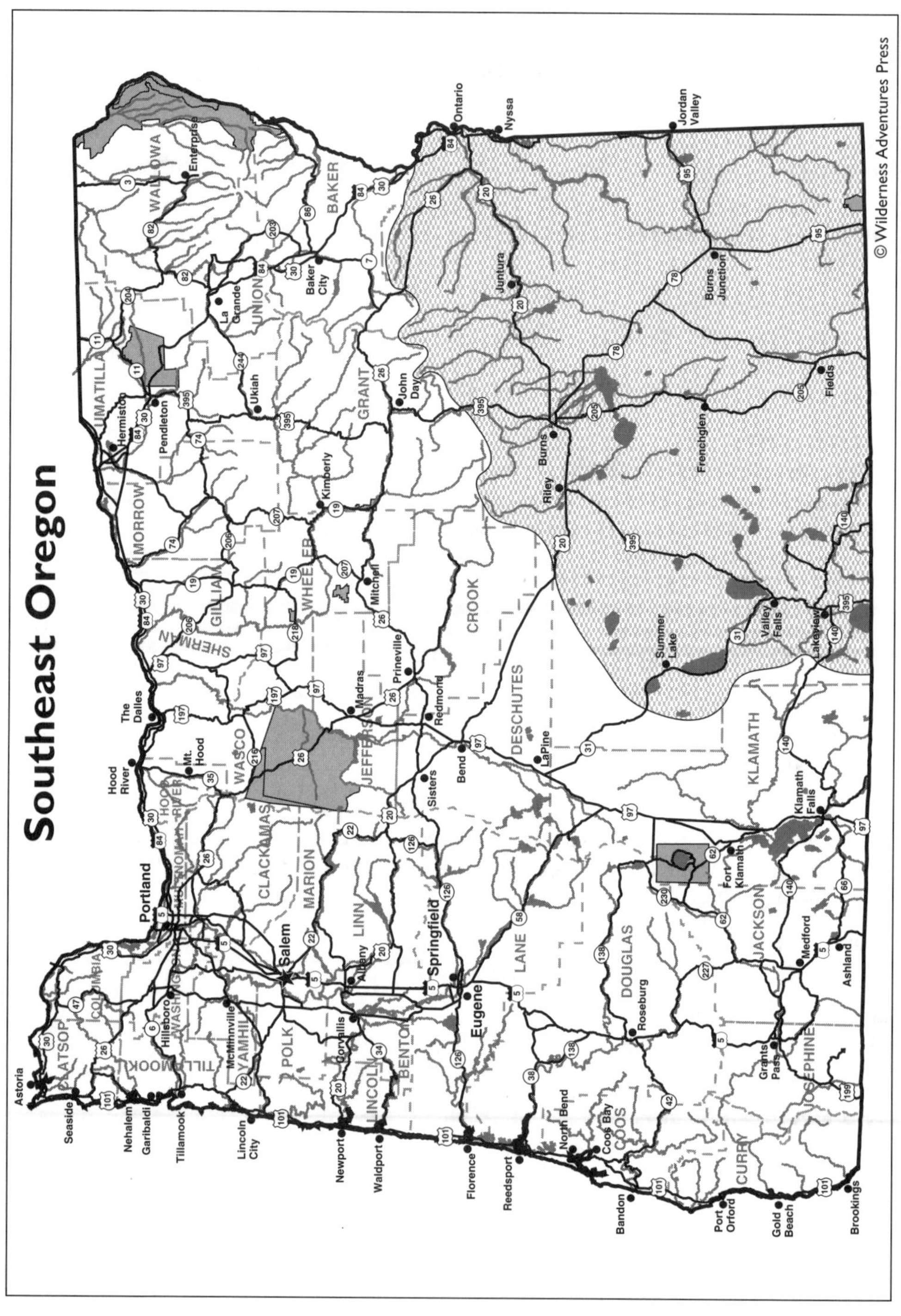
Southeast Oregon
© Wilderness Adventures Press
Astoria
Seaside
Nehalem
Garibaldi
Tillamook
Lincoln City
Newport
Waldport
Florence
Reedsport
North Bend
Coos Bay
Bandon
Port Orford
Gold Beach
Brookings
Portland
Hillsboro
McMinnville
Salem
Corvallis
Albany
Eugene
Springfield
Roseburg
Grants Pass
Medford
Ashland
Hood River
The Dalles
Mt. Hood
Madras
Prineville
Redmond
Sisters
Bend
LaPine
Fort Klamath
Klamath Falls
Summer Lake
Valley Falls
Lakeview
Hermiston
Pendleton
Ukiah
La Grande
Enterprise
Baker City
John Day
Kimberly
Mitchell
Burns
Riley
Juntura
Ontario
Nyssa
Jordan Valley
Burns Junction
Frenchglen
Fields
CLATSOP
COLUMBIA
TILLAMOOK
WASHINGTON
YAMHILL
POLK
LINCOLN
BENTON
LINN
MARION
CLACKAMAS
MULTNOMAH
HOOD RIVER
WASCO
SHERMAN
GILLIAM
MORROW
UMATILLA
WALLOWA
UNION
BAKER
GRANT
WHEELER
JEFFERSON
CROOK
DESCHUTES
LANE
DOUGLAS
COOS
CURRY
JOSEPHINE
JACKSON
KLAMATH

Southeast Oregon

Eastern Oregon's desert presents a rare challenge when casting one's fly: keeping one's mind on the task at hand. The desert has a way of drawing an angler's attention. You can make your best cast of the day in the best looking foam line in the best looking run and still find your line of vision drift from an eloquently presented dry fly to the towering blue skies of this arid landscape.

This is a place that remains wild, where small canyons harbor exquisite streams complete with lush riparian zones, and where the only sounds you hear may be the riffles that surround you.

Oregon is host to many quality trout streams that run through pristine rainforests, rugged high desert canyons, and various conifer forests throughout the state. These are streams that one can focus on as the surrounding trees and canyons tunnel your vision to the waters that run through them. Eastern Oregon waters, on the other hand, are invaded by side canyons and dry lake beds that beg to be explored. The colors of your surroundings change with each passing minute, shadows come and go as high clouds try to survive their journey across this dry land. It is far too easy to be distracted here. With nothing to block your view, it is an almost hopeless task to keep your eye on the fly.

In spite of all these distractions, these desert waters contain something that will make you pay attention: large and weighty trout. Some outstanding blue ribbon flyfishing awaits anglers venturing into eastern Oregon. Tailwaters hold browns and rainbows, while lakes and reservoirs, containing large as well as unique fish, offer floating opportunities. There are also smaller streams with correspondingly smaller fish that are perfect for an angler to fish alone, knowing that there will be no one upstream. This may be the area's real attraction—to lose oneself without actually being lost.

Deciding where to fish in Oregon is a matter of how much time is available and what kind of experience is desired. Excellent waters and fishing are available within a short distance from Portland or Bend, but there are also greater numbers of anglers on the water. Conversely, eastern Oregon's fisheries require driving long distances but offer incomparable solitude.

Fish that live in desert waters have to survive blazing hot summers and chilly winters. We can only hope that these trials make them strong enough to withstand pressure from fishermen. Anglers should always tread lightly wherever they fish, but it is especially important to do so in desert watersheds. Although the desert looks tough and unforgiving, it is also one of the most easily damaged and most difficult lands to reclaim. Of all Oregon's diverse environments, this may be its most vulnerable to human activity.

A flyfishing expedition to eastern Oregon requires extra planning. Keep in mind the following:

You should enjoy driving, because you'll be doing a lot of it. You can reduce your wear and tear as well as your stress levels by being prepared. Have good lumbar support in your car, a large gas tank, a spare tire that you're sure is road ready, a toolbox (it's a good idea to carry an extra fan belt), a cooler, summer coolant/antifreeze, and plenty of water (you might need some for your radiator). Four-wheel drive can be necessary in some locations, so check road conditions before you leave. Radio reception in these remote areas is not consistent, so take some music and/or books on tape to help keep you alert. On my last trip to eastern Oregon, I was able to listen every night to the World Series from a Salt Lake City station, but don't count on this happening to you.

You should also be prepared to camp in this part of Oregon. While there is an occasional oasis to be found, you really can't cover the region very well if you plan your trip around places with lodging and food. Camping will give you the flexibility to fish several locations in this immense area or spend multiple days in one area. And beyond that, this is spectacular country in which to camp.

Night in the desert is when things really start to happen. I'll never forget watching the stars come out while camped next to the Malheur or listening to the wind trying to rip my suburban from the Owyhee plateau. At one autumn campsite, I was joined by some mule deer hunters who had been having no luck finding game. The next morning I woke up to the sight of 20 muleys milling through their camp while the hunters were still fast asleep. I've counted hundreds of shooting stars on any given August night and have been blessed to see the sun rise over Mann Lake, with the towering Steens Range for a backdrop.

Southeast Oregon is probably not for the angler looking for sure-fire hookups. This is not to say that the fishing is poor. All things considered, it may be the best trout flyfishery in the state. If you're looking for numbers and size, other regions may be a better choice. However, if you want open space that is uncluttered by people and fish that put your angling skills to the test, eastern Oregon won't disappoint you.

This is truly a place where each stream has a secret, each cast holds wondrous possibilities, and each fish caught imprints itself on your memory.

THE DONNER AND BLITZEN RIVER

Picture yourself in an arid and inhospitable land that is being deluged by torrential rain—the kind of hard rain that, in a desert, can change the shape of the landscape in moments. Between deafening claps of thunder, you can hear the sound of hooves approaching at full gallop. The horses and riders are racing Mother Nature, attempting to get across the swelling stream before it can no longer be crossed.

In 1864, Colonel George M. Curry and his men found themselves in this situation while on a campaign against the Snake Indians. With thunder and lightning crashing overhead, the Colonel, who had studied German, named the little river, "Dunder und Blitzen," which means thunder and lightning. Settlers later Americanized it to Donner and Blitzen.

The Donner and Blitzen is a small stream originating in the Steens Mountains. It flows freely through a desert canyon picking up life and size from several smaller tributaries.

In the world of flyfishing, the word "spiritual" is often overused, but it is really the best way to describe the entrance to the Donner and Blitzen River canyon at Page Springs. Many a flyfisher has been faced with a long downstream hike after losing track of time and distance while casting on this river. Each bend in the river casts an irresistible spell, luring flyfishers inexorably upstream to see what wonders are to be found in the next new hole or riffle.

Big flies are the norm here, with both dries and nymphs working equally well on most summer and fall days. Try using large parachute and Wulff patterns on the surface. Standard nymphs, such as hare's ears, Prince nymphs, and pheasant tails in a variety of sizes will move plenty of fish. Leaders can be kept in the 9-foot range, while 3X, 4X, and 5X tippets will handle most situations.

Working upstream with strike indicators and nymphs is very productive, but on most days a well presented attractor dry fly will bring the river's biggest fish out of hiding. There is not much need for a hatch chart on the Donner and Blitzen. General mayfly, caddis, and attractor patterns will all work fine. Some skill is required, but fish aren't overly fussy about particular insects. Now open to fishing year-round, winter fishing here centers on midges and the occasional baetis emergence. Temperatures fluctuate from the fifties to the teens throughout the winter. This fluctuation will often trigger conditions similar to spring run-off on the river. Always call ahead for current information.

Most eastern Oregon rivers can be fished with 4- and 5-weight rods, and the Donner and Blitzen is no exception. You won't find much refuge from the sun, so be prepared for heat. Even in fall, a water bottle is necessary equipment. Most of the year, wet wading or the use of lightweight waders is appropriate, while neoprene waders are pretty much out of the question except in winter. And one other thing: like other desert rivers, Donner and Blitzen has its share of rattlesnakes. Besides being careful yourself, it's probably best to leave your canine companion at home during the warmest months.

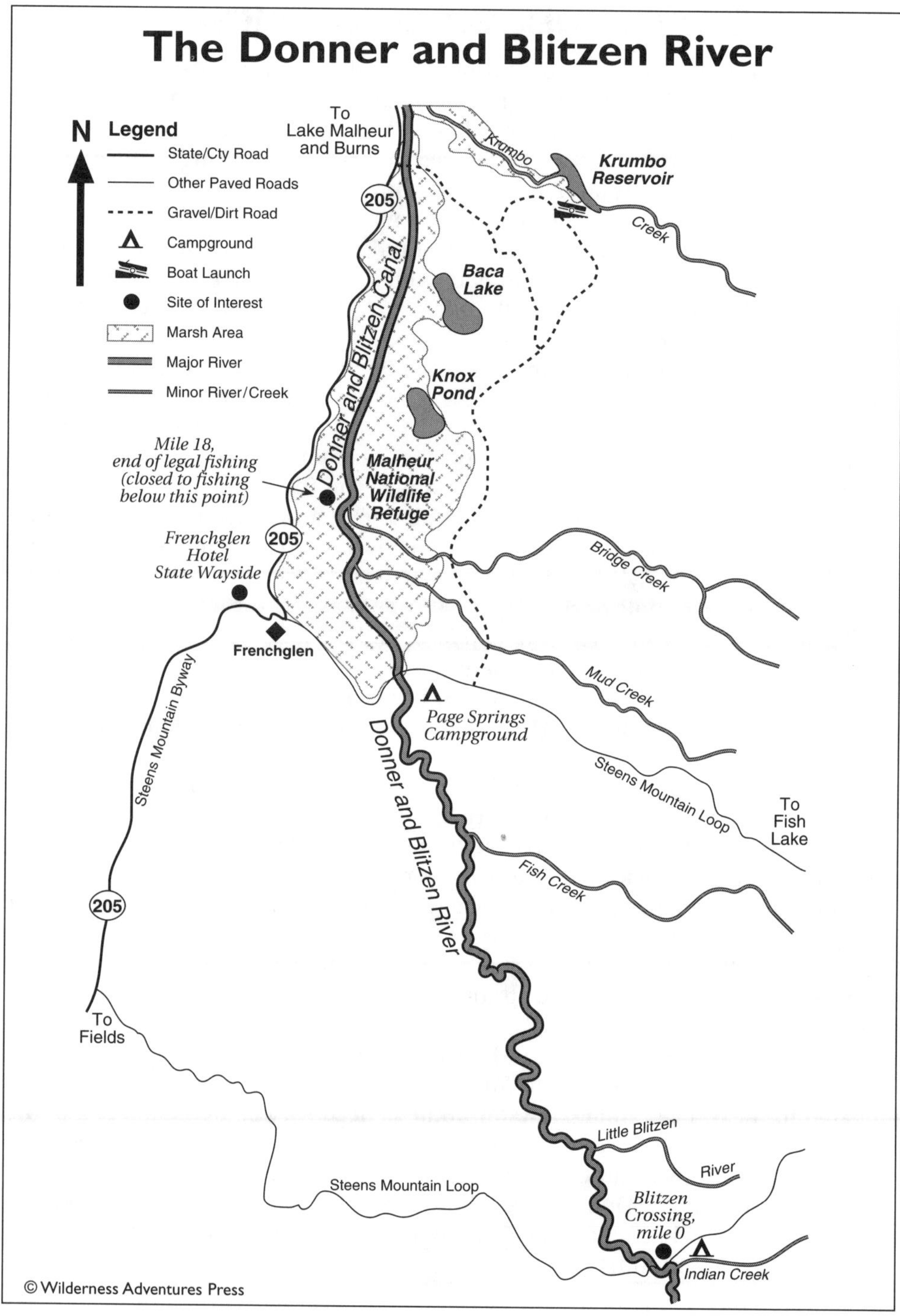
The Donner and Blitzen River
N
Legend
State/Cty Road
Other Paved Roads
Gravel/Dirt Road
Campground
Boat Launch
Site of Interest
Marsh Area
Major River
Minor River/Creek
To
Lake Malheur
and Burns
Krumbo
Krumbo
Reservoir
Creek
205
Baca
Lake
Knox
Pond
Donner and Blitzen Canal
Mile 18,
end of legal fishing
(closed to fishing
below this point)
Malheur
National
Wildlife
Refuge
Frenchglen
Hotel
State Wayside
205
Bridge Creek
Frenchglen
Mud Creek
Page Springs
Campground
Steens Mountain Byway
Donner and Blitzen River
Steens Mountain Loop
To
Fish
Lake
Fish Creek
205
To
Fields
Little Blitzen
River
Steens Mountain Loop
Blitzen
Crossing,
mile 0
Indian Creek
© Wilderness Adventures Press

The Damsel Flies, a women's flyfishing club in Eugene, work together to unlock the Donner and Blitzen.

Both fish and angler are at the mercy of the sun on these desert waters. This river's largest fish will only be visible when the sun is off the water. The crack of dawn and the waning minutes of dusk are not only the best fishing times but the most comfortable for anglers.

The Donner and Blitzen offers fish in many sizes. All these fish share the common traits of being hard fighters as well as being able to grow bigger when put back. This river has the ability to grow nice size fish quickly. If the Oregon Department of Fish and Wildlife keeps protective regulations on this piece of water, it will remain an excellent fishery.

I cannot say enough about catch and release in the Oregon desert. These fish have plenty to contend with in this uncommon piscatorial environment. We can all do our part to conserve these fish. If you really think about it, why would anyone want to drive several hundred miles to kill a beautiful native trout? Especially in Oregon where stocking, historically speaking, has become an all too common quick fix for overzealous anglers looking for bragging rights and full freezers. If you want to keep fish, stop at one of the local reservoirs for your dinner.

The best access to Donner and Blitzen is at one of two points. The first is Page Springs Campground. You can park there and fish downstream as far as Bridge Creek,

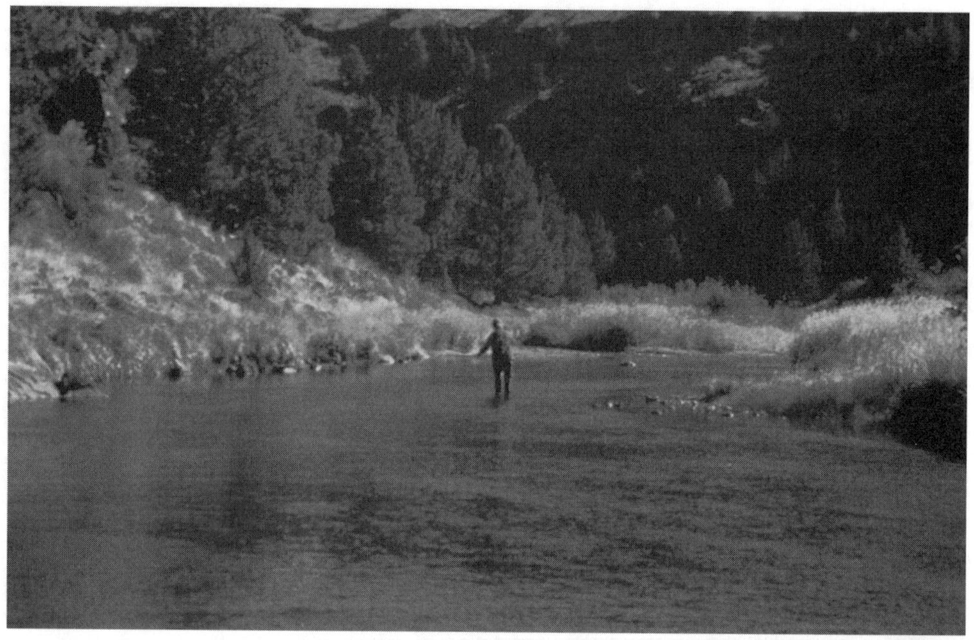

Cathy McCartney is drawn up and up into the Blitzen canyon.

which is the second tributary downriver from the campground. You can also fish upstream from the campground as far as you're willing to walk.

Page Springs to Fish Creek is an entire day of fishing for one person. Another access is the Blitzen Crossing on Steens Mountain Loop Road off Highway 205. Here you may fish upstream into Big Indian Creek or the Little Blitzen, which form the Donner and Blitzen near this crossing. Downstream, an angler can explore the Donner and Blitzen's main stem.

Page Springs Campground is located 4 miles from Frenchglen—I mention this because Frenchglen is one of the few oases that eastern Oregon's desert offers. Frenchglen Hotel has been in business since 1916 and offers beds and meals with a slice of history. Steens Mountain Inn, 541-493-2738, run by Lance and Missy Litchy, is another choice for dinner and lodging as well as the best source for up-to-date fly-fishing information. You'll find Frenchglen a hospitable place to stay and/or eat.

Donner and Blitzen is a very nice little river, but it may not be everyone's cup of tea, what with hot weather and long distances. Beginning flyfishers can find easier places to hone their skills. These desert fish can be quite spooky, and some stealth is needed to catch them.

Remember that Donner and Blitzen needs river-friendly fishermen in order to continue being an excellent fishery. Pinch your barbs, use stout tippets, and handle the fish carefully.

Stream Facts: Donner and Blitzen River

Seasons

- Malheur Lake upstream to Bridge Creek: Closed to all angling the entire year.
- The main river and all its tributaries upstream from and including Bridge Creek are open all year.

Special Regulations

- Artificial flies and lures only. Two trout may be kept at an 8-inch minimum length and only one over 20 inches. I highly recommend catch and release on these waters—both fish and environment here are fragile.

Trout

- Redband rainbows are in the main river system.
- Lahontan cutthroat, bass, brook trout, and stocked rainbows can all be found in the surrounding lakes.

Flows

- Flows vary from 5 cfs on up and can change in a hurry due to snowmelt or hard rain.

River Characteristics

- The river runs through a small desert canyon with a gentle gradient. Water consists of riffles and runs accentuated by many boulders.

Maps

- DeLorme *Oregon Atlas and Gazetteer*

Side Trips from Frenchglen

Krumbo Reservoir

Krumbo Reservoir is a short jaunt from Frenchglen and can be reached from a 4-mile long access road that branches east from Hwy 205 north of Frenchglen. It holds both trout and bass and is a popular reservoir for local fishermen. By the way, in the 900 square miles around Frenchglen, the local population is about 50 people. At least, so I've been told.

Josh Warburton, owner of Steens Mountain Resort, fishes black woolly buggers and swears by the renegade: "However she falls, wet or dry." This reservoir is stocked with rainbows that can grow up to 6 pounds in a hurry. This is a small impoundment that is best fished from float tubes or by bank angling rather than boats. Krumbo Creek is also worth exploring and can be reached via Moonhill Road and Diamond Valley Road, also from Hwy 205.

Wild Horse Lake

Lance Litchy, owner of Steens Mountain Inn, told me never to leave this area without first driving the Steens Mountain Loop Road. This is good advice, especially since much of the fishing in the area is accessible from this road. Take the loop road out of Frenchglen, eventually reaching the east rim summit of the Steens Mountains. This is about 20 miles, and fully 1 mile above Alvord Desert. At 9,700 feet, this is the highest point in Oregon that can be reached by vehicle.

Proceed to the Wildhorse Lake viewpoint, where you will find a trailhead for the lake. The trail runs downhill about a mile to this glacial cirque lake, where Lahontan cutthroat grow to a fair size. In most years, access to the lake is not possible until July due to snowpack on the loop road.

When it is accessible, pack in a float tube, some basic flies, such as zug bugs, woolly buggers, and Wulff patterns. Then enjoy the scenery along with the fishing. Don't forget a sinking line and some lunch for those slower times of day.

Fish Lake

To reach Fish Lake, take the Steens Mountain Loop Road for about 15 miles east of Frenchglen. Here you will find a wonderful BLM fee campground tucked into an aspen grove. While the lake is usually open by Memorial Day, in some years it can be as late as July 4. This is also a glacial cirque lake that grows stocked rainbows in the 14-inch range.

Fish Lake also has a nice population of reproducing brook trout that can grow as large as 17 inches. No motors are allowed on the lake, but canoes and other unmotorized craft are great here. Standard alpine flies, such as alpine emergers, Prince nymphs, and zug bugs, will work fine in this lake. If there is peacock herl on the fly, the fish will probably eat it.

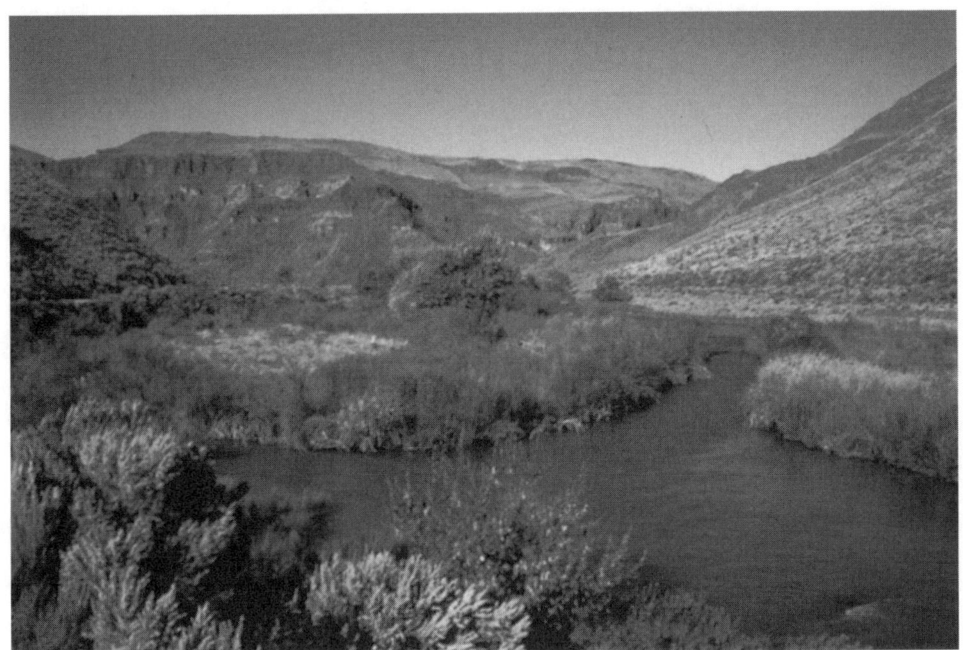

Blue skies, sagebrush, and canyon walls await fly anglers in southeast Oregon.

Indian Creek and The Little Blitzen

These two streams join near Blitzen Crossing on the Steens Mountain Loop Road to form the main Donner and Blitzen. According to fellow Oregon flyfisher Greg Veasey, "The tributaries of the Donner and Blitzen pretty much represent some of the finest in small stream fishing—and I mean small.""

Not only are the streams small, the fish here are small as well. With the proper light tackle and attitude, one can have an enjoyable day on these magical pieces of water. "This is the stuff 1- and 2-weight rods were made for," says Veasey. If you don't mind a hike and like dabbing for trout, Fish Creek can be fun as well.

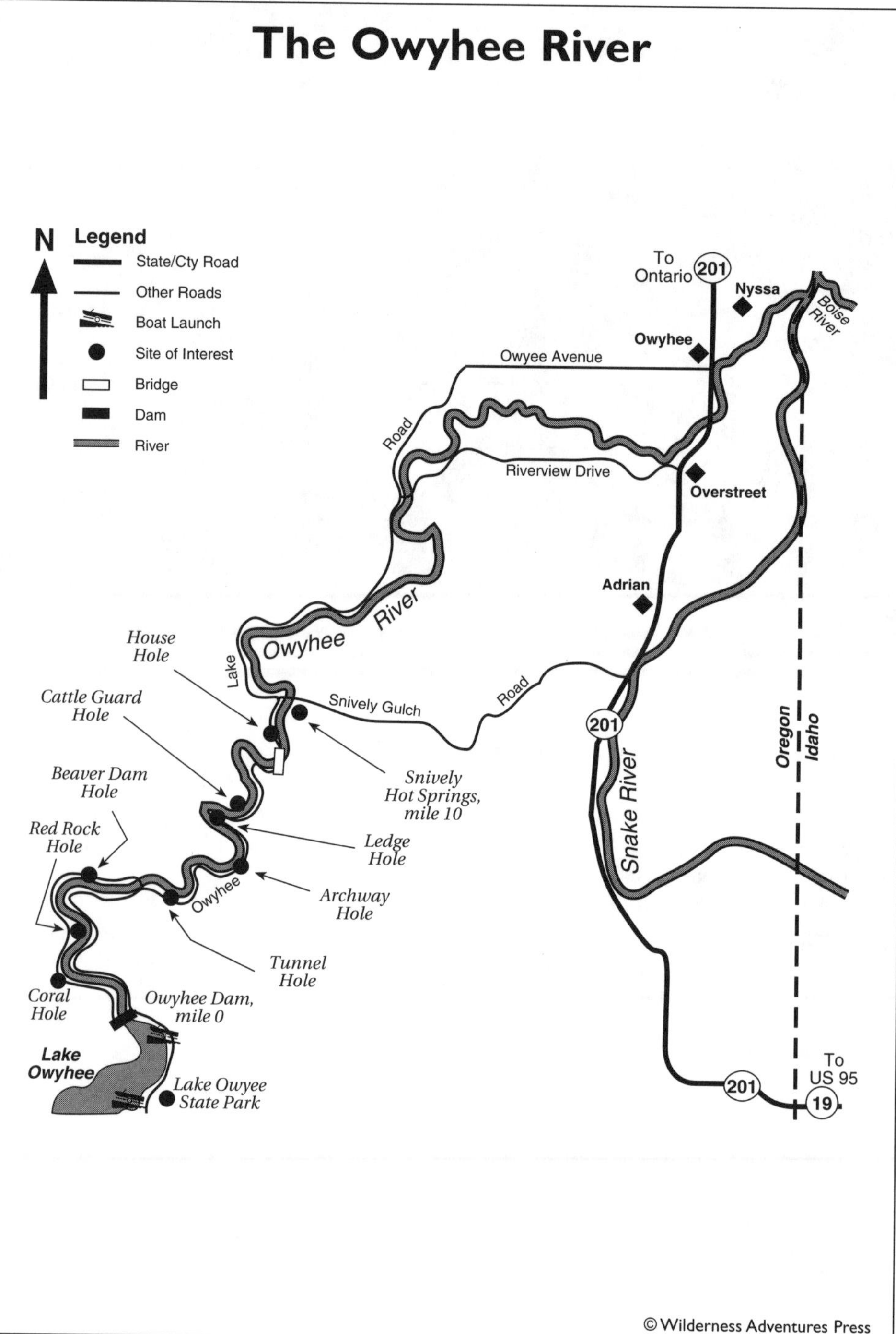
The Owyhee River
N
Legend
State/Cty Road
Other Roads
Boat Launch
Site of Interest
Bridge
Dam
River
To Ontario
201
Nyssa
Boise River
Owyhee
Owyee Avenue
Road
Riverview Drive
Overstreet
Adrian
Owyhee River
Lake
House Hole
Snively Gulch Road
201
Snake River
Oregon
Idaho
Cattle Guard Hole
Snively Hot Springs, mile 10
Beaver Dam Hole
Ledge Hole
Red Rock Hole
Owyhee
Archway Hole
Tunnel Hole
Coral Hole
Owyhee Dam, mile 0
Lake Owyhee
Lake Owyee State Park
To US 95
201
19
© Wilderness Adventures Press

The Owyhee River

When I was a child, I spent many a hot summer's day pulling crappie out of Owyhee Reservoir. My cousin and I would catch as many as our fathers were willing to clean. I didn't know it at the time, but the water I was fishing in the reservoir was feeding one of Oregon's finest tailwaters. My family went to the Owyhee country every summer for 14 years. It was during the later years of my youth when flyfishing found me. I, in turn, had finally found the Owyhee River, right under my nose. Unbeknownst to most of the state, the locals around Ontario and Nyssa had been flyfishing this river for years with hardly anyone taking notice.

By the time I was fishing the Owyhee, drought years had already taken their toll on this trophy tailwater. I caught fish but not in the numbers and size I had hoped for and heard about. The rainbows were becoming second class citizens to a growing brown trout population as irrigators battled Mother Nature.

While the drought certainly hurt the Owyhee River, it didn't decimate it. Currently, brown trout are the biggest fish in the Owyhee, but rainbows are making a strong comeback, according to Bernie Babcock, an avid fly angler from Ontario and possibly eastern Oregon's leading desert fishing authority. "It was not uncommon to have 20 fish over 20 inches in a day while on the Owyhee," according to Babcock, and I can readily believe that this was true.

I remember, one summer in my childhood, floating in truck innertubes down the Owyhee. Two things struck me immediately. The first was how cold the water was, and the second was how many dead bugs were floating down the river with me. I had obviously, but unknowingly, launched right in the middle of a large spinner fall. I didn't know what the insect was, but there were so many of them that I was horrified. These insects covered every square inch of the water. At the age of 10, I never made the connection between aquatic insects and fish—I just knew that I was covered in bugs.

These prime conditions lasted into my early teens. Year in and year out, giant rainbows quietly indulged their appetites just 5 miles from my panfish and me. If you listen carefully, very late at night in the darkness of eastern Oregon, you can still hear the faint sound of me kicking myself.

The Owyhee received its name in a peculiar way. Two Hawaiian miners, who had come to eastern Oregon to strike it rich, staked a claim near this river, originally named the Sandwich Island River. Instead of finding their fortune, they were killed by Snake Indians in 1819. Fellow miners memorialized them by naming the river after the two miners' homeland, Hawaii, which was commonly spelled "Owyhee" in this region a century ago. Eventually, the entire region was given the same name. About the only attributes shared by the Owyhee region and the state of Hawaii are the presence of hardened lava and hot summers.

It will take an angler more than a day or two to unlock the nuances of this fine desert tailwater. Anglers need to be patient and particularly observant to get results, but will be amply rewarded for their efforts.

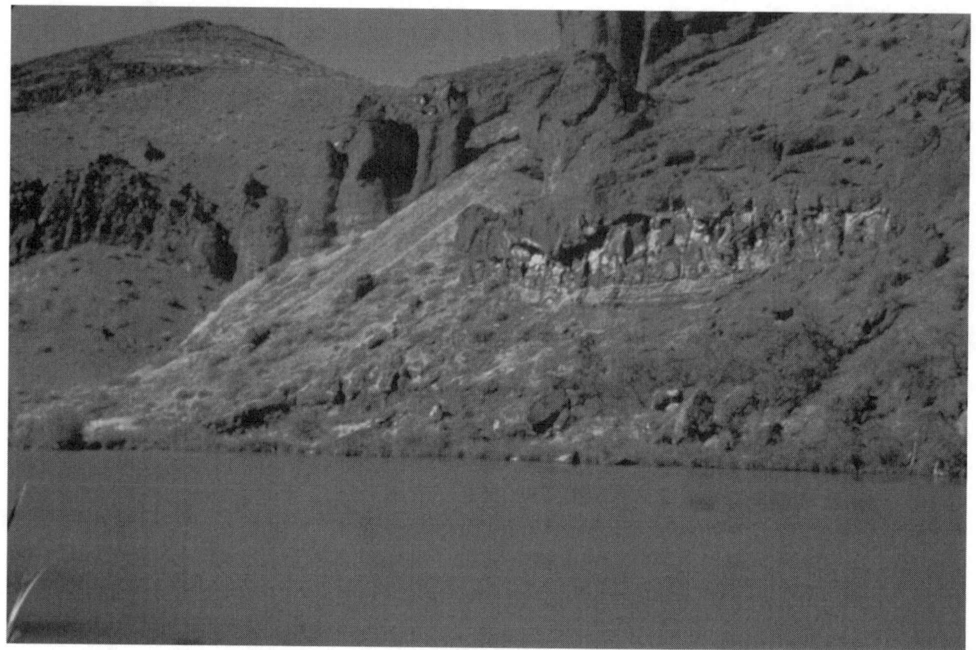

The Owyhee is big but not deep when water levels are down.

While nymphing is an Owyhee mainstay, it can be a tough technique to employ for two reasons. First, the river almost always runs a little off color. Not only does this make wading difficult, it is also a real challenge to find troughs and buckets. That beautiful riffle you've been nymphing for the last 20 minutes without a strike could turn out to be only 4 inches deep. Even the most able-bodied angler is better off using a wading staff here.

The other reason that nymphing is difficult is that the bottom of the Owyhee is loaded with fly-eating lava rock. Plan on using and losing plenty of flies when fishing subsurface. Although difficult, nymphing is not impossible here, but the angler who studies the river to find its slots is definitely a step ahead. That's why it's necessary to spend more than a day or two before passing judgment on the quality of this desert fishery.

Dry fly time on the Owyhee is special. For the frustrated and perplexed angler, these hours can be a big relief. Finding fish is suddenly much easier, as heads materialize to devour the consistent Owyhee hatches. These are the times when less experienced Owyhee fishers can hook their share of fish as trout poke their heads through the water's surface during the low-light hours of morning and evening.

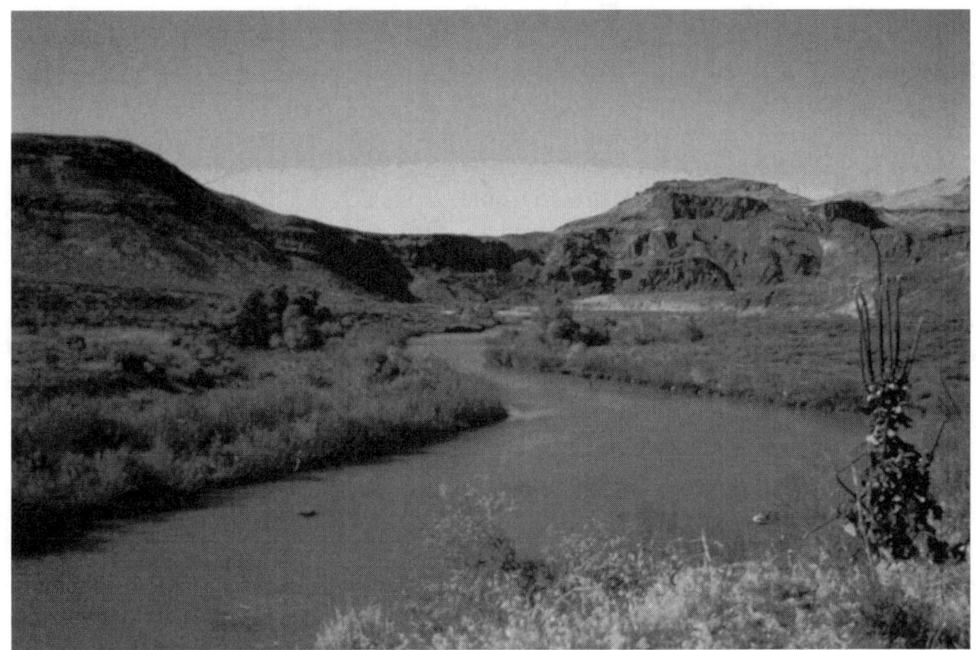

The Owyhee River runs through true desert country. Be ready for it with plenty of sunscreen and drinking water.

If it's big fish you're after, the Owyhee is home to some husky brown trout. In a recent Oregon Fish and Wildlife fish shocking survey, an 11-pound brown trout turned up. And if you can find one 11-pounder, you can bet there are others. These big boys don't get that size by eating insects, so you'll need baitfish imitations to hook up with one. A well-presented streamer works well, but once again, be prepared to lose lots of flies to the lava rock. It wouldn't hurt to use a hook sharpener on any flies you do manage to free from the rock.

In addition to standard trout gear, remember to bring a wading staff and a camera to the Owyhee. The canyon provides breathtaking scenery, with its ever-changing colors and lighting, especially at dawn and dusk.

Take the well-marked roads south of Nyssa to reach the Owyhee tailwater. Look for Owyhee Reservoir signs and proceed on a well paved road out of the small wayside of Owyhee. Eventually, the road runs parallel to the river upstream to the dam. Watch for Snively Hot Springs on your left. This is a good place for a soak and is also the beginning of prime fishing water. From here all the way to the dam, plentiful access and fishable waters are available.

Stream Facts: Owyhee River

Seasons
- Open all year from the mouth to Owyhee Dam.

Special Regulations
- Catch and release only for all brown trout.
- General regulations apply to rainbows.

Trout
- Rainbows in the 10- to 20-inch range.
- Browns in the 10- to 30-inch range.

River Miles
- From Snively Hot Springs to the Owyhee Dam: About 10 miles of river, most of which is paralleled by the Owyhee River Road.

River Characteristics
- The Owyhee is a desert river with all the trimmings: sagebrush, rocks, and rattlesnakes. The river has a permanent tint but is almost entirely wadeable with the exception of a few deep holes.

Maps
- DeLorme *Oregon Atlas and Gazetteer*

OWYHEE RIVER MAJOR HATCHES

Insect	J	F	M	A	M	J	J	A	S	O	N	D	Flies
Aquatic Scud				■	■	■	■	■	■	■			San Juan Worm #14
Aquatic Worm				■	■	■	■	■	■	■			Olive Scud #10-16
Caddis (*Rhyacophila*)	■	■	■	■	■	■	■	■	■	■	■	■	Olive Hare's Ears, Beadhead Olive Hare's Ears, Green Rock Worm, Killer Caddis, Elk Hair Caddis #12-18
Slate-wing Mahogany Dun					■	■	■	■	■				A.P. Nymph, Peacock Mahogany Dun, Parachute Mahogany Dun #14-18
Pale Evening Dun									■	■	■	■	Beadhead Pheasant Tail, Pale Morning Dun Parachute #16
Callibaetis Mayfly					■	■	■	■	■				Beadhead Hare's Ear, Brown Parachute Adams #14-18
Medium Brown Stone			■			■	■	■	■				Prince Nymph, Stimulator, Royal Trude, Low Floating Adult Stone (brown and black) #10-12
Grasshoppers						■	■	■	■				Parachute Hopper, Dave's Hopper, Turck's Tarantula #8-12
Ants & Beetles						■	■	■	■				Parachute Ant, Hi-Vis Beetle, Yellow Humpy #8-12

Hatch Chart Prepared by Bernie Babcock

Side Trips from the Owyhee River

Owyhee Reservoir

Owyhee Reservoir offers some great opportunities for largemouth bass, crappie, and if you're so inclined, carp. There is excellent fishing to be found on Owyhee Reservoir, but you should be aware that if you plan on eating any fish a health advisory has been posted due to mercury contamination. Check current regulations for guidelines on eating reservoir fish. My suggestion is that you return all fish to the water.

To reach the best bass fishing areas, you will need to use a powerboat. There are several boat launches just beyond the dam. The best fishing spots are usually found near rocky points and shorelines. Many anglers run their boats up the reservoir to fish near Pelican Point Flight Strip. This sight offers bass the shallows and structure they prefer many times of the year.

Crappie are found throughout the reservoir. In high water years, flooded trees and bushes surrounding the state campground offer nonstop action for both crappie and bass. Wading or float-tubing this area work equally well.

Float-tubers need to exercise common sense and caution on this reservoir. High winds can blast through the Owyhee canyon, usually in the evening. Occasionally, an afternoon wind will whip the reservoir into white caps. Because this can happen very fast, it is best to keep close to shore. Other than that, the reservoir is generally very placid, but you shouldn't let that lull you into a false sense of safety.

Carp, the poor man's saltwater fish, inhabit the reservoir as well and often travel in large schools, milling around near the surface looking for morsels. Fishing with a partner can offer a fun tactic for fishing these huge fish. The road from the dam provides an excellent view of the carp's cruising schools. After spotting some of these, one angler float tubes while the other spots from the bank.

Carp often take leeches, nymphs, and the occasional dry fly. Once you hook up, be prepared for a hard fight. You'll need a 6-weight rod for both carp and bass.

Upper Owyhee River

The upper Owyhee, from the town of Rome downriver, winds through some of Oregon's most dramatic scenery. It is only accessible by raft or kayak and can only be fished at low water. Whitewater enthusiasts prize the Owyhee's upper reaches in big water years. Water in this canyon can be overwhelming—always use the services of an experienced guide.

Although the upper Owyhee attracts very little fishing activity, it does offer a truly unique fishing opportunity. Hire a river guide for five days during a low-water year for an excellent desert fishing experience. Since low-water years don't offer much in the way of rapids, the guide may seem perplexed at your request, so you'll have to explain that your purpose is fishing rather than a whitewater experience. Take along large attractor patterns, bass poppers, and an assortment of buggers and streamers, and you'll be all set for the upper Owyhee.

Plan on seeing lots of bass, catfish, and small redband trout.

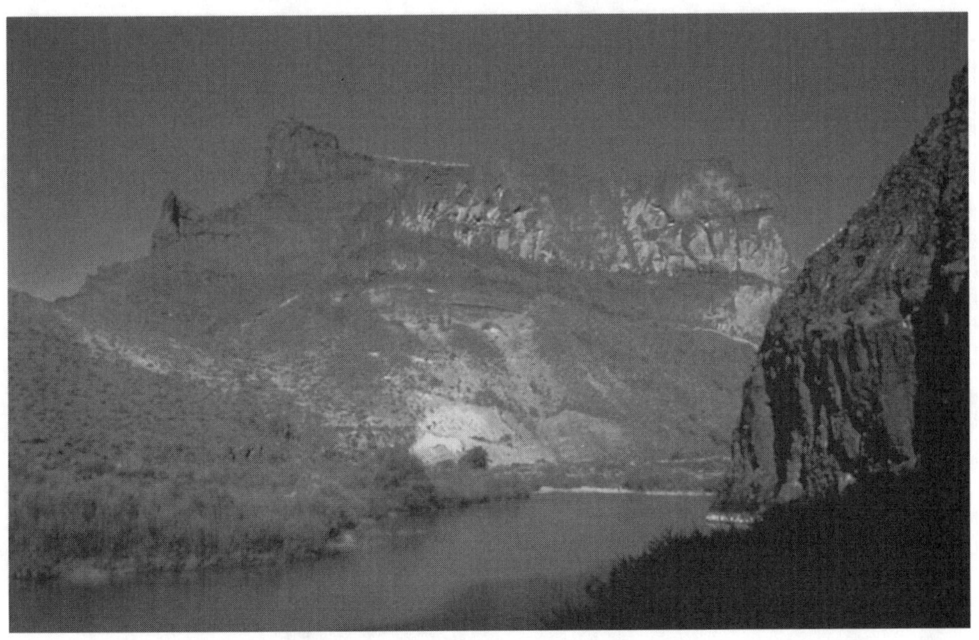

Shadows and colors change the scenery on the Owyhee all day.

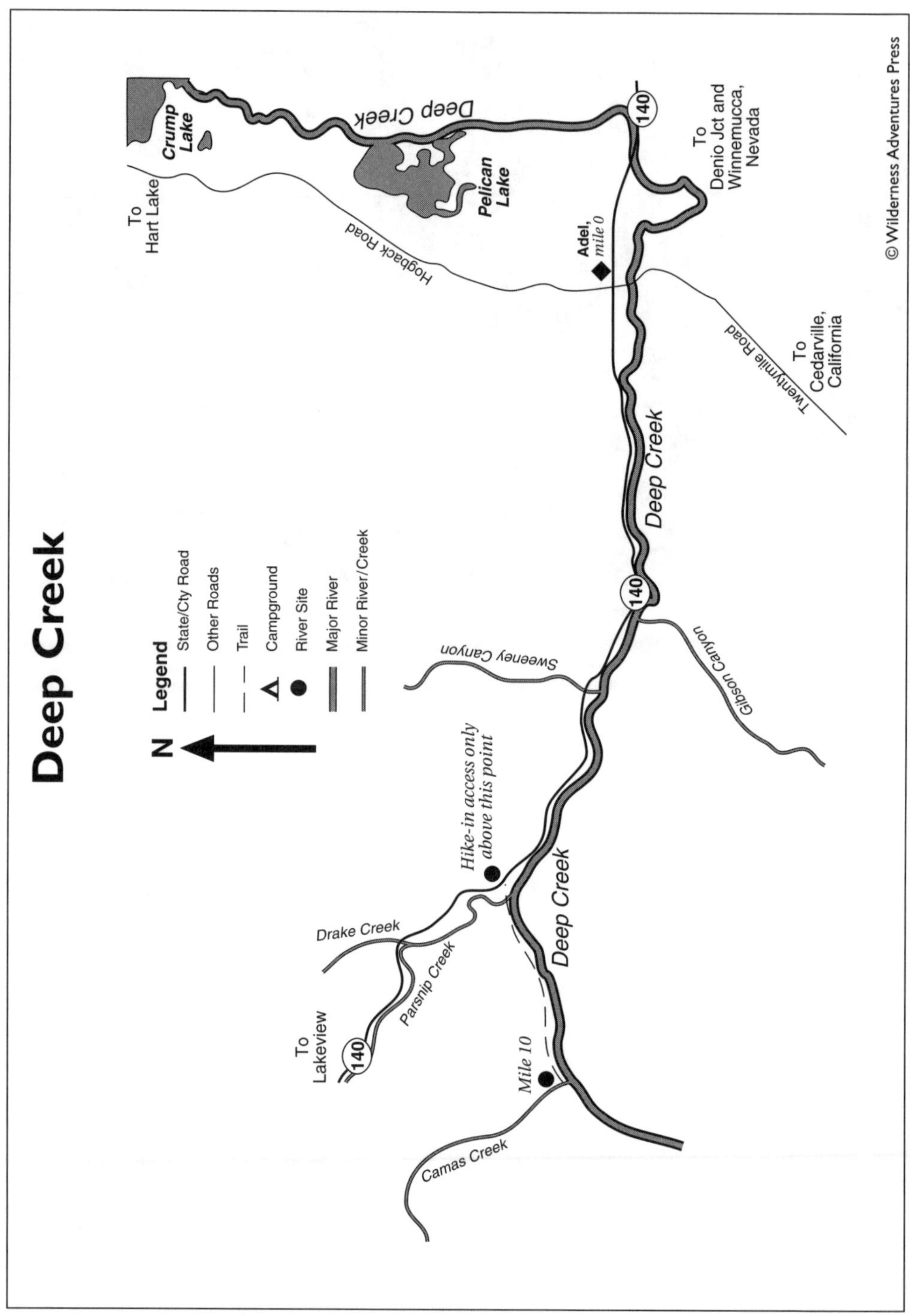
Deep Creek
N
Legend
State/Cty Road
Other Roads
Trail
Campground
River Site
Major River
Minor River/Creek
To Hart Lake
Crump Lake
Deep Creek
Pelican Lake
Hogback Road
Adel, mile 0
140
To Denio Jct and Winnemucca, Nevada
Twentymile Road
To Cedarville, California
Deep Creek
140
Sweeney Canyon
Gibson Canyon
Hike-in access only above this point
Deep Creek
Drake Creek
Parsnip Creek
To Lakeview
140
Mile 10
Camas Creek
© Wilderness Adventures Press

Deep Creek

Walk into almost any fly shop in Oregon and mention Deep Creek, and you'll probably be greeted by a blank stare. Deep Creek is far from everywhere and close to nowhere. Rolling out of Fremont National Forest, this tumbling desert creek becomes a perfect flyfishing stream by the time it reaches Adel, a small wayside on Hwy 140. It is full of rainbows up to 16 inches. Although summertime with its accompanying heat doesn't offer much in the way of fishing, spring and fall offer fly-fishers some fast action.

Downstream from Adel, much of the property alongside the creek is private. Hwy 140, which follows the creek upstream from Adel, offers easy access to Deep Creek. Eventually the creek turns south from the highway and into a beautiful gorge. From the highway, an angler can follow the river on foot as far as Camas Creek, where it becomes significantly smaller.

Deep Creek is a fantastic fishery and has remained so because of its distance from any large population centers. No special regulations have been imposed on this stream, and stocking hasn't taken place in approximately 10 years. While there is a small but hard-core contingent of local anglers, the rest of us have to drive many hours to reach Deep Creek and then hope for good conditions once we get there.

Spring and fall offer the best conditions, especially because the water is cooler. Many local anglers are out hunting in the fall, so that can be an excellent time to have the river to yourself. When fishing these seasons, most attractor files work well, and stimulators, Wulffs, and an assortment of parachute Adams are sufficient for dry flies. If nymphing becomes necessary, beaded pheasant tails, Prince nymphs, and hare's ears will all produce.

Once again, I recommend catch and release on this stream. Southeast Oregon's fisheries are special because they haven't received the pressure that so many Oregon streams endure. Regardless of what the regulations say, anglers should impose even stricter limitations on themselves.

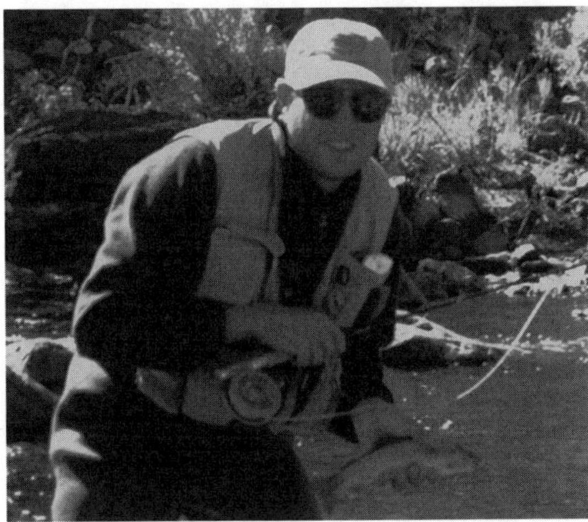

You can catch fish this size all day long on Deep Creek.

Deep Creek has a lot of character and holding water.

Stream Facts: Deep Creek

Seasons

- Open all year.

Regulations

- Limited to 5 fish per day with an 8-inch minimum length, and only one over 20 inches.

Trout

- Strictly rainbows from 7 to 17 inches.

River Miles

- From Hwy 40, 5 to 6 miles are accessible from the road, while another 2 miles are accessible by walking from the highway upstream.

River Characteristics

- Deep Creek is truly deep in many places, and this should be kept in mind while wading. You will definitely get the sense of climbing a stream when fishing here. The creek passes through boulder fields and gentle glides as it approaches Adel, with very few riffles in its course. Although the highway is in close proximity, it is hardly a distraction from the hard fighting fish found in Deep Creek.

Maps

- DeLorme *Oregon Atlas and Gazetteer*

MANN LAKE

When I was young, one of the places I kept hearing about in fly shops was Mann Lake. Anglers would utter the name with a certain sense of pride, part of which could be attributed to just making the long journey there. Living in Portland, Mann Lake was just about as far as you could drive to flyfish and still be in Oregon. Mann Lake's distance from Portland, where I grew up, helped fuel its mystique for me. If so many Portland area anglers were willing to drive there, it must be something special. When I eventually did travel to Mann Lake, I discovered that seeing the Steens Mountains alone made the trip worthwhile.

There comes a point in every flyfisher's life when enough fish have been caught and the elusive monster trout seem less elusive than ever. Suddenly, you find yourself receiving more and more enjoyment from the experience beyond the fishing. Packing is no longer a pain but a ritual. Taking time to have a real lunch, as opposed to three candy bars while mending a swinging nymph, becomes more appealing. Little by little, you find yourself knowing all the names of the surrounding flora and fauna. Perhaps more than anything else, the road trip often becomes as memorable as the fishing. Having your best friend, best dog or favorite music with you as the hours and miles stack up becomes a pleasurable, if not surreal, experience.

The farther you go, the more you begin to know and appreciate the people and the natural world around you. Sometimes it takes more than the right fly to catch trout—sometimes you must go somewhere very far away and fish the right fly. Mann Lake is the kind of road trip worth taking.

The lake is stocked semiannually with juvenile Lahontan cutthroat that grow to 14 inches within a year and become a respectable 18 to 20 inches in a short time after that. As soon as the lake thaws from its winter freeze, it is a prime time to fish. Midsummer heat not only makes the water too warm for good fishing, it is inhospitable for anglers. Cooler fall temperatures create a second season on the lake.

Mann Lake can be a float-tuber's paradise, but a desert wind can have the water whipped into white caps in a very short time. If a wind comes up, it is usually wise to either get closer to shore or off the lake altogether.

When planning a trip to Mann Lake, wind and heat should be two of your primary considerations. Area fisheries biologist Wayne Bowers stresses, "Be sure to bring your own shade and your own water. Also make sure that your tent is tied down or you may find it in the middle of the lake." Tying your tent to your vehicle is definitely a good idea, and Bowers isn't kidding about water and shade, either. Although you can camp in several spots around the lake, there is NO escape from the sun and drinkable water is NOT available.

From the north, you can reach Mann Lake on SR 78 south from Burns. The highway crosses the Steens Range and eventually meets up with Fields-Denio Road, where you should turn right. Mann Lake will be on your right when approaching from the north. From Frenchglen, take SR 205 south until you reach Catlow Valley Road. Turn left and continue to Fields, where you turn north (left) onto Fields-Denio Road until you reach Mann Lake, which will be on your left. From either direction,

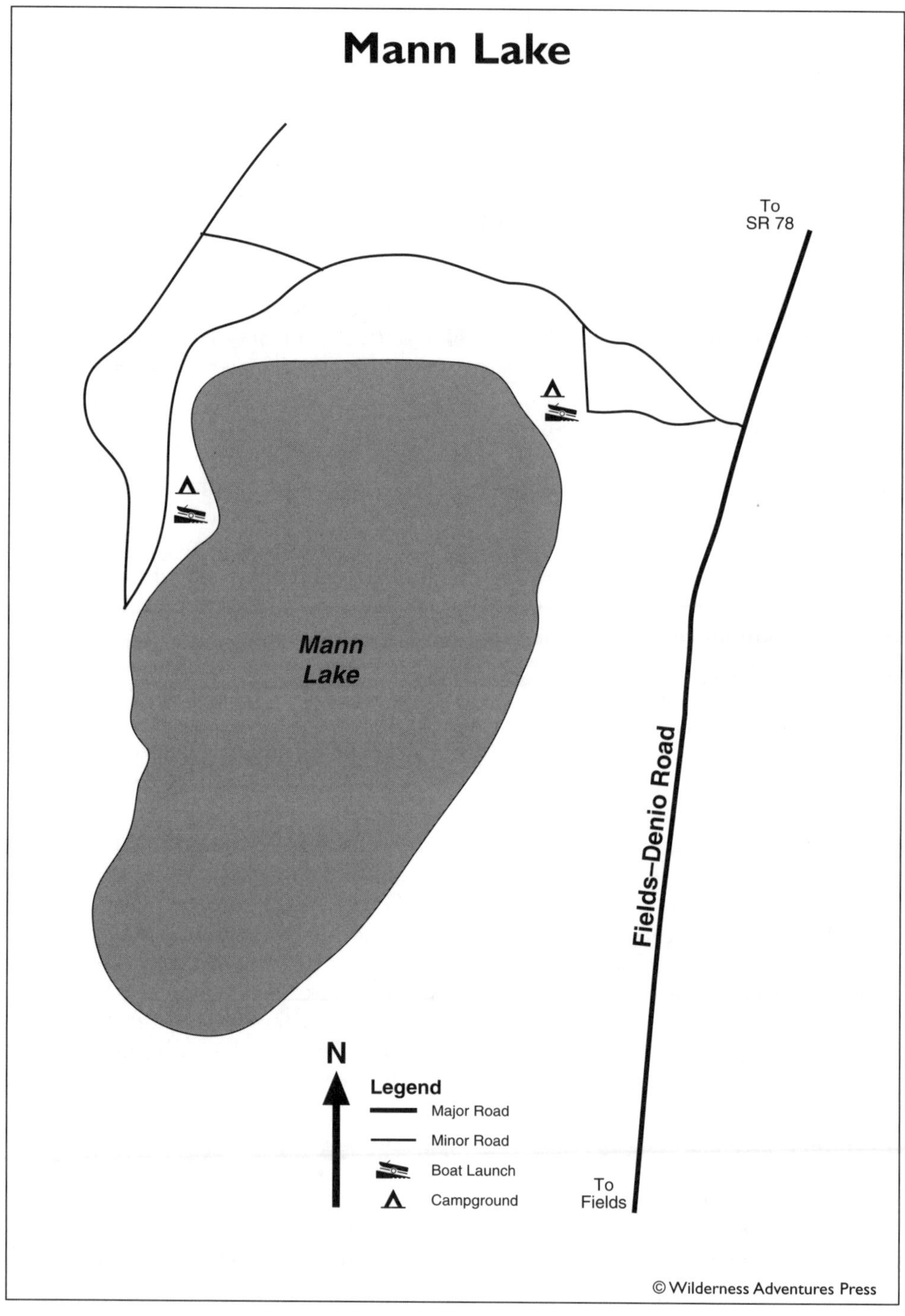

Mann Lake
To
SR 78
Mann
Lake
Fields–Denio Road
N
Legend
Major Road
Minor Road
Boat Launch
Campground
To
Fields
© Wilderness Adventures Press

Mann Lake sits directly below the Steens Mountains.

you will be traveling on a fair amount of dirt road and will be a long way from any services. Make sure your vehicle is up to the trip before you leave.

Unimproved camping is easily found by following the dirt road that goes about halfway around the lake. As there are no immediate supplies available here, be prepared to camp or drive long distances every day.

Mann Lake isn't particularly difficult to fish, and its deepest spot is only about 16 feet. A dry line will suffice most of the time, but when the wind blows it helps to have a slow sinking or sinktip line. Most situations can be covered with a 9-foot leader and 3X, 4X, and 5X tippets.

The lake is loaded with snails, scuds, damselflies, leeches, water boatmen, and some callibaetis mayflies. Standard imitations of these lake dwellers will all produce hookups. You can also try weighted brown renegades for the snails using a slow retrieve or a tight line with no retrieve. Other imitations include epoxyback scud patterns for scuds and woolly buggers in blacks and greens for damsels and leeches. Prince nymphs and zug bugs are good imitations for much of the aquatic life found in the lake.

By mid-March, when ice-off occurs, Mann Lake's Lahontan cutthroats are often voraciously hungry. This is an excellent fishing time, but a call to the local fish and wildlife office (541-573-6582) to make sure the ice is gone can save you a long trip for nothing. Also check on any recent fish kills, since desert lakes are susceptible to this from time to time.

Fall is also a good time to visit Mann. Many anglers abandon fishing to pursue big game and waterfowl, so many of Oregon's waters are pleasantly vacant. While

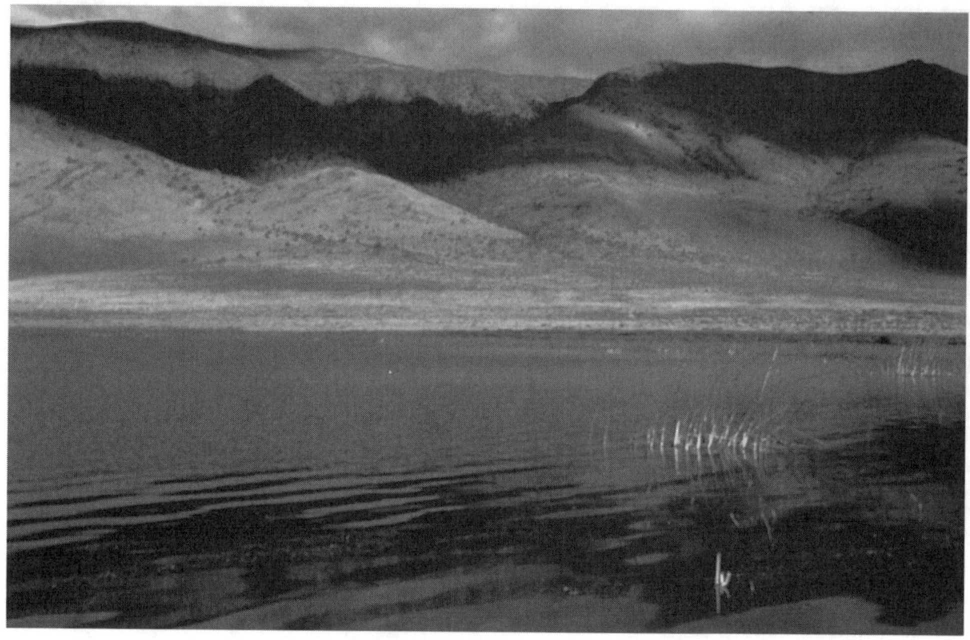

Reed-lined banks at Mann draw fish into the shallows.

hunters may be in the surrounding countryside as well as campgrounds, you will most likely have the lake to yourself with perhaps a handful of other anglers.

Don't let distance discourage you from making a trip to Mann. As far as lakes go, there aren't many like this one. If you have never fished a desert lake or seen the Steens Mountains, then grab your rod and fill your tank. Mann will offer a memorable experience.

At peak fishing times, Mann is a great fishing experience. It is a true desert lake that offers scenery unlike any other lake in Oregon. With the Steens Mountains towering to the west and the Alvord Desert expanse to the east as well as the lake's beautiful Lahontan cutthroat, you will have memories for a lifetime.

SIDE TRIPS FROM MANN LAKE

Juniper Lake

This small lake lies north of Mann Lake on Fields-Denio Road. It is a smaller lake, but Oregon Fish and Wildlife also stock it with Lahontan cutthroat. It is close enough to Mann Lake that it can be fished on the same day, and its seasons are much the same as Mann. Use the same techniques and flies as those suggested for Mann Lake. This fishery offers anglers something to fall back on if Mann Lake is having an off day.

Lake Facts: Mann Lake

Seasons

- Mann Lake is open all year; although it fishes best in the spring after ice-off and again in the fall after temperatures cool.

Special Regulations

- Two trout per day, 16-inch minimum length.
- Restricted to artificial flies and lures.
- Tributaries are closed.

Trout

- Lahontan cutthroat that are stocked as juveniles but grow to a fair size in a year and trophy size in two years, but there aren't many fish over 20-inches.

Lake Size

- The lake is over 200 acres but varies depending on the previous year's snowpack. It averages 8 to 10 feet deep and is about 16 feet in the deepest spots.

Lake Character

- Mann is a true desert lake, where heat and wind are your enemy. It is one of Oregon's most remote fishing lakes that is still accessible by road. The lake has historically been prone to fish kill, so call Oregon Fish and Wildlife for current status, 541-573-6582.

Roads

- There is only one that wraps halfway around the lake on the north.

Maps

- *Atlas of Oregon Lakes*
- DeLorme *Oregon Atlas and Gazetteer*

MANN LAKE MAJOR HATCHES AND BAITFISH

Insect	J	F	M	A	M	J	J	A	S	O	N	D	Flies
Scuds			■	■	■	■	■	■	■	■	■		Epoxyback Scuds #12-16
Damselflies				■	■	■	■	■	■				Zing Wing Damsel, Parachute Damsel, Damsel Wiggle Nymph #10-12
Callibaetis					■	■	■						Grey Soft Hackles, Quigley Cripples, Callibaetis Ostrich Nymph #14-18
Water Boatmen			■	■	■	■	■	■	■	■	■		Hare's Ears, A.P. Nymphs #10-12
Leeches			■	■	■	■	■	■	■	■	■		Woolly Buggers, Marabou Leeches, Mohair Leeches #6-10
Minnows			■	■	■	■	■	■	■	■	■		Woolly Buggers, Zonkers, Prince Nymphs #6-10
Snails			■	■	■	■	■	■	■	■	■		Brown Weighted Renegades, Hare's Ears, Borger Snails #10-12

MALHEUR RIVER

Yet another fragile desert fishery, the Malheur River offers anglers four to five months of prime trout fishing. These months, as with other eastern Oregon streams, are in the spring before irrigation is at its peak and again in fall when irrigation is discontinued. February, March, and sometimes April are the peak spring months, while October and November are the best months in fall.

The Malheur River is relatively clear and is warmer than other streams in the area, such as the Owyhee. Trout don't seem affected by the warmer water, which is responsible for an abundance of baitfish that rainbow certainly don't ignore. If there are back-to-back good water years, rainbow can grow quite large and become very susceptible to a variety of streamer patterns.

Bernie Babcock of Ontario talks excitedly about fish chasing his favorite streamer patterns. And he speaks of fish leaving a wake in the shallows while chasing his flies. Nymphs are important as well. According to Babcock, "The river is absolutely loaded with big olive scuds. The fish get big eating them." He insists that a #10 olive scud is essential for a Malheur River fly box.

Other nymphs that work well here include most peacock patterns, such as Princes, zug bugs, and olive hare's ears will also do the trick.

Dry fly activity is limited to a medium brown stonefly in spring, Tricos in summer and fall, and baetis throughout the fishable months.

To really appreciate the Malheur, a flyfisher should appreciate the art of streamer fishing. Streamer fishing's appeal here is due to the excitement of a tight line take and the opportunity to hook the river's biggest fish, which are a mix of reproducing hatchery rainbows and eastern Oregon's native redband trout.

Along with a variety of minnows, the Malheur River also hosts a large population of crayfish and cranefly larva. Woolly buggers will work for all of these in brown, green, and olive colors. In the Malheur's deep holes, don't hesitate to use beadheaded buggers.

When asked about presentation, Bernie Babcock replied, "You have to fish close to the bank on the Malheur. Fish hold tight, especially where there are boulders in the water. You really have to be ready when you swing your fly behind any rock on this river."

When streamer fishing, be prepared to fish heavy tippets all the way up to 8 pounds. A tight line take of a big fish on the Malheur is impressive but only if your fly doesn't snap off. Remember that these fish are trying to kill what the fly represents.

Access to the Malheur River is from Juntura, Oregon, on US Hwy 20. Don't blink, or you'll miss this small town. Just west of Juntura on Hwy 20, you will find the Juntura-Riverside Road, which is gravel but easily traveled most of the year.

You'll find the first access at the second cattle guard on this road. To the left of the cattle guard, there is a dirt road leading down a small valley, twisting and turning about a mile to the river. This road will require four-wheel drive. Once on the river,

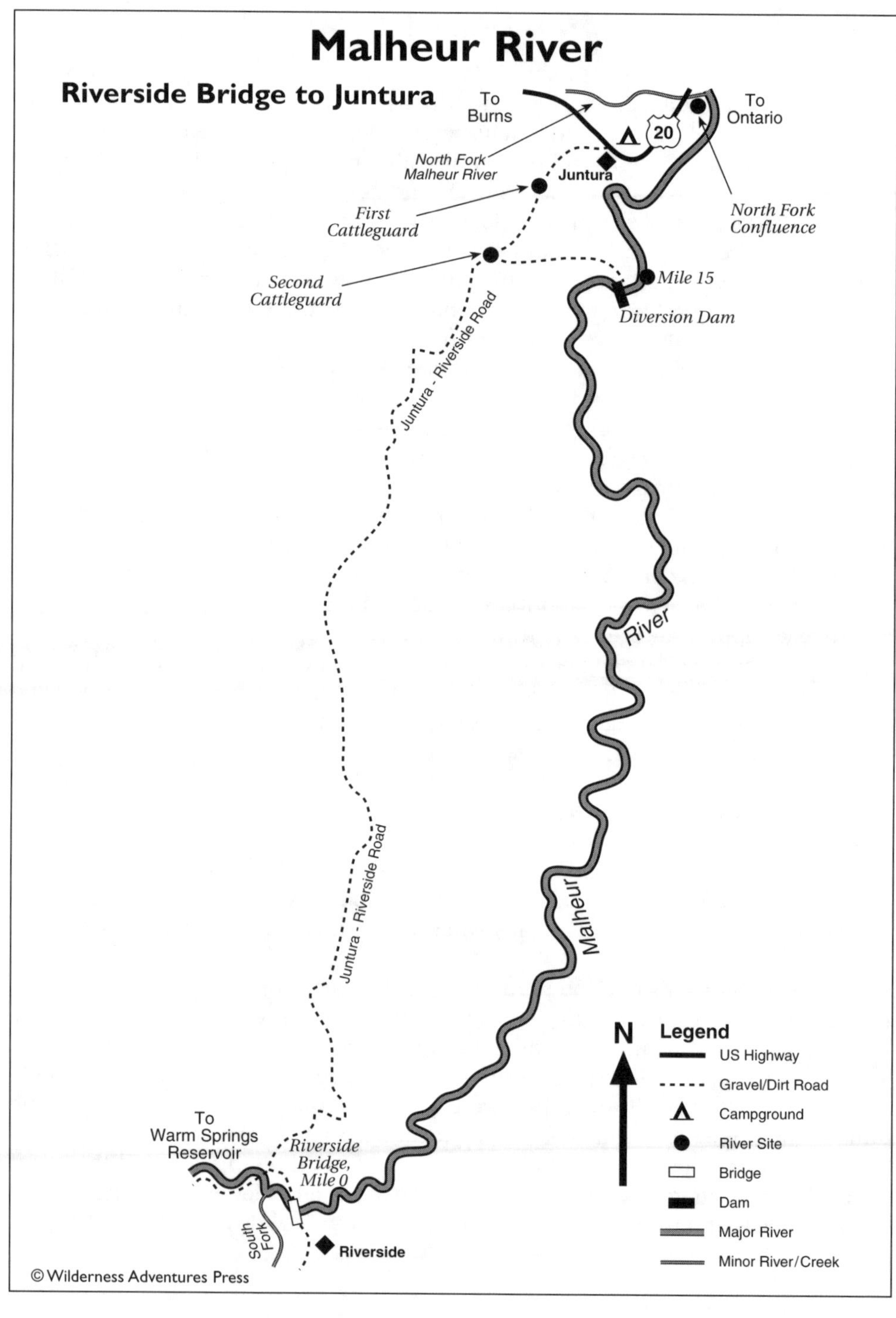

Malheur River
Riverside Bridge to Juntura
To Burns
To Ontario
20
North Fork Malheur River
Juntura
First Cattleguard
North Fork Confluence
Second Cattleguard
Mile 15
Diversion Dam
Juntura - Riverside Road
River
Juntura - Riverside Road
Malheur
N
Legend
US Highway
Gravel/Dirt Road
Campground
River Site
Bridge
Dam
Major River
Minor River/Creek
To Warm Springs Reservoir
Riverside Bridge, Mile 0
South Fork
Riverside
© Wilderness Adventures Press

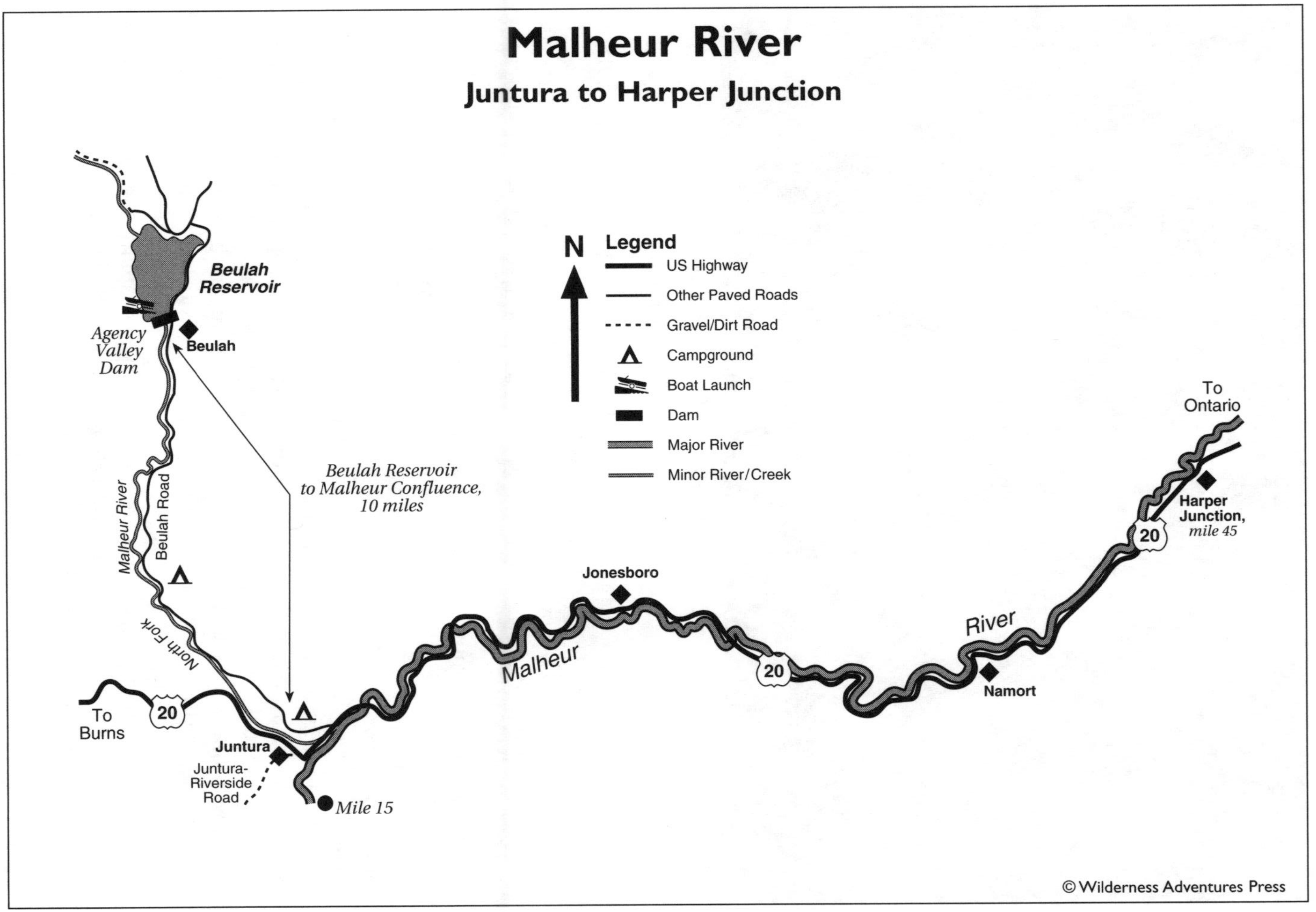
Malheur River
Juntura to Harper Junction
N
Legend
US Highway
Other Paved Roads
Gravel/Dirt Road
Campground
Boat Launch
Dam
Major River
Minor River/Creek
Beulah Reservoir
Beulah
Agency Valley Dam
Beulah Road
Malheur River
North Fork
Beulah Reservoir to Malheur Confluence, 10 miles
20
To Burns
Juntura
Juntura-Riverside Road
Mile 15
Malheur
Jonesboro
20
River
Namort
20
Harper Junction, mile 45
To Ontario
© Wilderness Adventures Press

Big skies dominate the Malheur River.

anglers can walk upriver as far as they are willing to go. To cover the most distance comfortably, I suggest wet wading or breathable waders.

This stretch is not fished as much as the upper river, and you can often have it to yourself. Unfortunately, cattle have done damage to the banks here, but the surrounding desert landscape is as beautiful as any found in Oregon. The river's banks and the fishing both improve as you travel upriver.

Riverside Bridge is the next access on the Juntura-Riverside Road. The bridge is only a few miles downstream from Warm Springs Dam. From here, you can either walk or boat downriver. If you decide to boat from here, you should be aware that you will have to go all the way to the access previously mentioned. This takes at least two days, so camping is a necessity. Because of the lack of boat ramps, especially at the take-out, as well as many shallow riffles, drift boats are not practical here. Pontoons or small rafts are the best choices for this section of the Malheur.

Below Juntura, where the river is still stocked, you can gain access via Beulah Road heading north to Beulah Reservoir, which is also worth a flyfisher's time in good water years.

Mule deer and bighorn sheep are often the only company encountered on the Malheur. There are no special regulations to protect the trout in this river, so practice catch and release on this fine Oregon tailwater.

Stream Facts: Malheur River

Seasons

- Open all year. Like other rivers in eastern Oregon, productive flyfishing is limited to spring and fall.

Special Regulations

- No special regulations; limit is 5 fish per day, 8-inch minimum length, and only 1 trout over 20 inches may be kept.

Trout

- Native redband trout are present as well as rainbows that reproduce from previous stockings. It can be assumed these fish have crossbred as well. There are some smallmouth, but not in sufficient numbers to warrant fishing for them.

River Characteristics

- The stream looks much like a spring creek when it leaves Warm Springs Dam. It eventually warms and becomes colored as it nears Juntura. There are many miles of water to fish with a good mix of riffles, deep pools, and shallow boulder-filled glides.

Boat Ramps

- There are no official ramps although small rafts or personal craft can be launched from the Riverside Bridge and taken out at the lower access near Juntura.

Maps

- DeLorme *Oregon Atlas and Gazetteer*

MALHEUR RIVER MAJOR HATCHES AND BAITFISH

Insect	J	F	M	A	M	J	J	A	S	O	N	D	Flies
Medium Brown Stonefly		X	X	X									Stimulators, Rubberlegged Hare's Ear #10-12
Cranefly		X	X	X									Woolly Buggers #10
Olive Scud		X	X	X					X	X	X		Epoxyback Scud #10
Blue-winged Olives		X	X						X	X	X		Parachute Adams, Gulper Special #14-18
Trico							X	X	X				CDC Stalcup Trico #18
Minnows								X	X	X			Woolly Buggers and Beadhead Buggers in brown, light olive, and black #4-10
Crayfish		X	X	X				X	X	X			Woolly Buggers, Crayfish Imitations, Brown Furnace #4-10

NOTE: The Malheur is not a great dry fly river due to the abundance of bigger prey. Streamer fishing dominates the action in the Malheur, although nymphing will produce nice fish as well.

JACKS LAKE

The Summer Lake region of Oregon is often overlooked by flyfishers. Its close proximity to well-known Bend area fisheries keeps angler numbers low here. Jacks Lake is nestled right in the heart of the Summer Lake area, sitting at the base of 3,000-foot high Winter Ridge. It hosts Donaldson rainbows, known for their size and fight. These fish reach lengths of 28 inches and are an excellent fly target.

This is a private lake, and the Summer Lake Inn charges to fish it. If you don't mind paying for access, this is a very enjoyable place to cast a fly. Expect to pay around $100 a day to fish Jacks Lake. The Inn only allows six anglers a day on the lake, and Darrell Sevens, who runs the Inn, says that rarely happens. Special arrangements can be made if you want to visit Jacks Lake with a group of more than six anglers.

Summer Lake Inn offers rooms and cabins that have all the comforts of home. With its proximity to quality fishing and controlled angler numbers, the Inn has been and continues to be an attractive place for anglers to gather with friends.

Jacks Lake is 3,000 feet by 400 feet, and it is a springfed lake. Float-tubing or pontoons are needed for the most effective fishing. Standard stillwater gear and flies will generate hookups. This lake is operated as a catch and release fishery, ensuring the chance of hooking some really nice fish.

The lake's depth can reach 25 feet in places, and fish use this depth in the summer months. Rick Coxen has fished the Summer Lake region with a fly rod for years and continues to return to Jacks Lake. "I've fished the lake in all seasons and done well, but the spring and fall, when the water temperatures are cooler, are definitely the best fishing."

Coxen says there are great populations of leeches, scuds, and midges. Bring the appropriate flies to match these aquatic appetizers. Fish in the spring and fall with an intermediate full-sinking line. Bring a dry line for occasional hatches as well. As summer progresses and water temperatures rise, go to a faster sink rate to get to fish holding over cool springs coming from the lake's bottom.

There are occasions in winter when the lake is ice-free and fishable. Call Darrell Sevens at the Summer Lake Inn (800-261-2778) for access and the most current information. Typical ice-out for winter is usually the first part of April. The season continues to be strong through May, drops off slightly in the summer, and picks up once again until November. According to Coxen, catch rates for anglers with decent stillwater skills are excellent. And if you're working on your stillwater skills, this is a good place to learn without the frustration of down time you may experience on Oregon's bigger waters.

Summer Lake Inn also has a small lake at the lodge, which is a good place for kids and novices to hone flyfishing skills. There are several new additions to Summer Lake Inn's fisheries that are showing promise, especially Foster Lake. Summer Lake Inn is located on Hwy 31, about a hundred miles south of Bend. The area all around Summer Lake offers multitudes of flyfishing opportunities with little pressure.

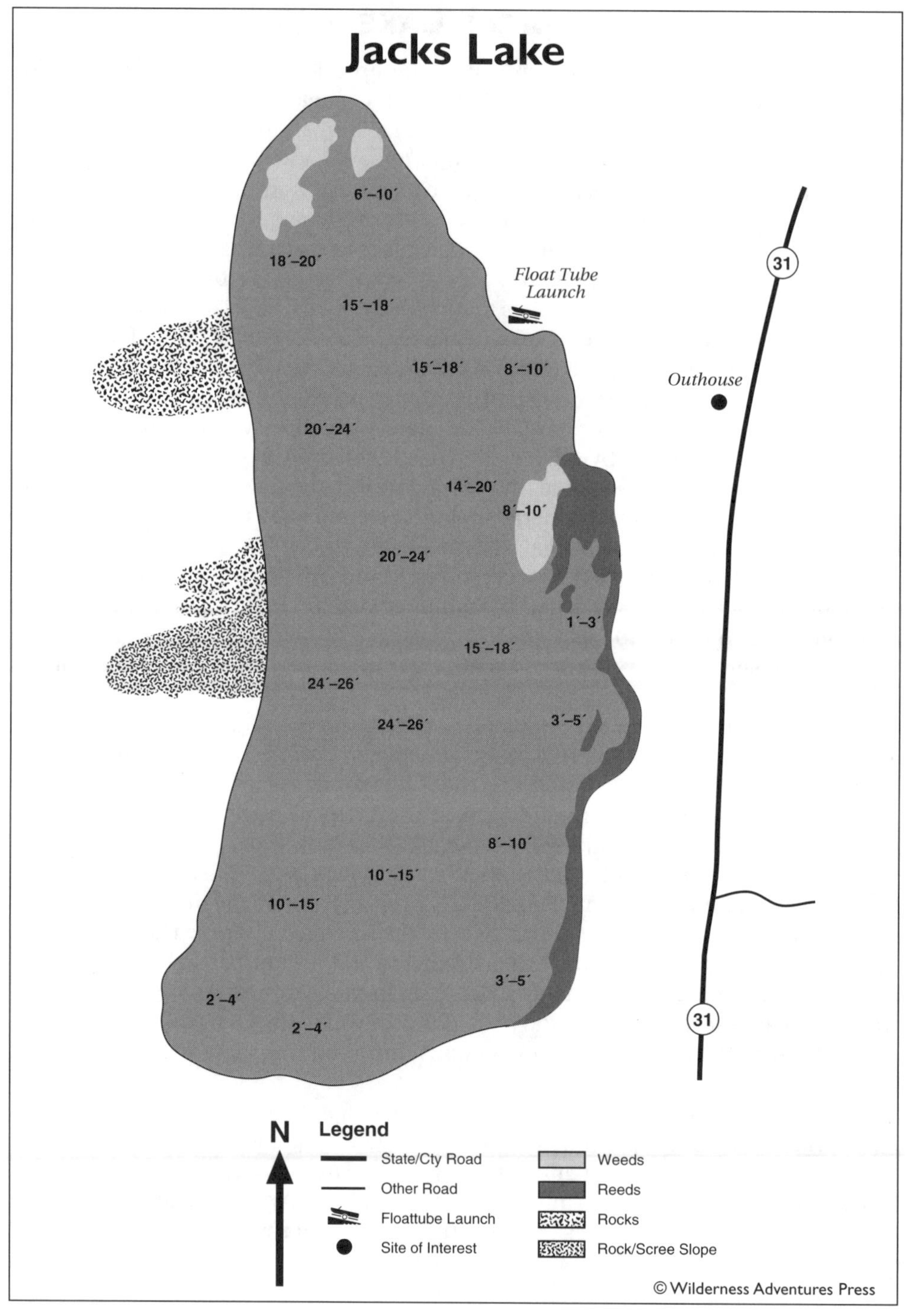
Jacks Lake
6´–10´
18´–20´
15´–18´
Float Tube Launch
15´–18´
8´–10´
Outhouse
31
20´–24´
14´–20´
8´–10´
20´–24´
1´–3´
15´–18´
24´–26´
24´–26´
3´–5´
8´–10´
10´–15´
10´–15´
3´–5´
2´–4´
2´–4´
31
N
Legend
State/Cty Road
Other Road
Floattube Launch
Site of Interest
Weeds
Reeds
Rocks
Rock/Scree Slope
© Wilderness Adventures Press

ANA RIVER

This little river in the Summer Lake area has unique characteristics that make fishing it both interesting and difficult. Its source is a small springfed reservoir that keeps the river's temperature constantly in the high 50s. Its fish are spooky, and according to Rick Coxen, "There is definitely a need to be sneaky on the Ana. The fish have plenty of food, so a poorly fished fly is likely to be ignored."

More experienced flyfishers will appreciate the technicality of fishing the Ana, although it is not regarded as a blue ribbon fishery. The river is treated more like an irrigation ditch than a fishery. Like most desert waters, fishing can either be excellent or a total disappointment. Good and poor water years affect the river's productivity, and fishing pressure waxes and wanes accordingly.

Coxen says there are fish in the Ana River that can grow as big as 24 inches. "I like to fish in May and June and again in October. The fall can be a good time to catch some of the bigger fish in the Ana." But he adds that you should exercise caution when fishing the Ana in the autumn. Numerous duck hunters come to the area and jumpshooting ducks on the water is a favorite tactic. Wear bright colors when fishing here in the fall.

To gain access to the river, you can walk downriver from the reservoir or by taking Church Road opposite the Summer Lake Store. The road proceeds out of the Summer Lake Rest Area. Continue on the road until it crosses the river, where you can then pull off and walk upriver.

Both native and planted trout live in the river. Parachute patterns are a favorite of Rick Coxen's on the Ana. He also regards caddis imitations, such as the elk hair and parachute, as excellent choices. Beadhead hare's ears and pheasant tails are effective patterns to use when fishing subsurface. At times in summer, according to Coxen, damsel activity can become a consideration.

With its proximity to other Summer Lake fly waters, the Ana River is a nice complement to the other small lakes and streams. For a change of pace, consider the Ana for a day's fishing.

SIDE TRIPS IN THE SUMMER LAKE REGION

Sycan River

The Sycan's headwaters sit atop Winter Ridge at an elevation of 7,200 feet. Beaver have been left to their own devices in the area, and they have created ponds full of small fish that love to eat flies. This is an excursion that beginners and kids would love. Brook trout are the main target here, and there seem to be plenty of them. The most basic flies, such as Wullfs and parachutes, work very well. Terrestrials are always a good bet for beaver ponds, and no brook trout can resist a renegade. The Fremont National Forest map is a must for getting around on the many roads in the area.

Thompson Valley Reservoir

Thompson Reservoir's fishing quality, like most shallow desert reservoirs, is dependent on precipitation from year to year. But these reservoirs always seem to

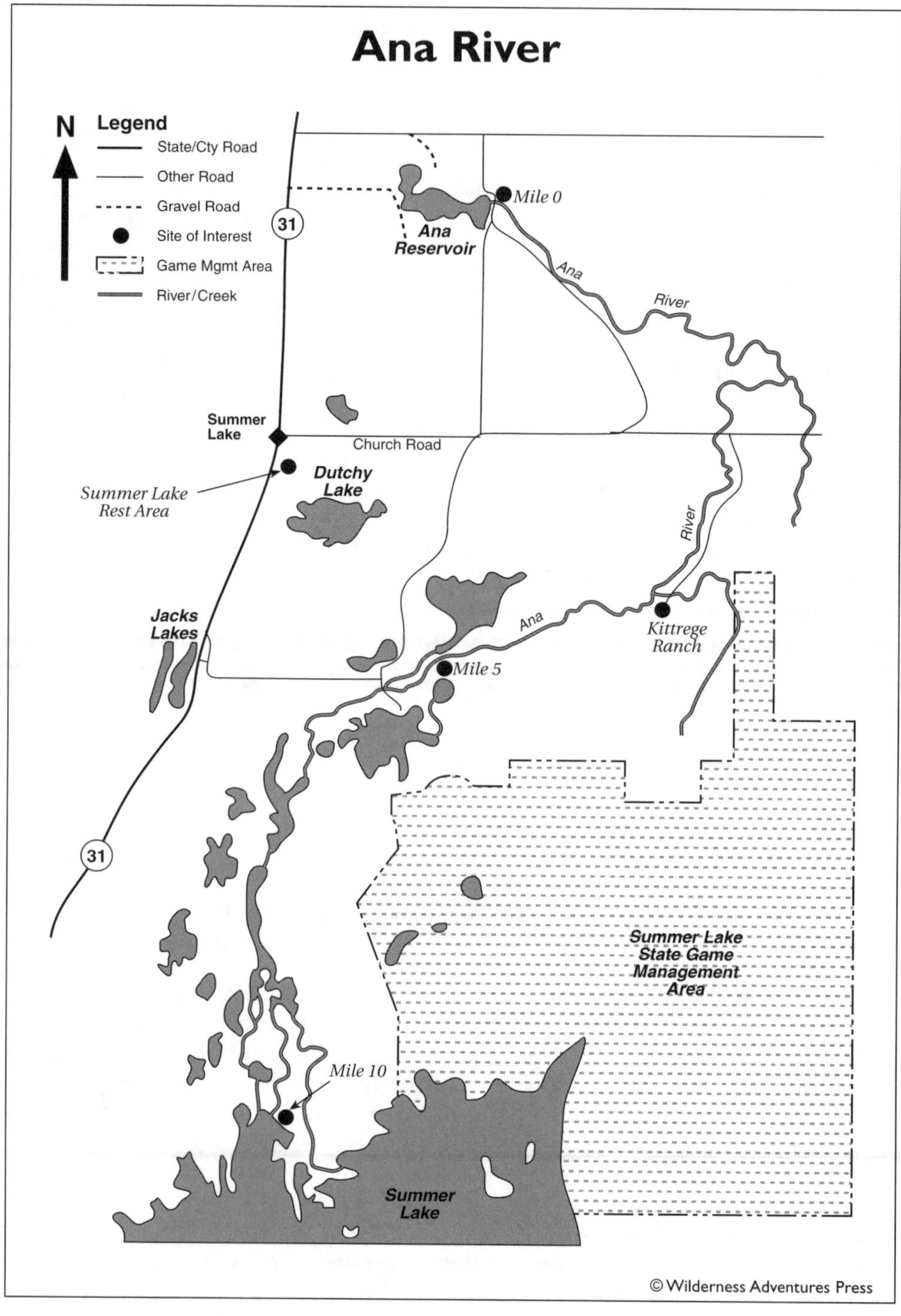

Ana River
N
Legend
State/Cty Road
Other Road
Gravel Road
Site of Interest
Game Mgmt Area
River/Creek
31
Mile 0
Ana Reservoir
Ana
River
Summer Lake
Church Road
Dutchy Lake
Summer Lake Rest Area
River
Kittrege Ranch
Ana
Jacks Lakes
Mile 5
31
Summer Lake State Game Management Area
Mile 10
Summer Lake
© Wilderness Adventures Press

The Ana River as it flows from the Reservoir.

produce plenty of trout food, and fish grow fast in these conditions. Thompson's shallows hold many 5-pound fish.

Basic patterns will catch fish in Thompson—take buggers in brown, olive and black. An intermediate sinking line will produce plenty of hookups, provided there are fish in the water column. Call the local fish and wildlife office to get information on the most recent stockings and holdover success rates..

Thompson Valley Reservoir is near Silver Lake. Just west of Silver Lake on State Hwy 31, take Silver Creek Marsh Road (primary forest road 27), which will take you to the reservoir. Watch for roads leading to the reservoir. There are two campgrounds on the lake. A float tube or some other small craft will give you more fishing opportunities here.

Duncan Reservoir

Duncan Reservoir is another stillwater fishery near Silver Lake. In good water years it hosts populations of really nice rainbows. According to Rick Coxen, there is good damselfly activity in the summer that brings big fish close to the banks as migrating nymphs head for the shorelines. Try twitching nymphs near the bottom when damselflies are present. Duncan is small and great for float-tubing. Like most desert waters, spring and fall are great times to be on the water.

Bob Gaviglio gets a rise on a nice fish at Lake of the Dunes.

To reach Duncan Reservoir, take Hwy 31 east from Silver Lake until you reach Emery Road. Turn right and go a short distance where you will find another road on the right. This road will take you to the reservoir and its boat ramp.

Lake of the Dunes

This is a small, manmade lake near Ana Reservoir that is a fee fishery. There is one small spring lake that has some good fish, which grow big and smart as the year progresses. A small cabin is available to rent if you want to stay at the lake.

This is a good place to fish with friends, especially if you stay the night. As night falls, the Summer Lake region is engulfed in wonderful solitude. During the day, the lake's spring creek type conditions ensure hours of interesting fishing. This isn't a good choice for beginners, but it's a great place to lock the gate and shut the world out for a day or two.

Contact The Fly Fisher's Place in Sisters, OR, at 541-549-FISH to make reservations. Don't forget your flying ant patterns.

CHEWAUCAN RIVER

The Chewaucan River, pronounced "She-wau-can" by locals, is a Native American name meaning place of the potato. It is a little desert stream that is best fished when water is a bit high. Its rainbow trout population is generally on the small side with the occasional 14- to 17-inch trophy being caught. The river is very easy to wade and has a ton of access from the forest road that parallels the river.

The Chewaucan may be one of Oregon's most beautiful autumn fisheries. Autumn's low light and colors bring a special beauty to the river. And the low-water conditions make the trout spooky and reluctant to move for even the most delicately presented fly. Fish can be caught in autumn but not as readily as in spring.

Rick Coxen has fished the Chewaucan for years and says, "This is a good year-round fishery that can produce nicely in May and June. Most fish are 8 to 12 inches and respond to most attractor patterns well."

Rick adds that the tributaries of the Chewaucan are great little streams that have native redband rainbows as well as some stocked fish. Try Dairy Creek, Coffee Pot Creek, and Elder Creek if you want to try flyfishing in the smallest of waters. He says that you can, on occasion, catch larger fish than you might expect in these small streams.

Concerning fly choice, Rick says, "I like muddler minnows and spruce flies and will fish attractor patterns if the fish are willing to rise. June has great mayfly activity and is a good time to fish dries on the river."

Chewaucan is relatively shallow with intermittent pools and some thigh deep runs. An angler's best tactic is to stay on the move. Fish tend to hang out together in the river's better pools. Often, it's just a matter of working upriver with dries or down-river with small streamers long enough to cast over some of these spots. Walking will also get an angler away from the more heavily fished spots near the many campsites on the river.

This river is a great place to break out your lightest fly tackle—light rods, lines, and reels. A 3-weight rod is perfect here. Long casts aren't necessary, and the Chewaucan's smaller fish will seem much bigger on light tackle. If you encounter the bigger fish, a 3- or 4-weight outfit should still provide enough backbone to land these trout.

Don't let fish size fool you into being overconfident. I have to admit I've lost my share of Chewaucan's smaller fish. This river has plenty of structure, and trout learn to make use of it very quickly. I've seen few places where fish make for cover as rapidly as those living in the Chewaucan. You will see a strike, a flash, and then be wrapped in tree limbs before you can even think about steering the fish. This river is deceptively quiet, and if you're not attentive, you'll be spending more time tying on flies than fishing.

In spite of having a number of trees lining its banks, the Chewaucan is still very much a desert stream. Bright sunlight on the water makes fish very wary, but they can still be caught with nymphs and indicators during midday. A well-presented streamer can coax some of the river's biggest fish, which are in the 18-inch range, out of their holding spots. Most fish average 8 to 12 inches.

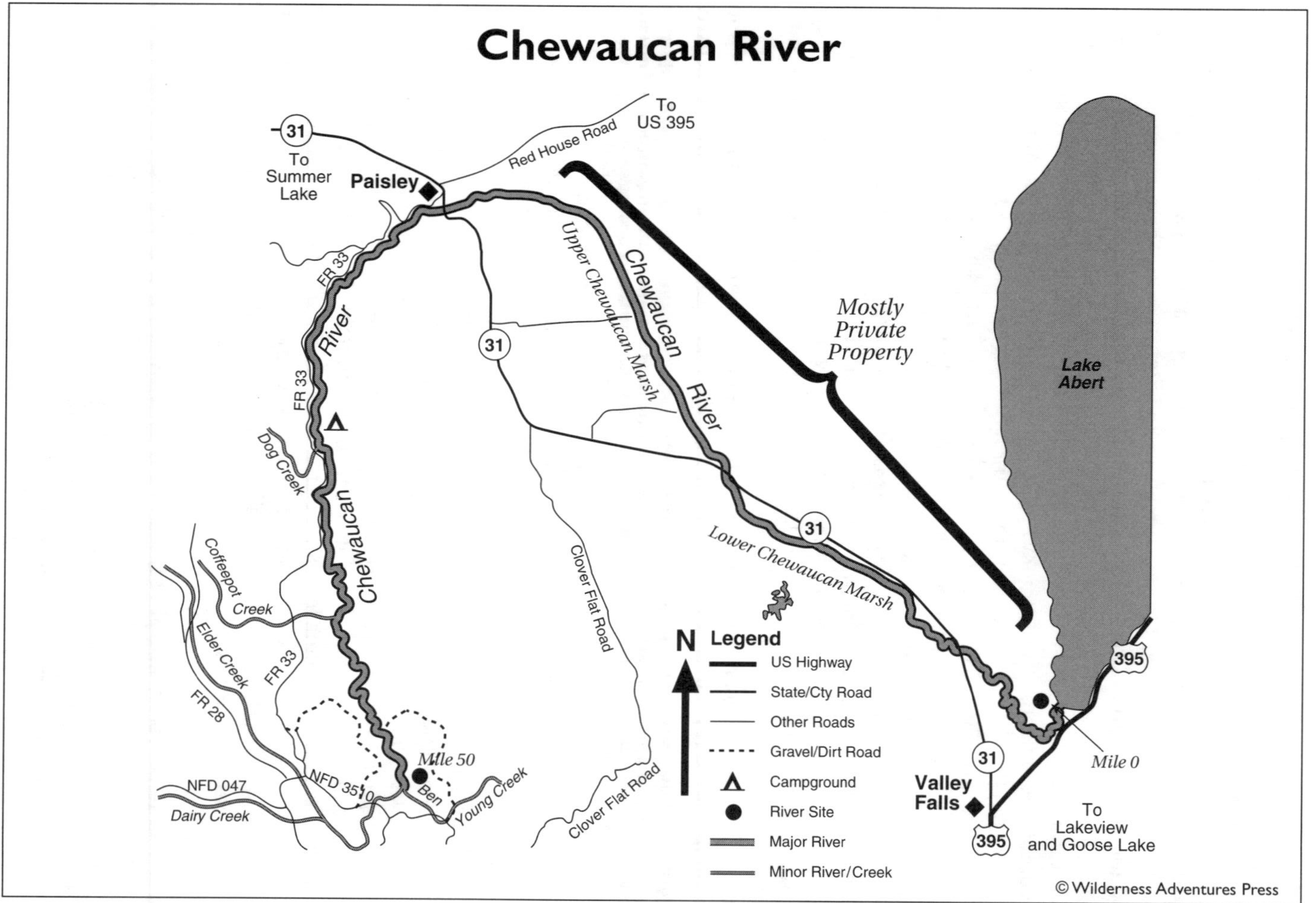
Chewaucan River
31
To Summer Lake
Paisley
Red House Road
To US 395
FR 33
River
FR 33
Dog Creek
Chewaucan
Coffeepot Creek
Elder Creek
FR 33
FR 28
NFD 047
Dairy Creek
NFD 3510
Mile 50
Ben
Young Creek
31
Upper Chewaucan Marsh
Chewaucan River
Clover Flat Road
Clover Flat Road
Mostly Private Property
31
Lower Chewaucan Marsh
Lake Abert
395
Mile 0
31
Valley Falls
395
To Lakeview and Goose Lake
N
Legend
US Highway
State/Cty Road
Other Roads
Gravel/Dirt Road
Campground
River Site
Major River
Minor River/Creek
© Wilderness Adventures Press

The Chewaucan River flows through lightly wooded land.

Attractor patterns work well on the Chewaucan as will an assortment of parachute Adams and elk hair caddis to match the river's mayfly and caddis hatches. Stimulators and Wulff patterns will entice fish most days. Pheasant tails, both beaded and nonbeaded, are a good nymph choice, as are hare's ears, Prince nymphs, and woolly worms.

Easy access to the Chewaucan River is available on Forest Road 33, heading west from Paisley, which is located on State Hwy 31. Forest Road 33 parallels the river for approximately 12 miles, offering numerous spots to stop and fish.

As for the Chewaucan's tributaries, most are accessible from forest service roads that have hike-in spots at bridges and camps. Maps available from Fremont National Forest are your best bet for tributary access.

This area is a beautiful place to spend time fly casting, and since there are plenty of stocked fish in these waters for a meal, return wild fish to the river so that they will continue to thrive in these waters.

Chickahominy Reservoir

Sagebrush and trout can both be found at Chickahominy. While sagebrush can be found year in and year out, trout need water to thrive in this dry country. Like almost every other stillwater in this part of the state, put a couple of good water years back to back and the reservoir is awesome. The down side is that it only takes one bad year to ruin it.

Chickahominy is a producer of big rainbows in the 20-inch range. These fish grow quick and plump on a variety of reservoir morsels. Damselflies are a key player in the shallows of the reservoir. Also look for scuds, leeches, and mayfly nymphs to draw strikes. As they do in other desert stillwaters, a variety of buggers in several colors and sizes will suffice most of the time. The damsel may have to be imitated more precisely if there is a big migration and the fish are keying on them.

Chickahominy Reservoir is located just off Hwy 20 (Central Oregon Hwy), about 30 miles west of Burns. Boats are allowed on the reservoir, but tubes and pontoons will suffice. There is good vegetation along the banks of the reservoir, and large fish often cruise the edges, especially on cloudy days and during low-light periods. Chickahominy is best visited in spring or late fall, since this is some seriously hot country in the summer. There is a small campground on the reservoir, but there is limited shade available.

Standard stillwater gear will suffice on the reservoir—try to throw a heavy rod like a 6-weight if the season and temperatures are warm. This will aid in landing fish without tiring them too much. Sinking lines are a plus, but the reservoir's edges can be fished with a floating line.

The nature of the area is such that a quick phone call to Oregon Fish and Wildlife for current fish populations is not a bad idea. It is a long way to go cast a line if conditions aren't prime. However, when conditions are prime, it's worth the drive from anywhere. This fragile system's ability to recover from major fish kills is remarkable. With help from the Oregon Department of Fish and Wildlife, Chickahominy will continue to be a productive fishery in good water years and deserving of a fly angler's attention.

SOUTHEAST HUB CITIES

Frenchglen, Oregon

Elevation–4,200 • Population–9

ACCOMMODATIONS

Steens Mountain Inn / 541-493-2738

Lance and Missy Litchy own and operate this mercantile complete with lodging that includes rooms and/or a house that they rent out in Frenchglen. They serve a great lunch and dinner daily in the Buckaroo Room. Basic supplies can be found here, including essential fly shop items. Gas is available when the owners are in town.

The Frenchglen Hotel / 541-493-2825

Built in 1916, this is the other building in town. John Ross operates this historic and quaint hotel. Breakfast, lunch, and dinner are served in a homelike atmosphere. Relaxing on the hotel's front porch here is one of the best and only attractions in Frenchglen.

Steens Mountain Resort / 800-542-3765

Josh Warburton runs the show here and is a great source for any questions you may have about the surrounding area. The resort offers RV sites, tent sites, and cabin rentals. The resort is on the loop road only a few miles from Frenchglen and very near the banks of the Donner and Blitzen. Basic supplies are available as well as laundry facilities. If Josh can't answer any questions you have about the area, probably no one can.

Page Springs Campground

A nice place to camp on the Donner and Blitzen. Cost is $6 per night. The campground has pit toilets and water during the peak season. In the winter there is no charge and no water. Page Springs is also a popular river access. There is no charge to park at the trailhead for day use.

Nyssa, Oregon

Elevation–2,850 • Population–2,178

Accommodations

Lake Owyhee Resort, on Owyhee Reservoir / 541-339-2444 / Don't take the word "resort" too literally—basic supplies are available, including cabin rentals and RV hookups

Arrowhead Motel, 710 Emison Avenue / 541-372-3942

Restaurants

Twilight Cafe and Lounge, 212 Main Street / 541-372-3388

Hacienda Durango, 207 Main Street / 541-372-0227

Wong's Chinese Cafe, 208 East Main Street / 541-372-2632

Ferdinand's Family Pizza, 400 Thunderegg Boulevard / 541-372-3585

Fly Shops and Sporting Goods

Kline's Hardware / 541-372-3545 / Licenses available

Cambo's Outdoorsmen (Ontario, OR) / 541-889-3135 / Licenses available plus some fly tackle

Hospitals

Valley Family Health Care, 17 South 3rd Street / 541-372-5738

Holy Rosary Medical Center, 351 SW 9th Street, Ontario, OR / 541-889-3135

Airports

Boise Air Terminal, 3201 Airport Way, Boise, ID / 208-383-3110 / Northwest, Horizon, Delta, Southwest Airlines

Auto Rental

Avis Rent-A-Car, 3201 Airport Way, Boise, ID / 208-383-3350

Budget Rent-A-Car, 3201 Airport Way, Boise, ID / 208-383-3090

Dollar Rent-A-Car, 3201 Airport Way, Boise, ID / 208-345-9727

Hertz Rent-A-Car, 3201 Airport Way, Boise, ID / 208-383-3100

Auto Service

Nyssa Co-Op Supply, 18 North 2nd Street / 541-372-2254

Hittles Automotive Repair, 711 Park Avenue / 541-372-3451

Les Schwab Tire Center, 204 Thunderegg Boulevard / 541-372-2297

Bud's Conoco, 101 Thunderegg Boulevard / 541-372-3113

For More Information

Nyssa Chamber of Commerce
14 South 3rd Street
Nyssa, OR 97913
541-372-3091

Lakeview, Oregon

Elevation–4,872 • Population–2,880

ACCOMMODATIONS

Best Western Skyline Motor Lodge, 414 North G Street / 541-947-2194 / Pets OK with $10 dollar charge
Lakeview Lodge Motel, 301 North G Street / 541-947-2181 / Pets OK
Interstate 8 Motel, 354 North K Street / 541-947-3341
Rim Rock Motel, 727 South F Street / 541-947-2185 / Pets OK
Heryford House Bed and Breakfast, 108 South F Street / 541-947-4727

RESTAURANTS

Eagle's Nest Food and Spirits, 117 North E Street / 541-947-4824
Plush West Dinner House, 9 North F Street / 541-947-2353
El Aguila Real, 407 North G Street / 541-947-5655
King's Cafe, 27 North F Street / 541-947-2217
Pizza Villa, 44 South G Street / 541-947-2531

SPORTING GOODS

Lakeview Sporting Goods, 3 North F / 541-947-4486
Coast to Coast (True Value) Hardware, 4 North E Street / 541-947-2210

HOSPITALS

Lake District Hospital, 700 South J Street / 541-947-2114

AIRPORT

Klamath Falls Airport, 6801 Rand Way (Klamath Falls) / 541-883-5372

AUTO RENTAL

Budget Rent-A-Car, 6819 Rand Way (Klamath Falls) / 541-885-5421
Hertz Rent-A-Car, 6815 Rand Way (Klamath Falls) / 541-882-0220
Sears Car and Truck Rental, 6819 Rand Way (Klamath Falls) / 541-885-5620
Enterprise Rent-A-Car, 1945 South 6th Street (Klamath Falls) / 541-850-9000

AUTO SERVICE

Bob Lake's Midtown Gas, 126 North F Street / 541-947-2268

FOR MORE INFORMATION

Lakeview Chamber of Commerce
126 North E Street
Lakeview, OR 97630
541-947-4892

Adel, Oregon

Services

Adel Store / 541-947-3850 / Only place in the immediate vicinity / Carries basic supplies as well as a cafe / RV hookups with water, power, and sewer (call ahead in the fall because hunters grab these spaces quickly)

Burns, Oregon

Elevation–4,000 • Population–2,900

Accommodations

Ponderosa Best Western, 577 West Monroe / 541-573-2047
Royal Inn, 999 Oregon Avenue / 541-573-5295
Silver Spur Motel, 789 North Broadway Avenue / 800-400-2077
Bontemps Motel, 74 West Monroe Street / 800-229-1394
Orbit Motel, Hwy 20 West and Hwy 395 North / 541-573-2034

Restaurants

Ye Olde Castle, 186 Monroe Street / 541-573-6601
Pine Room Cafe and Lounge, 543 West Monroe Street / 541-573-6631
Figaro's Italian Kitchen / 541-573-5500
The Elkhorn Cafe, 457 North Broadway Avenue / 541-573-3201
Sage Country Inn Bed and Breakfast / 541-573-7243

Fly Shops and Sporting Goods

Kiger Creek Fly Shop, 120 NW Circle Drive (Hines, OR) / 541-573-1329

Hospital

Harney District Hospital, 557 West Washington / 541-573-7281

Airport

541-573-6139

Auto Rental

Teague Ruel Motor Co., 82 South Harney / 541-573-2863

Auto Service

C and C Auto, 67 East Railroad Avenue / 541-573-6932
The Auto Shop, 320 West Main / 541-575-1776

For More Information

Harney County Chamber of Commerce
18 West D Street
Burns, OR 97720
541-573-2636

Ontario, Oregon

Elevation–2,800 • Population- 10,500

Accommodations

Best Western Inn, 251 Goodfellow Lane / 541-889-2600 / Pets OK
Colonial Inns of Ontario, 1395 Tapadera Avenue / 541-889-9615 / Pets OK / Kitchenettes
Budget Inn, 1737 North Oregon Street / 541-889-3101 / Pets OK
Oregon Trail Motel, 92 East Idaho Avenue / 541-889-8633 / Pets OK / Kitchenettes

Restaurants

Alexander's on the River, 1930 Southeast 5th Avenue / 541-889-8070
Brewskey's Broiler, 49 Northwest 1st Street / 541-889-3700
Fiesta Guadalajara, 336 South Oregon Street / 541-889-8064
Sizzler, 830 Southeast 1st Avenue / 541-889-5005

Fly Shops and Sporting Goods

Cambo's Outdoorsman, 160 North Oregon Street / 541-889-3135
Rite Aid Drug Store, 1440 South Park Boulevard / 541-889-3184

Hospitals

Holy Rosary Medical Center, 351 Southwest 9th Street / 541-889-5331
Physician's Primary Care Center, 335 Southwest 13th Street / 541-889-8410

Airport

Boise Air Terminal, 3201 Airport Way, Boise, ID / 208-383-3110 / Northwest, Horizon, Delta, Southwest Airlines

Auto Rental

Boise Air Terminal, 3201 Airport Way, Boise, ID
Avis Rent-A-Car / 208-383-3350
Budget Rent-A-Car / 208-383-3090
Dollar Rent-A-Car / 208-345-9727
Hertz Rent-A-Car / 208-383-3100

Auto Service

Claire's Automotive, 541-889-2664

For More Information

Ontario Chamber of Commerce
88 Southwest 3rd Avenue
Ontario, OR 97914
541-889-8331

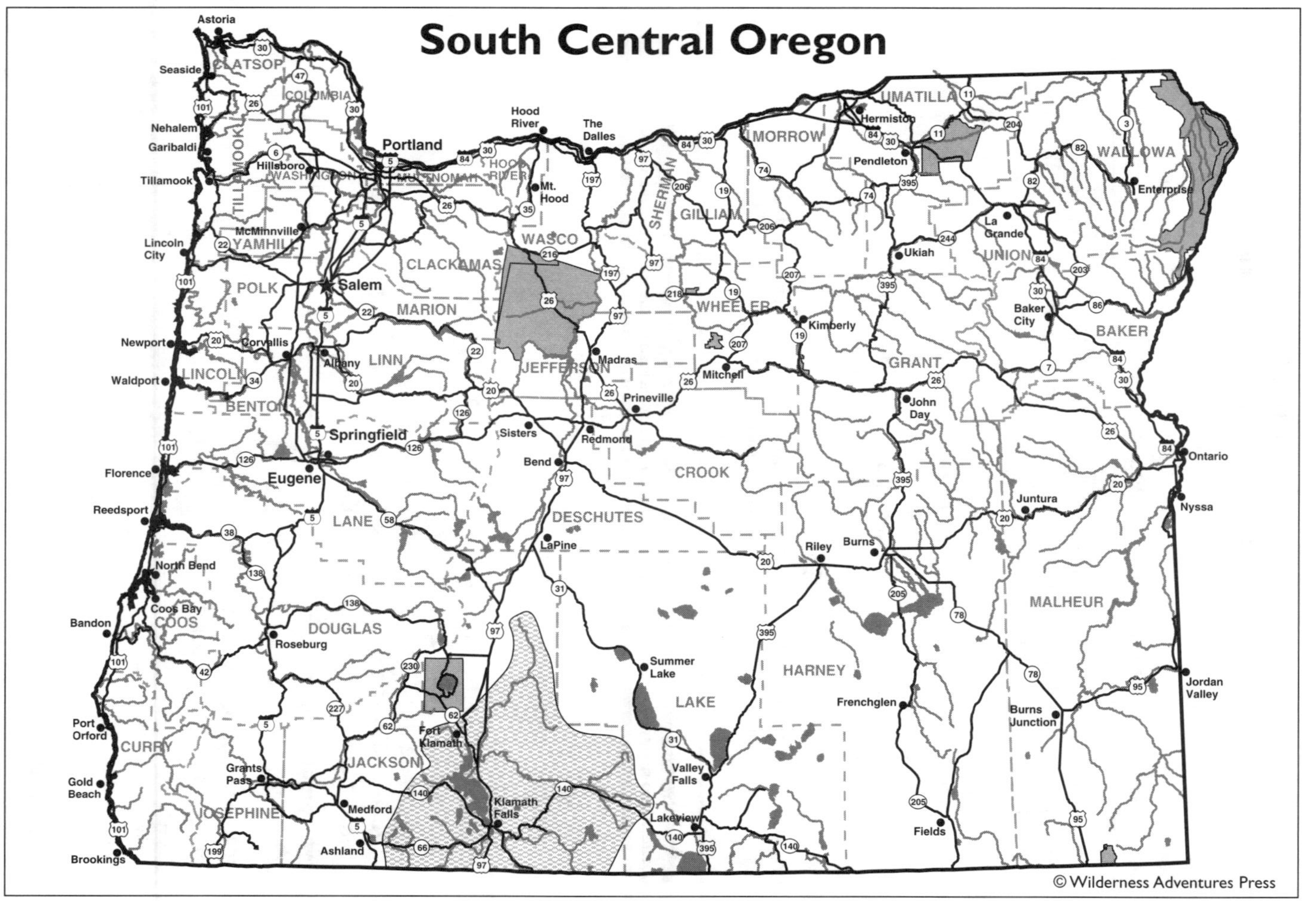

South Central Oregon
Astoria
Seaside
Nehalem
Garibaldi
Tillamook
Lincoln City
Newport
Waldport
Florence
Reedsport
North Bend
Coos Bay
Bandon
Port Orford
Gold Beach
Brookings
Portland
Hillsboro
McMinnville
Salem
Corvallis
Albany
Springfield
Eugene
Roseburg
Grants Pass
Medford
Ashland
Fort Klamath
Klamath Falls
Lakeview
Valley Falls
Summer Lake
LaPine
Bend
Sisters
Redmond
Prineville
Madras
Hood River
The Dalles
Mt. Hood
Mitchell
Kimberly
John Day
Ukiah
Pendleton
Hermiston
La Grande
Baker City
Enterprise
Ontario
Nyssa
Juntura
Burns
Riley
Frenchglen
Fields
Burns Junction
Jordan Valley
CLATSOP
COLUMBIA
TILLAMOOK
WASHINGTON
YAMHILL
POLK
LINCOLN
BENTON
LINN
MARION
CLACKAMAS
MULTNOMAH
HOOD RIVER
WASCO
SHERMAN
GILLIAM
MORROW
UMATILLA
UNION
WALLOWA
BAKER
GRANT
WHEELER
JEFFERSON
CROOK
DESCHUTES
LANE
DOUGLAS
COOS
CURRY
JOSEPHINE
JACKSON
LAKE
HARNEY
MALHEUR
© Wilderness Adventures Press

South Central Oregon

Fly anglers nationwide have pictures of leviathan trout. Usually in the background there is a wide-eyed, crazed looking angler supporting the fish. Most of the anglers in these pictures will tell you that the fish in the scene is not a fluke. They will tell you they went on a trip knowing that a photo like this was not only possible, but probable. They will tell you that it wasn't the fish of a lifetime because they plan on catching another one this year. Most likely, they will tell you that they were fishing in south central Oregon.

The fertile waters of the Klamath Basin grow big trout and contain legendary fisheries. The size and nature of south central Oregon's rivers and lakes make it a place where much of the fishing is done with guides and out of boats. There are people who don't like using guides and will tell you so with great passion. Chances are they've just never had a good guide. Spending a day with someone whose office is the water, is a treat and an eye opening experience. If you can't get a referral to a good guide, trial and error is the only way to find one. If guides and boats aren't your style or in your budget, this part of Oregon also offers some great opportunities to adventurous anglers willing to go it on their own.

More time and planning may be needed to fish this part of the state, but it is worth it. Whether you're sweating it out behind the oars or paying a professional guide, in this part of Oregon it's quite possible that you'll wind up in a picture behind a big fish, complete with a crazed smile on your face.

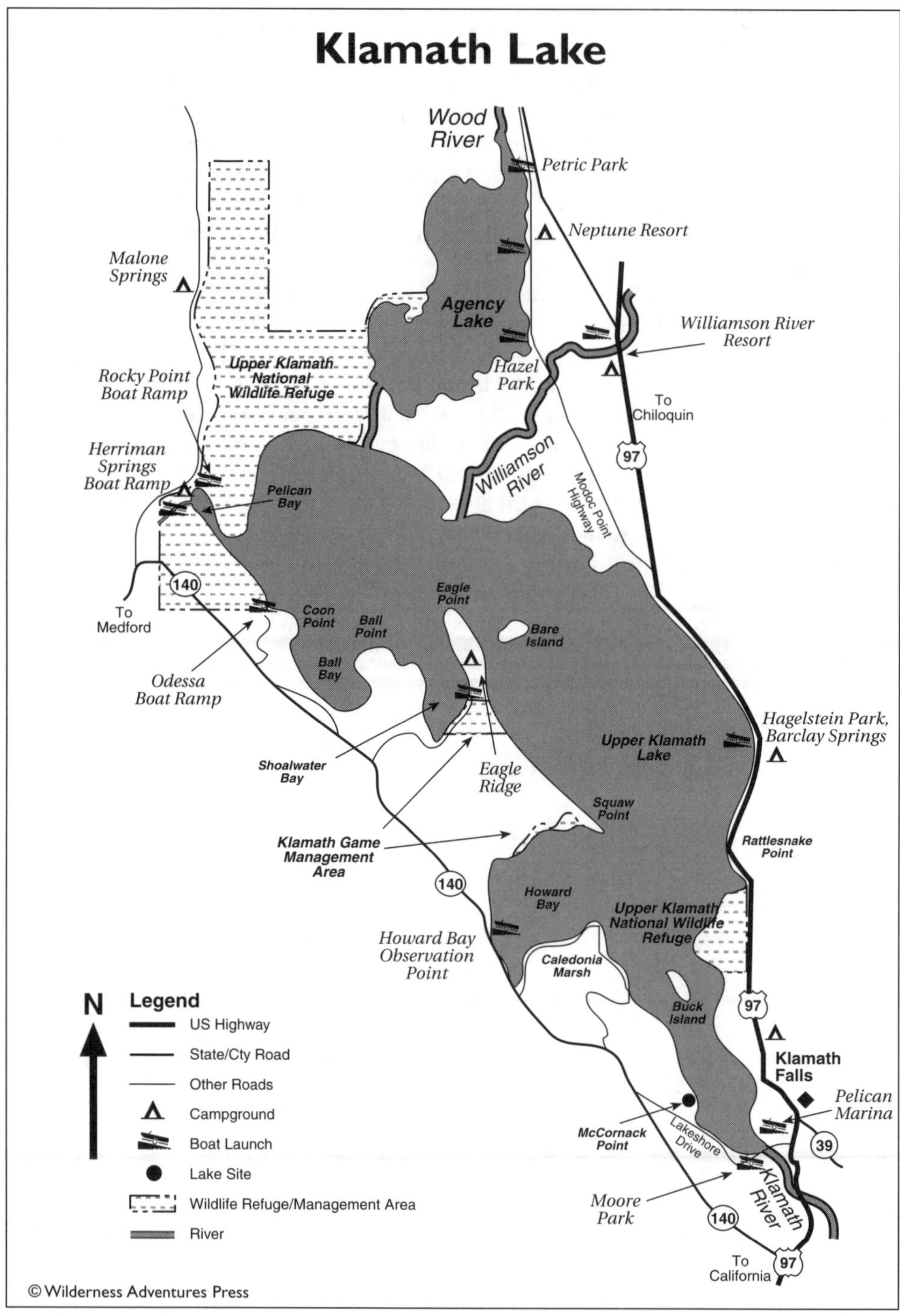
Klamath Lake
Wood River
Petric Park
Neptune Resort
Malone Springs
Agency Lake
Williamson River Resort
Upper Klamath National Wildlife Refuge
Rocky Point Boat Ramp
Hazel Park
To Chiloquin
97
Herriman Springs Boat Ramp
Pelican Bay
Williamson River
Modoc Point Highway
140
To Medford
Eagle Point
Coon Point
Ball Point
Bare Island
Ball Bay
Odessa Boat Ramp
Hagelstein Park, Barclay Springs
Upper Klamath Lake
Shoalwater Bay
Eagle Ridge
Squaw Point
Klamath Game Management Area
Rattlesnake Point
140
Howard Bay
Upper Klamath National Wildlife Refuge
Howard Bay Observation Point
Caledonia Marsh
Buck Island
97
Klamath Falls
Pelican Marina
McCornack Point
Lakeshore Drive
39
Moore Park
140
Klamath River
To California
97
N
Legend
US Highway
State/Cty Road
Other Roads
Campground
Boat Launch
Lake Site
Wildlife Refuge/Management Area
River

KLAMATH LAKE

Klamath Lake is an enormous body of water that grows enormous fish. The sheer size of it makes it seem almost unfishable with a fly rod. However, several features make it a flyfisher's dream. The lake is 25 miles long but with an average depth of only 7 feet. It is considered a super tropic lake, meaning the shallow depths will warm the water significantly in the summer months. This causes intense aquatic growth, creating an abundance of food for hungry trout.

Klamath grows huge fish quickly. A wild trout in Klamath Lake will grow to 20 inches in only three years. The depth of the lake and the warming waters create enough hardship that hatchery fish are unable to survive here. The trout in this system reproduce naturally and have adapted to taking advantage of cool springs and tributaries in the lake's consistent menu.

The lake's huge populations of shiners and chub help the biggest fish to get even bigger. Ken Morrish, manager of the Ashland Outdoor Store, says, "an angler who is proficient in stillwater fishing can have 23- to 24-inch fish be their average—the guys who regularly fish Klamath frown upon an 18-incher."

Essentially, Klamath Lake has no winter flyfishing season. Klamath Basin's cold and unpredictable winter weather discourages any angler venturesome enough to try fishing at this time of year. Not to mention that much of the lake is frozen. The fishing season really starts with spring's warmer temperatures. Denny Rickards, author and long-time Klamath Lake guide, says, "Once the season begins on Upper Klamath, you really have to divide the lake up into two parts." Rickards calls the two parts the inside and outside.

The inside refers to the areas of clear water on the lake's north end, including Pelican Bay and the mouths of the Williamson and Wood Rivers. (Wood River flows into the north end of Agency Lake, which is separated from Upper Klamath by a channel. The two lakes are fished as if they were one.) The tributaries and springs in all these areas offer cool, clean water to the lake's trout. These waters can be as much as 10 degrees cooler than water in the main lake. The prime season in these places lasts from June through October, and they can be fished throughout the day.

The outside encompasses the main lake, where conditions for fish are much tougher. Rickards says anglers use this as a morning fishery from about mid-June to mid-September. In this harsher environment, the bite goes off by noon due to the warming water. This is when it's time to head back to the inside to cast flies.

Another big difference between the two areas is what the trout eat. According to Rickards, "Fish on the outside eat baitfish and leeches. It is hardly an insect fishery at all. The inside is more of an insect fishery, but baitfish and leech patterns will work in these cool waters as well."

Ever-changing conditions on Klamath mean that anglers should be prepared to change tactics throughout the day. For example, you may have to switch from weedbeds that have been producing hookups on streamers during the morning to areas with cooling springs 2 miles away that produce strikes on nymphs in the afternoon.

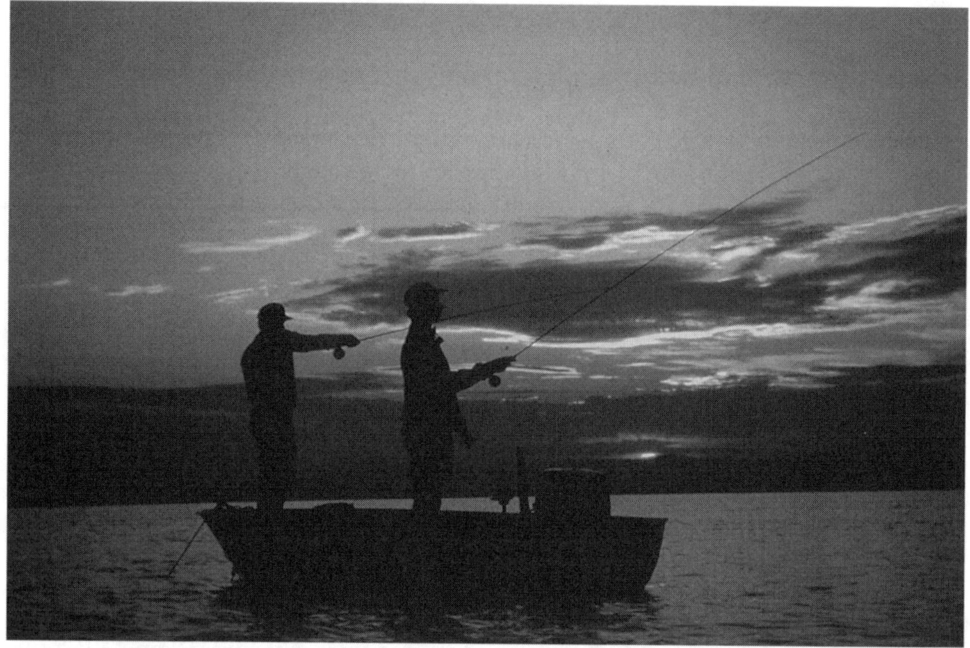

Most fishing out of boats is done with 5- and 6-weight rods rigged with intermediate sinking lines. (Photo by Ken Morrish)

Because fish change their eating habits throughout the day and because of the lake's size, Klamath is really a boat fishery. Distances that need to be covered to shift from one hot spot to the next make human powered craft, such as tubes and oar-powered boats, very impractical. If you want to fish Klamath the way it should be fished, get a boat. If you don't have ready access to a boat or you don't want to tow your own, there are some boat rentals available on Klamath Lake. Try the Rocky Point Resort, 541-356-2287, or Harriman Springs Resort, 541-356-2331.

Fish begin to move slowly up the rivers by August and continue to do so into September and October. River mouths and channels become even more important at this time of year. By the first week of November, winter's first snows are showing up in the Klamath Basin, and temperamental weather once again forces anglers off the lake.

Klamath's rich waters are packed with trout food. Its myriad insect life is dominated by Chironomids. Ken Morrish talks of midge activity so heavy that you need your windshield wipers on when driving near the lake. Along with giant midges, the lake has prolific damselfly, dragonfly, and callibaetis mayfly populations. Fish will occasionally rise to all of these insects during an emergence or a spinner fall, but hard core Klamath anglers rarely bother with the rise and continue to strip flies subsurface for the lake's biggest fish.

One of Klamath Lake's big rainbows. (Photo by Ken Morrish)

Even though insect life is prolific on Klamath, the lake holds unparalleled numbers of chub and shiners, which means that fly anglers can fish streamers almost exclusively to the lake's biggest fish. Given an opportunity to browse on thousands of midges or one chub, fish are usually going to take the baitfish.

A variety of flies will work on Klamath. Rickards says that all streamer patterns will take fish on the lake but some work better than others. Rickerts uses what he calls a seal bugger that is tied with seal fur, leaving a long, sparse tail for action. Standard woolly buggers fished in both dark and light colors will imitate most baitfish. Leeches tied with mohair or marabou can be deadly. Zug bugs, Prince nymphs, and other peacock-bodied flies are always a standard for any stillwater situation. Hare's ears and various soft hackles will imitate a variety of aquatic insects as well. While the right fly is important, fishing each imitation correctly can make an incredible difference in number of hookups.

If you need to brush up on your stillwater skills or are just starting out, I highly recommend Denny Rickards' recent book on stillwater angling. Most of the skills covered in the book were learned right here on Klamath Lake. He also goes through a list of the custom flies he's developed specifically for stillwater fishing. Learning to tie some of these patterns and then reading how to fish them properly will put you at a great advantage when fishing Klamath.

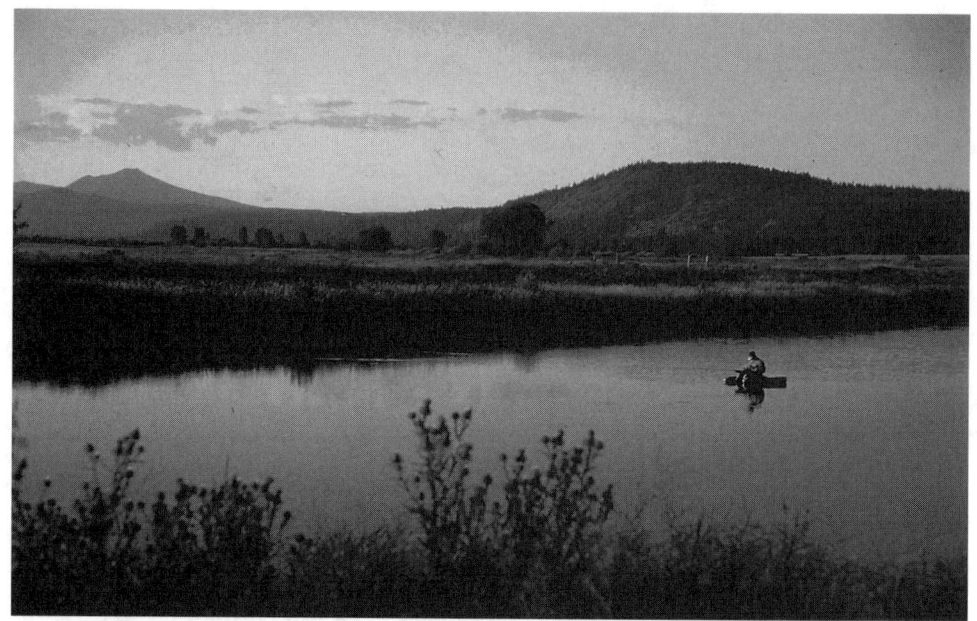

A beautiful day to fish on Klamath Lake, and this flyfisher has plenty of room. (Photo by Ken Morrish)

Fishing out of boats with 5- and 6-weight rods rigged with intermediate sinking lines is the norm on Klamath. Rickards explains, "Even though the water is shallow, the use of floating lines scare the fish here. I watch people struggle all the time over fish that could have been taken with a sinking line."

Rickards also recommends clear stillwater lines when fishing the inside waters, although the clarity at any given spot is really the deciding factor. This also determines what leader strength to use. Six pounds is common when fishing streamers, but this may change from place to place. Rickards uses 12-foot leaders, although some people prefer to throw shorter ones if they have trouble casting big flies on long leaders.

To catch Klamath's biggest fish, use a fly that is a proven producer, then find a combination of depth and strip that hooks fish. Once you lock in on a combination, be ready for some arm-jarring pulls. Always be ready to switch flies and techniques if the fishing slows down. Once you are familiar with the trout's movements and habits, each outing on Klamath will be successively more rewarding.

Because fish may change their habits due to weather conditions or time of year, it can't hurt to keep a log of conditions that includes water temperature, time of day, and depth. Serious anglers sometimes take the extra steps to record barometer readings and moon phases when the fishing is red-hot to lock in on Klamath trout.

Take the time to really look at the water—you may be surprised how many fish are cruising just under the surface near banks. Be patient and look for a target before you begin to cast randomly. A target is much better than a blind cast anytime. Oftentimes, you will have to blind-fish, but it is always a good idea to look first.

Camping and boat launches are available all around the lake. The western shore is the most popular and also has good amenities. It can be reached on Hwy 140 from the town of Klamath Falls, which sits at the lake's southernmost point. Follow the east shore on Hwy 97 and Modoc Point Road, also from Klamath Falls.

Casting to giant cruisers in Klamath Lake is as exciting as flyfishing can be. Be patient on this big water, and each time out you will find it easier and easier to be successful. Considering the average size of a Klamath Lake rainbow, it is easy to justify trying to learn as much as possible about the lake's nuances.

Lake Facts: Klamath Lake

Season

- Open all year.

Special Regulations

- One trout per day.

Fish

- Wild rainbows over 10 pounds are considered big, 20-pound fish are occasionally landed.
- Brown trout

Lake Size

- One hundred square miles at full pool. The lake occupies roughly 64,000 acres; depths over 24 feet are not common, and average depth is around 7 feet.

Lake Characteristics

- A huge but shallow lake, Klamath tends to warm significantly in the summer, pushing fish toward springs and river inlets on the north end. Klamath Basin can get very windy, and caution should be used on the lake at all times.
- A short channel connects Klamath with 8,200-acre Agency Lake.

Boat Ramps

- There are at least a dozen boat ramps. The northernmost ramps, such as Rocky Point and Harriman Springs for Klamath Lake, may be the best choices. Agency Lake is accessible from Henzel Park or Neptune Resort. Some ramps are public, but some are on a fee basis. Most of the pay-to-launch ramps offer basic supplies, and a few have boat rentals.

Maps

- *Oregon Atlas of Lakes*

KLAMATH RIVER

One of the problems encountered when doing a book like this is deciding which waters to include and which ones not to include. I decided that one way to choose was to tour Oregon, visiting local guides and fly shops and asking their opinions about the waters in their area.

In Welches, Oregon, near Mt. Hood, I stopped in at the local fly shop and asked about fishing the Sandy River. On the way to my truck, a customer who had overheard my conversation cornered me, wanting to know what I was going to write about the Klamath River. "Nothing," was my reply, "No room for it."

Apparently, that was the wrong answer. For the next few minutes, he proceeded to let me know just how good the fishing is on the Klamath River and just how ignorant I was.

About two weeks later, after some slow steelhead fishing on the Rogue, I decided to head to the Klamath. I soon found myself in a fly shop in Keno trying to get directions to the river before it got too dark. I subsequently found the river and for the next two days was treated to some great fishing. In the process, I learned a lot more about southwest Oregon than I had previously known.

So, to my friend in the parking lot: Be careful what you ask for, you might find a few more anglers on the water next time you head to the Klamath River. But I'm sure he'll be happy to know that his favorite river has been accorded its rightful place among Oregon's flyfishing waters.

Because of its proximity to famous rivers like the Wood and Williamson as well as Upper Klamath Lake, Klamath River is one of the most overlooked flyfisheries in the state. Locals in the area know this and have learned to fish it extremely well.

All the nutrient-rich waters that make Klamath Lake a world class fishery eventually form the Klamath River. Although river access can be a scramble at times, an angler can find solitude and big rainbow trout opportunities that make it worth the effort. Flowing from Keno Dam, which forms Lake Ewauna, the Klamath is a big river that demands strong gear and strong muscles to fish it. Much of the fishing is found by descending into a sloping canyon downriver from the dam. Once on the water, you will find that it is a place for big nymphs and stout lines. As Skip Levesque, my friend and former owner of The Fly Shack in Keno, puts it, "You are looking for a slot in the river—a deep trough that holds deep-bodied fish."

The upper section, commonly referred to as the Keno stretch, is a 6-mile section from Keno Dam to J.C. Boyle Reservoir. An occasional pool and riffle interrupt the turbulent flows through this section. Swinging large flies with a lot of weight is a good way to fish the deepest pools but be prepared to lose a lot of flies. Losing flies is a good trade-off when what you think is a snag suddenly begins ripping line off your reel!

Rainbows in this upper stretch can go to 7 pounds. I know some serious fishheads who tell me 7 pounds may be small here. Ken Morrish, manager of The Ashland Outdoor Store, says that, "The combination of sculpins and a major crawdad population are something the fly angler cannot ignore here."

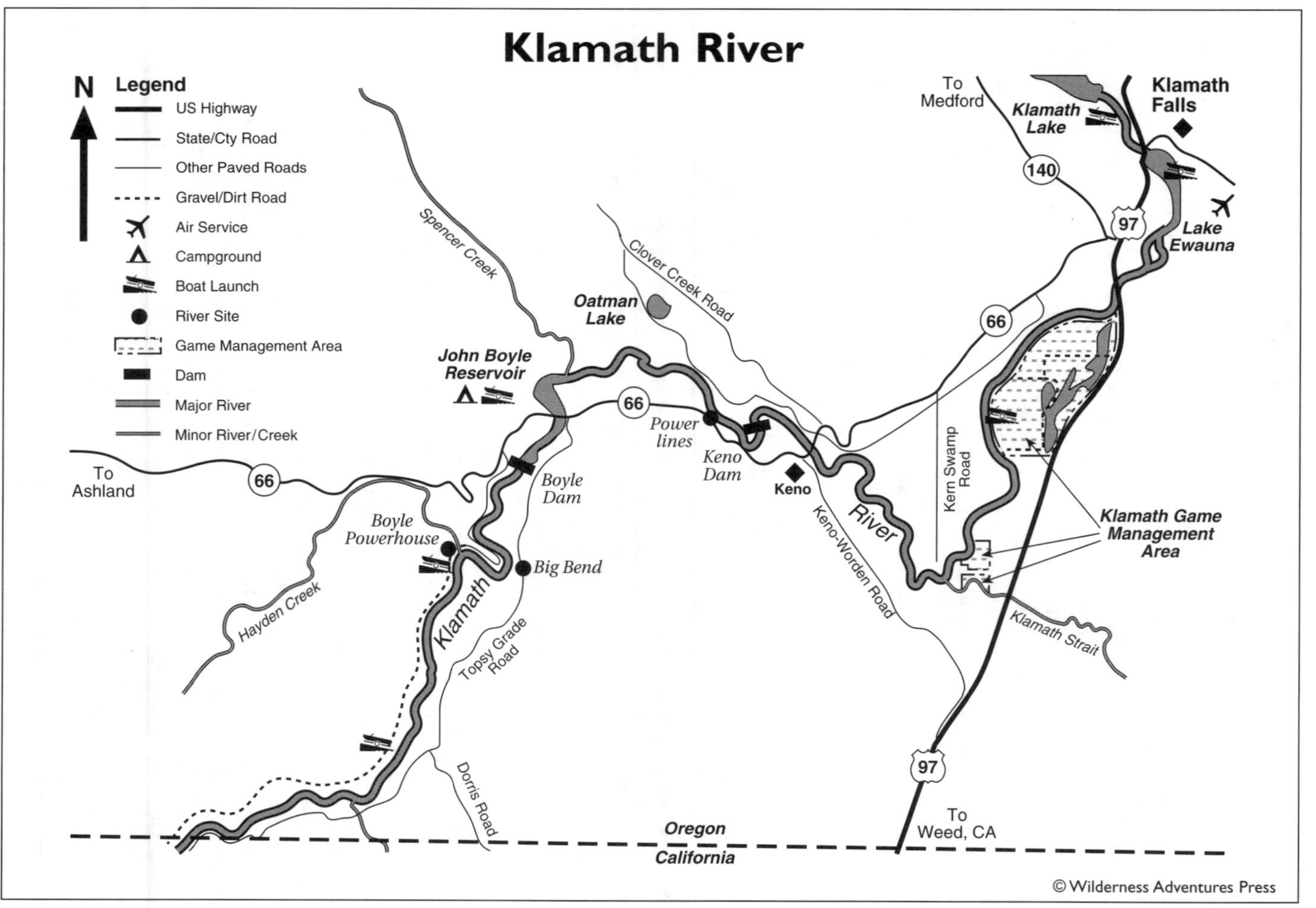
Klamath River
N
Legend
US Highway
State/Cty Road
Other Paved Roads
Gravel/Dirt Road
Air Service
Campground
Boat Launch
River Site
Game Management Area
Dam
Major River
Minor River/Creek
To Medford
Klamath Lake
Klamath Falls
140
97
Lake Ewauna
Spencer Creek
Clover Creek Road
Oatman Lake
John Boyle Reservoir
66
Power lines
Keno Dam
Keno
River
Kern Swamp Road
Klamath Game Management Area
To Ashland
Boyle Dam
Boyle Powerhouse
Big Bend
Keno-Worden Road
Klamath Strait
Hayden Creek
Klamath
Topsy Grade Road
Dorris Road
To Weed, CA
Oregon
California
© Wilderness Adventures Press

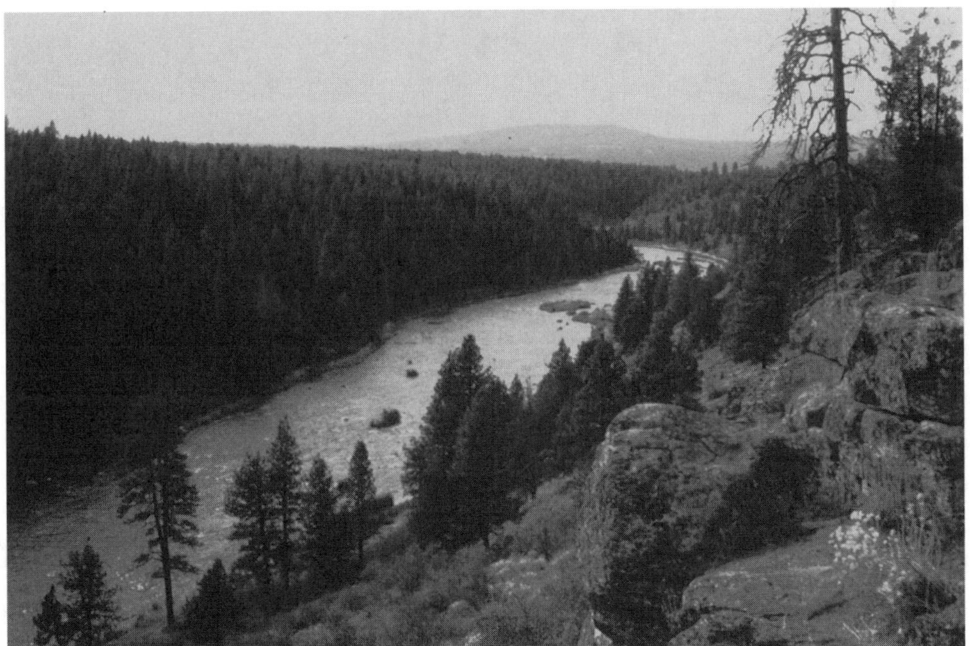

Fishing the Keno stretch of the Klamath River means climbing down to it.

Riffles do hold some fish but locals definitely concentrate on "the slot." Once you find this deep water, heavily weighted nymphs and good size indicators will help you find fish. Skip won't go to the river without a few Schlappen-buggers. He ties this like a woolly bugger—basically, it's a ton of ostrich herl wrapped with a black hackle. Using a 3X long heavy wire hook, tie a tail with 5 or 6 strands of herl, and then tie in a webby black hackle at the rear of the fly as well. Wrap the herl up the hook shank for the body and simply palmer the hackle forward, making the turns closer together where the abdomen should be. I watched Skip fish this fly one day and was treated to a lesson in local knowledge. Other flies that Skip recommends include size 10 and 12 black or brown woolly worms, equally large Prince nymphs, hare's ears, and common stonefly patterns.

Most of the action for larger fish in this stretch is going to be with weighted nymphs and large streamers. Due to the numbers of sculpin and crawdad found here, giant streamers will move the biggest rainbows. Crawdad patterns are not cheap to buy or easy to tie, but you should always take a few into the Keno stretch. Dry fly time in this upper water usually brings up smaller rainbows, and general attractor patterns, such as Wulffs and humpies, will draw strikes. Matching the hatch is not extremely important.

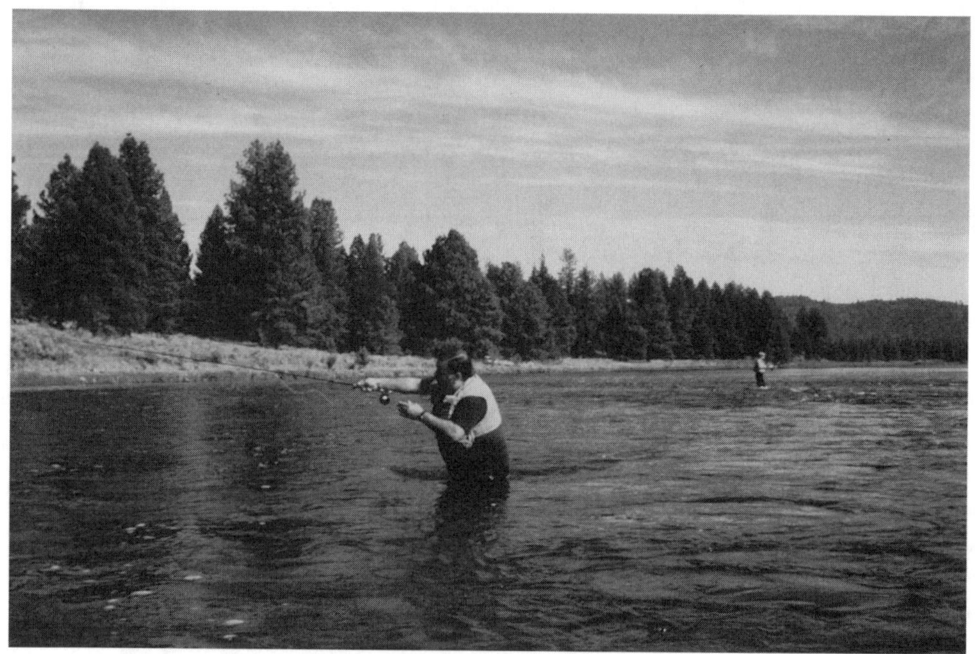

Skip Levesque works some of his favorite water on the Klamath.

To get to the river's south side, there are some steep trails accessible from Hwy 66. From J.C. Boyle Reservoir to Keno, there are several pullouts located by the powerlines that cross the canyon. You can find trails to the river from many of these pullouts. There are trails under the powerlines as well. Because these trails are primitive and on a 70-degree slope, only the hardiest of anglers should try them. It is treacherous going down the trails, and a long, hard climb back out.

There are two easier access points on the river's north side. Heading toward Klamath Falls on Hwy 66, go over the bridge from Keno, take the first left (Pucket Road) to Clover Creek Road and turn left again. Continue to Old Wagon Road and turn left. At the first and only stop sign, turn right to the metal powerlines. From here you can park and hike down to the river.

This is also a place to exercise caution. Once in the canyon, you can hike upriver or downriver. If you aren't able to hike steep canyons, you can continue past the powerlines to the top end of J.C. Boyle Reservoir. A few miles past the powerlines look for a dirt road on the left at the wooden bridge. Water releases cause constant depth changes in this area. A pool in the morning may become a riffle by lunchtime. In spite of these depth changes, this area does hold fish and provides some easier wading. Although the wading is easier, a wading staff is strongly recommended everywhere on the Keno stretch. From the reservoir an angler can scramble upriver, but the going is slow and tough.

The Klamath River at the mouth of the Keno stretch.

Some things to keep in mind about fishing the Klamath River: In summer, the upper Klamath's waters become warmer, causing the fish to be stressed. Therefore, the fishery is closed to angling from June 15 through October 1. Although the public is allowed to fish the Keno stretch, much of the land is privately owned. Please treat this area with respect and courtesy to ensure continued access. Always pack your garbage out, pick up any trash that others have left, and tread lightly on the river's banks.

It is important to know that the Keno stretch is physically demanding. It requires a commitment to get to the river, so allow yourself plenty of time for access. Always be sure to tell someone where you are when fishing alone, especially on this stretch. Be sure to carry water, even if temperatures are low. You will be rewarded for your efforts with very memorable fish.

Downriver from J.C. Boyle Reservoir, the river becomes slightly more user friendly. Fish size drops a bit but numbers increase, as do dry fly opportunities. A road paralleling this portion makes access much easier than on the upper river.

The first stretch, between J.C. Boyle Reservoir and the Boyle powerhouse, is about 6 miles. Because water is diverted to run the power plant, an angler can count on fishable flows here in most summer months. This stretch is loaded with small fish and is a great beginner and novice fishery. This is some of the least technical water in this part of the state. When water is low enough and clear enough, basic beadhead patterns will catch fish holding beneath the surface. By mid-June a good hatch of little yellow sallies is prevalent, accompanied by periodic stonefly and salmonfly hatches. Generally, hoppers will hook plenty of fish in the summer months. When in doubt, most attractor patterns from size 10 to 16 will catch fish.

Below the power plant, the river once again becomes less user friendly. Fish size increases at this point but so does the river's size. The terrain in this section is rugged, and rattlesnakes are present. Water levels here are subject to change on a daily basis.

Because the power plant operates during the day, this is a morning and evening fishery. Rafters make use of the river during the day when there are Class V rapids. Boat fishing is neither practiced nor recommended in this stretch. Should you decide to wade, use extreme caution if you fish in the morning. Know what time the power plant starts operating so that you can be out of the river before the plant releases water. People have been caught out in the middle of the river by the morning's first rush of water.

Big dries, such as hoppers and stimulators, as well as standard beadhead nymphs will work well here. Although there are quality fish to be caught in this section, it is not for everyone. The going is tough, the weather can be scorching hot, and the fishing is limited to certain hours. A wading staff is a must in this stretch.

Here again, locals who have the luxury of fishing it consistently during prime hours do quite well. This section can provide some great fishing and good numbers of sizable fish when conditions permit. Don't expect instant results your first time out.

Overall, the Klamath offers experienced anglers some great opportunities to catch trophy trout. In the right places, it also offers beginners the chance to hook up with good numbers of fish. The Klamath might not be the type of river that is considered "classic" fly water, but it's a great place to find adventure when you're ready for something new and different.

Stream Facts: Klamath River

Season

- From Keno Dam to J.C. Boyle Reservoir: Open to angling January 1 to June 15 and October 1 to December 31.
- Boyle Dam to California border: Open all year. Catch and release only from June 16 to September 30.

Special Regulations

- Keno Dam to J.C. Boyle Reservoir: One trout per day; restricted to artificial flies and lures.
- Boyle Dam to California border: One trout per day. Catch and release for trout June 16 to September 30. Restricted to artificial flies and lures. Closed from Boyle Dam to downstream side of bridge at flume crossing.

Fish

- Keno stretch has rainbows that can exceed 7 pounds.
- Boyle Dam to Boyle powerhouse has small but plentiful rainbows.
- Powerhouse to California border has rainbows in the 4- and 5-pound class.

Flows

- River flows vary on a daily basis. Call 800-547-1501 for up-to-date levels.

River Characteristics

- Most of the river is extremely rugged. Wading is always an issue—use a wading staff and acquaint yourself with the dam's operating hours. Getting to the river as well as moving up and down its banks is extremely difficult with the exception of the areas right above Boyle Reservoir and right below it. I can't say it enough: Use caution when fishing the Klamath River.

Access

- Keno stretch: Drop down into the canyon from Hwy 66 on the south side; take the secondary road after crossing the bridge from Keno to get on the south side. This is private property but open to anglers if it is not abused. Below J.C. Boyle Reservoir, Klamath River Road follows the river for long stretches.

Maps

- DeLorme *Oregon Atlas and Gazetteer*

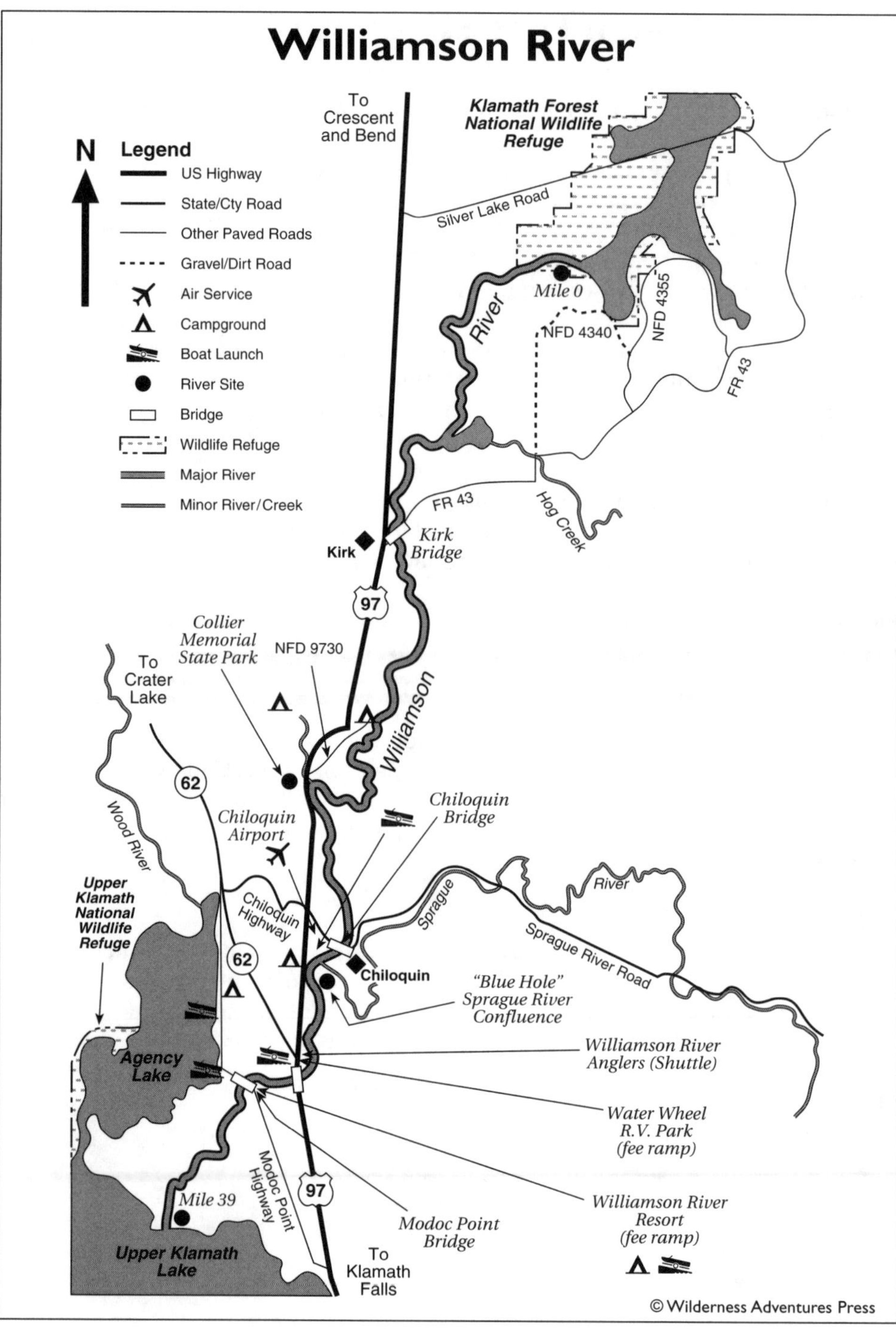
Williamson River
To Crescent and Bend
Klamath Forest National Wildlife Refuge
Legend
US Highway
State/Cty Road
Other Paved Roads
Gravel/Dirt Road
Air Service
Campground
Boat Launch
River Site
Bridge
Wildlife Refuge
Major River
Minor River/Creek
Silver Lake Road
Mile 0
River
NFD 4340
NFD 4355
FR 43
FR 43
Hog Creek
Kirk
Kirk Bridge
97
Collier Memorial State Park
NFD 9730
To Crater Lake
Williamson
62
Wood River
Chiloquin Airport
Chiloquin Bridge
Upper Klamath National Wildlife Refuge
Chiloquin Highway
Sprague
River
Sprague River Road
62
Chiloquin
"Blue Hole" Sprague River Confluence
Agency Lake
Williamson River Anglers (Shuttle)
Water Wheel R.V. Park (fee ramp)
Modoc Point Highway
97
Mile 39
Williamson River Resort (fee ramp)
Modoc Point Bridge
Upper Klamath Lake
To Klamath Falls
© Wilderness Adventures Press

WILLIAMSON RIVER

Few places in the U.S. can claim to have a river in which an 18-inch rainbow is considered small. Oregon's Williamson River is such a place, although it is not a typical trout stream, and its fish don't always act like fish found in other rivers.

The Williamson is the main tributary that fills Klamath Lake. Its source is in Winema National Forest, and it gradually gains size as it meanders toward Klamath Lake. About 12 miles from the lake, it begins to hold the sizable rainbows that have given it a national reputation.

Much of the river is lined by large parcels of private property, forcing anglers to use boats. Long-time Williamson anglers often stake out the best holding spots for trout and fish them for long periods. Fish here are very migratory, often acting more like steelhead. If ever there was a place to hire a guide, the Williamson may be it.

The Williamson River is one of the few places where 10-pound rainbows will occasionally rise to hatches. If seeing the nose of one of these monster rainbows doesn't make you throw a tailing loop, nothing will. The rise on the Williamson can be a hair-raising event.

When insects aren't present, an angler may be forced to fish more deeply with heavy sinktips and large flies. As Judy Carothers of Williamson River Anglers stresses, "The Williamson is never a place where someone should come to learn how to flyfish. The size of the tackle and the trout can be overwhelming. It is also a place where the right gear is a necessity. We see all kinds of people who come here thinking this is like every other trout stream they have fished, only to find out that their gear is useless here."

Judy is right in saying that a novice angler shouldn't come to the Williamson to learn. First, it is very difficult to fish from a boat unless basic skills have been mastered. Add sinking lines and sizable flies, and the beginning angler will have a very disappointing experience. A frustrating experience is no way to get someone hooked on flyfishing, regardless of the size of the fish. A 12-pound rainbow is not that exciting when you've hooked yourself six times trying to catch it. It's not a bad idea to let inexperienced anglers catch plenty of small fish as they learn. That way, when they do finally come to the Williamson to catch that fish of a lifetime, they can truly appreciate its size.

As far as gear is concerned, no one should be fishing this river with anything less than a 5- or 6-weight. When casting heavy lines and flies, there should be enough backbone in the rod to play the fish. This will benefit both the angler and the fish. Many of Williamson's leviathan fish come upriver from Klamath Lake seeking cooler, clearer water. In effect, stress has pushed them into the river, and any additional stress from anglers using improper tackle is a punishment they don't deserve.

There is a decent population of resident fish in the Williamson River, but the presence of many of the biggest fish is due to conditions in Klamath Lake. The migration of Williamson River rainbows is thought to be caused by the combination of spawning urges as well as the need to relieve the stress caused by warming waters in Klamath Lake.

Fish ready to spawn are slowly drawn upriver much the way they are in other bodies of water. On the Williamson, however, it is believed that the trout go upriver in the fall, hold throughout the winter, and then spawn, much like steelhead. Rainbow trout found here are unique and are thought to be a landlocked strain of the original Klamath River steelhead. Fish leave the lake because of their need for cool, clean water and shallow gravel.

Williamson trout meander up the river in a pre-spawn mode, eating as they go. Whether or not these fish are actually staging months before the spawn remains a mystery. Regardless, they are in the system available to the flyfisher.

Other fish in Klamath Lake stay in the lake until spring and are consequently more ripe when they enter the river. They head upriver at a faster pace than the former group. After spawning, fish are preoccupied with regaining fat stores depleted during mating. While brown and brook trout do inhabit the river, they are a small percentage of the catch.

The Williamson season begins on the last Saturday in May. June fishing offers sporadic hatches but also provides a good opportunity to use heavier tippets. This may be an angler's best chance to wrangle one of the Williamson's biggest fish without breaking it off.

As summer approaches in southwest Oregon, Klamath Lake's shallow waters begin to warm to a level uncomfortable for trout, and they begin to seek refuge elsewhere. Some head to springs in the lake and other tributaries, but many enter the Williamson River. Once in the river they begin to act like typical river fish, dining on the river's different fare.

Fish that head up the Williamson River are treated to a variety of insects. Starting around the first week of July, one of the best hatches seen on the river is the Hexagenia. Avid Oregon flyfisher and tier Bob Quigley tells me that this giant mayfly brings up the biggest fish in the system. It is an evening hatch continuing into the darkness of night. In a good year, the hatch may last four to six weeks with levels of intensity varying. Quigley says; "I've seen this Hex as early as the third week in June and sporadically until the end of the season. It won't happen every night, but given the right weather conditions, it is always possible to see it during the season."

Note that, even though the hatch may last well into the night, an angler is only allowed to fish for one hour after sunset. To prevent a violation during this event, I suggest checking local papers for the time of sunset and then setting a wristwatch alarm accordingly.

As summer progresses anglers will encounter more hatches. There are good amounts of caddis, with the October caddis being the biggest and bringing up good sized fish. Pale morning duns, pale evening duns, and callibaetis make up the bulk of frequently seen mayflies. Hoppers are present and can move fish to a well-placed imitation. Tricos and midges are also present, and although small, always tend to

Mike Witthar hefts a fair-sized Williamson River rainbow taken on a Turck's Tarantula.

hatch in good enough numbers to bring up fish. Big fish eating these tiny flies are often hooked but not often landed.

The Williamson is a bug factory and therefore a good draw for hungry trout. To catch these fish, anglers use a variety of rods and lines. Commonly, local fly anglers have floating lines rigged on 5- and 6-weight rods, as well as 6- and 7-weight rods rigged with intermediate sinking lines or heavier for certain runs. Local guides have a huge advantage on this river, since they have learned to match gear and techniques to particular runs and holes in every stretch. Dry flies and suspended nymphs, fished with strike indicators, are used with floating lines. Big streamers and nymphs are generally fished down and across with sinking lines. Fish commonly strike on the drift as the fly swings but will also smash a fly on the retrieve as well. Try hand twists and erratic stripping techniques to draw strikes on the retrieve.

Early in the season 12-foot leaders tapered to 4X and 5X will handle most nymphing situations, and 12-foot leaders from 4X to 6X will take care of the dries. By late summer, water levels have dropped and fish have been exposed to a lot of angling pressure. Leaders as long as 15 to 18 feet may have to be used and may need to be tapered down to 7X.

Flyfishing on the Williamson is at its peak in August, September, and the first part of October. Many fish are in the system, and hatches are most frequent during this time. During these months, there can be many anglers on the river, so make a point of being courteous during these less than solitary days on the water. By the end of October, anglers become scarce as the first signs of winter approach.

Access is problematic on the Williamson. There are only a few spots in which an angler can wade and only a few boat ramps for launching and retrieval. At Collier Memorial State Park off Hwy 97, an angler can walk and wade some productive water. Small craft can be launched here, but angling from a floating device is not allowed.

As far as take-out access, be aware that the only decent spots are private. There is a public take-out at Chiloquin, but it isn't very good. Inquire at Williamson River Anglers for current take-out information. It is always wise to have your put-in and take-outs prearranged when floating the Williamson.

Right below the town of Chiloquin, boats can be launched for the most popular float on the river. Boaters leave here and are quickly over the "Blue Hole," where the Sprague River joins the Williamson. From here the river is bigger and fishes very well from a boat. Fly anglers drift this stretch to just below the Hwy 97 bridge and pay a small fee to take out at the Water Wheel RV Park. There is also a pay-to-walk stretch of river available at the Water Wheel. Again, be sure to prearrange shuttle service and take-outs. By late summer, this popular stretch flows and acts much like a spring creek and can be made a whole day float or a 4-hour drift.

From Hwy 97, a few anglers float the short stretch down to the Williamson River Resort, which requires a row through some slack water. This spot also requires a fee. There is an area to fish well above Collier State Park, but it is small and the fishing can be hard to find at times. If you feel like exploring, talk to Judy and Steve Carothers at Williamson River Anglers.

The Williamson River's trout are the basis for its national reputation. It contains some of the biggest rainbows in the state, and as far as rivers go, some of the biggest rainbows in the Lower 48.

Stream Facts: Williamson River

Seasons
- From the mouth to Kirk Bridge: Open the last Saturday in May through October 31.
- Kirk Bridge to headwaters: April 25 to October 31.

Special Regulations
- Mouth to Modoc Point Road Bridge: Limit is 1 trout per day.
- Modoc Point Road Bridge to Chiloquin Bridge: 1 trout per day from last Saturday in May to July 31. Catch and release from August 1 to October 31. Restricted to artificial flies and lures. No angling from motor-propelled craft while motor is operating.
- Chiloquin Bridge to Kirk Bridge: 1 trout per day from the last Saturday in May to July 31. No limit on size or number of brook trout. Catch and release and restricted to artificial flies and lures August 1 to October 31. No angling from a floating device that supports the angler.
- Kirk Bridge to Headwaters: Two trout per day except no limit on size or number of brook trout. Restricted to artificial flies and lures. No angling from a floating device that supports the angler.

Trout
- Rainbows dominate the system. Some are resident and some are visitors from Klamath Lake; 10-pound fish are not uncommon, and a few 15-pound fish are caught every season.
- Browns and brook trout are occasionally in the catch.

River Characteristics
- The Williamson is mostly a boating river with some bank access. It acts and feels much like a spring creek in the summer months. Good insect populations keep fish and fisherman busy. When fish aren't biting and water levels are up, anglers bring out their sinktips and streamers to entice trout. This is a good river to make use of a guide and also provides outstanding scenery, so don't forget your camera.

Fishing Access
- Access is very limited with most ramps and wading available on a fee basis, but most people who fish the Williamson will tell you it's worth it. Williamson River Anglers is a good resource for access information and shuttles.

Maps
- DeLorme *Oregon Atlas and Gazetteer*

WILLIAMSON RIVER MAJOR HATCHES

Insect	J	F	M	A	M	J	J	A	S	O	N	D	Time	Flies
Pale Morning Dun					■	■							Morning	PMD Thorax, PMD Cripple, PMD Spinner, PMD Parachute #16
Pale Evening Dun						■							Evening	PMD Thorax, Quill Body PED, PED Spinner #16
Green Drake					■	■							PM	Green Drake Cripple, Extended Body, Hairwing Drake, Epoxyback Green Drake Nymph #10-12
Black Drake					■	■	■	■					Afternoon Evening	Hairwing Drake, Quigley Cripple #10-12
Hexagenia						■	■						Evening Dark	Paradrake, Grizzly Wulff with Yellow Floss Body, Michigan Caddis, Yellow May Hatch Matcher, Comparadun #4-8
Blue-winged Olive									■	■			PM	Sparkle Dun, Parachute Adams, Gulper Special #16-18
Callibaetis								■	■				PM	Quigley Cripple, Adams, Ostrich Nymph, Floating Nymph, Parachute Adams #16-18
Brown Quill									■	■			PM	Rusty Spinner, Mahogany Dun #16-20
Trico							■	■	■	■			Morning	Stalcup CDC Trico, Zing-wing Spent Trico, CDC Spent Trico, Parachute Trico #20-24

Hatch Chart Prepared by Judy Carothers

WILLIAMSON RIVER MAJOR HATCHES (cont.)

Insect	J	F	M	A	M	J	J	A	S	O	N	D	Time	Flies
October Caddis													Evening	Royal Stimulator, Orange Stimulator, Orange Soft Hackles #6-8
Caddis													Morning Evening	Elk Hair Caddis, Hemingway Caddis, Peacock Caddis #16-18
Midges													Evening	Sly's Midge, Griffith's Gnat, Midge Pupa #14-18
Ants													All day	Parachute Ant, Thorax Ant, Flying Ant #14-16
Grasshoppers													PM	Dave's Hopper, Turck's Tarantula, Parachute Hopper, #8-12
Streamers (most important)													All Day	Matuka's, Marabou Muddlers, Woolly Buggers, Articulated Leeches, Zonkers, Bunny Leeches, Muddlers, Mohair Leeches #6-14

Hatch Chart Prepared by Judy Carothers

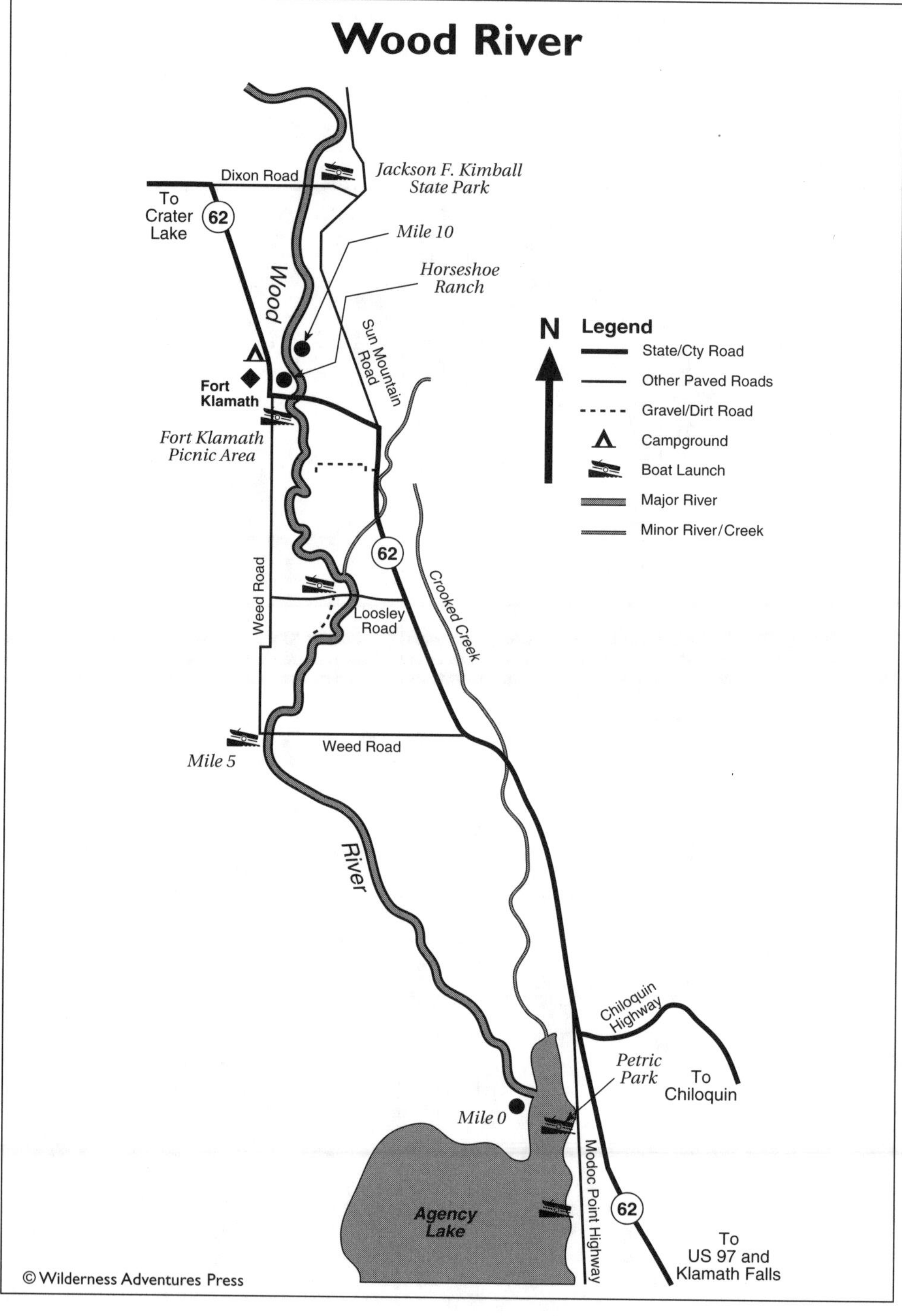
Wood River
Jackson F. Kimball State Park
Dixon Road
To Crater Lake
62
Mile 10
Horseshoe Ranch
Wood
Sun Mountain Road
Fort Klamath
Fort Klamath Picnic Area
N
Legend
State/Cty Road
Other Paved Roads
Gravel/Dirt Road
Campground
Boat Launch
Major River
Minor River/Creek
62
Weed Road
Loosley Road
Crooked Creek
Weed Road
Mile 5
River
Chiloquin Highway
Petric Park
To Chiloquin
Mile 0
Modoc Point Highway
Agency Lake
62
To US 97 and Klamath Falls
© Wilderness Adventures Press

Wood River

The Wood River is much like the Williamson. It is a smaller river but equally big fish occasionally move into it. It is a twisting and turning spring creek, supporting a decent brown trout population as well as hosting moving Agency and Klamath Lakes rainbows.

Much of the land along the river is private property, which limits the amount of access for floating. While there are floatable stretches, the current can create problems in some spots. With few boat ramps, planning becomes very important on this river. Keep in mind that it can be hard to control hand-carried individual craft. You could ruin the fishing for a bank angler if you are not in control of your craft. If you decide to float the Wood River, take a thorough look at the river and its access points.

Walking and wading the banks is really the best way to fish the Wood River. Search the eddies and cutbanks with nymphs and streamers or look for risers during the frequent hatches. Most of the bank access requires permission as well as a fee. For access to long stretches of the river and for a reasonable rod fee, contact the Horseshoe Ranch at 541-381-2297. They have an exceptional lodge and about 6 miles of bank access. Since access is based on bookings, always call ahead.

Some limited public access and small craft launch sites are available at Kimball State Park and the Fort Klamath Picnic Area. Floating this upper section can be very tight and tricky. Access is also available at Loosely Road crossing, Weed Road crossing, and Petric Park on Agency Lake, which can be used as a take-out.

The Wood River can be fished effectively with 5- and 6-weight rods, while floating lines and short sinktips cover most situations. Long leaders tapered from 4X to 7X are common. Insect life is much like the Williamson, with two exceptions: there is no Hex hatch and there is much more hopper activity.

Overall, the Wood is a superb fishery once you overcome access issues. If your time is limited, use a guide or pay the rod fee at Horseshoe Ranch. If you choose to float, be courteous and acquaint yourself with Oregon's trespass laws. If you have doubts about what you're doing, then you're probably trespassing. Consult Judy and Steve Carothers at Williamson River Anglers for the most current Wood River information.

WOOD RIVER MAJOR HATCHES

Insect	J	F	M	A	M	J	J	A	S	O	N	D	Time	Flies
Pale Morning Dun													Morning	PMD Thorax, PMD Cripple, PMD Spinner, PMD Parachute #16
Green Drakes													PM	Hairwing Drake, Green Drake Cripple, Extended Body Drake, Epoxyback Green Drake Nymph #10-12
Callibaetis													PM	Quigley Cripple, Adams Ostrich Nymph, Floating Nymph, Parachute Adams #16-18
Brown Quill													PM	Rusty Spinner, Mahogany Dun #16-20
Caddis													Morning Evening	Elk Hair Caddis, Hemingway Caddis, Peacock Caddis #16-18
October Caddis													PM Evening	Royal Stimulator, Orange Stimulator, Orange Soft Hackle #6-8
Grasshoppers													PM Evening	Dave's Hopper, Turck's Tarantula, Parachute Hopper #8-12
Ants													All day	Parachute Ant, Flying Ant, Thorax Ant #14-16

Hatch Chart Prepared by Judy Carothers

The Wood River is a beautiful spring creek.

WILD BILLY LAKE

Wild Billy Lake is located 45 miles east of Chiloquin. It is a fee fishery restricted to fly angling with small barbless hooks and maintained as a catch-and-release fishery. Anglers will find three trout opportunities here: Donaldson trout up to 12 pounds, Kamloops trout that grow to 10 pounds, and to ensure that there are plenty of hook-ups, there are stocked Mt. Lassen rainbows, one-third of which grow to over 5 pounds.

The lake is about 200 acres, has an average depth of 12 feet with the deepest spot near 21 feet, and no motors are allowed. A few prams are kept at the lake for angler use; however, you may want to take a float tube or other device along in case all the prams are being used. Pressure on the lake is limited to a maximum of 24 man-days a week, which keeps the fish strong and catchable. Plan on spending up to $150 per rod on Wild Billy or call 541-747-5595 for information on group rates.

Take a variety of stillwater patterns to Wild Billy. There are enormous populations of Chironomids, leeches, and fathead minnows. Damselflies, dragonflies, and callibaetis mayflies also figure into the equation at Wild Billy. Fathead minnows really keep the fish large and strong in the lake and are good to keep in mind if the fishing is slow or insects are scarce. Standard stillwater set-ups for trout will work here. Sinking lines and stout leaders are keys to hooking and landing the lake's largest fish.

Take the Sprague River Road east from Chiloquin and follow the Sprague for approximately 45 miles; then turn onto Ivory Pine Road. The lake is about a mile from the intersection. There are a couple of campsites and picnic areas at the lake, but it has no other improvements. Call well in advance to fish Wild Billy.

SOUTH CENTRAL HUB CITY
Klamath Falls, Oregon

Elevation–4,105 • Population–18,765

ACCOMMODATIONS

Cimmarron Motor Inn, 3060 South 6th Street / 800-742-2648 / Pets OK / $
Best Western Klamath Inn, 4061 South 6th Street / 800-528-1234 / Pets OK / $$
Quality Inn and Suites, 100 Main Street / 800-732-2025 / No pets / $$
Red Lion Inn Klamath Falls, 3612 South 6th Street / 541-882-8864 / No pets / $$$
Best Western Olympic Inn, 2627 South 6th Street / 800-600-9665 / No pets / $$$

CAMPGROUNDS

KOA Kampgrounds of Klamath Falls, 3435 Shasta Way / 541-884-4644

RESTAURANTS

Mollies, 3817 Hwy 97 North / Open 24 hours / 541-882-9591
Klamath Grill, 715 Main / Breakfast and lunch / 541-882-1427
Sergio's, 327 Main / Mexican / 541-883-8454
Diamond Grill, 4480 South 6th / 541-884-0743
Steak Country Restaurant, 205 Main / 541-883-3901

FLY SHOPS AND SPORTING GOODS

Williamson River Anglers, Jct. Hwy 97 and 62 / Licenses / 541-783-2677
Big "R," 6225 South 6th Street / Licenses / 541-882-5548

HOSPITALS

Merle West Medical Center, 2865 Dagget Street / 541-882-6311

AIRPORT

City of Klamath Falls International Airport, 6801 Rand Way / 541-883-5372
Horizon Air / 800-547-9308
United Express / 800-241-6522

AUTO RENTAL

Budget Rent-A-Car, 6819 Rand Way (at airport) / 541-885-5421
Hertz Rent-A-Car, 6815 Rand Way (at airport) / 541-882-0220
Avis Rent-A-Car, 6817 Rand Way (at airport) / 541-882-7232

AUTO REPAIR

Les Schwab Tire Center, 5757 South 6th Street / 541-882-6623
Ace Towing and Auto Repair, 501 South Broad Street / 541-884-9388

FOR MORE INFORMATION

Klamath County Department of Tourism
1451 Main Street
P.O. Box 1867
Klamath Falls, OR 97601
800-445-6728 or 541-884-0666

Klamath Falls Chamber of Commerce
701 Plum Avenue
Klamath Falls, OR 97601
541-884-5193

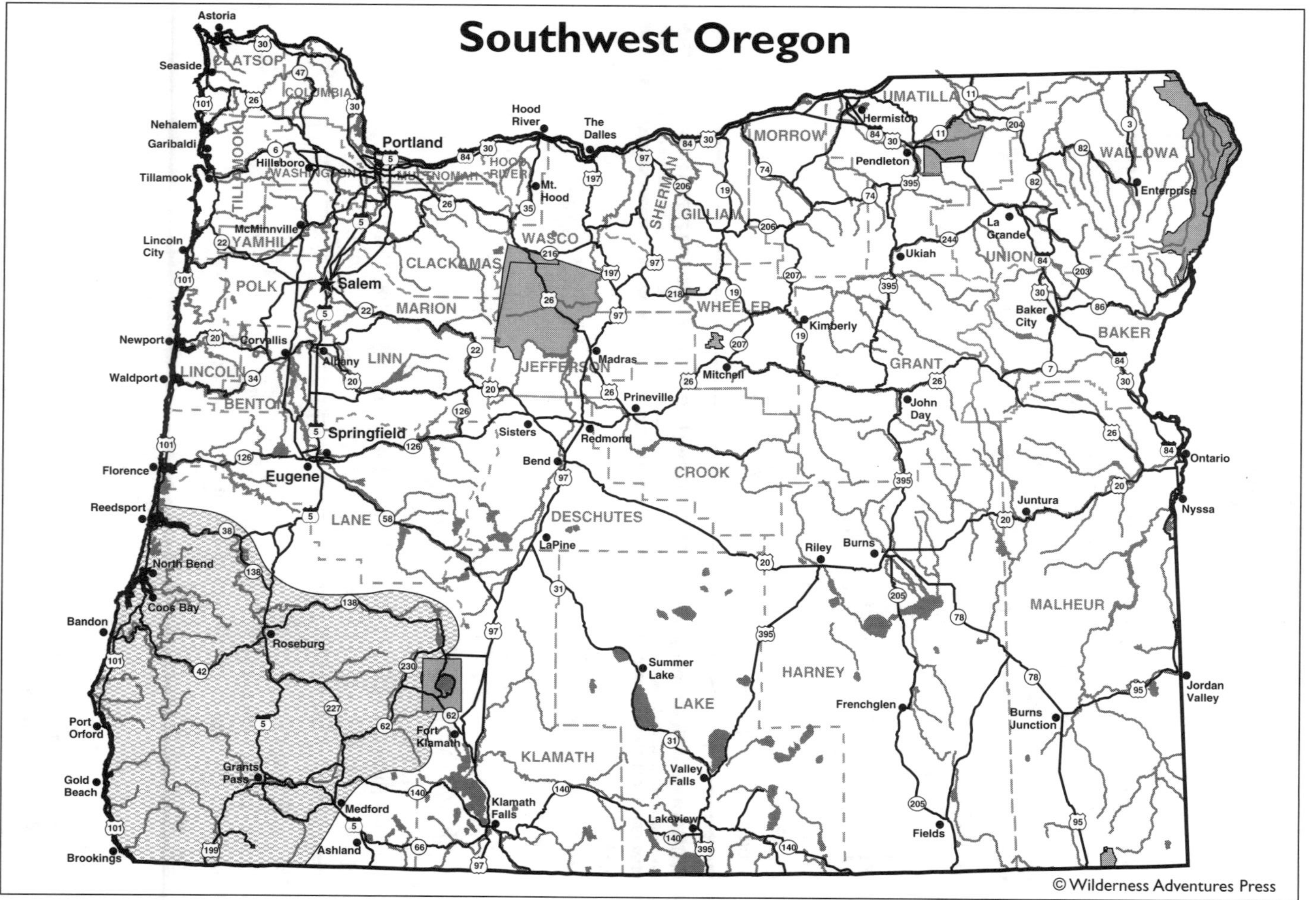
Southwest Oregon
Astoria
Seaside
Nehalem
Garibaldi
Tillamook
Lincoln City
Newport
Waldport
Florence
Reedsport
North Bend
Coos Bay
Bandon
Port Orford
Gold Beach
Brookings
Hillsboro
McMinnville
Portland
Salem
Albany
Corvallis
Eugene
Springfield
Roseburg
Grants Pass
Medford
Ashland
Hood River
Mt. Hood
The Dalles
Madras
Prineville
Redmond
Sisters
Bend
LaPine
Fort Klamath
Klamath Falls
Summer Lake
Valley Falls
Lakeview
Mitchell
Kimberly
John Day
Ukiah
Pendleton
Hermiston
La Grande
Baker City
Enterprise
Ontario
Nyssa
Juntura
Burns
Riley
Frenchglen
Fields
Burns Junction
Jordan Valley
CLATSOP
COLUMBIA
TILLAMOOK
WASHINGTON
YAMHILL
POLK
LINCOLN
BENTON
LINN
MARION
CLACKAMAS
MULTNOMAH
HOOD RIVER
WASCO
JEFFERSON
SHERMAN
GILLIAM
MORROW
UMATILLA
UNION
WALLOWA
BAKER
GRANT
WHEELER
CROOK
DESCHUTES
LANE
KLAMATH
LAKE
HARNEY
MALHEUR
© Wilderness Adventures Press

Southwest Oregon

This may be the shortest chapter in this book, but this region contains two of the best steelhead streams in the nation. Both the North Umpqua and the Rogue River are storied waters. They have been written about and photographed for much longer than most of us have been alive. Classic runs of fish coupled with breathtaking scenery await the fly angler in southwest Oregon.

Presidents, authors, and unknown fish-heads have been casting flies to bright steelies for generations. A lot of anglers know about these rivers, and great steps have been taken to ensure the quality of the fishing. This means that even though they are crowded at times, things generally go pretty smoothly when you're on the water. Like anyplace else, there are peak times when the river is crowded and quieter times when an angler can cast a line with nobody else in sight.

These are big rivers, where the screaming of your reel will be muffled by rushing waters and the only thing around as you lift a brilliantly colored steelhead from the water is ancient rainforest.

These rivers will test both your skills and patience while giving you a glimpse of something natural and far removed from daily life. Steelhead don't care who won the game or whether your stock made money this week—they only care about completing a cycle that has been taking place as long as the surrounding forests have stood. Luckily for us, we have an opportunity to join them in southwest Oregon and perhaps find ourselves not caring about much besides a bright-sided, hard-fighting fish.

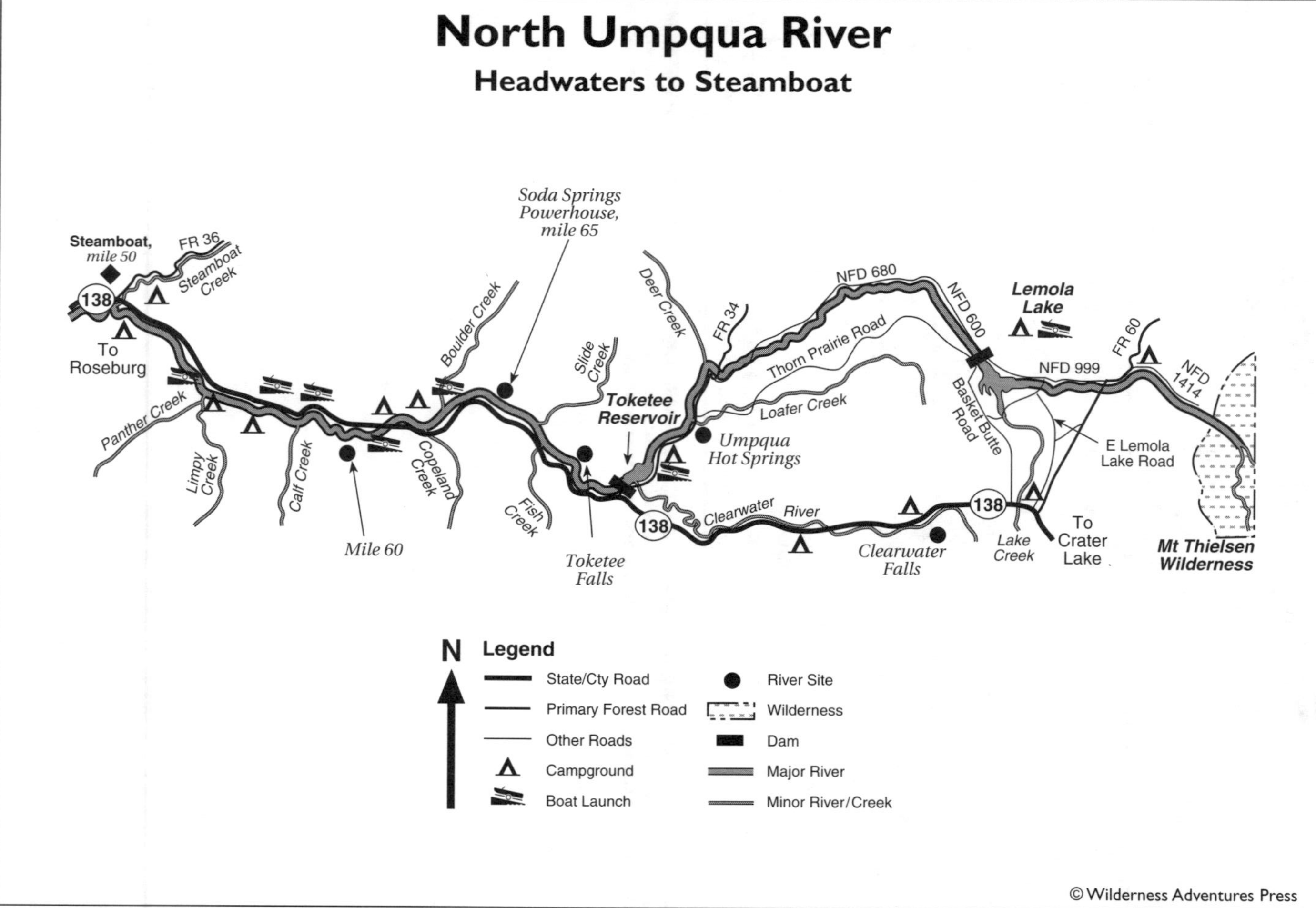
North Umpqua River
Headwaters to Steamboat
Steamboat, mile 50
FR 36
Steamboat Creek
138
To Roseburg
Panther Creek
Limpy Creek
Calf Creek
Mile 60
Copeland Creek
Boulder Creek
Soda Springs Powerhouse, mile 65
Slide Creek
Fish Creek
Toketee Falls
Toketee Reservoir
Deer Creek
FR 34
138
Umpqua Hot Springs
Loafer Creek
Thorn Prairie Road
NFD 680
NFD 600
Clearwater River
Clearwater Falls
Basket Butte Road
Lemola Lake
NFD 999
FR 60
NFD 1414
E Lemola Lake Road
138
Lake Creek
To Crater Lake
Mt Thielsen Wilderness
N
Legend
State/Cty Road
Primary Forest Road
Other Roads
Campground
Boat Launch
River Site
Wilderness
Dam
Major River
Minor River/Creek
© Wilderness Adventures Press

North Umpqua River

Emerald waters pool, then cascade down through a remaining slice of Oregon rainforest. In the cool depths of the river, a silver steelhead hen pulls alongside another fish of equal size that is slightly more tinted with a rose-colored stripe. Seconds later, they are joined by two others.

The sun begins to rise into blue summer skies, taking the chill out of the morning air. An enormous boulder, just left of center stream, offers a big shadow. The fish pull close together and begin moving toward the boulder. The group moves, but as I watch them from my perch 12 feet up a tree, I can detect no individual movements. The midriver boulder just seems to suck them in. In the distance I hear a truck door close, so I climb down the tree to the river's edge.

Surprisingly, from where I've chosen to cast, I can still see a shadow within the shadow. I know that this is the group I saw from the tree. I rhythmically strip line off my reel and cast well above them. Not trusting the length of the cast, I mend three feet of line up and out of the rod tip. As the line tightens with the current and swings across river, I stare intensely into the water. The fly swings below me and sits. I lift the rod and let out the breath I've been unconsciously holding. Just as my line lifts from the water, I see a bright flash and a silver streak back to the boulder. Although I feel nothing hit the fly, I cannot stop smiling as I begin to cast again.

Even as you read this, a historic run of steelhead trout is somewhere in its yearly cycle on the North Umpqua River. It is a perfect match of fish and fly water. The nature of the river is such that steelhead can often be easy targets but are also afforded the opportunity to be impossible targets. The North Umpqua's banks are a national treasure, and those who come to fish should do their very best to make sure it remains this way.

Open to angling the entire year, there are significant stretches that are only open to fly angling. Summer steelhead, averaging around 7 to 8 pounds, enter the river in June and are fished productively with fly gear through the end of October. During the winter run in February and March, steelhead are much smaller in number but bigger in size, averaging 10 to 12 pounds. My friend, T.R. McCrystal, is among those who often fish the North Umpqua well after the prime season. It takes a lot of skill and steelhead savvy to find a rare fish after prime time, but T.R. and a few others seem to get it done just fine.

For the rest of us, summer offers prime water and the chance to use classic techniques. Down and across, tight line presentations are standard on the North Umpqua. Legally, you can use strike indicators and such, but this is really frowned upon by local anglers and angling groups. On the fly-only stretch of river, strict etiquette is observed. By familiarizing yourself with this etiquette, you will find your experience more fulfilling and pleasant. If you have doubts, ask a fellow angler or stop by the Steamboat Inn for advice. The whole world of fishing would be a better place if even a few of these rules of etiquette were universally adopted.

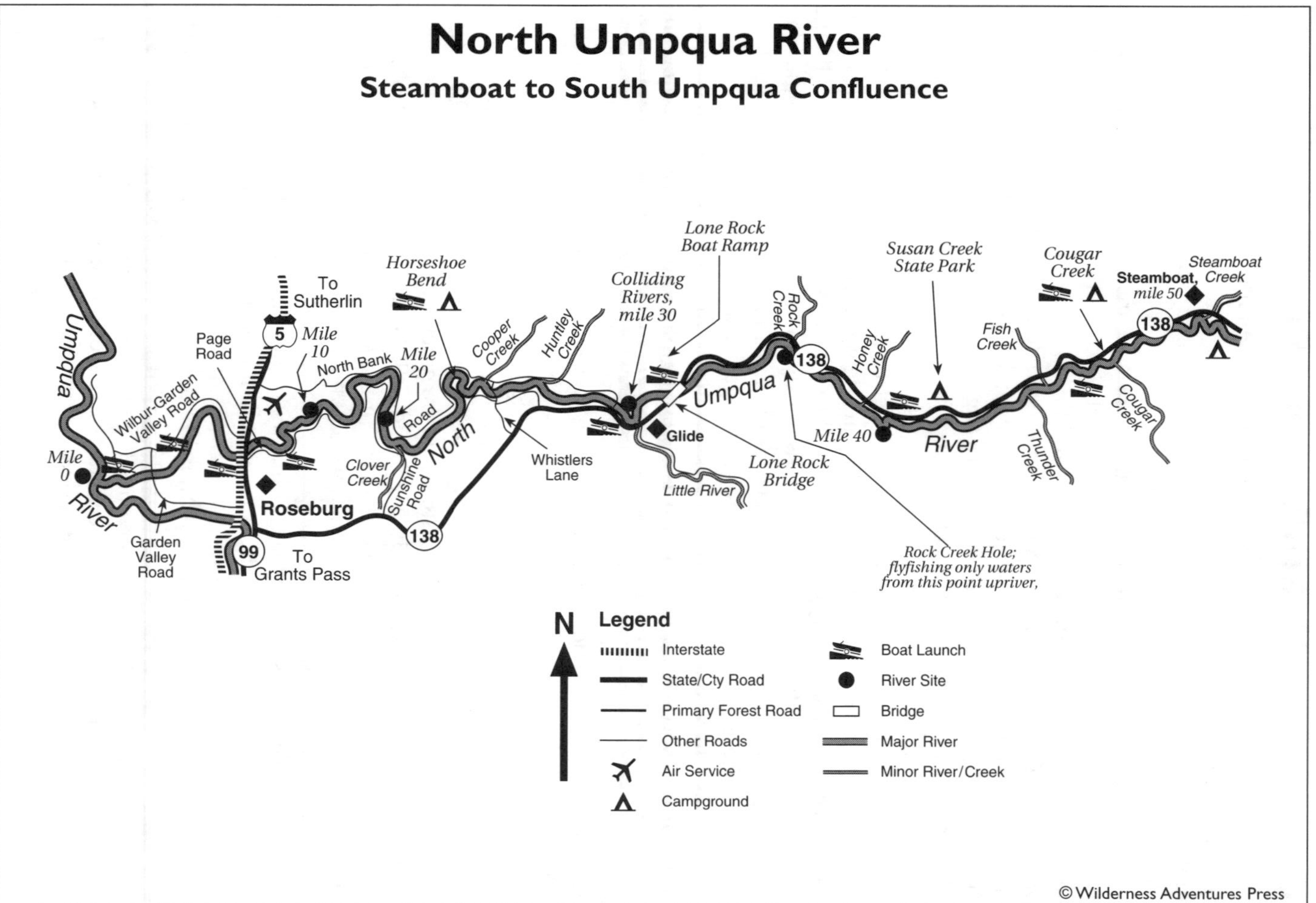
North Umpqua River
Steamboat to South Umpqua Confluence
Lone Rock Boat Ramp
Susan Creek State Park
Cougar Creek
Steamboat Creek
Steamboat, mile 50
Horseshoe Bend
Colliding Rivers, mile 30
To Sutherlin
5
Mile 10
Page Road
North Bank
Mile 20
Cooper Creek
Huntley Creek
Rock Creek
138
Honey Creek
Fish Creek
138
Umpqua
Wilbur-Garden Valley Road
Umpqua
Road
North
Glide
Mile 40
River
Mile 0
Clover Creek
Whistlers Lane
Lone Rock Bridge
Thunder Creek
Cougar Creek
River
Roseburg
Sunshine Road
Little River
Garden Valley Road
99
To Grants Pass
138
Rock Creek Hole; flyfishing only waters from this point upriver,
N
Legend
Interstate
State/Cty Road
Primary Forest Road
Other Roads
Air Service
Campground
Boat Launch
River Site
Bridge
Major River
Minor River/Creek
© Wilderness Adventures Press

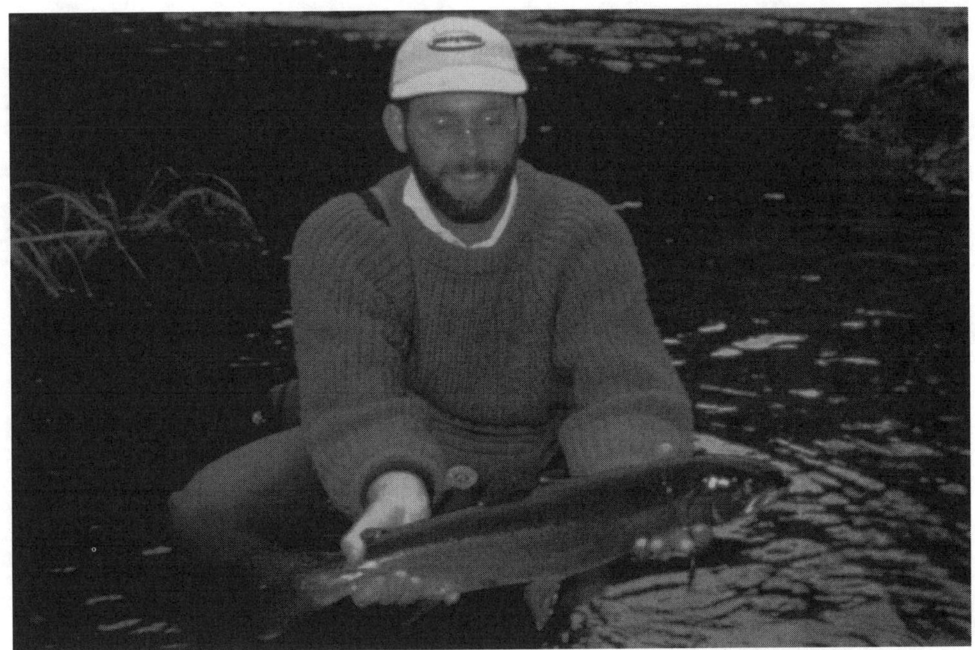

T.R. McCrystal holds a wild North Umpqua steelhead.

On the North Umpqua, fly anglers predominantly use a greased line technique in which the fly is presented above the fish and allowed to sink. As the line tightens, anglers then try to move the fly in front of the fish or to a likely holding spot. North Umpqua flyfishers also use a similar down-and-across technique with skated dry flies instead of wet flies.

Work your way down a run, covering all the likely holding areas—the places in which fish stop to rest or seek shelter from bright sunlight. While each person's pace varies, it is considerate to work through a run in a timely fashion. While it is generally acceptable to step in well upstream from another angler, you should never step in downstream.

Standard North Umpqua tackle consists of 9-foot rods all the way up to spey rod lengths, and common rod weights are 7, 8, and 9. Both single-handed and two-handed rods have their uses on the North Umpqua, and many anglers carry both. Ten-foot leaders tapered from 8 to 10 pounds are commonly used. More length may be needed in deeper slots.

Many flies, both traditional and nontraditional, are productive here. Traditional patterns include green-butted skunk, purple perils, and bombers, while less traditional flies may include Kaufmann's rubberlegged stoneflies, lead-headed leeches, and sofa pillows. And, of course, there are many local patterns as well as the ever-present "hot" fly. All can be found at Joe Howell's Blue Heron Fly Shop in Idleyld Park on State Hwy 138, 3 miles east of Glide, and at the Steamboat Inn, which is approximately 13 miles east of Glide on State Hwy 138.

Due to this river's physical aspects, waders and cleated boots are just about a necessity for flyfishers. There is a direct correlation between fishing success and having the right equipment for the stream. If you have to concentrate on your balance and foot placement, you won't have the patience and concentration that are necessary to fish successfully.

Access is no problem between the town of Glide all the way upriver to the Soda Springs powerhouse, which is the end of the fishing section. Almost every hole and bucket has been named, and they are too numerous to mention here. You will find one run after another in this section. With so many holding spots available, fishing can be difficult. If there was only one water type it would be easy, but different fish hold in different types of water depending on where they are in the system.

From Glide, State Hwy 138 follows the river for nearly 45 productive miles, most of which is fly-only water. From about 5 miles east of Glide to the Soda Springs powerhouse, the river is flyfishing only upstream from the Rock Creek confluence. Steamboat Creek joins the North Umpqua in the middle of the fly-only section, and this is where you will find the Steamboat Inn. The Inn offers great lodging and meals as well as basic fly supplies. It also sits next to what is called "The Camp Water." Steelhead can be found here in great numbers before pulling up into Steamboat Creek or continuing on upriver.

Steamboat Creek and all other tributaries from the mouth of Soda Springs are off limits to all fishing. These waters serve as major spawning grounds.

The river has a mix of both hatchery and wild steelhead, and if you want to keep any fish, you should check the special regulations for this area. No wild fish can be kept above Rock Creek. Note that almost all steelhead caught above Steamboat Creek are wild.

If you want to extend your fishing season, the river also has a decent winter run of steelhead. Even though the water levels can be higher in winter, die-hard flyfishers probe the depths with sinktips when water color is good. Sinktips are used to swing the fly deeper than a dry line will allow. During summer a dry line is all you need, but it's wise to carry both for winter fishing. Technique is essentially the same as in the summer, but river levels can make fishing more physically demanding. Winter-run steelhead are less numerous than summer-run fish in the North Umpqua.

While the most popular fishing takes place on the fly-only water, there is a popular float from Lone Rock boat ramp above Glide to the Colliding Rivers boat ramp and on down. Boats are just about the only way to get to this section's banks. If you gain access by boat, you will find great spots to get out and fish some nice holding water.

McCrystal pointed out something interesting to me, "The boat fishery starting at Lone Rock and the fly-only stretch near Rock Creek are separated by a 5-mile piece of water that is the most overlooked stretch on the North Umpqua. The access is

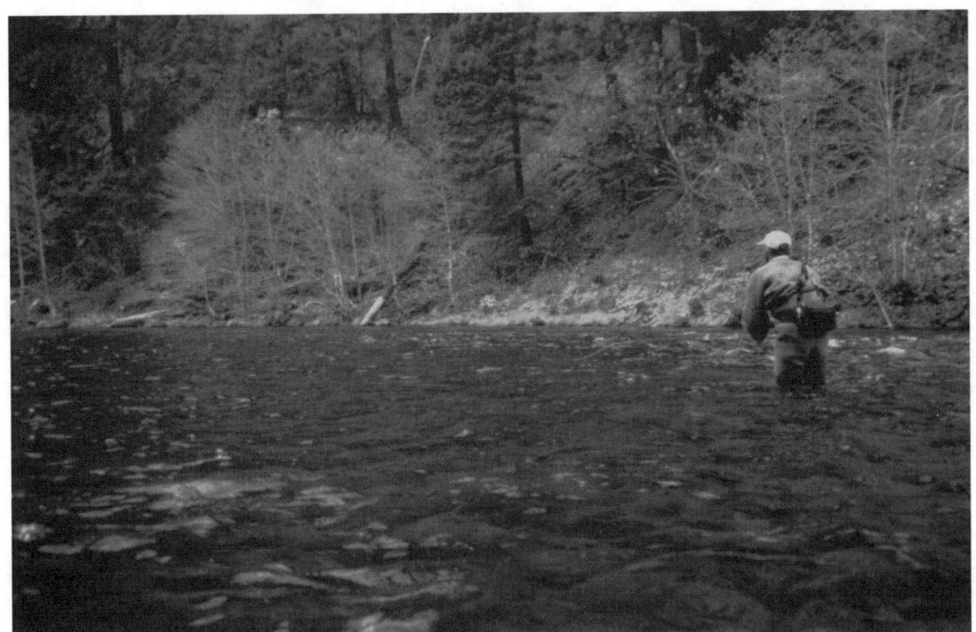

An endless amount of holding water awaits fish and anglers on the North Umpqua.

spotty, but very possible. Small, individual craft can be floated in this section. As long as the angler gets out to fish, it is perfectly legal." My friend, Ken Morrish, would refer to this as "creative access."

The North Umpqua is an inspiring river with a great flyfishing history. Take your time while on the river and learn as much as you can about it. It will teach you some awesome lessons in steelhead behavior and steelhead technique.

Stream Facts: North Umpqua River

Seasons

- From mouth to deadline at Soda Springs powerhouse: Open for steelhead the entire year.
- Above Soda Springs Reservoir: Open for trout April 25 to October 31.

Special Regulations

- From mouth to fly area boundary above Rock Creek: Closed for trout. Non-finclipped steelhead may be kept; 1 per day, 5 per year. Open for finclipped coho salmon August 16 to December 31. Open for chinook salmon January 1 to July 31. Closed between old Hwy 99 bridge and Winchester Dam.
- No angling from a floating device that supports the angler upstream from BLM recreation site located above the Lone Rock Bridge (Hwy 138).
- Closed from markers located upstream from Rock Creek, upstream 700 feet to the fly area boundary.
- From fly area boundary upstream to Soda Springs Dam: Closed for trout. Only adipose clipped steelhead may be kept. Open for finclipped coho salmon August 31 to December 31. Restricted to the use of a single barbless fly (see page 7 of Oregon regulations), any type of rod and reel permitted but no metal core lines and no added weight or attachments except a bubble or similar floating device.
- Closed from Soda Springs Dam downstream about half-mile to marker below powerhouse enclosure.
- No angling from a floating device that supports the angler.
- All tributaries from mouth to Soda Springs Dam closed.
- Upstream from Soda Springs: 2 trout per day. No limit on size or number of brook trout taken.

Fish

- Steelhead are the targets for fly anglers on the North Umpqua although trout and chinook are all present at times.

River Characteristics

- The North Umpqua is a big river to wade even during low flows. It runs through rugged terrain, and stream cleats are recommended. The river has runs, riffles, glides, and deep pools, all of which hold fish.

Flows

- Winter flows during storms can bring the river up to 3,000 cfs.
- Normal summer flows are a minimum of 900 cfs.

River Access

- From the town of Glide up to Soda Springs Dam, there is about 45 miles of fishable water with a lot of access from Hwy 138.

Steelhead flyfishing on the North Umpqua. (Photo by Ken Morrish)

- The fly water on the North Umpqua is not boated. There are plenty of access points to the river along Hwy 138. The river below Glide has ramp access at Lone Rock boat ramp and at Colliding Rivers with more ramp access downstream.

Maps
- DeLorme *Oregon Atlas and Gazetteer*

Area Fly Shops
- Blue Heron, 109 Hargis Lane, Idleyld, OR 97447 / 541-496-0448
- Steamboat Inn, 42705 North Umpqua Hwy, Steamboat OR 97447 / 800-840-8825

South Umpqua River

Steelhead populations in the South Umpqua are not nearly as large as they are in the North Umpqua. Logging has warmed the water and made it second rate and has essentially destroyed any summer runs. Ken Morrish describes it as a "sleeper" winter-run steelhead fishery, because there is decent fishing in February and March when cooler winter flows are accompanied by higher volumes of water. When the water is clear, standard down-and-across fishing with sinktips is the method that fly anglers will find most successful. The type of access is wade fishing from roadside pullouts.

Summertime flows are reduced to a crawl, and the river becomes a smallmouth bass fishery. Trout-sized fly tackle in conjunction with buggers and nymphs are used on the bass. Road access is continuous on most of the river's reaches.

There is an upstream fishing deadline at Jackson Creek Bridge. See Oregon regulations for seasons and harvest information.

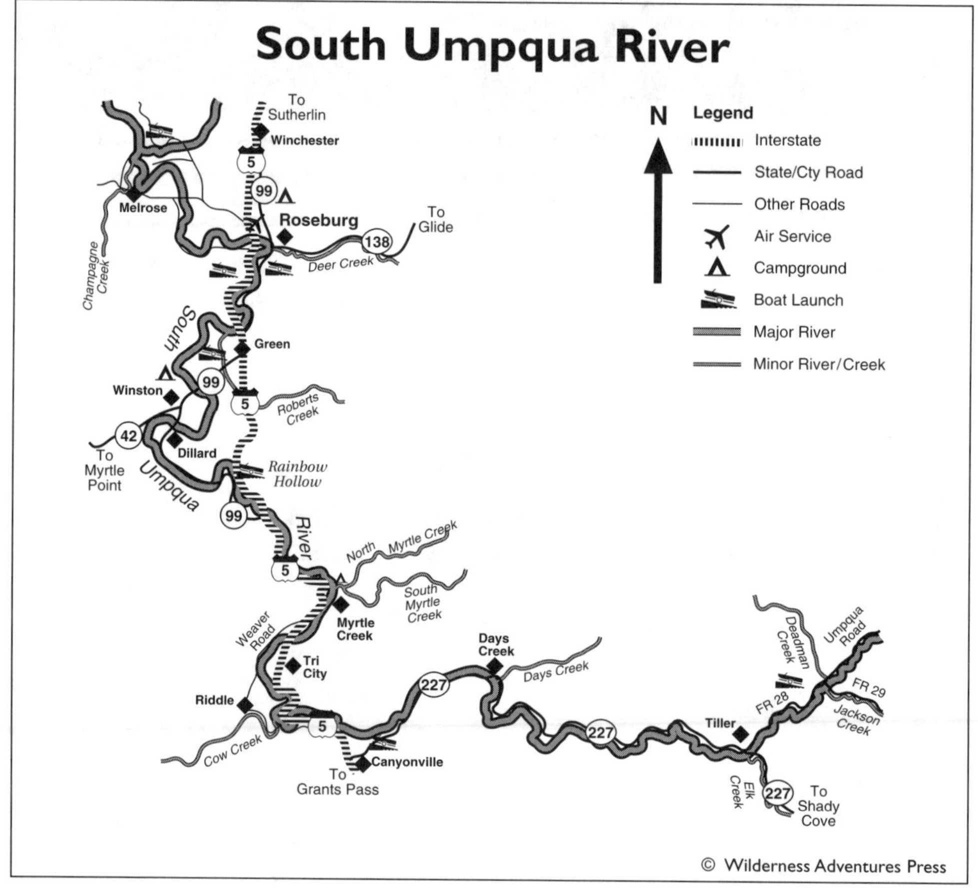

ROGUE RIVER

The three words that best describe the Rogue River are fun, fun, and fun. A big river that rolls through the valleys and coastal mountains of southern Oregon, the Rogue changes its appearance according to the terrain, but its fishing quality remains consistent. Although the river receives a lot of pressure, there are many remote stretches in which an angler can find an untouched pocket of fish if he is willing to make the effort.

The Rogue River holds one of the greatest "half-pounder" fisheries in existence as well as bigger, adult steelhead in the 8- to 12-pound range. Both bank anglers and boaters can do well on the Rogue. Fly angling can be an absolute ball here.

Half-pounders are small, sexually immature steelhead that have entered the river system prematurely. They eventually head back to the ocean but with any luck, not before they see a few flies. They can be extremely aggressive and willing to attack a fly. They are generally only 12 to 18 inches in length and look like nice bright, miniature steelies. When you feel the fight that these fish put up in contrast to their size, you'll find it hard not to laugh. You'll get the feeling that if they were any bigger, you would break them all off. What these half-pounders lack in size (3 pounds would be considered big), they make up in numbers and their willingness to take a fly. And despite their size, they look and act much like their bigger brothers.

Ken Morrish, manager of the Ashland Outdoor Store, insists that, "Fished with the right gear, the half-pounders will always bring an angler back for more." He suggests heavy trout tackle, such as 5- and 6-weight rods. Match these with floating lines and light sinktips—10-foot intermediate sinktips or mini 5-foot sinktips, like those made by Teeny, are fine. Add a leader tapered to 6-pound tippet and some basic steelhead and trout flies and you are all set to enjoy this fishery.

Morrish says that half-pounders can be found from the mouth as far upstream as the town of Grants Pass, although not many are found above Gold Ray Dam. They enter the river in good numbers in July. As summer progresses, the action picks up and fish can be caught well upriver. This fishery remains active for these little steelhead through November, but August, September, and October are when the bulk of them are around and conditions permit fishing to them.

Most of the half-pounder fishing action takes place from Galice downriver about 65 miles to the tidewater at Gold Beach. There are three distinct sections within this stretch. The lowest stretch, from the tidewater to the Foster Bar boat access, is accessible by taking Jerry's Flat Road from Hwy 101 in Gold Beach, which eventually becomes Agness Road. Several well-maintained campgrounds and boat launches are available as well as bank access. Occasional pullouts along the road also have trails to the river.

While bank access is available, the best way to fish the Rogue is definitely from a drift boat. Near the ocean, the Rogue is big but not very technical boating water. Many guides have motors mounted on their boats to fish deep runs more than once, while others just do it the old fashioned way and rely on gravity. If you have never floated the

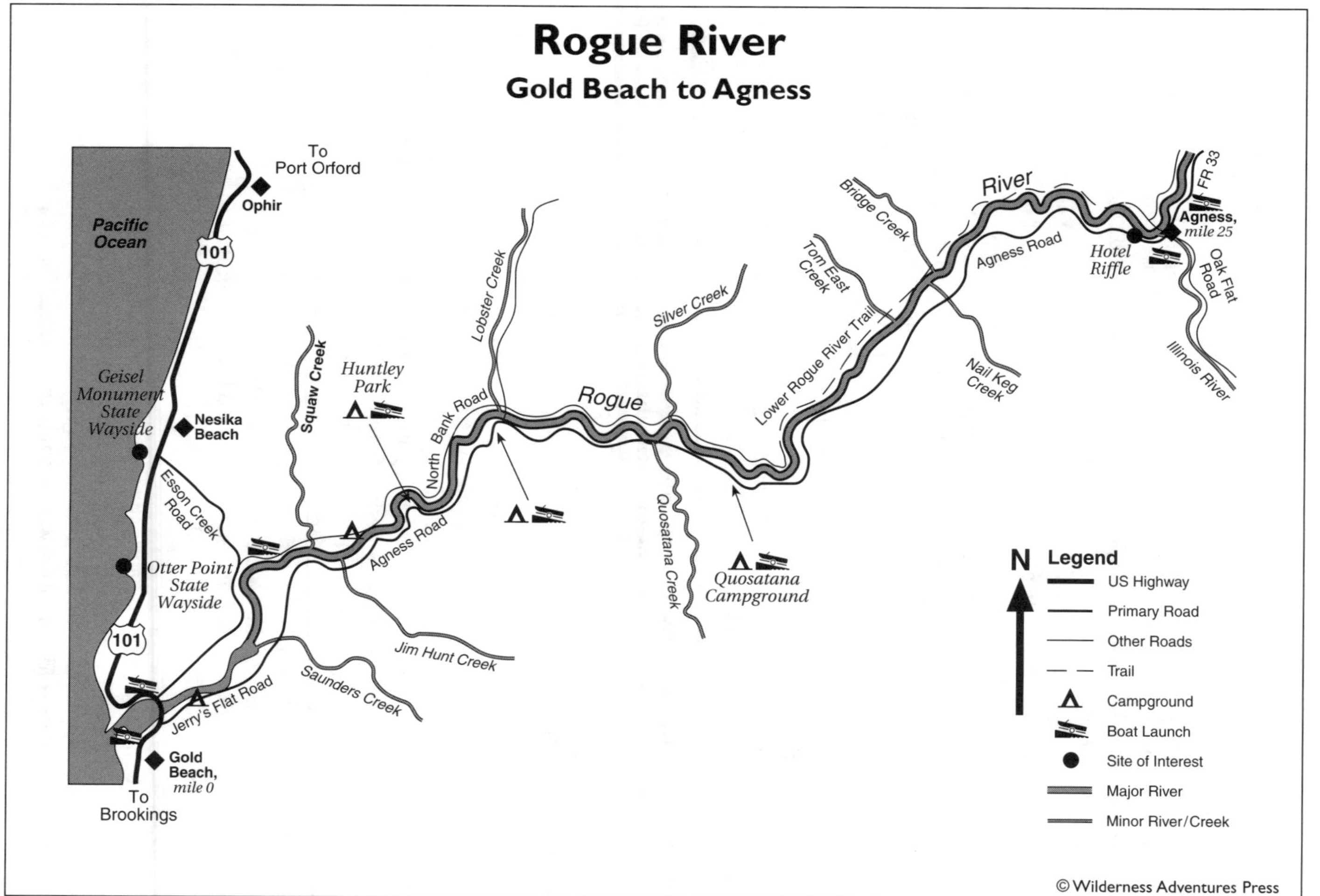

Rogue River
Gold Beach to Agness
To Port Orford
Ophir
Pacific Ocean
101
Geisel Monument State Wayside
Nesika Beach
Esson Creek Road
Otter Point State Wayside
101
Gold Beach, mile 0
To Brookings
Jerry's Flat Road
Saunders Creek
Jim Hunt Creek
Agness Road
Squaw Creek
Huntley Park
North Bank Road
Lobster Creek
Rogue
Silver Creek
Quosatana Creek
Quosatana Campground
Lower Rogue River Trail
Tom East Creek
Bridge Creek
Nail Keg Creek
River
Agness Road
Hotel Riffle
FR 33
Agness, mile 25
Oak Flat Road
Illinois River
N
Legend
US Highway
Primary Road
Other Roads
Trail
Campground
Boat Launch
Site of Interest
Major River
Minor River/Creek
© Wilderness Adventures Press

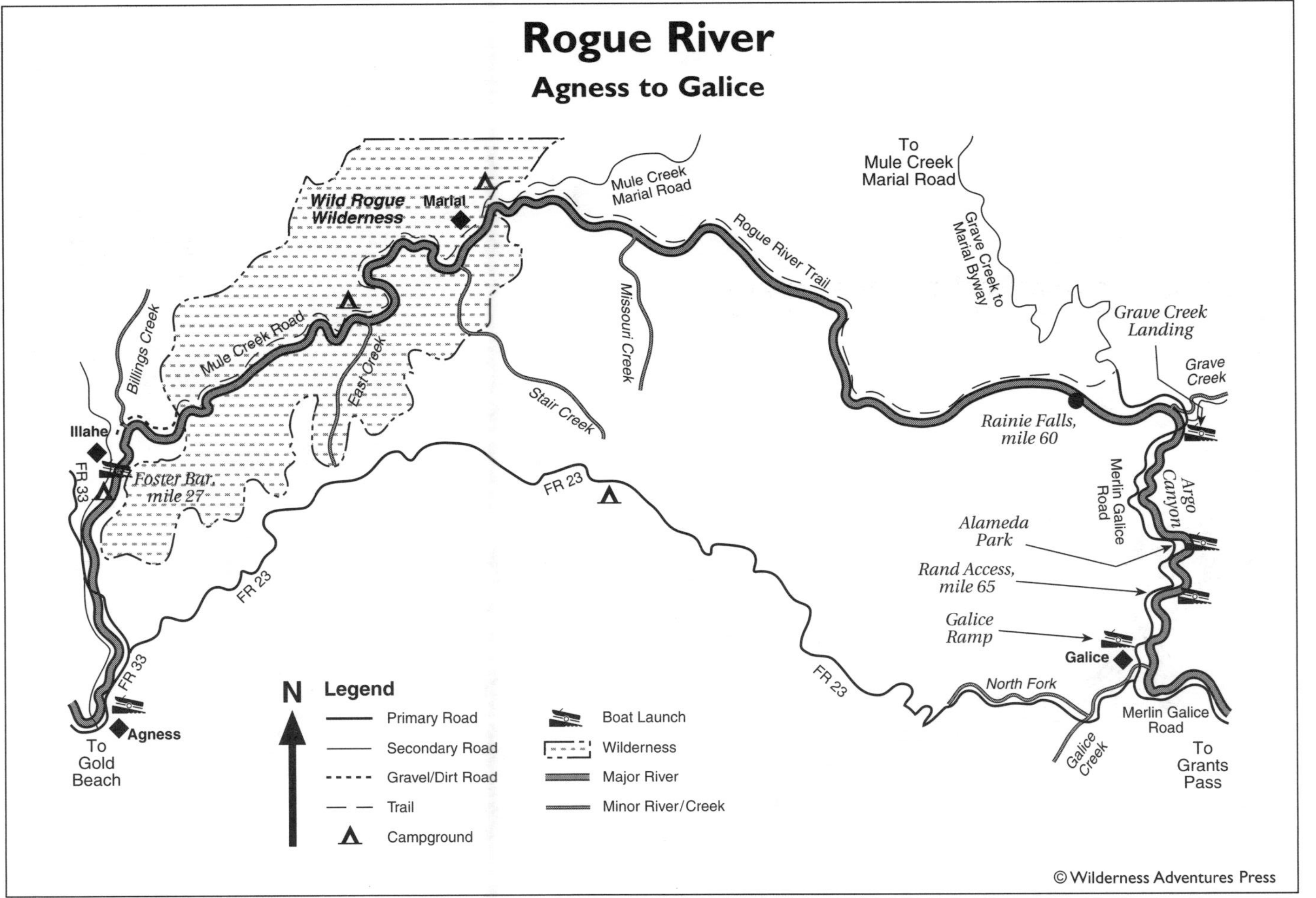
Rogue River
Agness to Galice
Wild Rogue Wilderness
Marial
Mule Creek Marial Road
Rogue River Trail
Missouri Creek
To Mule Creek Marial Road
Grave Creek to Marial Byway
Grave Creek Landing
Grave Creek
Billings Creek
Mule Creek Road
East Creek
Stair Creek
Rainie Falls, mile 60
Illahe
FR 33
Foster Bar, mile 27
FR 23
FR 23
Merlin Galice Road
Argo Canyon
Alameda Park
Rand Access, mile 65
Galice Ramp
Galice
FR 33
FR 23
North Fork
Agness
To Gold Beach
Galice Creek
Merlin Galice Road
To Grants Pass
N
Legend
Primary Road
Secondary Road
Gravel/Dirt Road
Trail
Campground
Boat Launch
Wilderness
Major River
Minor River/Creek
© Wilderness Adventures Press

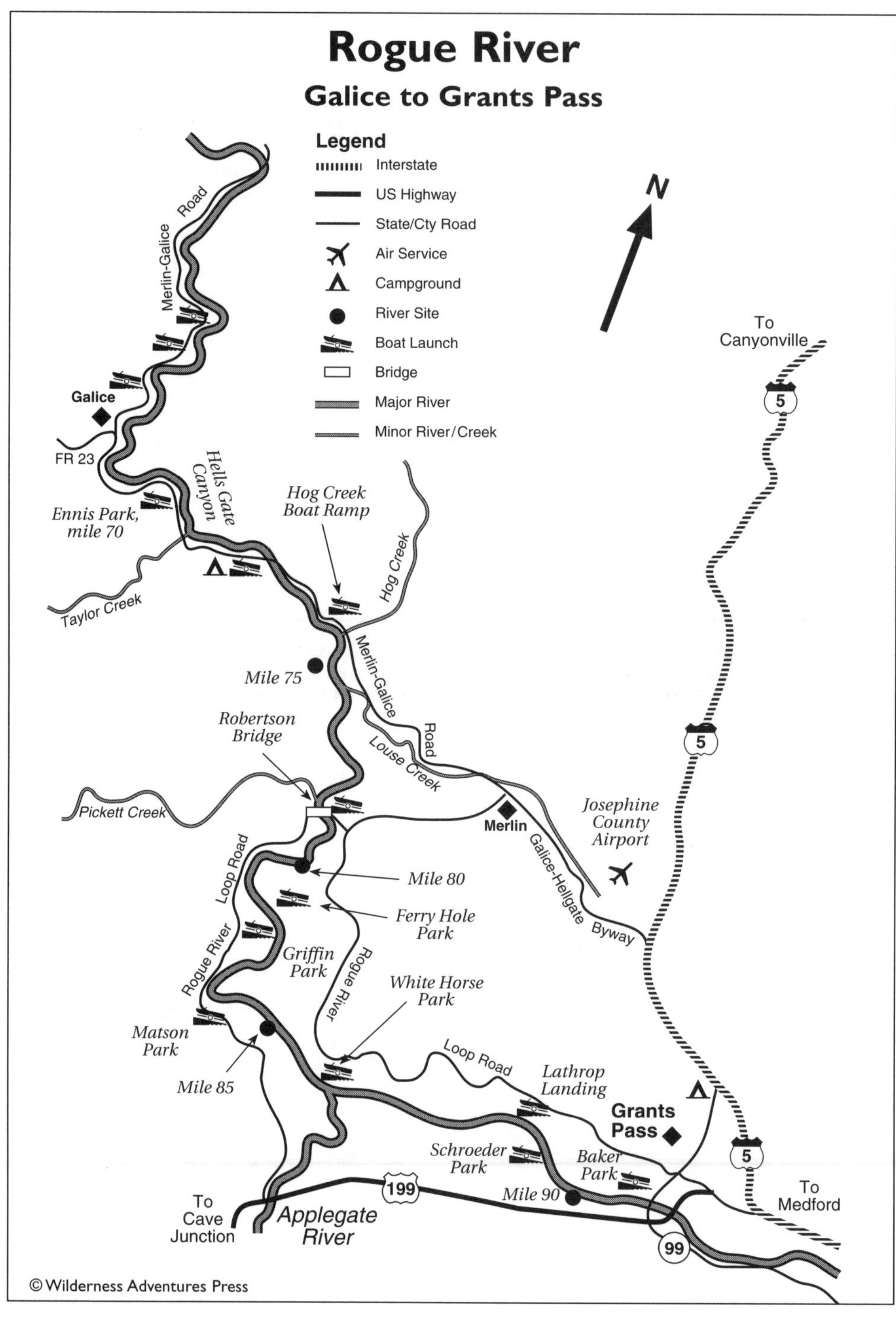
Rogue River
Galice to Grants Pass
Legend
Interstate
US Highway
State/Cty Road
Air Service
Campground
River Site
Boat Launch
Bridge
Major River
Minor River/Creek
N
Merlin-Galice Road
Galice
FR 23
Hells Gate Canyon
Ennis Park, mile 70
Taylor Creek
Hog Creek Boat Ramp
Hog Creek
Mile 75
Merlin-Galice Road
Louse Creek
Robertson Bridge
Pickett Creek
Merlin
Galice-Hellgate Byway
Josephine County Airport
To Canyonville
5
Loop Road
Mile 80
Ferry Hole Park
Griffin Park
Rogue River
Rogue River
White Horse Park
Matson Park
Mile 85
Loop Road
Lathrop Landing
Grants Pass
Schroeder Park
Baker Park
Mile 90
199
99
To Cave Junction
Applegate River
To Medford
© Wilderness Adventures Press

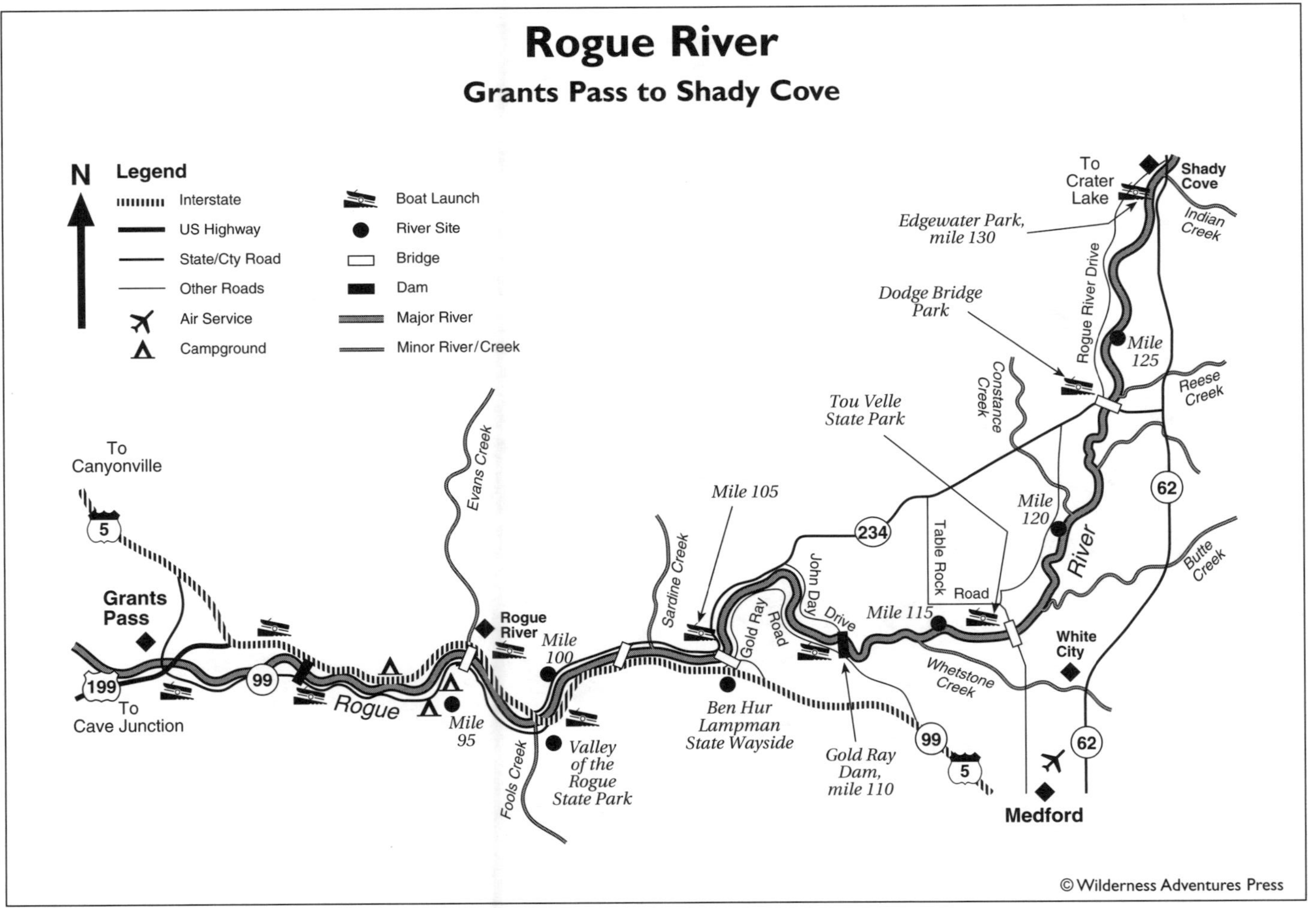
Rogue River
Grants Pass to Shady Cove
N
Legend
Interstate
US Highway
State/Cty Road
Other Roads
Air Service
Campground
Boat Launch
River Site
Bridge
Dam
Major River
Minor River/Creek
To Canyonville
5
Grants Pass
199
To Cave Junction
99
Rogue
Mile 95
Evans Creek
Rogue River
Mile 100
Fools Creek
Valley of the Rogue State Park
Sardine Creek
Mile 105
Ben Hur Lampman State Wayside
Gold Ray Road
John Day Drive
Gold Ray Dam, mile 110
234
Mile 115
Table Rock Road
Tou Velle State Park
Whetstone Creek
99
5
Medford
62
White City
Constance Creek
Mile 120
River
Dodge Bridge Park
Rogue River Drive
Mile 125
62
Butte Creek
Reese Creek
Edgewater Park, mile 130
To Crater Lake
Shady Cove
Indian Creek
© Wilderness Adventures Press

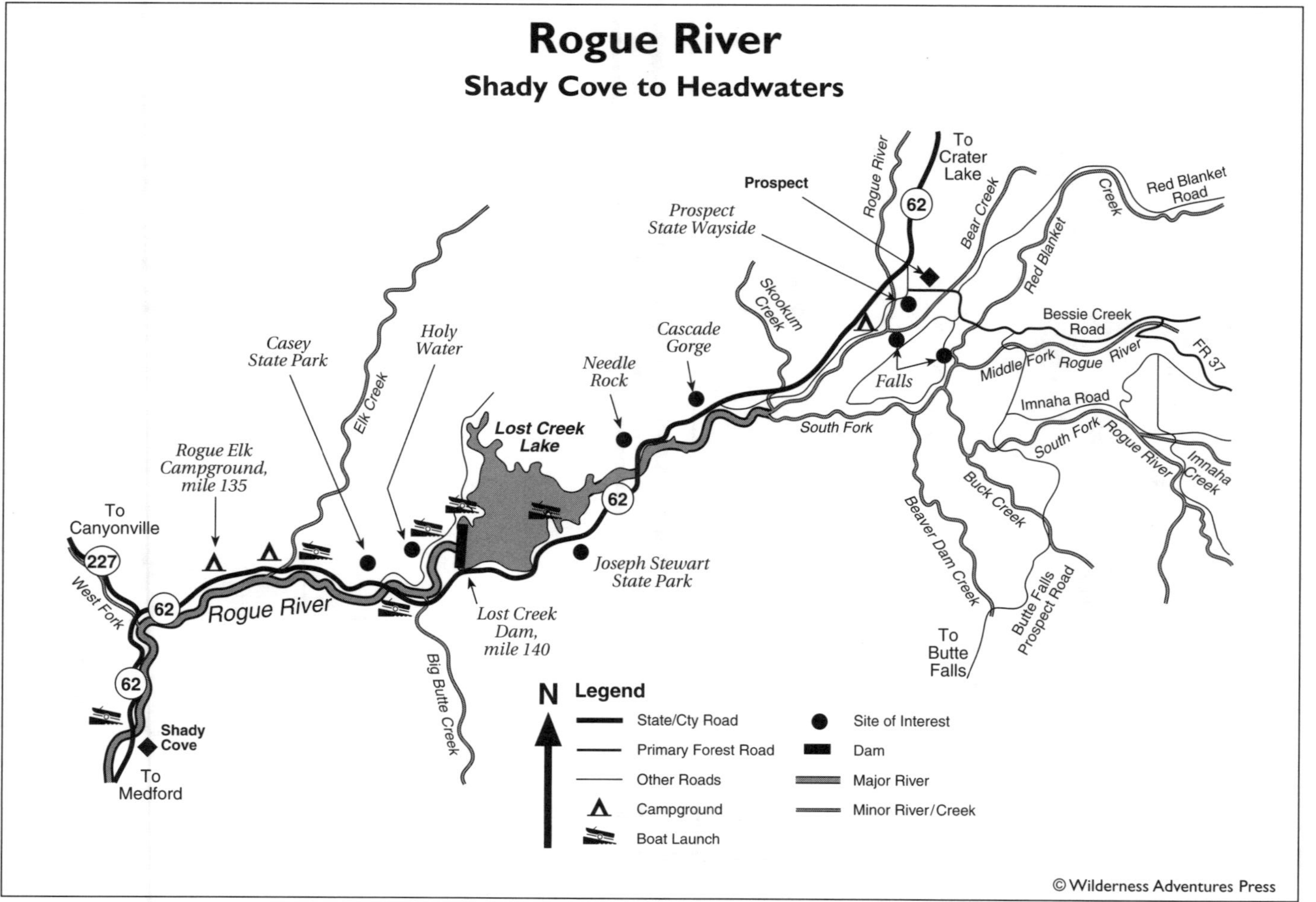
Rogue River
Shady Cove to Headwaters
To Crater Lake
Prospect
Prospect State Wayside
Rogue River
62
Bear Creek
Red Blanket
Creek
Red Blanket Road
Skookum Creek
Bessie Creek Road
FR 37
Middle Fork Rogue River
Falls
Imnaha Road
South Fork Rogue River
Imnaha Creek
South Fork
Buck Creek
Beaver Dam Creek
Butte Falls Prospect Road
To Butte Falls
Cascade Gorge
Needle Rock
Lost Creek Lake
Joseph Stewart State Park
Lost Creek Dam, mile 140
Holy Water
Casey State Park
Elk Creek
Rogue Elk Campground, mile 135
To Canyonville
227
West Fork
Rogue River
Big Butte Creek
Shady Cove
To Medford
N
Legend
State/Cty Road
Primary Forest Road
Other Roads
Campground
Boat Launch
Site of Interest
Dam
Major River
Minor River/Creek
© Wilderness Adventures Press

The Rogue River near Agness is big and powerful.

river, make sure you know what your take-out looks like. Also, jetboats on the river can be a hazard to nonpowered craft, so be aware when you hear one coming.

There is good boat access at Huntley Park, Lobster Creek, (south bank), Quosatana Campground, Hotel Bar River, (north bank) below Agness, and at Foster Bar. When the river is low, the stretch below Foster Bar and above Agness has some Class IV whitewater that should not be run by novices. Experienced boaters floating the Rogue for the first time should follow someone who knows the river or scout it well themselves. The end of the road is at Foster Bar, unless you're ready to hike or have a jetboat.

The section of river between Foster Bar and Grave Creek has been deemed Wild and Scenic, which means it has all the protection rights afforded that designation. Access from Foster Bar upstream is limited to hiking and boating. Jetboats are only allowed in this stretch for a few of the 30-plus miles of river. The rest is left to the hiker and floater. Boaters can plan three- to five-day floats through this stretch. There are a few backcountry lodges that can be used, but be sure to book well in advance. Boaters should be aware that the Wild and Scenic stretch is floated by permit only from May 15 through October 15. This is done on a lottery basis. For information about the lottery, contact Rand Ranger Station in the town of Merlin. If you can't get a permit, remember that the fishing is still good for a time after the October permit deadline.

The Rogue River has a lot of technical boating water. Novices have no place rowing through here, and experts who haven't run it before should either follow an experienced Rogue boater or get detailed information about its idiosyncrasies. People who aren't careful drown on the Rogue. During the summer, rafts are the primary means of entering the Wild and Scenic section, and by fall, when water levels have dropped, drift boats will be seen on this stretch.

If you really want to creep along and fish the entire scenic stretch, take the Rogue River Trail on the north end from Grave Creek to Foster Bar. You can day-hike from the south or north end for great fishing, or you can put your pack on and try the whole stretch. This could take a week or more if you fish hard, but it can put you on some of the Rogue's untouched water. Straight through, the trail would take at least three days to hike. It is a gorgeous hike, and the trail is well maintained.

The last good stretch of river for half-pounders is from the confluence of the Applegate River down to Grave Creek. Of several good floats in this section, the most popular is around Galice. Boaters can float from Galice to the top end of Argo Canyon or continue to Grave Creek. There are several good pullouts before Argo. This is a busy stretch and you'll find a lot of boat trailers around when you come into the Galice area during prime season. If you are not able to float, the Merlin-Galice Road offers bank anglers plenty of access to some great water through this same stretch. This is a heavily used area, so be polite and practice good etiquette. Both boaters and wade anglers should consistently move through runs, giving others an opportunity to fish.

Since all techniques used to fish the Rogue's half-pounders will consistently take fish, it boils down to your personal preference. A basic dry line trout setup is commonly used on the Rogue. Anglers use nymphs and a dead-drift strike indicator technique, much like fishing for trout on a small freestone stream. Upstream or up-and-across drifts from the bank, or long drifts from a boat using an indicator on the leader will take fish. Big trout nymphs, such as Prince nymphs, hare's ears, large beaded soft hackles and such, will draw plenty of strikes from these little steelhead.

Flyfishers also use greased line, down-and-across methods with traditional steelhead patterns. This is where sinktips are effective as well as dry lines. This swinging fly technique with a sinktip is a great way to take half-pounders out of some deep tailouts and out of thin water using dry lines. Morrish explained to me how much these little steelies like to sit in really fast riffles. "They hide out in the churning water, much like adult steelhead, but they like the current even faster and shallower than the adults, especially in hotter months like August. Fish use riffles to find oxygen during lower flows. They sit in all types of water, but the shallows are great fly water."

Don't hesitate to fish a dry line when searching for half-pounders. A fly swung just under the surface, and even riffle-hitched dries skated on top, will draw exciting takes from these little silver torpedoes.

One of the most common techniques employed on the river, especially by guides, is to "pull flies" from a boat. This is also known as "twitching" from a boat. Boaters slowly float downriver, hanging flies on light sinktips or dry lines from the

A guide has clients "twitching" or "pulling" for half-pounders between Galice and Grave Creek.

front of the boat. Anglers positioned in the front of the boat bounce the rod tip to move the fly a little. Although not a lot of casting takes place, it is an effective way to cover the water. According to Morrish, "Pulling flies is a traditional, as well as original, method used on the Rogue. Anglers hang flies like gold demons, brindle bugs, and red ants. A lot of half-pounders get caught this way."

The Rogue River draws a ton of these little steelhead, and they make for some very unique sport. There are other coastal rivers that have half-pounders, but the Rogue is one of the very best. Add in the Rogue's prolific adult steelhead, and suddenly all those empty boat trailers start making sense.

Adult steelhead enter the river in July, and a few get caught in the latter half of the month. These adult fish are usually in the 18- to 24-inch range with a few up to 30 inches. All the techniques used to catch half-pounders will also take these bigger fish.

The lower river, from Galice to the mouth, provides adult summer-run steelhead from July through October. These fish are caught as a bonus to the half-pounders. While there are some anglers who actively pursue adult steelhead rather than half-pounders, most fish for both. For those who want to increase their chances for adult

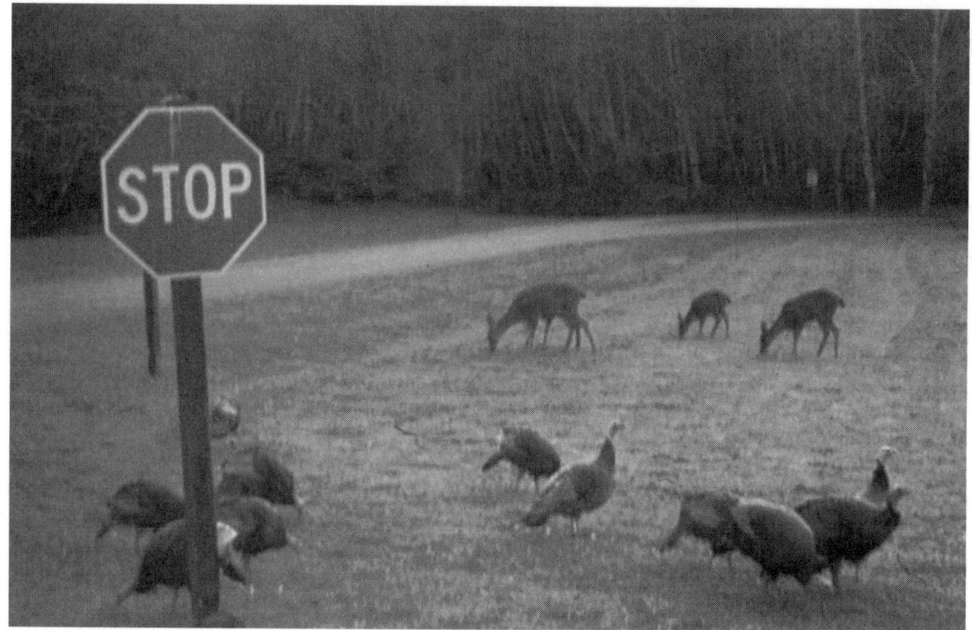

You are never camping alone on the Rogue between Gold Beach and Agness.

steelhead, bigger size steelhead flies and fishing slightly deeper than needed for half-pounders will often get results.

Anglers fish for winter-run steelhead in the lower river when levels drop and the water clears. Because the system is so large, it can take days or weeks after heavy rains for the Rogue's water to drop and clear. Heavier sinktip lines are the norm for fishing lower river winter fish.

From Grants Pass up to Medford, the river produces some adult steelhead action, but a more productive stretch is from Gold Ray Dam near Medford up to Shady Cove. This area can produce some good days, especially later in the season.

Typically in July and August, river flows are still high, usually around 2,400 cfs, but by September 15, flows drop to around 1,200 cfs, which is just after the beginning of a special fly-only season from the Gold Ray Impoundment to the markers below the Cole River Hatchery. That means no external weight on the line and no metal core lines may be used when flyfishing. This special season is from September 1 to October 31. The last half of September until the end of October is prime time for flyfishers. After October, the river fills with all kinds of anglers.

During the fly-only season, adult steelhead can be caught much like trout. Indicator techniques using 2X and 3X leaders are very effective from boats. Drop flies about 5 or 6 feet below an indicator and concentrate on riffles, pocket water, and cur-

Riffles and rocks create great holding water for steelhead in the Rogue system.

rent seams. Try to avoid the deep frog water. According to Ken Morrish, chinook salmon drop a lot of roe in the system at this time of year and are kicking up a lot of nymphs as they spawn. This fills the water sphere with plenty to catch a steelhead's attention and makes fishing them with indicators a great approach. Morrish's favorite patterns include big, black stonefly imitations, like Kaufmann's stonefly nymphs, big birds, and loosely dubbed, soft hackle hare's ears. He also likes to use caddis and egg imitations. All flies should be weighted, and fly tiers are at a big advantage here, considering the no external weight rules.

The Rogue River is host to a good winter run of steelhead that appears in December in the lower and middle stretches. The action really heats up in the lower reaches during February and March. The upper river above Hell's Gate Canyon is more of a March to April fishery. These fish can be slightly bigger than summer fish and weigh in around the 8- to 12-pound range. They are pursued as water levels drop and the water clears after winter rains. They respond to the same techniques used to catch summer-run fish, except that most indicator fishing is done with egg patterns and heavier sinktips are used for down-and-across methods. Spey rods are gaining popularity for handling heavier lines and higher waters in winter. The winter season provides a chance to catch both summer-run and winter-run steelhead in the upper sections.

Summer steelhead fishing on the Rogue River is done with 6- and 7-weight rods in the 9- and 10-foot range. In winter, heavier rods like 7- and 8-weights are used, from 9½ feet up through spey sizes.

The Rogue's steelhead fishery is top notch if you hit it just right. Even if there were no adult fish, the half-pounders would still make the river a worthwhile destination. There are extensive guide services available on the Rogue. Ken Morrish at the Ashland Outdoor Store is a great guy to speak with and very knowledgeable about the whole Rogue River system.

There is more to the Rogue than its wonderful steelhead fishery. For die-hard trout bums, check out the Rogue section dubbed "The Holy Water." This is a half-mile stretch from Lost Creek Dam downriver to a weir, which causes this section to be much like a spring creek. It holds trout in the 12- to 24-inch class and has some interesting dry fly opportunities.

During winter on this stretch, midges as well as leeches are used when trout are holding in deeper areas. Spring brings both good caddis activity and great blue-winged olive hatches. Summer features sporadic mayfly and caddis activity, highlighted by the salmonfly emergence. By the end of May through July, salmonflies are hatching out of the river below the dam and are corralled by it on their upstream migration. Morrish explains, "You get this freestone insect in spring creek conditions and suddenly salmonfly fishing becomes very technical. It is not uncommon to have a fish bump your dry salmonfly imitation 6 or 8 times without taking it. You can get 20 fish to roll it and strike it without ever hooking one of them."

Sounds frustrating, but at the same time, it seems like a lot of f-u-n, doesn't it?

Stream Facts: Rogue River

Season and Special Regulations

- Tidewater upstream to deadline markers located downstream from Cole River Hatchery diversion dam, including impoundments:
- Open for trout January 1 to March 31 and the last Saturday in May to December 31. Two adipose-clipped rainbow trout per day, 8-inch minimum length.
- Rainbow trout over 16 inches are considered steelhead and must be recorded on tag.
- Open for finclipped coho salmon September 1 to December 31.
- Open for chinook salmon and steelhead entire year. See exceptions below.
- Closed for chinook salmon:
  a. Rogue River mouth upstream to mouth of Illinois River, October 1 to December 31.
  b. Hog Gate boat landing, located at Hellgate, upstream to Gold Ray Dam October 1 to December 31.
  c. Gold Ray Dam upstream to ODFW markers located downstream from Cole River's hatchery August 1 to October 31.
- Nonadipose-clipped steelhead at least 24-inches in length may be kept; One per day, five per year, as part of a daily or annual salmon/steelhead catch limit January 1 to April 30 and December 1 through 31.
- Restricted to the use of barbless artificial flies (see Oregon regulations page 7), any type of rod or reel permitted but no metal core lines and no added weights or attachments except a bubble or similar floating device from Gold Ray Impoundment upstream to ODFW markers located downstream from Cole River Hatchery September 1 to October 31.
- Closed:
  a. Rainie Falls downstream 400 feet.
  b. Gold Ray Dam downstream to markers located downstream from lowest fishway entrance.
  c. Savage Rapids Dam downstream to markers located below the lowest fishway entrance.
  d. Cole River Hatchery diversion dam downstream to ODFW markers located downstream from hatchery, including hatchery outflow to the river.
  e. Ideal Cement Co. powerhouse diversion dam (including diversion canal) downstream to Gold Hill boat landing.
- Tributaries downstream from Cole River Hatchery: Closed, except as noted under Special Regulations in the Oregon Fishing Regulations booklet for Applegate River, Illinois River, Big Butte, and Little Butte creeks.
- Hatchery diversion dam upstream to Lost Creek Dam: Open to angling, catch and release only, entire year. Restricted to fly angling only with barbless hooks.

Approaching rapids on the upper Rogue River. (Photo by Ken Morrish)

- Mainstem and tributaries above Lost Creek Dam: Open to angling April 25 to October 31. Five trout per day, 8-inch minimum length. No limit on size or number of brook trout taken.

Fish

- Main targets for fly rodders in the Rogue are juvenile steelhead called "half-pounders." Runs of summer and winter adult steelhead are fished, and the upper water has a nice trout fishery for 12- to 24-inch fish and smaller.

River Characteristics

- The Rogue's length makes it hard to summarize. Much of it is gentle and user friendly, while much of it is remote, requiring great effort to fish. The one constant is the fishery. Many fish call the Rogue home, and the river does a good job of supporting these populations of trout and salmon.
- From the head to the mouth at the Pacific Ocean, the river traverses around 200 miles.
- There are many public ramps along the river. Foot access is from roads that follow the river as well as extensive trail systems.

Maps

- DeLorme *Oregon Atlas and Gazetteer*

APPLEGATE RIVER

A major tributary of the Rogue, Applegate River is about 35 miles long from Applegate Reservoir to its mouth on the Rogue, just above Galice. Public access is limited, and there is no fishing allowed from boats. Property owners along its banks own the land to the river's center. Thus, anglers have only the few public access points to reach the river. A road follows the Applegate river for its entire length, and there are public access points from this road.

A decent run of winter steelhead is open to fishing from January 1 to March 31, with most of the action in March. This river fishes well when it is running under 500 cfs. The same techniques and gear employed on the Rogue for winter steelhead are used on the Applegate.

There is also a trout season from May 23 until December 31. There is a resident population of rainbow and cutthroat trout. Standard nymphing techniques using a variety of beadhead nymphs and standard dries will get attention from all the trout. Please check current fish and wildlife regulations for harvest restrictions.

Illinois River

The Illinois is another major tributary of the Rogue, joining it right below Agness. The river's lowest reaches have a few miles of road access. Stray fish from the Rogue sometimes nose into the system in summer and fall, but it is primarily a catch-and-release winter steelhead fishery at its upper end. A few miles above the mouth, the Illinois goes into an extremely rugged canyon and is listed as Wild and Scenic. While there is a trail that follows it, access from the trail to the river is often limited.

Limited flyfishing is available upriver near the towns of Kerby and Selma. From there an angler can drive the Illinois River Road for about 20 miles to its termination at Briggs Creek, where there is a trailhead. The river is strictly catch and release for all fish, and fishing seasons are January 1 to March 31 and again from May 23 to December 31.

This is primarily a bank fishery that is reached from the road. A fly angler should concentrate on tailouts between rapids. An angler needs good distance and depth, and very heavy sinktips fished with two-handed rods is usually the best approach. Standard Western steelhead patterns work well if you can locate fish. One of the most challenging rivers in Oregon to catch a steelhead, the Illinois is not everyone's cup of tea.

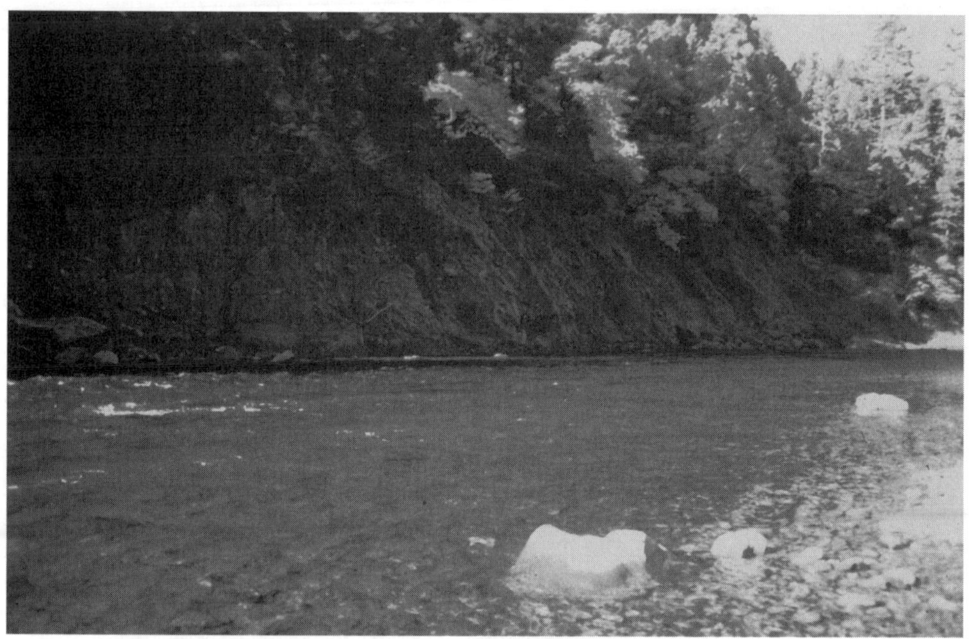

Tributaries of the Rogue are inviting to steelhead and hardy fly anglers.

SOUTHWEST HUB CITIES

Roseburg, Oregon

Elevation–465 • Population–29,500

ACCOMMODATIONS

Best Western Douglas Inn Motel, 511 Southeast Stephens Street / 541-673-6625
Windmill Inns of America Motel, 1450 Northwest Mulholland Drive / 541-673-0901

RESTAURANTS

The Apple Peddler, 1350 Northeast Stephens Street / 541-673-0503
Beef & Brew, 2060 Stewart Parkway Drove / 541-673-8030
Denny's Restaurant, 350 West Harvard Boulevard / 541-672-3134
The Gallery Restaurant, 809 Southeast Main Street / 541-673-6357
Hacienda Mexican Restaurant, 940 Northwest Garden Valley Boulevard / 541-672-5330
International House of Pancakes, 1370 Northwest Garden Valley Boulevard / 541-672-6709
La Hacienda Mexican Restaurant, 940 Northwest Garden Valley Boulevard / 541-672-5330
Roma Italian Restaurant & Lounge, 5096 Old Highway 99 South / 541-679-7100
Sizzler Restaurant, 1156 Northwest Garden Valley Boulevard / 541-672-5443

FLY SHOPS AND SPORTING GOODS

Northwest Outdoors Supply, 435 Southeast Jackson Street / 541-440-3042
Rite Aid Drug Store, 464 Southeast Jackson Street / 541-672-4896
Surplus Center, 515 Southeast Spruce Street / 541-672-4312
Kmart Stores, 2757 Stewart Parkway Drive / 541-673-5113

HOSPITALS

Douglas Community Hospital, 738 West Harvard Boulevard / 541-673-6641
Harvard Medical Park Business Office, 1813 West Harvard Boulevard / 541-672-8341

AUTO RENTAL

Enterprise Rent-A-Car, 1481 Northeast Stephens Street / 541-440-3030

AUTO REPAIR

Clyde from Glide Towing & Auto Repair, 2400 Old Highway 99 South / 541-957-5597
Fray's Automotive & Machine Service, 1350 Southeast Short Street / 541-672-4072
Koble's Automotive Service, 1320 Northeast Cedar Street / 541-672-0249
Mobile Tune Auto Repair, 504 Southeast Rose Street / 541-672-0622
Roseburg RV Repair, 1350 Southeast Short Street / 541-672-4072

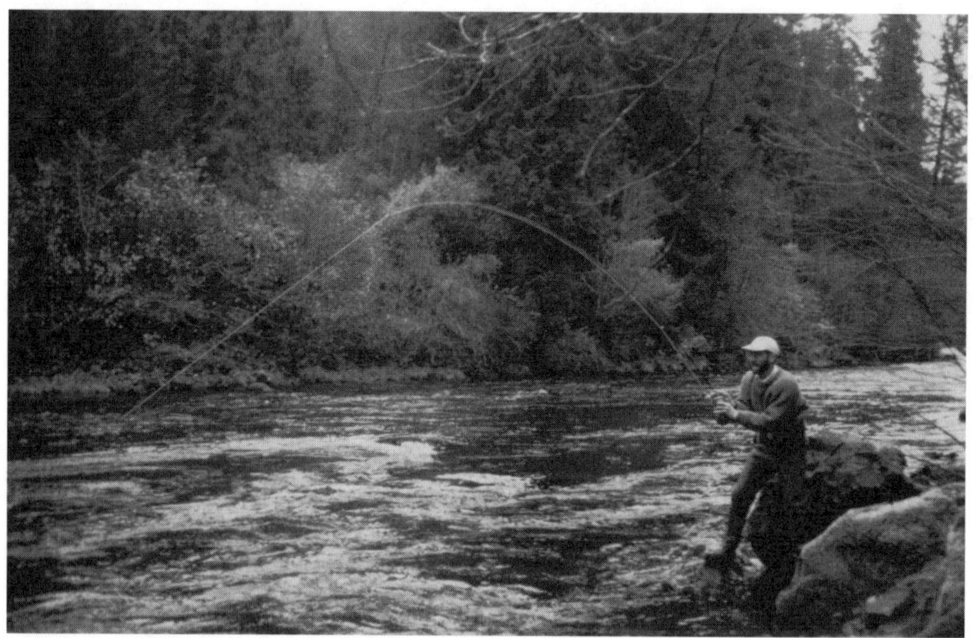

T.R. McCrystal tries to move a steelhead out of fast water.

For More Information

Roseburg Area Chamber of Commerce
410 Southeast Spruce Street
Roseburg, OR 97470
541-672-2648

Glide, Oregon

Accommodations

Steelhead Run Bed & Breakfast, 23049 North Umpqua Hwy / 541-496-0563
Colliding Rivers Drive-In, 19132 North Umpqua Hwy / 541-496-3205

Restaurants

Munchies Original, / 541-496-3112
Red Barn Restaurant, 20641 North Umpqua Hwy / 541-496-0246

Hospital

Glide Family Health Clinic, 20170 North Umpqua Hwy / 541-496-3504

Auto Repair

AAA Road Service (Clyde from Glide Towing), 151 Abbott Street / 541-496-0334
Glide Auto Service / 541-496-3286

Grants Pass, Oregon

Elevation–950 • Population–20,560

ACCOMMODATIONS

Best Western Inn at the Rogue, 8959 Rogue River Hwy / 541-582-2200
Holiday Inn Express, 105 Northeast Agness Avenue / 541-471-6144
Rod & Reel Motel, 7875 Rogue River Hwy / 541-582-1516
Shilo Inn Grants Pass, 1880 Northwest 6th Street / 541-479-8391
Bend o' the River, 7501 Lower River Road / 541-479-2547

CAMPGROUNDS

Have A Nice Day Campgrounds, 7275 Rogue River Hwy / 541-582-1421
Joe Creek Waterfalls RV Park, 699 Jumpoff Joe Creek Road / 541-479-7974
River Park RV Resort, 2960 Rogue River Hwy / 541-479-0046

RESTAURANTS

The Black Forest, 820 Northeast E Street / 541-474-2353
The Brewery, 509 Southwest G Street / 541-479-9850
Denny's Restaurant, 115 Northeast Morgan Lane / 541-479-4544
The Falls, 428 Southwest 6th Street / 541-474-1021
Maria's Mexican Kitchen, 105 Northeast Mill Street / 541-474-2429
Paradise Ranch Resort, 7000 Monument Drive / 541-479-4333
Sizzler Restaurant, 1871 Northeast 7th Street / 541-479-1034
Wild River Brewing & Pizza Co., 595 Northeast E Street / 541-471-7487

FLY SHOPS AND SPORTING GOODS

Bradbury's Gun North Tackle, 1809 Rogue River Hwy / 541-479-1531
TruValue Hardware, 324 Southwest 6th Street / 541-476-4488
WalMart, 305 Northeast Try Ln Str / 541-471-2822

HOSPITALS

Three Rivers Community Hospital and Health Center, 1505 Northwest Washington Boulevard / 541-479-7531
River City Urgent Care, 1215 Northeast 7th Street / 541-476-2804

AIRPORT

Grants Pass Aviation, 1441 Brookside Boulevard / 541-474-0665

AUTO RENTAL

Budget Car & Truck Rental of Grants Pass, 825 Northeast F Street / 541-471-6311
Enterprise Rent-A-Car, 1046 Court / 541-471-7800

AUTO REPAIR

Auto Care Center, 1693 Lynda Lane / 541-479-2024
The Autosmith, 301 Southeast J Street / 541-474-2886

L & M Automotive Service, 108 Union Avenue / 541-476-6271
Pro Automotive, 2133 Rogue River Hwy / 541-476-1579

For More Information

Grants Pass Chamber of Commerce
1501 Northeast 6th Street
Grants Pass, OR
541-476-7717

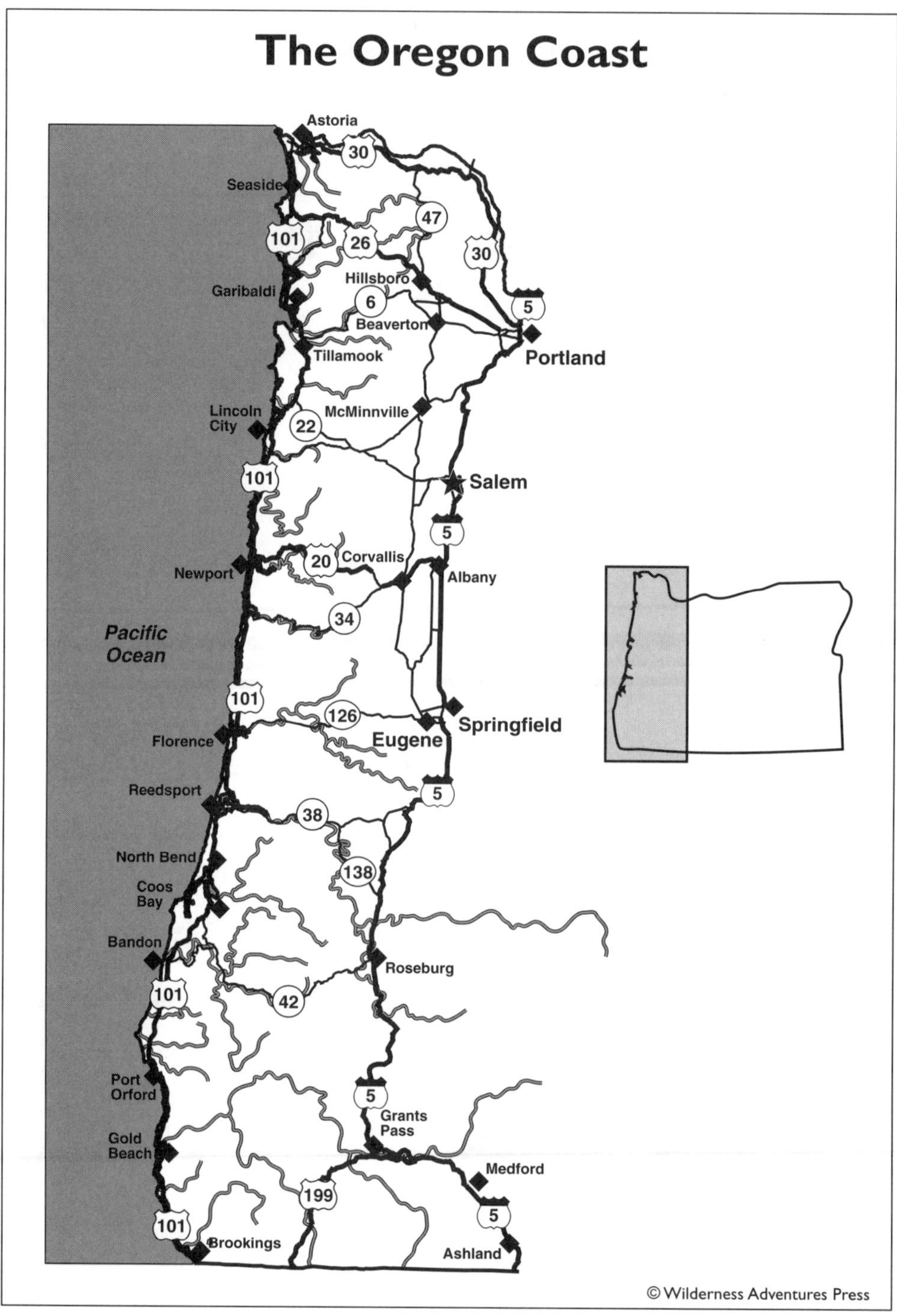
The Oregon Coast
Astoria
30
Seaside
47
101
26
30
Hillsboro
Garibaldi
6
5
Beaverton
Portland
Tillamook
Lincoln City
McMinnville
22
101
Salem
5
20
Corvallis
Newport
Albany
34
Pacific Ocean
101
126
Springfield
Florence
Eugene
Reedsport
5
38
North Bend
138
Coos Bay
Bandon
Roseburg
101
42
Port Orford
5
Grants Pass
Gold Beach
Medford
199
5
101
Brookings
Ashland
© Wilderness Adventures Press

The Oregon Coast

Unlocking the secrets of the Oregon coast fisheries is not something the traveling flyfisher is ever going to do. This doesn't rule out the possibility of stumbling into a grand day, when fish and fly angler meet in a run with no one else around. Finding a migratory fish is not always an easy thing to do, particularly if you are a migratory flyfisher.

So how does one find fish on the coast? The easiest answer is to be in the know. There are sources galore to find out when fish are running and a quick jaunt to the coast can put you in line with your fellow angler.

It may begin with a farmer who sees fish in the river that borders his property. Next, the neighbors are called, and the rods come out. The following day, a friend of a neighbor is invited to fish the property, who in turn goes to town soon after and tells the grocer, who then tells the guide's wife's brother-in-law, who tells the guide, who tells the pro shop, who tells the press, who tells you, who drives several hours, who arrives too late, and who had better get used to the words, "You should have been here yesterday."

That's not to say that the situation is hopeless. Do some research and then go with a good attitude. The experience is worth the effort regardless of how many fish are caught. Milton Fisher, one of a handful of coastal fly guides who was of great help to me in gathering information on the coast, says, "The opportunities here are endless. The Oregon coast is the most underutilized flyfishery in the state."

Another thing that flyfishers should keep in mind, according to Fisher, is that once most of the hatchery fish have run through a river and meat fishers have departed, many coastal rivers are then devoid of angling pressure. Unlike hatchery fish, wild fish enter rivers in a less uniform fashion and become available for flyfishing after the crowds and hatchery fish have vanished. Catch and release regulations are in effect for all wild fish, which means that there are some great fish available for sport fishers.

Following are some things to keep in mind for flyfishing Oregon's coastal rivers:

- Familiarize yourself with fish habits;
- Know the regulations and seasons;
- Keep abreast of weather and river flow levels;
- Take your chances and walk or float some rivers.

To land the main fly targets in coastal fisheries, an angler should take several rods and become proficient in various techniques. Steelhead, chinook, and sea-run cutthroat are all wonderful fly targets and can be found in most coastal systems at various times of the year. Although chum salmon and coho are present, there are only a few places where you can still fish for them.

The depletion of chum and coho runs has been well publicized in Oregon for many years. Reasons for this include: forestry practices that warmed rivers and caused silt to accumulate; offshore netting; bag limits that were too high; and poorly planned hatchery programs that were designed to supplement catch rates rather than saving native fish species in particular river systems.

These fisheries need support from the flyfishing community so that wild fish will continue to return to their native rivers. With catch and release practices and the possibility of quality coastal flyfishing gaining momentum among sport fishermen, coastal economies could certainly be given a boost from blue ribbon flyfisheries. Sport anglers can bring much-needed dollars to the area while having low impact on the land and rivers. Proper management and good sporting ethics can build these coastal systems into a solid resource.

However, in the meantime, opportunities are still available for fly anglers who understand the nature of these coastal waters—that success will vary from day to day and that one day of incredible conditions more than makes up for the fishless days. Fly anglers who are persistent will be rewarded when all the elements come together.

After much trial and error and by keeping careful logs on what was seen or caught or not caught, an angler can learn to predict when to fish and when to stay home. The number of waters an angler chooses to fish is a matter of personal choice. Being intimate with one or two bodies of water is a wonderful experience but knowing a variety of systems and having the knowledge to choose water in fishable condition on almost any day of the year will improve your coastal odds.

Techniques

Many nonresident anglers have the notion that Oregon's coastal fish really aren't interested in taking a fly. But the nature of steelhead and salmon fishing everywhere is that these fish are either snapping at everything one day or totally ignoring them another day. Considering the success of bait and spin fishing on the coast, it would be hard to argue that flies won't entice these fish as well.

Fly anglers who work and live on these rivers employ several techniques on migratory fish. These techniques aren't much different than standard trout and steelhead practices used elsewhere in the state and seem to be universally practiced by coastal guides.

Strike Indicators

Historically, this technique hasn't been used to catch migratory fish, and many in the flyfishing community frown on the technique. However, those same people also know how effective this technique is. Their objection is that it gives a flyfisher too much of an advantage. While that may be the case elsewhere, on Oregon's coast anglers need an advantage since coastal fish very often won't respond to traditional down and across techniques.

Strike indicators are useful for other situations, too, such as smaller streams and canyon waters that force anglers to throw over a fish's head. They also level the advantage that spin and bait anglers have. Few anglers practice flyfishing in groups, but when anglers of all types congregate around pools of chinook, a fly angler with an indicator can fish right in with everyone else and likely end up with a big advantage

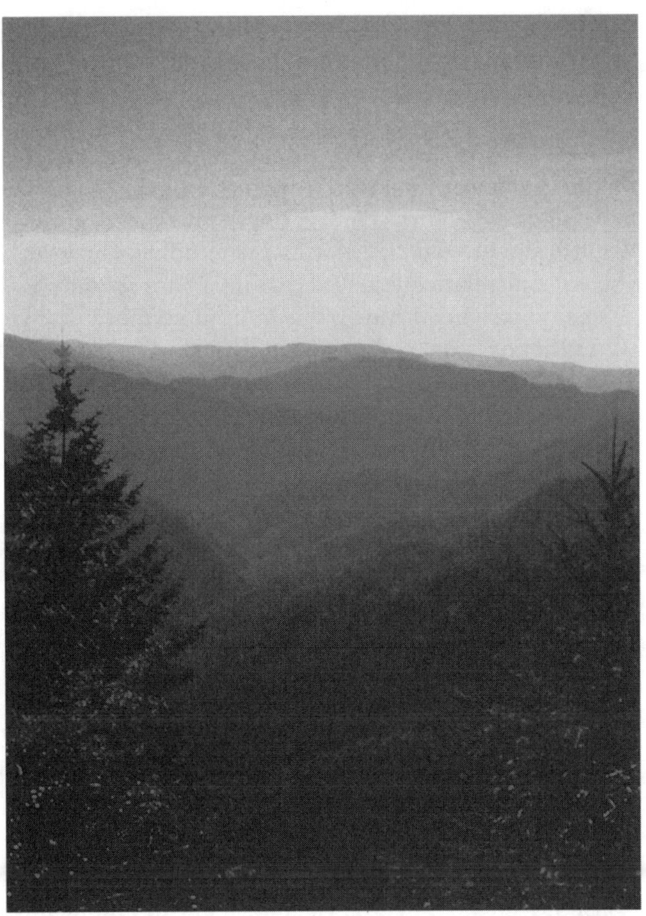

The Coast Range is big, rugged country with a lot of water running through it.

by showing fish something they haven't seen all day. If there are anglers immediately downstream, a swinging fly would be useless. Indicators are also helpful in pocket waters found in upriver sections of coastal streams and tributaries. Consider the use of strike indicators as an additional strategy for success on coastal waters.

When fishing with an indicator, work it just like you would for trout. Suspend the fly at the depth where fish are holding and watch for the take. Flies can vary from western steelhead patterns to glo-bugs to basic trout flies like hare's ears.

I'm not supporting the act of fishing in groups of anglers, as flyfishing is solitary by nature. But the use of indicators is plausible in even the most unlikely of situations. A fly angler is more likely to hear comments on the coast about flyfishing itself rather than a jab at overusing an indicator. It is a method to even up the odds; use it if you want to.

Swinging Flies

Traditionally, the method most often used to catch migratory fish on a fly is to swing flies down and across runs. Since there are a variety of conditions found on Oregon's coast, fly rodders make use of floating lines and a variety of sinktips and shooting heads. The key is to cast across a run and mend the line in order to swing the fly at the right depth and speed, which is a matter of trial and error. Once you have made a catch at a certain depth and speed, commit it to memory. The next time you fish the run, you'll know just what to do. Once you have discovered what works, you will feel relatively secure that if fish are present, you can get a hook-up.

Good steelhead runs have definite qualities that you can learn to read. Look for water that moves but doesn't pool. There can also be soft currents inside faster ones laced with boulders that provide cover and holding spots. Another water type is what my friend, Brett Drummond, calls pyramid water. This is water that riffles over waist-deep gravel, providing cover for ascending fish.

It's possible to swing flies for chinook as well, which could entail swinging a fly through deep pools and runs. You may need to swing your fly from top to bottom as well as from side to side within the water stratus of the pool. Chinook are taken in many coastal rivers using shooting heads and prams, and some can be taken with sinktips and waders as you would take a steelhead. And while sight fishing for chinook as they roll upriver can be great sport, fishing for dark fish in gravel isn't.

Sea-run cutthroat are also taken by swinging flies in different water types. The most significant is slow water, be it a pool high up a coastal tributary or near structure in brackish tidewater. Cutthroat in soft riffles and pocket water will also strike a swinging fly very hard. Stripping the fly while on the swing will add life to the fly, and to save your elbow some wear and tear, a quick hand twist will also work at times.

When to Fish

The Oregon coastal range is the first to catch the clouds off the Pacific Ocean. Coastal rivers are affected by rains all year, and obviously more so in some seasons than in others. As incoming clouds hit the coastal ranges and dump rain, rivers swell up and color as torrents of water spill into the watersheds. Often, the water runs a very short distance back to the ocean. High water provides the shield that entices migratory fish, such as chinook and steelhead, to move out of the ocean and into the rivers to spawn. As levels drop, which can happen any time from within hours to several days, water regains its clarity and fish start to seek cover in deep pools or riffles that are just out of the main current.

Optimum times to fish coastal rivers are when water begins to rise, when it is dropping, and immediately after it has stabilized. Information on river levels (cfs) is available by phone, 503-261-9246, and most are updated daily. Smaller streams that don't have a listed report usually coincide with reports for nearby larger rivers. There are also locations on the internet to obtain this information. Check "www.dfw.state.or.us" and go to their weekly fishing report or go to "www.fishinginoregon.com."

Catching coastal fish is a matter of knowing when and where to go. Locals on the coast know how many days or hours it will take for an individual system on the coast to begin clearing and when runs are due. A few kind words to the local shop owner or gas station attendant may be all that's needed to get valuable information.

The three primary targets on Oregon's coast for fly rodders are steelhead, chinook and sea-run cutthroat, which all enter coastal systems at various times of the year.

Steelhead

Coastal steelhead have both a summer and a winter run that overlap in many rivers. There are also hatchery and wild steelhead, and of course, all wild fish are catch-and-release. They can by differentiated yet again as adult fish and half-pounders (the small premature steelhead).

Winter-run fish enter coastal systems in October and continue to fill rivers until March. December and January can provide good action mostly to hatchery-reared fish, while February and March tend to have more wild fish in the rivers. Wild winter steelhead are perhaps one of the ultimate targets in the world of fly angling. These fish are incredibly powerful and will fight an angler every step of the way.

Steelheading, especially in winter, is truly an activity for the hardy angler with plenty of time. For the rest of us, there are guide services available. Be choosy when selecting an Oregon coastal guide. Find one who guides for flyfishing only and who emphasizes preservation rather than number of fish netted. Prepare a list of questions that will help you determine which guide has the qualities that suit you.

Summer-run steelhead percolate through coastal rivers from April to October, and consequently, many systems hold fish year-round. Summer runs are typically smaller than winter runs, but the steelhead in the system during these months are feisty and strong. They can sometimes be wary and unwilling to take a fly, but they also have a reputation for exploding on flies when the time is right.

Steelhead gear varies quite a bit. Because coastal water levels fluctuate considerably, it's important to take a variety of sinktips. Match your lines for 7- through 9-weight rods in the 9-foot range as well as spey sizes for the largest rivers. The most commonly used leaders are from 8 to 12 pounds in lengths determined by water clarity and depth.

Chinook

The chinook salmon, also sometimes called king salmon, is the largest of the Western salmon species and a highly respected game fish. Chinook runs are predominantly in fall and spring. Fall fish are usually darker, bigger, and more numerous than those running in spring. Spring chinook are brighter in color and somewhat smaller in size, although they are quite hard fighters. Small is a relative term, because these fish can weigh up to 40 pounds.

Chinook generally travel in groups and prefer to enter freshwater systems during high tides and good water flows. On shorter coastal rivers, a general rule of thumb, according to Milton Fisher, is that when water is high, fish higher up the system, and conversely, when water is low, fish lower in the system. This rule is applicable to all migratory fish in shorter coastal river systems.

In the fall, chinook start showing up in good numbers by late October, and fishing should stay productive into December. Spring runs start in May and are present until July.

Chinook can be spotted both on the move and holding in pools. When chinook are moving up a system, enticing them with a fly can be difficult but not impossible. Fish that are holding in pools are more susceptible to flies. Chinook hold in large pools as well as in riffles like steelhead. When fish find a deep pool, they often mill around until they're ready to make their next push upstream.

Spin anglers commonly surround deep pools filled with chinook, but if you're willing to keep hiking upstream or explore less popular rivers, it's possible to find a pool that you can fish by yourself. This can be an event, because when chinook are on the bite, it's possible to hook every fish in the pool.

These big bruisers will test your stamina as well as your skill, so gear is a major consideration. Since chinook will fight hard, stout rods in the 9- to 12-weight range are essential. You should also have a reel with good drag and a short, stout leader attached to a variety of lines, including a lot of weighted lines. This gear is often required to hook and hold a fish as big as a chinook.

Shooting heads are also used on coastal rivers, often fished out of boats. Chinook hold mainly in the mid- to bottom depths, which means that you will need a variety of interchangeable tips to suspend flies at those depths. Since chinook are not extremely leader shy, you may use stout leaders to do battle with these tough fish. With a good pair of polarized glasses, you can sometimes spot fish in pools before you cast. You can also spot them as they roll or fin near the surface when moving upriver. This is the first telltale signal that they are in the system.

Sea-run Cutthroat

The sea-run cutt is a great game fish that has a cult following. Some fly anglers marvel over the unpredictability and character of these coastal denizens. The sea-run cutt is an available target to fly anglers from July through September. The sea-run cutt doesn't follow a migratory route but does enter the ocean. On their return, they are met by anglers in estuaries and rivers when the first rains of summer raise river levels.

The sea-run cutt grows to trout proportions with a steelhead attitude. In the summer months, baitfish imitations fished in the tidal portions of creeks and rivers can produce a ton of fun. Anglers also fish high in coastal systems as the cutts move up rivers and streams. Many anglers catch them on dries and also come in contact with summer run steelhead in the process. Although the fish are elusive and unpredictable, they make the moment they are encountered memorable. Sea-runs grow plump on the ocean's bounty, turning them into supercharged trout. The sea-run cutt will usually inhabit a home river and wander down to saltwater if food becomes a factor.

The sea-run cutt can be found high in river systems, in places where slack water allows them to be the predators they are. Rather than using the current for food, the aggressive sea-run cutt will actively hunt for a meal. Swinging and stripping flies is a common technique employed to catch sea-runs. A floating line is often advantageous to the fly angler in search of cutts, and a sinktip helps cover deeper pools. A sinking line is also important when fishing tidal waters.

When fishing estuaries from small boats, anglers should concentrate on structure where fish may wait in ambush for a well-tied streamer. Low-light periods are key times when looking for sea-runs. This fish is a predator and will hunt with darkness as its cover.

Sea-runs can be fished with your trout gear. Be sure to clean your gear after fishing saltwater. Fishing for sea-runs is like treasure hunting—it becomes intriguing and addictive when hard fought success finally jolts your rod tip. Actively hunt sea-run cutthroats the way they pursue their prey, and you will find success.

The Coastal Rivers

Providing a list of places to fish the Oregon coast is definitely a task worthy of an entire book. Oregon's coast is loaded with water and to list every riffle that holds a migratory fish at some time during the year is just not possible. There is a strong local contingent on the coast who vigorously guard information concerning their particular favorite places and times to fish. What I hope I have done at the beginning of this chapter is help draw a mental map of where and how fish can be found. Anglers with a willingness to explore will find work does pay off eventually. No angler, local or otherwise, is likely to frown on someone for finding out certain things about a special run of fish in a coastal river at a certain time of year if that person has paid his dues. I have been told not to write about certain places because the pressure will be too great and new faces are not welcome. I personally would rather see a few extra flyfishers in Oregon coastal waters, and I encourage all flyfishers in Oregon to look at the coast as a land of opportunity.

The preservation and enhancement of wild and productive coastal fisheries can supply anglers with lifetime memories and give local communities a chance to show off their back yard. The catch and release ethic that permeates flyfishing makes wild fish a very renewable resource. The potential for world class flyfisheries on Oregon's coast is limitless—not that there aren't a few already. I definitely recommend that flyfishers get out their maps, rods, and regulations, and make an appointment with a big fish in a secluded spot.

The rivers listed here are each quite good at given times, and these rivers are no secret to the angling world. Take a quick look at fish catch statistics compiled by the Oregon Department of Fish and Wildlife, and you will find over a hundred different places listed for fishing on the coast and near the mouth of the Columbia River. Some are big, tumbling rivers with smaller tributaries, and some are small, coastal streams that may run only a few miles to the ocean.

Fly anglers often catch fish from beaches on river mouths. Flyfishing offshore from boats is another option that is becoming more popular. Rivers hold many hike-in opportunities, and pontoon boats take anglers into remote areas. The variety of angling opportunities on the coast is overwhelming. It is important to practice good etiquette at all times on the coastal systems, avoid confrontation, and release wild fish. If you like what you find on the coast, then by all means, do everything in your power to get it back to its natural state.

The Coastal Rivers

Columbia River to Tillamook

Columbia River
WASHINGTON
Astoria
Clatskanie
Seaside
Jewell
River
Veronia
St. Helens
Cannon Beach
Manzanita
Nehalem
Nehalem
Buxton
Vancouver, Washington
Wheeler
Miami
Garibaldi
Kilchis River
Wilson River
Willamette River
Bay City
Hillsboro
Forest Grove
Portland
Trask River
Tillamook
101
30
5
202
47
26
53
6
8
84

N

Legend
Interstate
US Highway
State/Cty Road
River

The Coastal Rivers

Tillamook to Newport

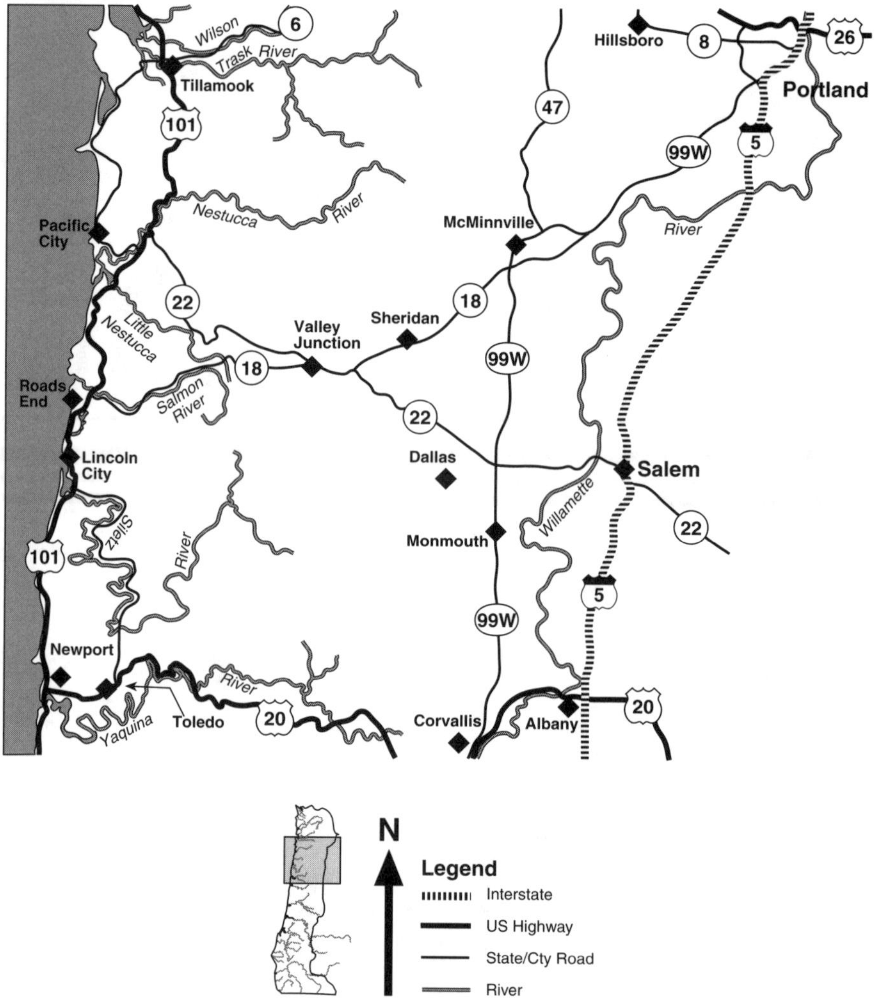

N

Legend

- Interstate
- US Highway
- State/Cty Road
- River

The Coastal Rivers

Newport to Florence

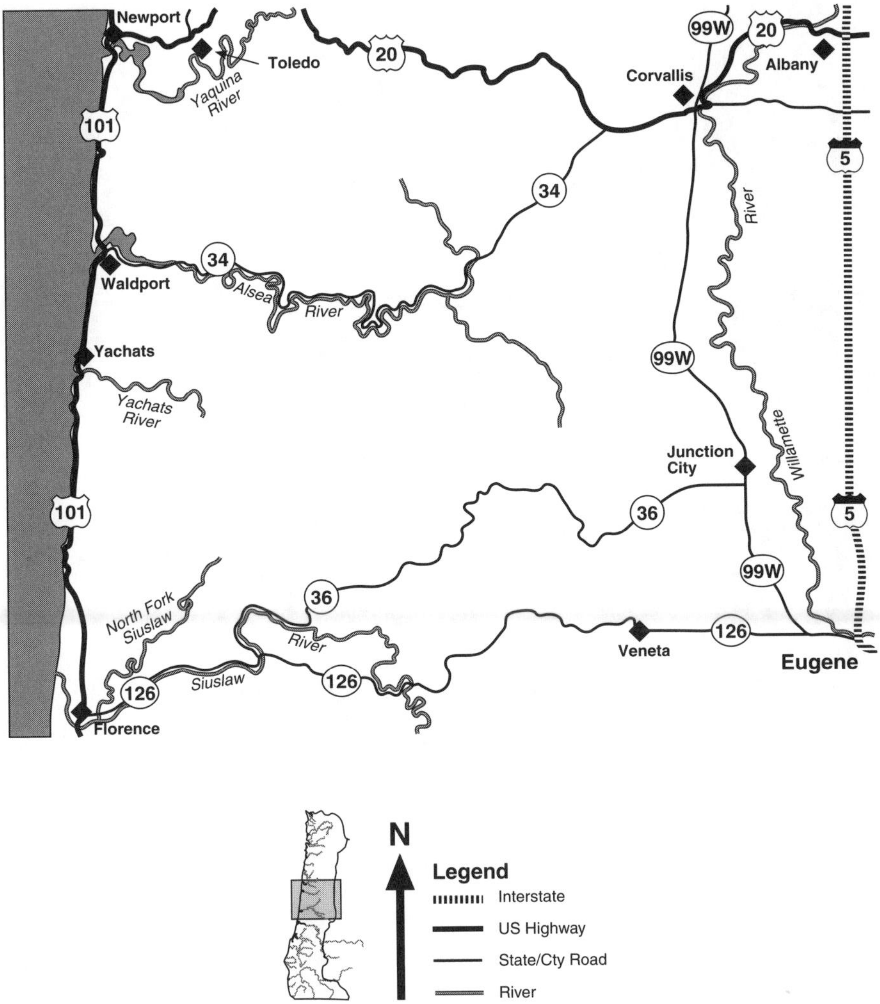

Newport
Toledo
Yaquina River
20
101
Corvallis
99W
20
Albany
5
34
River
Waldport
34
Alsea River
Yachats
Yachats River
99W
Junction City
Willamette
36
101
5
99W
North Fork Siuslaw
36
River
126
Veneta
126
Eugene
Siuslaw
126
Florence

N

Legend
Interstate
US Highway
State/Cty Road
River

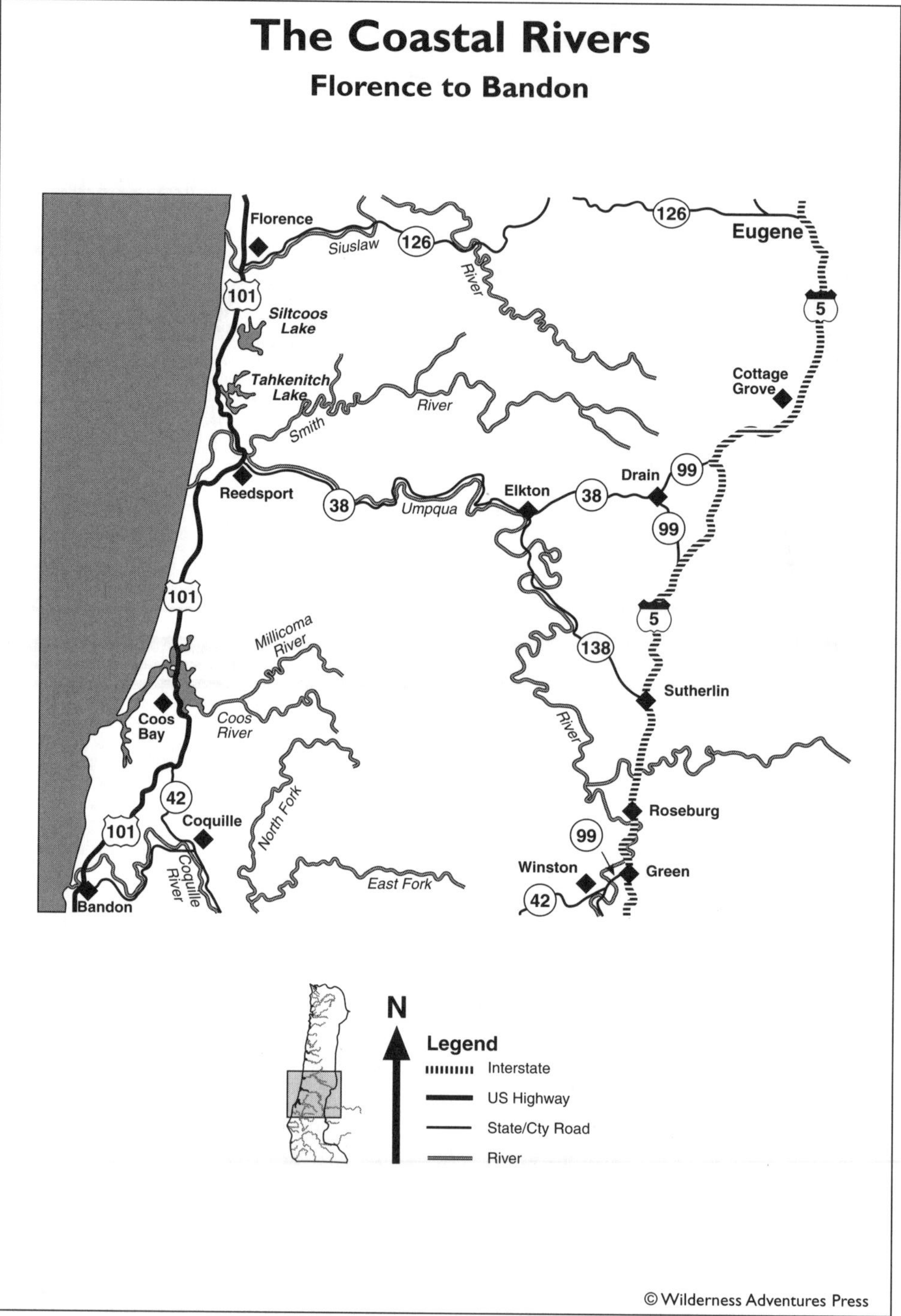
The Coastal Rivers
Florence to Bandon
Florence
Siuslaw
126
River
126
Eugene
101
Siltcoos Lake
5
Tahkenitch Lake
Smith
River
Cottage Grove
Reedsport
38
Umpqua
Elkton
38
Drain
99
99
101
5
Millicoma River
138
Sutherlin
Coos Bay
Coos River
River
North Fork
42
Coquille
Roseburg
101
99
Coquille River
Winston
Green
East Fork
42
Bandon
N
Legend
Interstate
US Highway
State/Cty Road
River

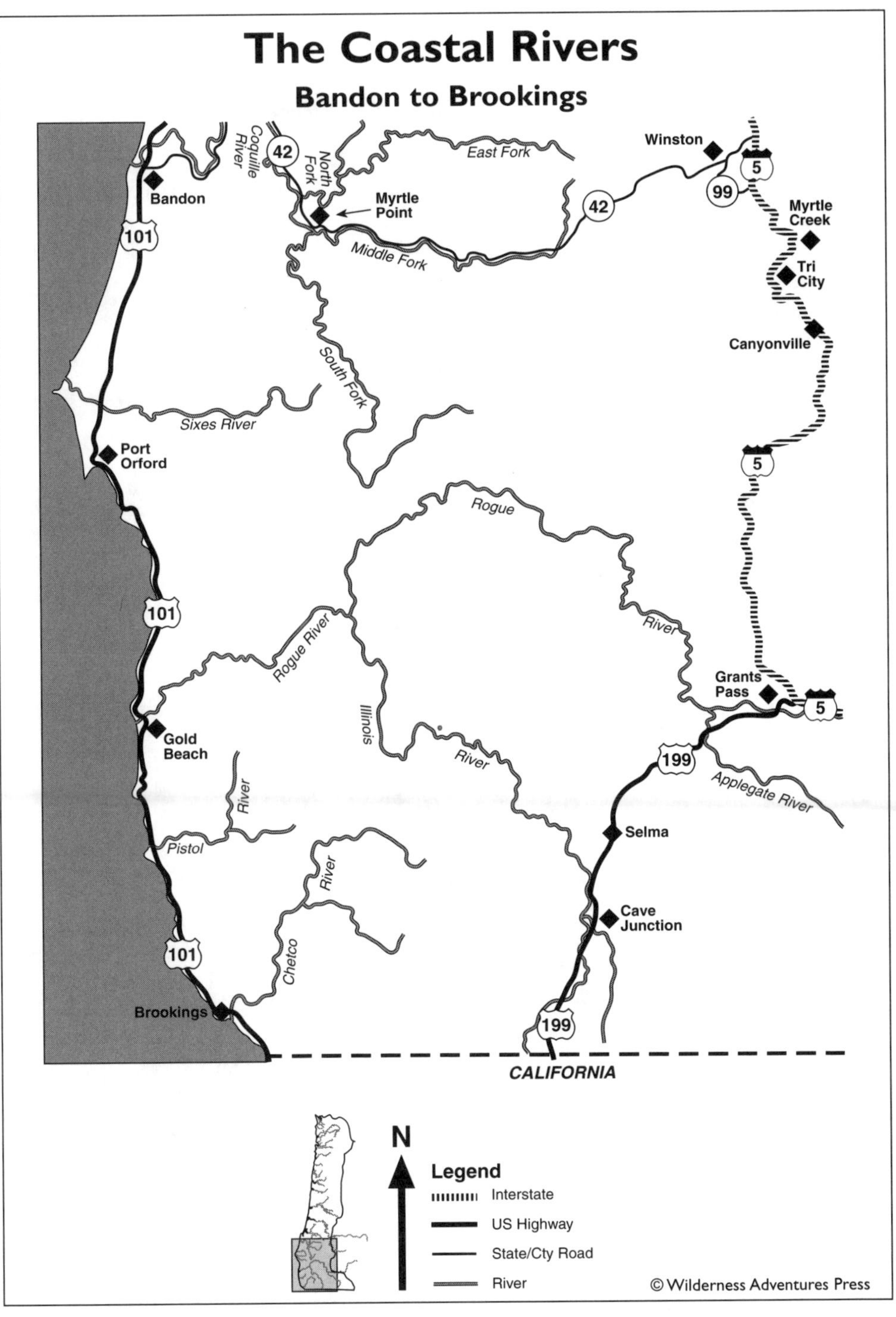
The Coastal Rivers
Bandon to Brookings
Bandon
Coquille River
42
North Fork
East Fork
Winston
5
99
Myrtle Point
42
Myrtle Creek
101
Middle Fork
Tri City
Canyonville
South Fork
Sixes River
Port Orford
5
Rogue
101
River
Rogue River
Grants Pass
5
Illinois
Gold Beach
River
199
Applegate River
River
Selma
Pistol
River
Cave Junction
101
Chetco
Brookings
199
CALIFORNIA
N
Legend
Interstate
US Highway
State/Cty Road
River
© Wilderness Adventures Press

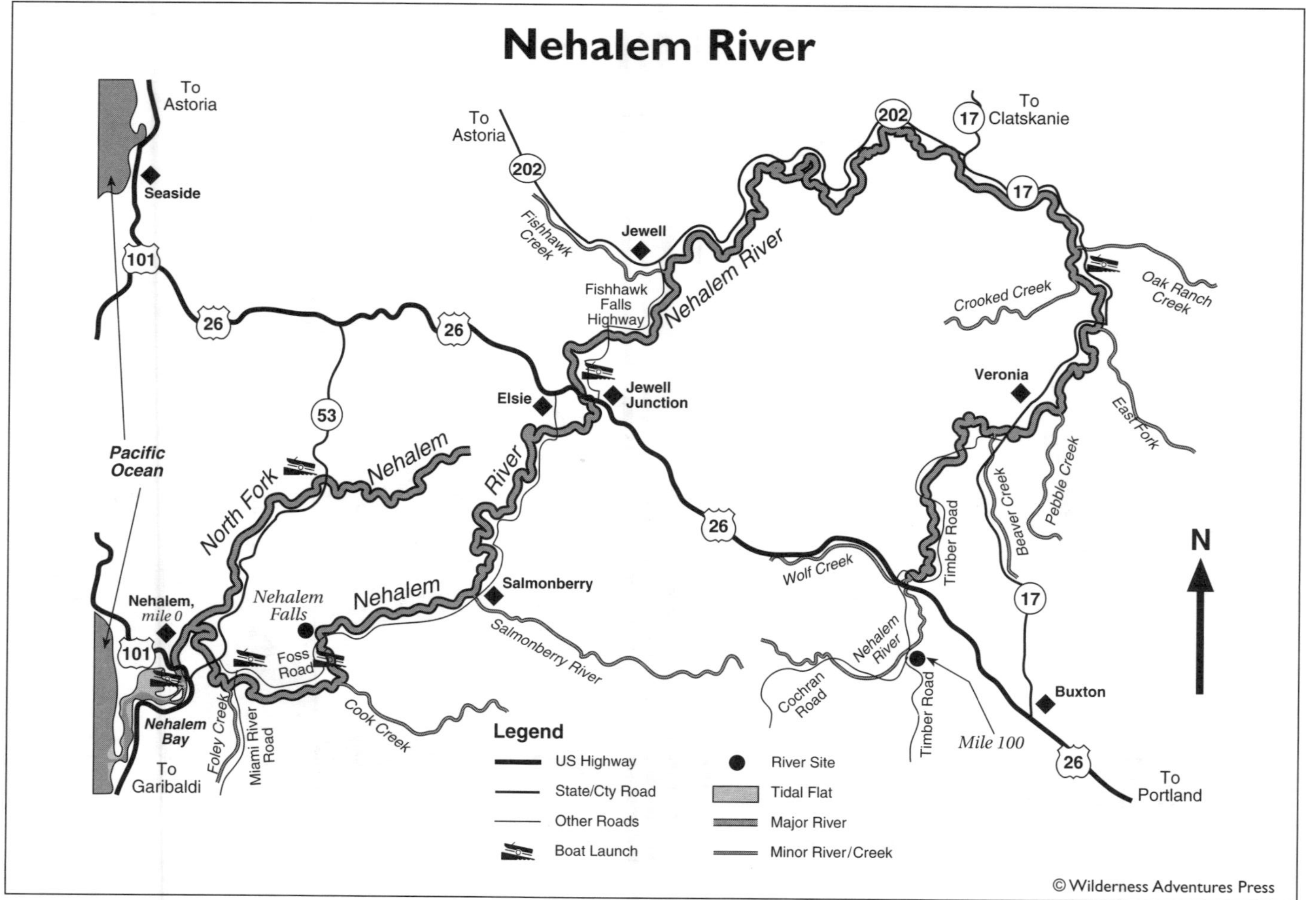
Nehalem River
To Astoria
Seaside
101
26
Pacific Ocean
To Astoria
202
Fishhawk Creek
Jewell
Fishhawk Falls Highway
Nehalem River
202
17
To Clatskanie
17
Oak Ranch Creek
Crooked Creek
Veronia
East Fork
Pebble Creek
Beaver Creek
Timber Road
26
53
Elsie
Jewell Junction
North Fork
Nehalem
River
Nehalem, mile 0
Nehalem Falls
Nehalem
Salmonberry
Salmonberry River
Wolf Creek
Nehalem River
Cochran Road
Timber Road
Mile 100
17
Buxton
26
To Portland
N
101
Foss Road
Nehalem Bay
Foley Creek
Miami River Road
Cook Creek
To Garibaldi
Legend
US Highway
State/Cty Road
Other Roads
Boat Launch
River Site
Tidal Flat
Major River
Minor River/Creek
© Wilderness Adventures Press

NEHALEM RIVER

Oregon's third longest river is the Nehalem, but it's hard to see this on a map as the river twists and turns almost into a circle. You'll find plenty of access throughout its length and fair numbers of steelhead, chinook, and sea-run cutthroat.

The Nehalem River is known primarily for its winter-run steelhead, which are present in good numbers through the holiday season. For decent action on wild steelhead, check this river out in February.

Tom Anderberg, owner of TK Fly Supply in Forest Grove, describes the river as good-sized with longer, slower runs than some found on other area rivers. He also assures me that the river is very slick—consider stream cleats or at least studded boots on the Nehalem.

With a lot of private property on its banks, lower sections are generally floated to gain access. Smaller water opportunities can be found in the Nehalem's tributaries for those who want to do some exploration off the main river.

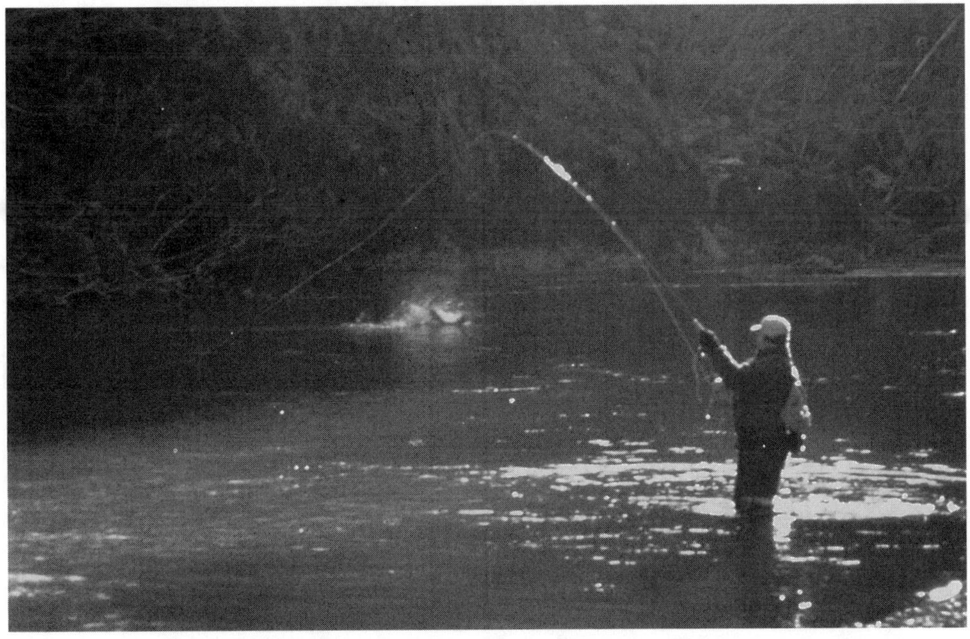

Winter steelheading on the Oregon Coast. (Photo by Ken Morrish)

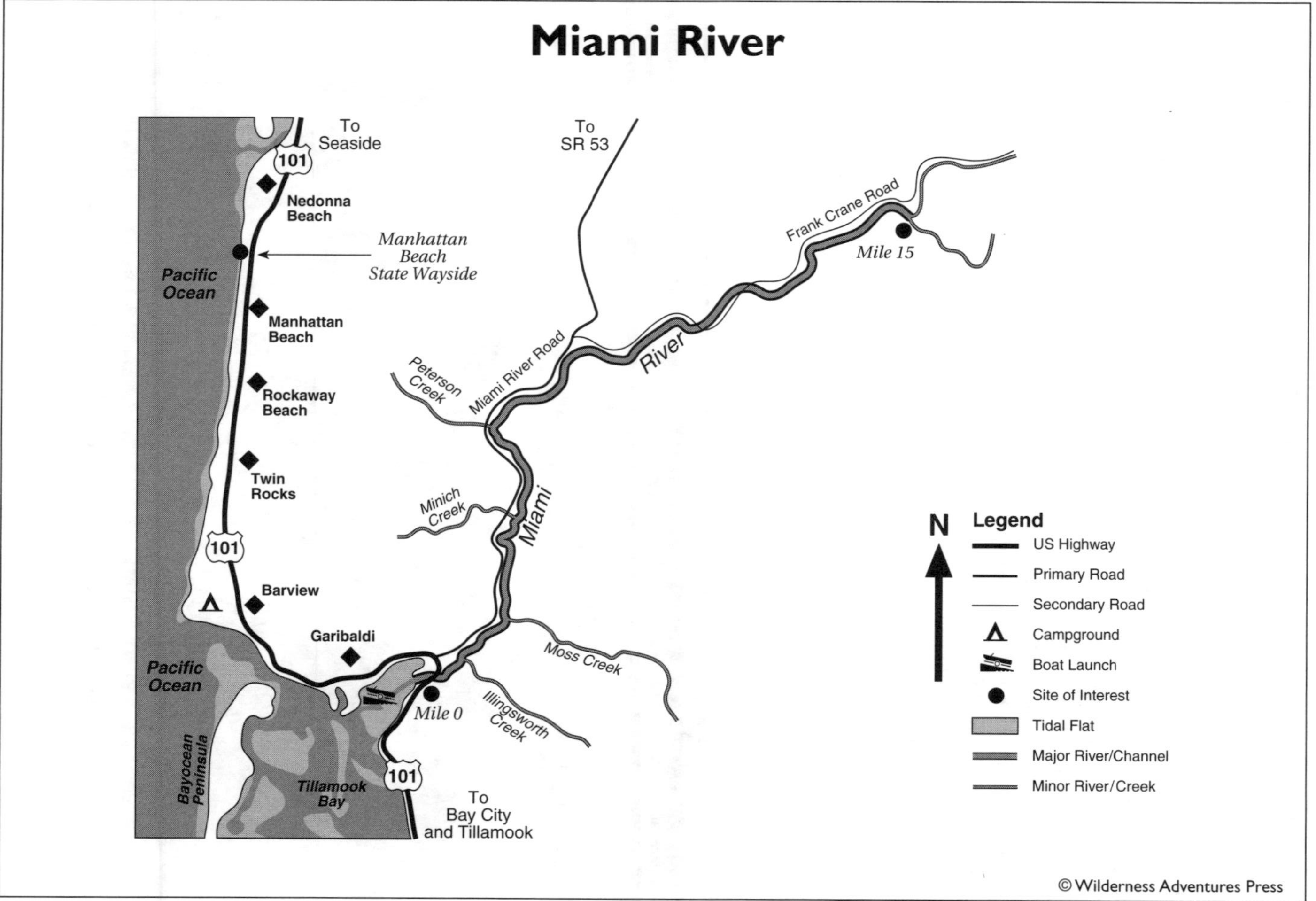

Miami River
To Seaside
101
Nedonna Beach
Manhattan Beach State Wayside
Pacific Ocean
Manhattan Beach
Rockaway Beach
Twin Rocks
Barview
Garibaldi
Pacific Ocean
Bayocean Peninsula
Tillamook Bay
To Bay City and Tillamook
Mile 0
Illingsworth Creek
Moss Creek
Minich Creek
Peterson Creek
Miami River Road
To SR 53
Miami
River
Frank Crane Road
Mile 15
N
Legend
US Highway
Primary Road
Secondary Road
Campground
Boat Launch
Site of Interest
Tidal Flat
Major River/Channel
Minor River/Creek
© Wilderness Adventures Press

MIAMI RIVER

The northernmost fishable river flowing into Tillamook Bay, the Miami is host to steelhead, chinook, and sea-run cutthroat, as well as a run of chum salmon that is open for catch and release only. When asked what would tempt chum, Tom Anderberg was quick to answer, "You have to show them green. They may eat other things, but a green glo-bug or a green popsicle are great bets when fishing over chum. You can fish with an indicator or by using a greased line technique. Quartering up with a fly hung loose, then a slow swing quartering down, will draw strikes from chum."

Among the migratory fish in coastal waters, chum salmon stand out from the crowd due the tiger-like stripes they develop as they move upriver toward their spawning areas. Their size is usually somewhere between steelhead and chinook, and even though they are fished on a catch-and-release basis only, hardware fishers also find them enjoyable to fish. Anglers fishing for chinook quite often find themselves with a chum on the end of their line—just remember that they must be returned to the river.

For those intentionally fishing for chum, try to get on the river on a weekday and hope bad weather or circumstances keep others at home. The Miami is a smaller river that makes spotting fish relatively easy, even in the few spots deep enough that the bottom isn't visible. Once you've spotted them, cast either on the swing or with an indicator.

In December, the Miami has a hatchery run of steelhead. If you're looking for big fish in small water, check the Miami out in February, when big steelhead show up.

Public access on the Miami is limited to a few roadside wade opportunities or floating in small craft. There is also some reasonably priced private access that is marked along the river. These can be an alternative when public areas are crowded. Treat all access, public and private, with respect.

Again, with several excellent fisheries available within a short distance from one another, north coast fishing offers anglers a nice variety and the chance to get on another river quickly if crowds or conditions on one river aren't favorable.

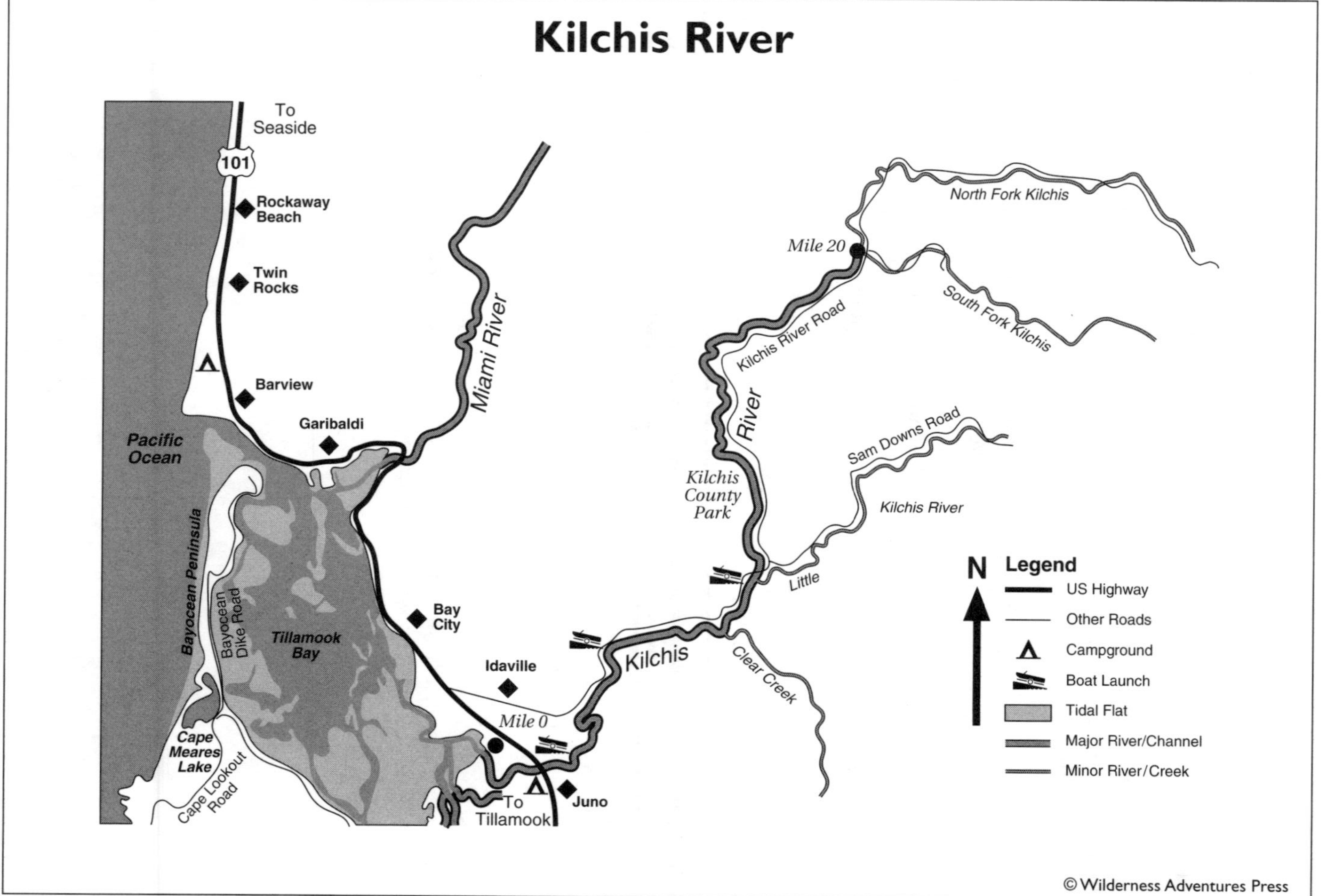
Kilchis River
To Seaside
101
Rockaway Beach
Twin Rocks
Barview
Garibaldi
Pacific Ocean
Miami River
Bayocean Peninsula
Bayocean Dike Road
Tillamook Bay
Cape Meares Lake
Cape Lookout Road
Bay City
Idaville
Mile 0
To Tillamook
Juno
Kilchis
Clear Creek
Little
Kilchis County Park
River
Kilchis River Road
Mile 20
North Fork Kilchis
South Fork Kilchis
Sam Downs Road
Kilchis River
N
Legend
US Highway
Other Roads
Campground
Boat Launch
Tidal Flat
Major River/Channel
Minor River/Creek
© Wilderness Adventures Press

KILCHIS RIVER

Like the Miami, the Kilchis has a run of chum salmon that are available on a catch and release basis in October and part of November. The river also hosts steelhead, chinook, and sea-run cutthroat. The Kilchis is a beautiful setting, so besides your fishing gear, bring your camera when fishing the river's upper sections.

Access is limited, especially in the lower sections. A pontoon boat will serve an angler well on this little river. The Kilchis is another river that clears quickly after heavy rains, making it a good starting point for a day of fishing.

Coastal rivers are subject to a variety of special regulations, and the Kilchis is no exception. Make sure you carry an up-to-date copy of Oregon's regulations at all times, because the rules change fairly often on individual rivers, as well as from river to river. Two regulations that are constant: always release wild fish and all sea-run cutthroat.

The Kilchis is known for its winter-run steelhead, which are in the river from November until March. Use standard techniques and flies to hook up with steelhead on the Kilchis.

August can have some decent sea-run cutthroat show up in the river. Sometimes all it takes to move good numbers of sea-runs upriver is a small burst of rain at this time of year. In the lower river, concentrate your efforts in areas having structure or slower moving water.

This is a very nice fishery, especially when crowds thin out. If you can time your trip during a lull in the crowds, you'll find this a very satisfactory fishing experience.

Brian Gefroh can see his targets holding at the head of a slow run.

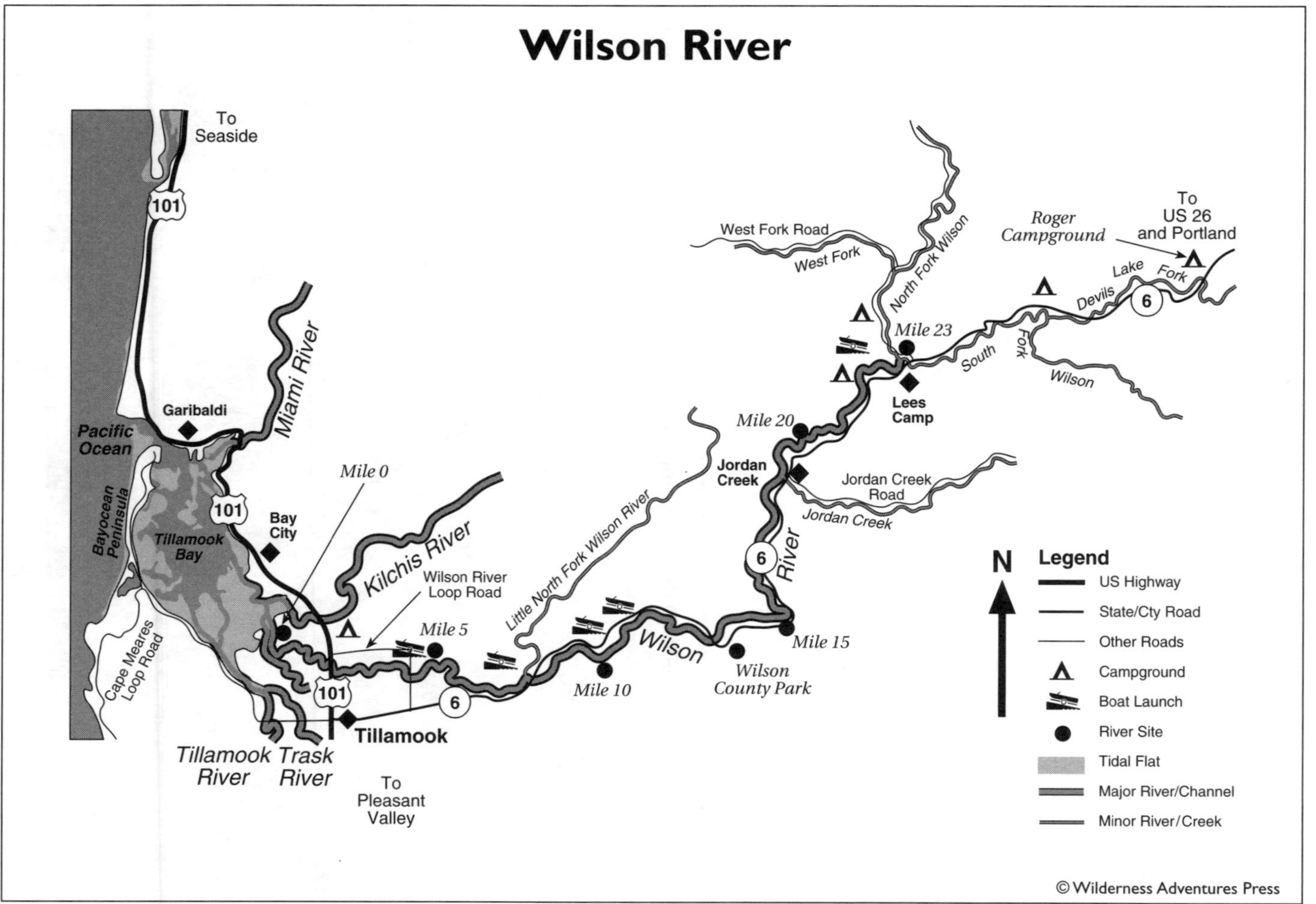

Wilson River
To Seaside
101
Garibaldi
Pacific Ocean
Miami River
Bayocean Peninsula
Tillamook Bay
Bay City
Mile 0
Kilchis River
Wilson River Loop Road
Mile 5
Cape Meares Loop Road
Tillamook
Tillamook River
Trask River
To Pleasant Valley
Little North Fork Wilson River
Wilson
Mile 10
Wilson County Park
Mile 15
6
River
Jordan Creek
Jordan Creek Road
Jordan Creek
Mile 20
Lees Camp
Mile 23
West Fork Road
West Fork
North Fork Wilson
South Fork Wilson
Roger Campground
Devils Lake Fork
To US 26 and Portland
N
Legend
US Highway
State/Cty Road
Other Roads
Campground
Boat Launch
River Site
Tidal Flat
Major River/Channel
Minor River/Creek
© Wilderness Adventures Press

WILSON RIVER

This well-known coastal river produces good numbers of steelhead, chinook, and sea-run cutthroat. According to Tom Anderberg, owner of TK Fly Supply in Forest Grove, "The Wilson fishes year around now, especially since sea-run cutts have come back."

Sea-run cutthroat are an important target for flyfishers, filling in the lull between steelhead and chinook runs. Currently, regulations are catch and release only for cutts on the entire coast. There is the potential for Oregon to have a world class sea-run cutthroat fishery, but anglers fear that once the numbers are high enough, limits will once again be allowed. Cutthroat populations would then be good enough to be interesting but hardly world class.

As more flyfishers visit the coast, the Oregon Department of Fish and Wildlife will have to consider flyfishing when implementing policy and regulations. According to Anderberg, "There is no doubt in my mind that the potential of the sea-run cutt fishery alone would make Oregon coastal rivers destination fisheries in the summer months."

Tillamook and nearby communities, as flyfishing destinations, would benefit in several ways: More visitors to spend money on accommodations, restaurants and sporting goods, as well as other services; during the day, anglers don't clog city streets because they are out fishing; they generally retire for the night fairly early in order to get out on the water early the next morning; and perhaps an increase in flyfishing activity would attract some new businesses to the community.

The Wilson is already a destination for flyfishers, and the addition of a noteworthy sea-run cutthroat fishery would only make it better. Anderberg says the whole river is accessible. In its lower waters, which border farmland, anglers most often fish through in boats. Bank anglers can get on the upper river from Hwy 6, which has plenty of pullouts and trails.

Techniques employed on the Wilson for steelhead and chinook include swinging flies and using indicators with slack line techniques. Anderberg likes to use a floating line with some weight if needed. Sinktips are useful to move fish hugging the bottom. Tom suggests using marabou patterns in red and black or black and orange for steelhead. Glo-bug patterns are also effective.

Like many guides who work the coast, he uses different techniques when guiding than when fishing on his own, which means that he relies on his advanced skills rather than special equipment to produce hook-ups. Some prefer to use traditional techniques in all situations. It's really a matter of personal choice—indicators and slack lines can be helpful for anyone and are almost a necessity in certain conditions.

Fishing for sea-run cutts is done much as it is for westslope cutthroat. In August when fish enter the rivers in full force, streamer fishing is employed. Tom suggests the spruce fly, which may even attract a steelhead as well.

Once in the river, treat sea-runs as you would any other trout. Dry flies, such as Wulffs and elk hair caddis, can be effective at times. If using basic nymphs, try

Princes or Teeny nymphs with a greased line technique or with an indicator. Look for soft water, riffles with deep buckets, and the calmest water near structure or shadows. Standard techniques with bright flies like glo-bugs work on the Wilson River, and insect patterns are also a staple employed by area guides. Both Milton Fisher and Tom Anderberg make use of subtle patterns like stoneflies, hare's ears, Teeny nymphs, and other similar flies.

While steelhead can be found all year, chinook are present in spring and fall. Searuns can show up as early as July and be present into October. When flows are manageable in significant stretches of water, pontoon boats can be used effectively on the Wilson River. According to Anderberg, 5.4 feet is the optimum depth for using pontoons on this river, while 8 feet is on the verge of being too high. Up-to-date information on river levels can be obtained by calling 503-261-9246 or on the internet at www.fishinginoregon.com.

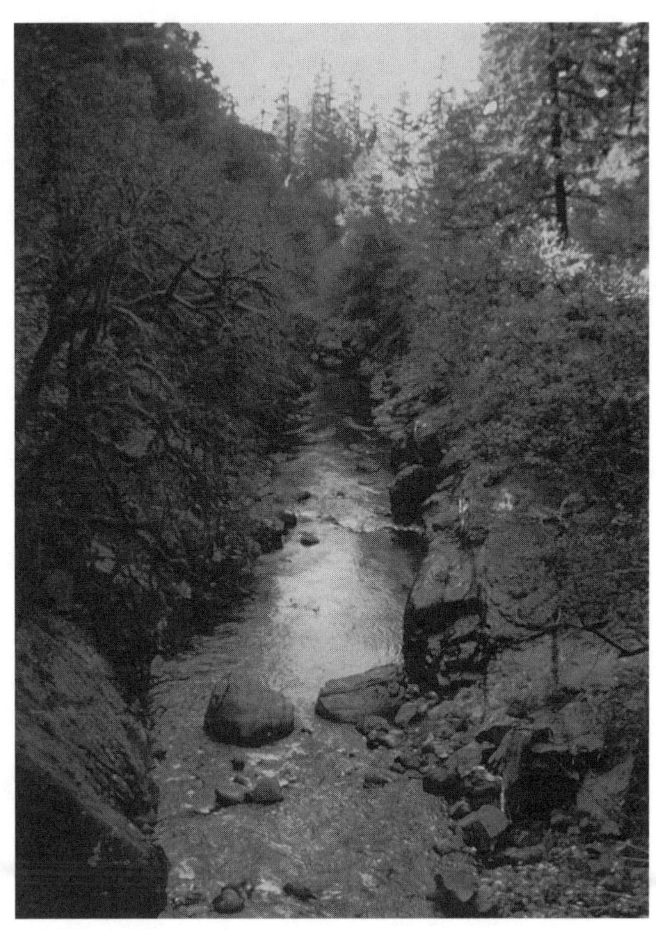

Sea-run cutthroat get well up into coastal streams like this one.

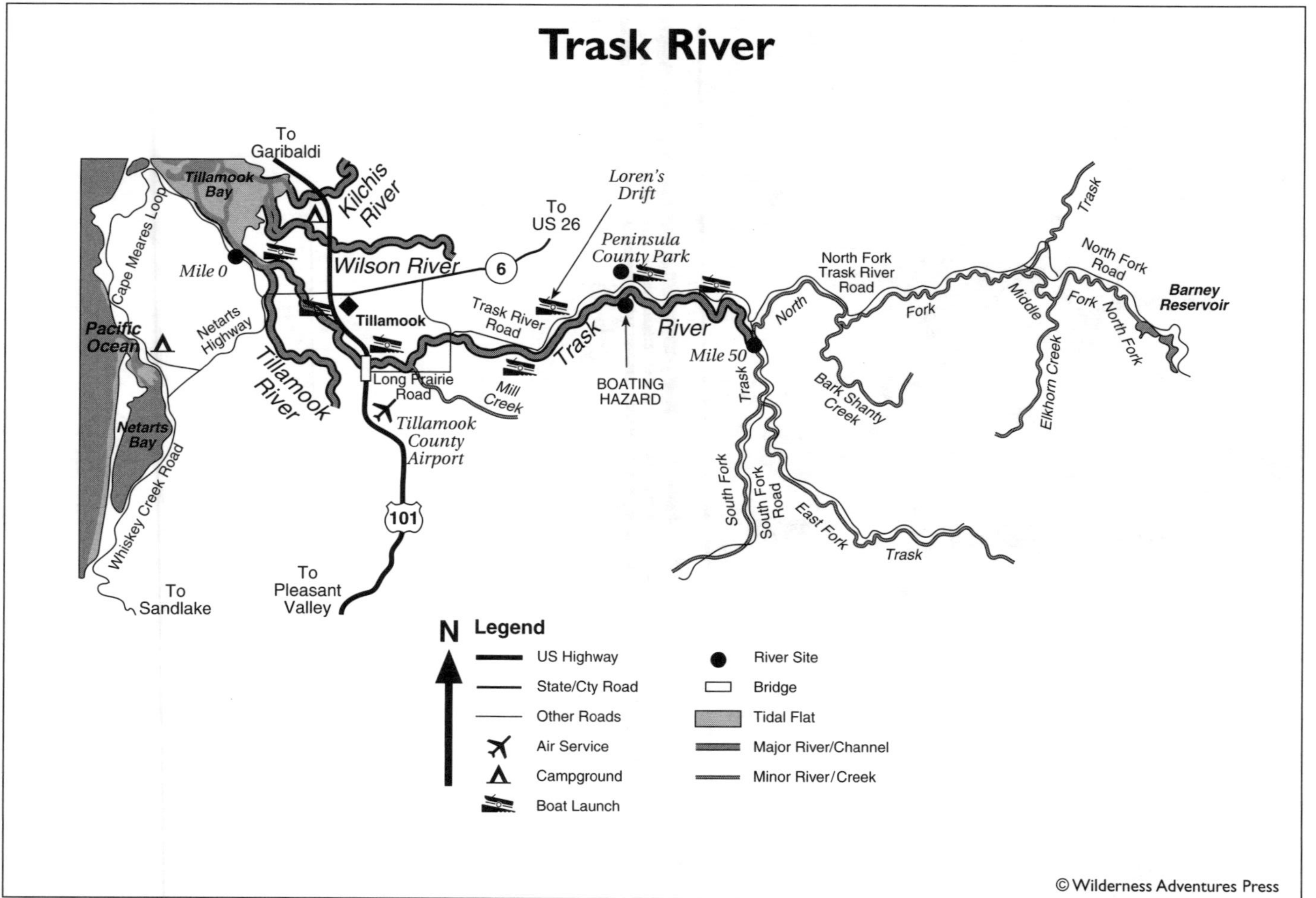
Trask River
To Garibaldi
Tillamook Bay
Kilchis River
To US 26
Loren's Drift
Peninsula County Park
Cape Meares Loop
Mile 0
Wilson River
6
Tillamook
Trask River Road
Trask
River
North Fork Trask River Road
North
Fork
Middle
North Fork Road
Fork
North Fork
Barney Reservoir
Trask
Pacific Ocean
Netarts Highway
Tillamook River
Long Prairie Road
Mill Creek
BOATING HAZARD
Mile 50
Trask
Bark Shanty Creek
Elkhorn Creek
Tillamook County Airport
Netarts Bay
Whiskey Creek Road
101
South Fork
South Fork Road
East Fork
Trask
To Sandlake
To Pleasant Valley
N
Legend
US Highway
State/Cty Road
Other Roads
Air Service
Campground
Boat Launch
River Site
Bridge
Tidal Flat
Major River/Channel
Minor River/Creek
© Wilderness Adventures Press

Trask River

Situated next door to the Wilson River, the Trask River shares many of the same traits with some variations. Access isn't as abundant on this river because there is more private property along its banks. Anglers become bottlenecked in public access areas, so many flyfishers opt to float the river, according to Tom Anderberg of TK Fly Supply. One of the more common floats is from Loren's Drift to the bridge on Hwy 101.

Anderberg says, "The Trask seems to have more big steelhead in it than neighboring rivers, and finding three and four salt fish is more common on the Trask." Along with excellent winter and spring runs of steelhead, there are fall and spring runs of chinook, a decent population of sea-run cutthroat in summer months, and a wild coho run that has an open season. Flyfishers will find a lot of fly water on the Trask, as well.

The same gear and techniques used on the Wilson and other coastal rivers are applicable on the Trask. And again, you won't have the place to yourself, so planning and preparation are important. Many locals will be on the river, and visiting anglers should do their best to make sure that they continue to be welcome. Practice stream etiquette, and if you object to other fishing practices that are legal, keep it to yourself.

In order to fish effectively on the north coast, anglers need to do their research ahead of time—check regulations, river flows, optimum times for flyfishing as opposed to bait fishing, when and where to hire a guide, where you can fish the banks and where floating is a better option. If you choose to use small craft like pontoons, be sure that you know how to use them safely. Good preparation will pay off in a quality fishing trip.

With its proximity to the other rivers draining into Tillamook Bay, the Trask is definitely worth checking out. It can be busy, but at the right times you will find this a productive fishery.

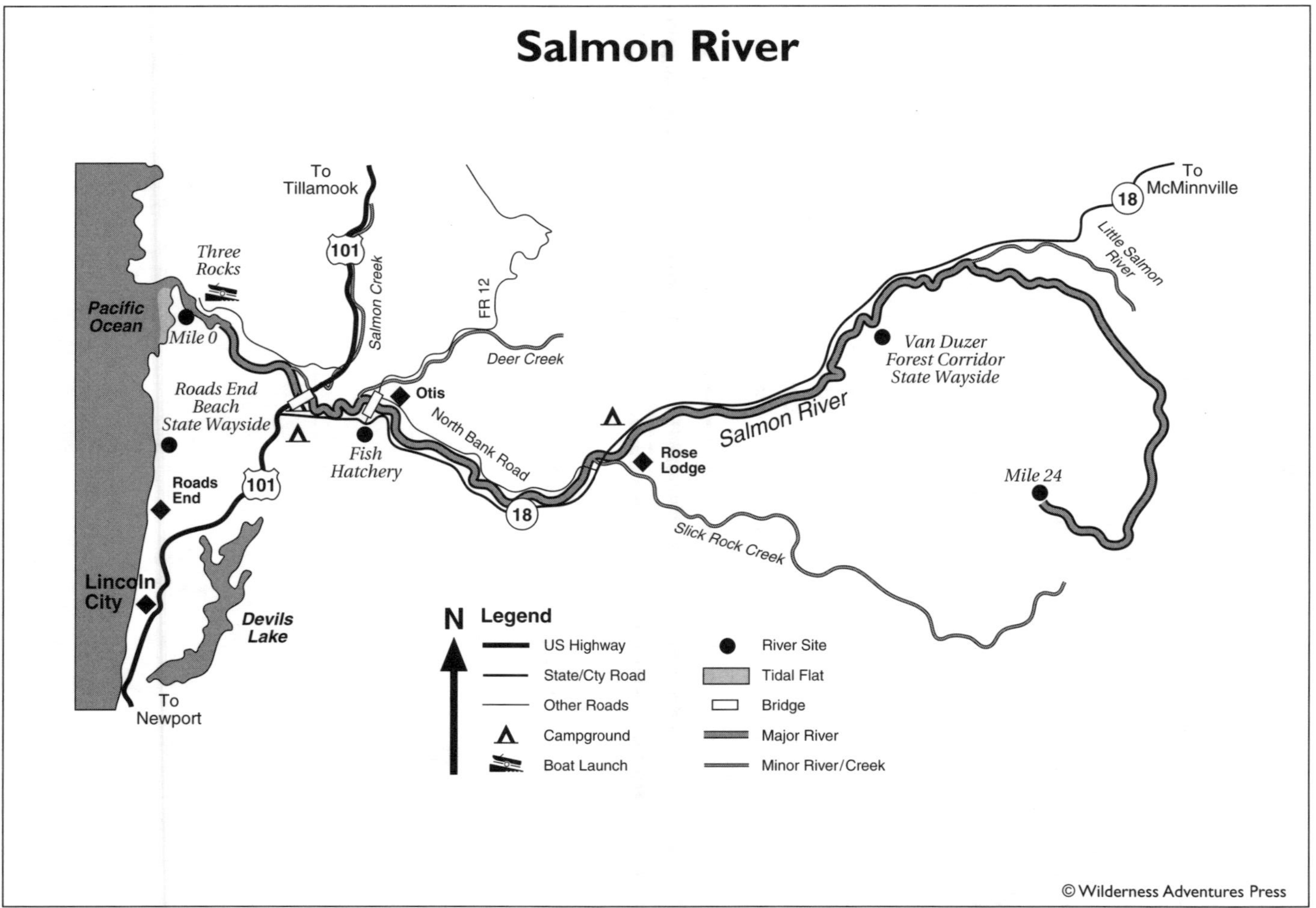

Salmon River
To Tillamook
101
Salmon Creek
FR 12
To McMinnville
18
Little Salmon River
Three Rocks
Pacific Ocean
Mile 0
Deer Creek
Otis
Van Duzer Forest Corridor State Wayside
Roads End Beach State Wayside
North Bank Road
Salmon River
Fish Hatchery
Rose Lodge
Mile 24
Roads End
101
18
Slick Rock Creek
Lincoln City
Devils Lake
To Newport
N
Legend
US Highway
State/Cty Road
Other Roads
Campground
Boat Launch
River Site
Tidal Flat
Bridge
Major River
Minor River/Creek
© Wilderness Adventures Press

Salmon River

A short, coastal river, the Salmon has good chinook runs, winter-run steelhead, and sea-run cutthroat. The Salmon's mouth is just north of Lincoln City and is paralleled for most of its length by Hwy 18, which connects to McMinnville from coastal Hwy 101. Chinook and steelhead are in the river in good numbers during fall and winter, while sea-run cutthroat can be found in late summer.

Access can be spotty due to the amount of private property on the river, but it can be found. On the lower reaches where fish first enter the river, access is mostly gained by using prams.

The Salmon clears more quickly than neighboring rivers and is a good choice soon after rains stop. December and January are usually the best times to find good runs of winter steelhead. Because this river is only about 25 miles long, some runs of fish can be quite dense. If an angler happens to be on the river on one of those magical winter days, the fishing can be memorable.

When water levels drop, there is more fly water available, and fish become more inclined to take a fly. There are some wade opportunities, but with its limited access, you'll have to look a littler harder for them on the Salmon.

Steelheading on the coast in winter. (Photo by Ken Morrish)

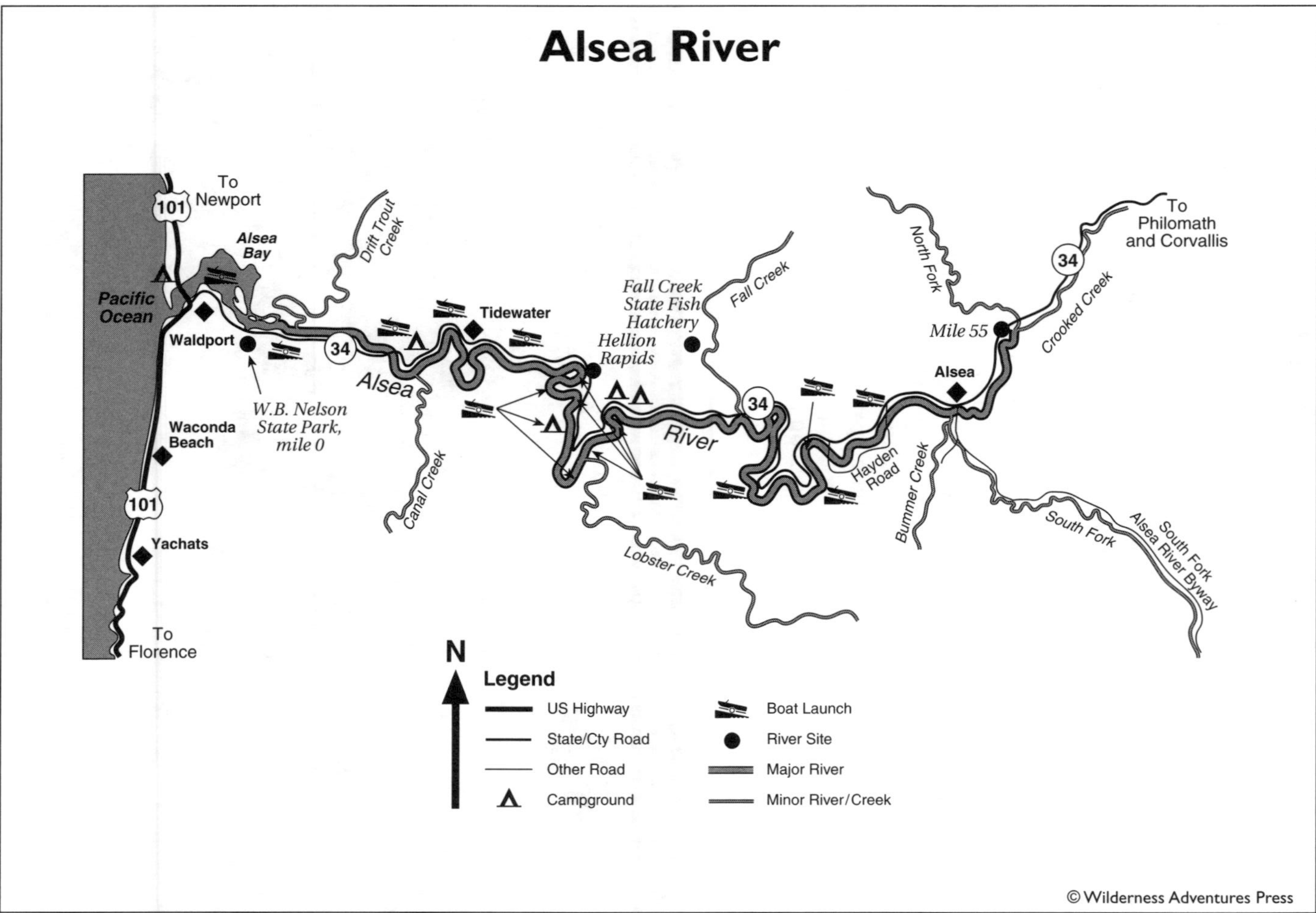
Alsea River
To Newport
101
Alsea Bay
Drift Trout Creek
Pacific Ocean
Waldport
Tidewater
34
Alsea
Fall Creek State Fish Hatchery
Hellion Rapids
Fall Creek
W.B. Nelson State Park, mile 0
Waconda Beach
Canal Creek
River
Lobster Creek
North Fork
To Philomath and Corvallis
Mile 55
Crooked Creek
Alsea
Hayden Road
Bummer Creek
South Fork
South Fork Alsea River Byway
Yachats
To Florence
N
Legend
US Highway
State/Cty Road
Other Road
Campground
Boat Launch
River Site
Major River
Minor River/Creek
© Wilderness Adventures Press

ALSEA RIVER

The Alsea makes a short, swift run to the Pacific from the coast range. The river has a nice winter steelhead fishery, as well as chinook and sea-run cutthroat and a resident population of cutthroat.

Winter steelhead are the primary target on the Alsea, and they can weigh between 5 and 20 pounds, although the average fish weighs around 8 pounds. The run is about 95 percent hatchery fish with a few wild fish showing up later. Brian Buggenhagen, Dan Reynolds, and Mike Gorhman own The Scarlet Ibis in Corvallis and fish the Alsea often. According to Brian, "The Alsea River steelhead are best fished in the fast, deep water. The steelhead will be in faster water at low levels and will use slightly lesser currents at higher levels."

Brian notes that there aren't many places with slow water on the Alsea. Prime time to fish the river's steelhead is January through March. The type of water found on the Alsea calls for deep-water techniques to catch bottom-dwelling winter runs. Indicator techniques will work to a certain extent. The Scarlet Ibis crew uses a hybrid line system that allows them to stay on the bottom when fishing the Alsea. If you're interested in this line setup, call The Scarlet Ibis at 541-754-1544. They can help with this setup as well as fly selection.

When steelhead aren't around, the Alsea has some nice cutthroat fishing. Generally, these fish are caught on swinging flies with a big emphasis on the color red, especially when salmon are in the system. Brian says they look for chinook on redds (spawning beds) and then cast red flies behind these fish to cutts looking for an easy meal. Riffles and places with cover for the often-shy cutthroat are good places to look when salmon are upstream. Alsea cutts are caught in the 12- to 20-inch range. Cutthroat are a great fly target these days on the Oregon Coast, and with the current catch and release regulations, this should only get better.

Chinook are found in the Alsea, but few flyfishers target these big fish in the Alsea's waters. Their eggs, on the other hand, help keep the cutthroat fishery healthy, which in turn makes for happy flyfishers.

Due to its proximity to the Willamette Valley cities of Corvallis and Eugene, the Alsea is a popular place. There are quite a few bait anglers here, but the Alsea may be one of the few rivers on the coast where flyfishers show up in greater numbers. The amount of pressure can be heavy at times, but the amount of access on the river helps ease this. It is primarily a wade fishery that has some drift boat opportunities in the lower water and pontoon opportunities in the upper stretches. Wade access can be found at many parks on the river as well as off of Hwy 34, which runs much of the Alsea's length.

Like all other coastal rivers, the Alsea is loaded with special regulations. Take the regulations with you and, perhaps, keep a lawyer on retainer when referring to these ever changing, often confusing rules.

The Alsea can produce nicely in the winter even with a lot of anglers. Try to fish weekdays if possible and remain courteous to everyone. During the off-times, explore the Alsea for sea-run cutthroat and enjoy this nice coastal river.

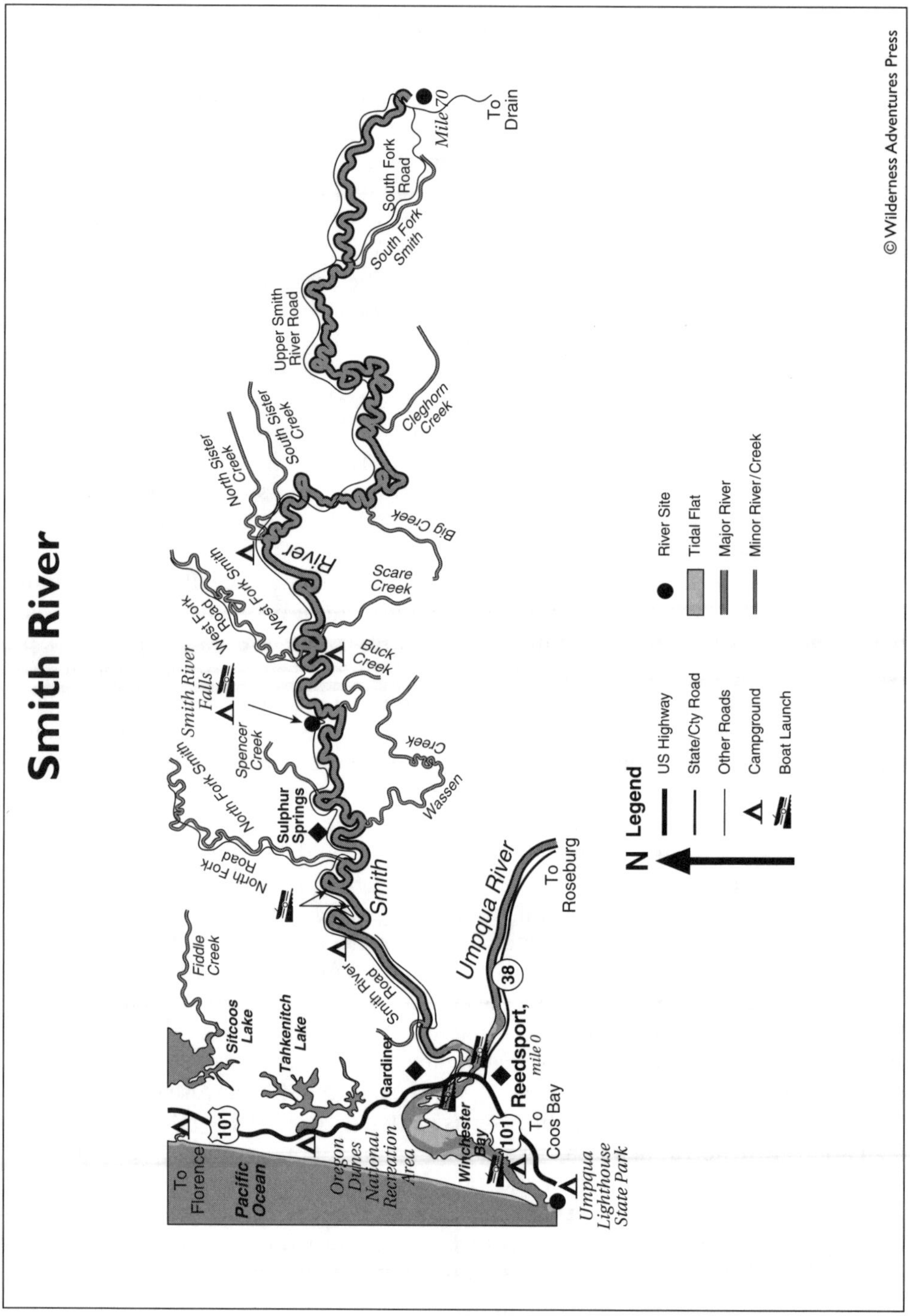
Smith River
© Wilderness Adventures Press
Legend
US Highway
State/Cty Road
Other Roads
Campground
Boat Launch
River Site
Tidal Flat
Major River
Minor River/Creek
N
To Florence
Pacific Ocean
101
Oregon Dunes National Recreation Area
Sitcoos Lake
Tahkenitch Lake
Fiddle Creek
Gardiner
Winchester Bay
Reedsport, mile 0
To Coos Bay
Umpqua Lighthouse State Park
38
Umpqua River
To Roseburg
Smith River Road
Smith
North Fork Road
North Fork Smith
Sulphur Springs
Spencer Creek
Wassen Creek
Smith River Falls
West Fork Road
West Fork Smith
Buck Creek
Scare Creek
River
Big Creek
North Sister Creek
South Sister Creek
Cleghorn Creek
Upper Smith River Road
South Fork Smith
South Fork Road
Mile 70
To Drain

SMITH RIVER

Anglers who want a new flyfishing experience will find the Smith River fills the bill. Since striped bass were introduced to the Pacific Coast some years ago, this river has become one of the West's best striped bass fisheries. These fish are big and aggressive, making them an excellent fly target using big streamers and poppers.

When stripers are in the river system, there are two types: those found in schools and single adults. Stripers found in schools are smaller (rarely over 20 inches) than their single adult counterparts. When you find yourself fishing to "schooling" stripers, use a 6-weight fly rod because these youngsters will fight as if they are a lot bigger.

Adult stripers are very predatory and tend to hang out alone. On the Smith, a legal striper worth keeping has to be 30 inches long, which gives an idea of their potential length and weight.

Stripers will be in the river in spring and fall. Although bank fishing can be done, boat fishing will help you cover the water more effectively. Good numbers of stripers can be found March through May as well as September and October when they are on spawning runs.

Striper fishing consists of casting and stripping flies like deceivers and foam poppers. In general, use heavy leaders and tackle if you're searching the water for singles. If you encounter school stripers, a switch from a 7- or 8-weight rod to a 5- or 6-weight rod will provide some great sport. When not in the river, stripers move out to Winchester Bay to forage.

You'll also find runs of fall chinook and winter steelhead in the Smith. Peak winter steelhead runs are in January. In summer, when sea-run cutthroats are moving farther upriver, anglers looking for productive fly water can pursue them into the Smith's forks.

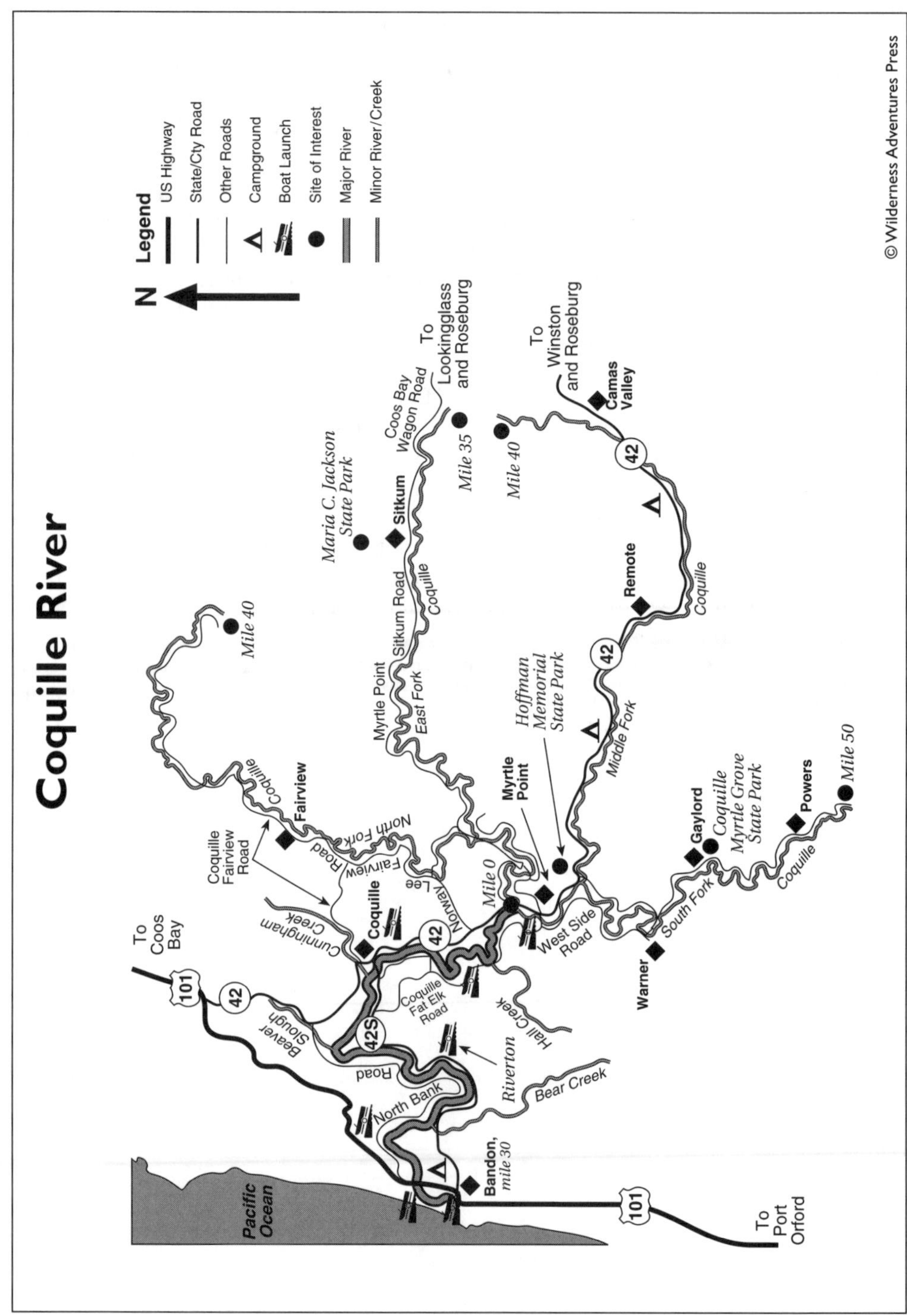
Coquille River
N
Legend
US Highway
State/Cty Road
Other Roads
Campground
Boat Launch
Site of Interest
Major River
Minor River/Creek
© Wilderness Adventures Press
To Coos Bay
101
42
42S
Pacific Ocean
Beaver Slough
North Bank
Road
Bandon, mile 30
To Port Orford
Riverton
Bear Creek
Coquille Fat Elk Road
Hall Creek
Cunningham Creek
Coquille
Coquille Fairview Road
Fairview
Fairview Road
North Fork
Coquille
Mile 40
Lee
Norway
Mile 0
West Side Road
Warner
South Fork
Myrtle Point
Hoffman Memorial State Park
Myrtle Point Sitkum Road
East Fork
Coquille
Sitkum
Maria C. Jackson State Park
Coos Bay Wagon Road
To Lookingglass and Roseburg
Mile 35
Mile 40
To Winston and Roseburg
Camas Valley
Remote
Coquille
Middle Fork
Gaylord
Coquille Myrtle Grove State Park
Powers
Mile 50
Coquille

Coquille River

The Coquille River can truly be called a system. The main river is relatively big and brush-lined. Very little flyfishing is done on the main river, where fishing is done primarily from boats, both motorized and human-powered. The Coquille's four main tributaries are what attract flyfishers.

In this extensive system, regulations vary from fork to fork, so unless you can memorize all the regulations, you should have them with you. In fact, you should have regulations with you on every coastal system, as seasons and limits change regularly.

Most sea-run cutthroat angling on the Coquille is done by bait and lure anglers who use trollers. But fly anglers will find opportunities here, as well. Look for sea-run cutts on the lower river when the tide is in and in the upper reaches during late summer. Anglers may find good action on sea-runs during low-light hours of summer.

The Coquille system hosts nice runs of steelhead with good catch rates from December through March. There will be both hatchery and wild fish, and all wild fish must be released. As I've mentioned on other coastal fisheries, wild fish opportunities open up as hatchery numbers decline.

Chinook can be found in the system as early as September. Parts of the Coquille system will have more placid water in autumn, and as these big fish move upriver, these spots can provide some great flyfishing opportunities. Stout rods are necessary for chinook, as the Coquille's forks have strong currents and plenty of structure in which fish can hang up your line.

The Coquille has plenty of access points for wade anglers in the forks of the river. The main river is a boat fishery with good ramp access. You will also find numerous spots worth visiting if only for their beauty, so treat the river and its banks kindly.

This is a perfect run to see migrating chinook salmon.

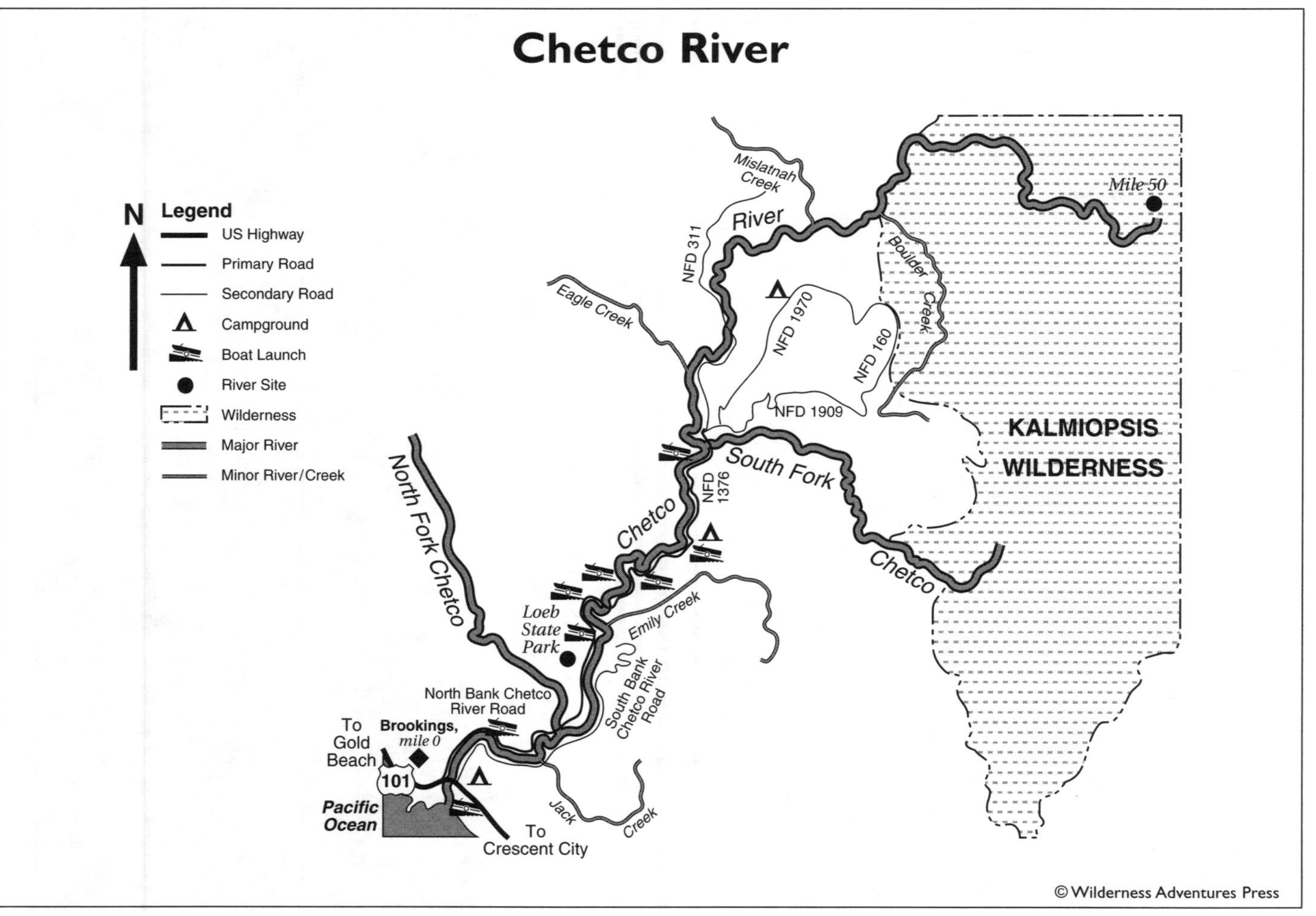
Chetco River
N
Legend
US Highway
Primary Road
Secondary Road
Campground
Boat Launch
River Site
Wilderness
Major River
Minor River/Creek
Mislatnah Creek
River
NFD 311
Mile 50
Boulder Creek
Eagle Creek
NFD 1970
NFD 160
NFD 1909
KALMIOPSIS
WILDERNESS
South Fork
NFD 1376
Chetco
Chetco
North Fork Chetco
Emily Creek
Loeb State Park
South Bank Chetco River Road
North Bank Chetco River Road
To Gold Beach
Brookings, mile 0
101
Pacific Ocean
Jack Creek
To Crescent City
© Wilderness Adventures Press

Chetco River

Flowing into the Pacific Ocean at Brookings, the Chetco River is the southernmost coastal river system to be included here. Much of the fishing done on this river is by northern Californians. While there are sea-run cutthroat in this fishery, they are mostly ignored because fall chinook and winter steelhead are the main attraction on the Chetco.

Chinook runs begin in October, and fly anglers who fish here regularly have developed very particular strategies and protocols. Because of this, these regulars feel somewhat proprietary about the Chetco. According to Ken Morrish, manager of the Ashland Outdoor Store, "The Chetco is primarily fished in two holes on the lower river, Morris and Tide Rock. They are fished out of prams, and there is a strict protocol practiced by long-time anglers. If you want to get in this line-up, familiarize yourself with the local customs or try to find someone who can show you the ropes. If you go out into those two holes not knowing what is what, it can become a very hostile place for a newcomer."

Morrish should know, since he wrote an extensive piece for *Wild Steelhead and Salmon* in the autumn 1997 issue. This is a must-read if you want to learn how to avoid conflict on the Chetco when chinook angling. Most fishing is done with shooting heads in numbers 2 through 4. Anglers mostly use 10-weights with 8- to 12-pound Maxima tippets. Anglers' favorite flies include small comet patterns tied from 6 to 8 that are stripped slowly to circling fish congregating for the upriver run.

The Chetco's strong winter steelhead fishery starts up by mid-December and closes on March 31. Always check regulations for current dates and limits. Morrish describes the Chetco as a big river without a lot of definition. "The runs are wide and the bottom gravelly, with little structure to define holding areas. The river gets a lot of boat traffic, especially by guides who may float it twice a day. There is still a lot of opportunity though. Check the soft water on the edges of more powerful looking runs." Morrish also recommends the use of a two-handed fly rod. "Distance can make a difference here."

Access is good on the Chetco for floaters and for wade anglers. Most of the pressure on the river is in the lower 10 miles. Morrish says that about 80% of fishing activity is located from Loeb State Park downriver to the mouth. This means that anglers who want to explore upriver opportunities are only limited by their own sense of adventure.

As I've said throughout this section, opportunity awaits the angler willing to explore, to get off the beaten track and take some chances. Oregon's coastal river systems hold excellent opportunities for a fly angler to cast a line at migratory fish, and each visit will contribute to your knowledge of the fish, the weather, and the seasons.

Tenmile Lakes

Among Oregon's serious warmwater anglers, Tenmile Lakes have the reputation of being Oregon's best bass lakes. This is true, but it is not common knowledge among flyfishers. Although a few more fly rodders are seen each year on Tenmile, the practice of flyfishing is a rarity here. There are two lakes: North Lake is around 1,000 acres, South Lake is around 1,600 acres, and having an average depth of around 15 feet.

Located in the beautiful coastal foothills, Tenmile Lakes hold largemouth bass up to 10 pounds, with the average in the 2- to 5-pound class. These are all strong, extremely aggressive fish that are best approached with 7- and 8-weight rods. Because of structure and plant life in the lakes, fish that are allowed to fight a long time will be lost. Use heavy tippets in the 6- to 8-pound range and in lengths that will allow a big fly to turn over.

Fish with poppers on the surface, varying the action from super obnoxious to a slight twitch. Once you find the formula, be ready for some great fishing. When fish won't rise from the shallows of Tenmile Lakes, try woolly buggers in different colors fished with erratic retrieves.

Fish for bass near structure in the lakes. These spots are best found by boat, and the size of the lakes pretty much dictates the use of a boat, anyway. Boats are available to rent at the Lakeside Marina. Call them for rental information and current conditions at 541-759-3312.

The lakes are fishable almost year-round, with spring and summer being peak seasons. Try this area if you really want some different fishing, and if local rivers blow out, it is a nice option to take your steelhead gear and fish for bass. Tenmile Lakes are located around 12 miles south of Reedsport, next to the small community of Lakeside.

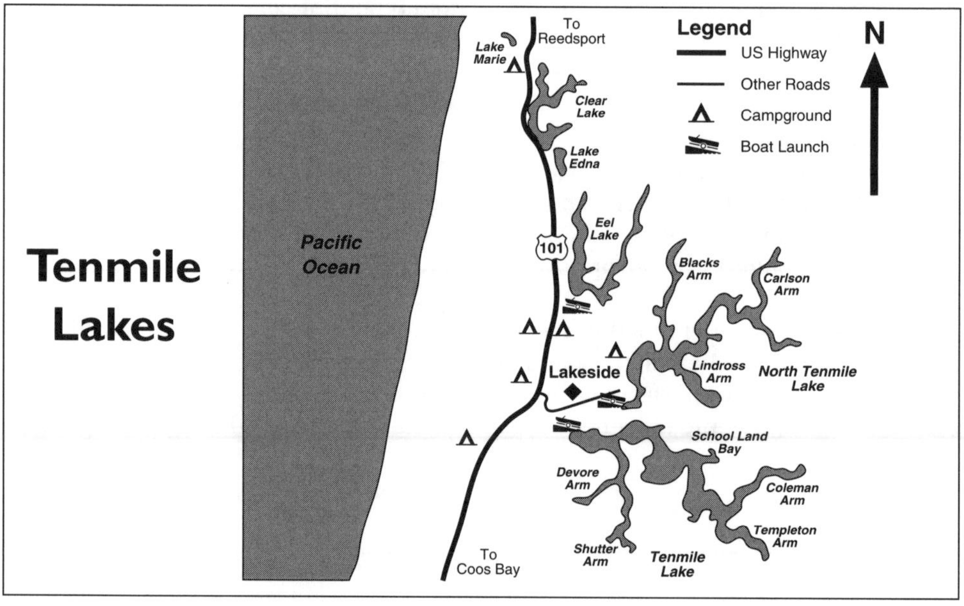

Oregon Coast Hub Cities
Gold Beach, Oregon
Elevation–16 • Population–2,069

Accommodations
City Center Motel, 94200 Harlow Street / 541-247-6675 / Pets OK / $
Drift In Motel, 94250 Port Drive / 800-424-3833 / Pets OK / $
Endicott Gardens Bed and Breakfast, 95768 Jerry's Flat Road / 541-247-6513 / $
Azalea Lodge, 29481 Ellensburg Avenue / 800-381-6635 / $$
Best Western Inn of the Beachcomber, 29266 Ellensburg Avenue / 800-528-1234 / $$$
Gold Beach Resort, 29232 Ellensburg Avenue (Hwy 101) / 800-541-0947 / $$$
Lucas Pioneer Ranch and Lodge, 3904 Cougar Lane (in Agness on the Rogue River) / 541-247-7443

Restaurants
Grant's Pancake and Omelette House, 94682 Jerry's Flat Road / 541-247-7208
Port Hole Cafe, 98812 Jerry's Flat Road / 541-247-7411
Rod 'n Reel Restaurant / 541-247-6823
Rogue Landing, 94749 Jerry's Flat Road / 541-247-5444
Spada's Restaurant, 29325 Neil Court / 541-247-7732

Sporting Goods
Rogue Outdoor Store, 29865 Ellensburg Avenue / 541-247-7142

Hospital
Curry General Hospital, 94220 Fourth Street / 541-247-6621
North Bend Medical Center, 94180 Second Street / 541-247-7047

Airport
Roseburg Regional Airport, 900 Southeast Douglas Avenue (Roseburg, OR) / 541-672-4931

Auto Rental
Certified Auto Rentals, 1410 Southeast Stephens Street (Roseburg, OR) / 541-672-1472
Enterprise Rent-A-Car, 1481 Northeast Stephens Street (Roseburg, OR) / 541-440-3030

Auto Service
D and J Texaco, 29619 Ellensburg Avenue / 541-247-7440

For More Information
Gold Beach Chamber of Commerce
1225 South Ellensburg #3
Gold Beach, OR 97444
800-525-2334

Tillamook, Oregon

Elevation–22 • Population–4,275

Accommodations

Tillamook Inn, 1810 Hwy 101 North / 503-842-4413 / Pets OK / $
Mar-Clair Inn, 11 Main Avenue / 800-331-6857 / $$
Shilo Inn, 2515 North Main Avenue / 800-222-2244 / $$$
Best Western Inn and Suites, Makinster Road / 800-528-1234
Kaufman's Streamborn (guiding and lodging on Oregon's north coast; Milton Fisher), 8861 Southwest Commercial Street (Tigard, OR) / 503-639-7004; 800-442-4359

Restaurants

Alice's Country House, 17345 Wilson River Hwy / 503-842-7927
The Barn Restaurant and Lounge, 1204 Ivy Street / 503-842-3664
Scotty's Sports Bar, 204½ Main Street / 503-842-8422
Cedar Bay Restaurant, 2015 First Street / 503-842-8288

Fly Shop and Sporting Goods

Kaufman's Streamborn, 8861 Southwest Commercial Street (Tigard, OR) / 503-639-7004; 800-442-4359

Hospital

Tillamook County General Hospital, 1000 Third Street / 503-842-4444

Airport

Tillamook Airport, 5005 Hwy 101 South / 503-842-7152
Portland International Airport, 7000 Northeast Airport Way / 503-460-4234

Auto Rental

Enterprise Rent-A-Car, 1623 West Burnside Street (Portland, OR) / 503-220-8200
Budget Rent-A-Car, 2033 Southwest 4th Avenue (Portland, OR) / 503-249-4555
Sears Car & Truck Rental, 2033 Southwest 4th Avenue (Portland, OR) / 503-249-6330
Hertz Rent-A-Car, 1009 Southwest 6th Avenue (Portland, OR) / 503-2249-5727

Auto Service

Mechtronics, 4360 Third Street / Tillamook, OR / 842-4361
Tillamook Mobile Home & RV Repair, 2150 Hadley Road North / 503-842-7702
Les Schwab Tire Center, 1220 North Main Street / 503-842-5543

For More Information

Tillamook Chamber of Commerce
3705 Hwy 101 North
Tillamook, OR 97141
503-842-7525

Oregon Game Fish

Rainbow Trout, *Oncorhynchus mykiss*

The rainbow's common name comes from a broad swath of crimson to pinkish-red usually seen along the midline of its flanks. The reddish band may be absent in lake dwellers, which are generally more silver in appearance. River rainbow coloration ranges from olive to greenish-blue on back, with white to silvery belly. They are marked with many irregularly shaped black spots on the head, back, and tail that extend below the midline.

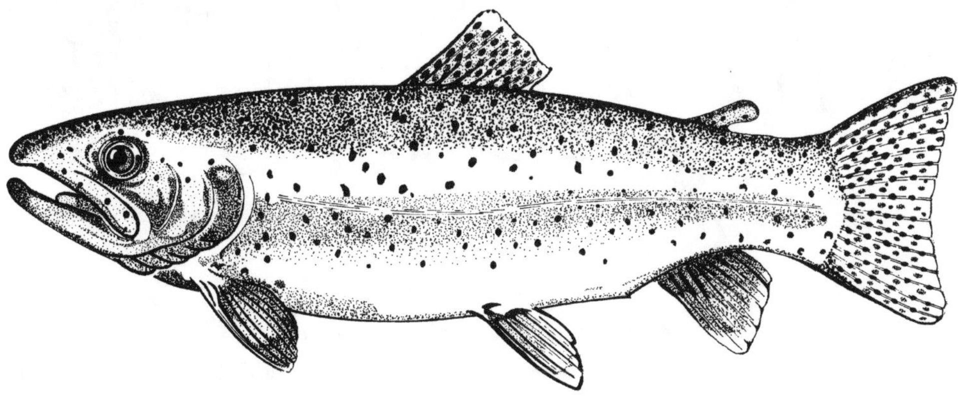

Oregon's redband or redside trout is basically a subspecies of rainbow trout that has a wider, deeper hued band and somewhat larger spots within the band. Long isolation in a certain area causes the slight variations in appearance, use of structure, and habit in subspecies.

Steelhead Trout, *Oncorhynchus mykiss* (Anadromous)

Steelhead adults are generally 18-40 inches in length. They have a profusion of small black spots on the upper head, back, dorsal fin, and tail. The upper head and back are greenish-brown. A reddish tinge on the gill plates and a red lateral stripe are darker the longer the fish is in fresh water. The inside of the mouth and the gum line are white. These are black on chinook salmon.

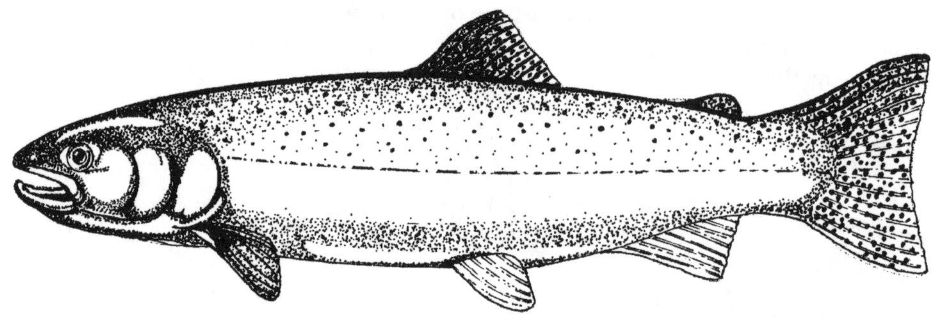

Brown Trout, *Salmo trutta*

The coloration of a brown trout is generally golden-brown with a dark-brown to greenish-brown back. The sides and belly range from light brown to lemon-yellow. There are well-spaced large black or brown spots mixed with a few red spots on the sides with light blue-gray halos. The adipose fin usually has an orange border. There are very few or no spots on the squarish tail. The brown was introduced to the United States from Europe in the 1800s.

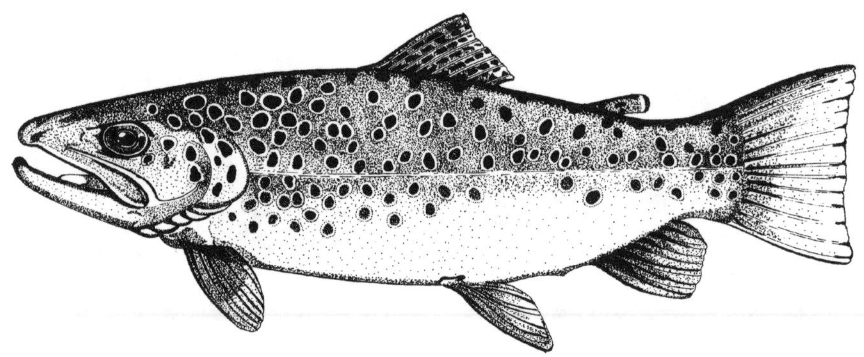

Brook Trout, *Salvelinus fontinalis*

The most distinctive markings on a brook trout are the white and black edges on the front of the lower fins, the wavy or worm-like markings on the back, and scattered red spots surrounded by a blue halo on the flanks. Brook trout are dark green or blue-black on the back to white on the belly. The belly and lower fins turn brilliant red on spawning males in the fall. The tail is square. Brook trout were introduced in the West in the 1880s.

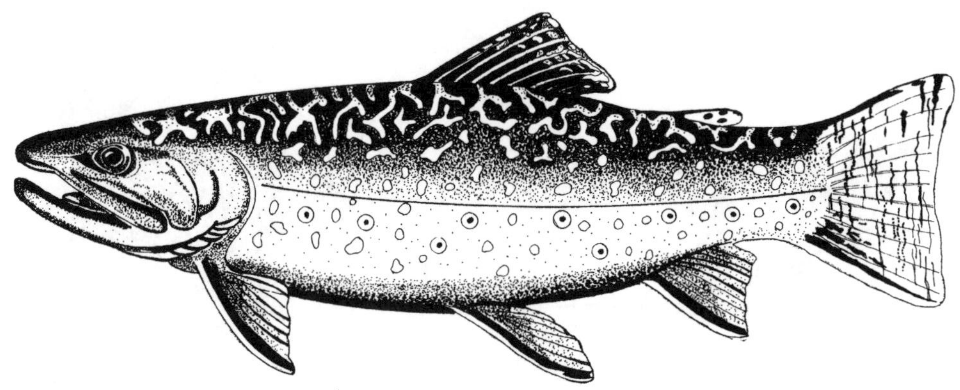

Bull Trout, *Salvelinus confluentus*

Bull trout are olive green to brown above and on the sides with shading to white on the belly. They lack the worm-like markings seen on brook trout, and the white border on the fins is less distinct. There are no spots on the dorsal fin. There are yellow spots on the upper body and red or orange spots on the flanks, but no blue halos around spots like in brook trout. The tail is square. Bull trout are a native species.

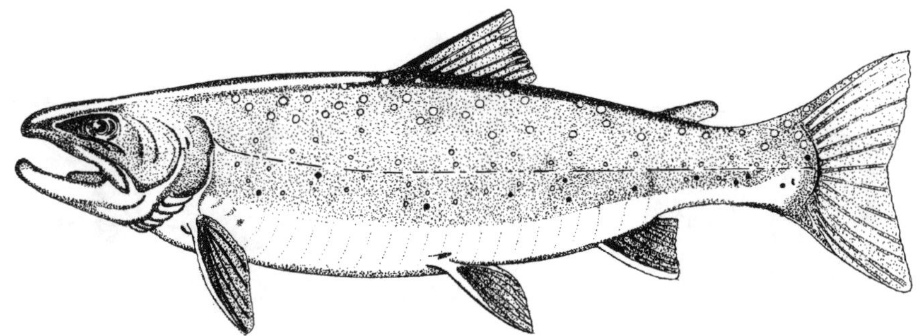

Westslope Cutthroat Trout, *Oncorhynchus clarki lewisi*

The coloration of a westslope cutthroat is richer than a Yellowstone cutthroat's, with many small, irregularly shaped black spots across the back, concentrating on the tail and rarely extending below the midline. The westslope variety is generally steel-gray on the flanks with an olive back and a white belly. Gill-plates are dusky-red and a pale-crimson swath extends along the flanks. The belly may be bright red during spring spawning season. An oval parr mark is also seen along midline.

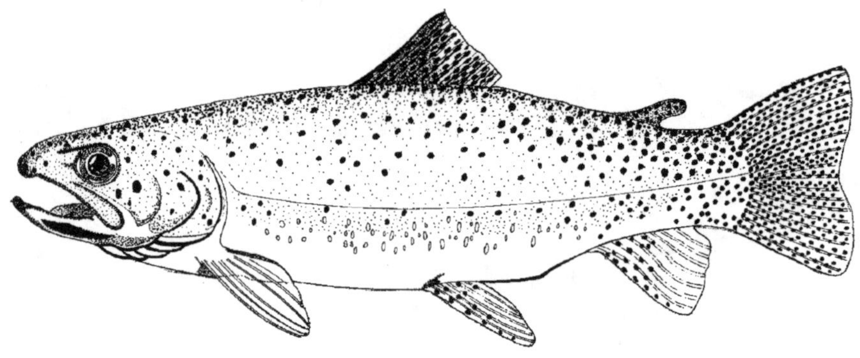

Sea-run (Harvest) Cutthroat, *Oncorhynchus clarki lewisi* (Anadromous)

Sea-run cutthroat are a silvery color and have more spots, especially on its side and belly, than their freshwater counterparts. The red markings under the lower jaw may be extremely faint. Sea-run cutthroat enter freshwater and feed all the way to their spawning grounds.

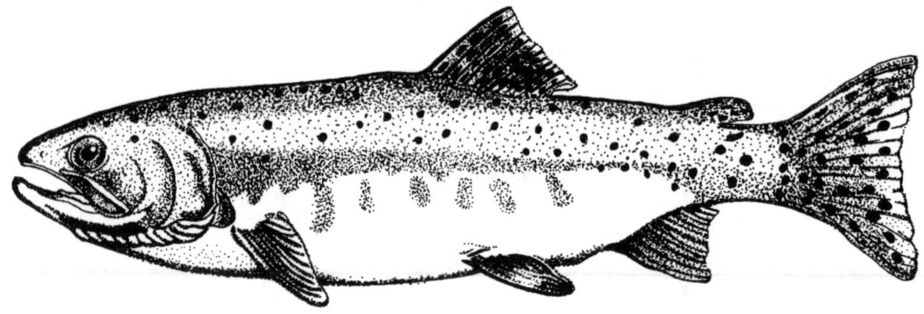

Largemouth Bass, *Micropterus salmoides*

Dark green on back and flanks, belly white. Dark, irregular horizontal band along flanks. Upper jaw extends behind eye. Deep notch in dorsal fin.

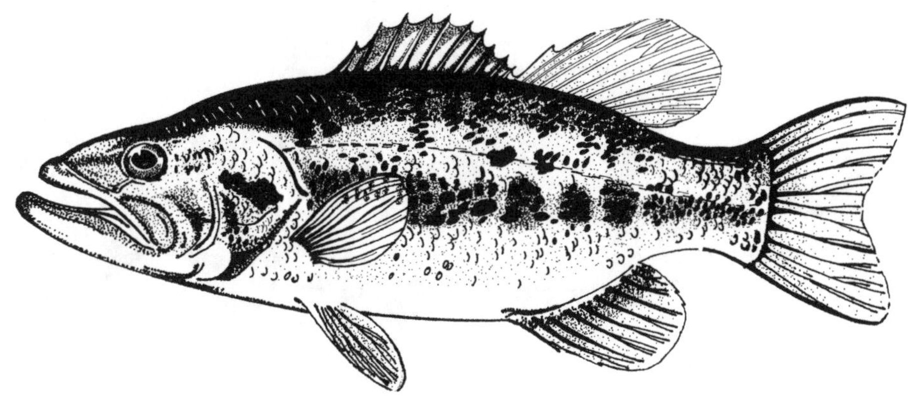

Smallmouth Bass, *Micropterus dolomieui*

Dark olive to brown on back, flanks bronze, belly white. Dark ventricle bands on flanks. Eyes reddish. Upper jaw ends in front of eye. Shallow notch in dorsal fin.

Chinook Salmon, *Oncorhynchus tshawytscha*

Also called king and tyee salmon, this is the largest of the Western salmons. They are a silvery color and have a white belly and dark-blue back. Small, dark spots are scattered on the upper half of the body, which become barely visible in freshwater.

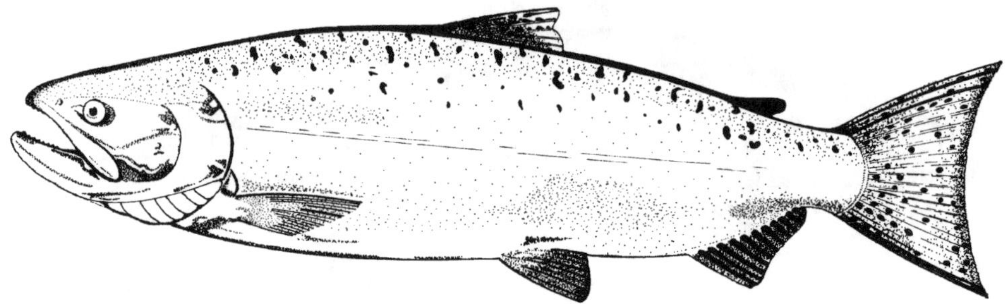

Kokanee Salmon, *Oncorhynchus nerka kennerlyi*

One of the smaller salmons, this is a landlocked form of sockeye salmon. The basic body color is platinum or silver, and the back can be blue or somewhat green in color. Because it is not a fully predacious species, it has a noticeably weaker jaw than other salmon.

Coho (Silver) Salmon, *Oncorhynchus kisutch*

Small black spots on the back and upper portion of the tail are found on this silver fish with a bluish back. Males in spawning season look quite reddish, which changes quickly after entering freshwater where it then becomes quite dark—almost black.

Catch and Release

Catch and release has become almost synonymous with the sport of fly angling. As anglers and the controlling agencies that oversee Oregon's fish stocks have learned, wild fish in a river are way more valuable than stocked fish on a dinner plate. I have heard of hatchery programs described as government subsidized feeding programs for anglers who won't stop filling limits after their own have been filled. In many cases this is true, but not always. Taking a fish on occasion is part of fishing, but taking a fish to have more fish than your buddy is not.

Oregon has many rural communities in which families have fished for generations. When wild fish numbers went down due to degradation in spawning grounds, be it from timber practices or cattle grazing, cries for hatchery programs were answered. Somehow, in most cases, fish numbers took precedence over fish genetics, and many wild stocks were lost while hatchery fish fared poorly.

The flip side of this coin are the waters in Oregon's highest population centers. Here, the sheer number of anglers taking fish was enough to hurt stocks of wild fish and send out cries for hatchery programs.

It seems as though things are coming full circle, with some attention being paid to restoring the magnificent fishing throughout Oregon, with a big emphasis on native fish. With this comes new regulations where catch and release is becoming mandatory. However, the only way this will help is if anglers learn to return fish without killing them in the process. Some will say it's too little, too late. But if Mother Nature is left alone long enough, anything can happen.

Releasing a fish is like anything else in flyfishing—doing it well takes time and experience. There are a few basic things to keep in mind when handling a fish.

- Always handle a fish with wet hands—this keeps the slime on them, which is what helps keep them warm in cold water. In winter, get your gloves wet or take them off, and bring extra gloves.
- Never let a fish flop on beaches or rocks. This could cause internal injuries that you won't see as the fish swims off, only to die a few hours later.
- Never squeeze a fish—this will also injure them internally. The more gently a fish is held, the less it will struggle. An open palm will work for trout almost every time once the fish has settled down.
- Use a net only if you are not comfortable handling a big fish. Nets fold fish and scrape off the slime that keeps them warm.
- Keep fish in the water as much as possible. New tools, such as the Ketchum Release, help keep fish in the water and allow anglers easy releases without handling the fish.
- If a fish has exhauted itself fighting your line, revive it before returning it to the water. A good rule is to revive a fish for at least as long as you fought it or until it swims off under its own power.

- The most important part of releasing fish really comes while fighting a fish. Don't wear a fish down. Use heavy enough tackle so that fish can be landed quickly, also learn how to fight a fish. Some anglers claim that a fish must be worn down before it can be landed. This is not true. A fish can be confused into the net while fighting it. An important technique to learn is how to rock a rod to keep a fish off balance. As the fish pulls one way, rock the rod in the opposite direction. As soon as the fish responds to the pressure, change direction again. Continue rocking the rod until the fish is close enough to land.

Catch and release is one of the few things that will ensure quality fishing in Oregon and will help preserve wild stocks. Learn from a friend or a guide how to be gentle with fish. Practice release techniques as you would practice casting or knot tying, and your personal fish mortality rates will almost become nonexistent.

Equipment Checklist and Travel Tips

When setting off on a fishing trip, make your travel list and check it twice. Nothing ruins a vacation more than forgetting to bring a key piece of equipment. Be paranoid; check off your rods, reels, and fishing vest a third time.

Come prepared for inclement weather and be physically fit to handle high-elevation trekking.

Summer Equipment Checklist

____ Rod selection depends on fish species. This could mean a 2-weight for an small fish in eastern Oregon or a 12-weight for coastal fishing. Take the appropriate rod or rods and make sure you take a spare anywhere in Oregon.

____ Fishing vest or fanny pack to hold tackle.

____ Forceps to remove hooks from fish; line nippers or fingernail clippers to trim leader tippets, trim flies.

____ Take a large selection of tapered leaders and tippet material geared to the fish species and a selection of sinking tips.

____ Fly floatant.

____ Nontoxic split shot.

____ Fishing net.

____ Stocking foot chest waders and wading shoes.

____ Wading staff if you plan to wade rocky, swift, or off-color waters.

____ Polarized sunglasses.

____ Stout fishing hat to protect neck and ears.

____ Lightweight rain jacket.

____ Wool or fleece sweater, windbreaker jacket, fingerless gloves for cool mornings and evenings.

____ Water bottle or canteen—take extra water when fishing in central or southeast Oregon. Dehydration can happen fast in these areas.

____ Sunscreen lotion.

____ Insect repellent.

____ Camera, extra film, and batteries.

Fall and Winter Equipment Checklist

In addition to the above, pack the following:

___ Neoprene chest waders.

___ Extra warm clothing to wear in layers.

___ Warm hat or wool ski cap that covers ears.

___ Neoprene gloves, wool gloves.

___ Heavy wool socks and polypropylene foot liners.

___ Get a windproof, waterproof lighter to start a fire.

___ High-energy snacks to munch on.

___ Full change of clothing in vehicle in case you get wet.

___ Parka and down vest for campwear, gloves or mittens.

Oregon Regulations

Learning the proper way to flyfish is something we all go through as novice fly anglers. The only thing harder than trying to flyfish effectively is learning how to keep up with fishing regulations.

Oregon is not alone when it comes to confusing fishing regulations, but the amount of migratory fish and the amount of people wanting to fill their freezers in Oregon has created a need for many regulations. Wading through these regulations is not easy, and calling the Oregon Department of Fish and Wildlife for answers can be a very trying experience. All I can suggest is to use the immediate sources—that is, guides and fly shops. These people are the best informed about restrictions in their areas and are always willing to help anglers clarify what special regulations are applicable on their favorite waters.

When you are off the beaten track in Oregon, especially on the coast, carry the regulations with you at all times. A detailed map will also help because many closures are indicated by such landmarks as bridges or hatcheries, etc. Knowing that you are fishing legally makes for a more relaxing experience.

Do your best to keep up with day-to-day changes, as well. Changes occur regularly due to the numbers of salmon and steelhead in Oregon's coastal waters as well as federal efforts to protect these often-threatened species. Wild fish are one of Oregon's biggest assets—keep them in the rivers and lakes and encourage others to do the same.

If you are doing your best to follow Oregon's regulations and find another angler who disregards the regulations, do the right thing by contacting the Oregon Department of Fish and Wildlife poacher hotline at 800-452-7888. Give as much information to them as possible, such as vehicle description and license number.

Oregon Department of Fish and Wildlife Regional Offices

ODFW Headquarters
2501 Southwest First Avenue
Portland, OR 97207
503-872-5268

Northwest Region
7118 Northeast Vandenburg Avenue
Adair Village
Corvallis, OR 97330-9446
541-757-4186

High Desert Region
61374 Parrell Road
Bend, OR 97702
541-388-6363 in Bend
541-573-6582 in Hines

Columbia Region
17330 Southeast Evelyn Street
Clackamas, OR 97015
503-657-2000

Southwest Region
4192 North Umpqua Highway
Roseburg, OR 97470
541-440-3353

Northeast Region
107 – 20th Street
LaGrande, OR 97850

Marine Program
2040 Southeast Marine Science Drive
Newport, OR 97365
541-867-4741

Oregon Fly Shops

Ashland
Ashland Outdoor Store
37 Third Street
Ashland, OR 97520
541-488-1202

Astoria
Salmon Republic
3292 Leif Erickson Drive, Lower Level
Astoria, OR 97103
503-325-7587

Bend
The Fly Box
1293 Northeast 3rd Street
Bend, OR 97701
541-388-3330

The Patient Angler
55 Northwest Wall Street, Bldg B, Suite 1
Bend, OR 97701
541-389-6208

Deschutes River Outfitters
61115 South Hwy 97
Bend, OR 97702
541-388-8191

Chiloquin
Williamson River Anglers
Junction Hwys 97 and 62
Chiloquin, OR 97624
541-783-2677

Corvallis
The Scarlet Ibis
905 Northwest Kings Boulevard
Corvallis, OR 97330
541-754-1544

Enterprise
The Wallowa Outdoor Store
110 South River Road
Enterprise, OR 97828
541-426-3493

Eugene
The Caddis Fly
168 West 6th Avenue
Eugene, OR 97401
541-342-7005

Home Waters Fly Fishing
444 West 3rd Avenue
Eugene, OR 97401
541-342-6691

Forest Grove
TK Fly Supply, Inc.
2635 Pacific Avenue
Forest Grove, OR 97116
503-359-1325

Gresham
Northwest Flyfishing Outfitters
17302 Northeast Halsey Street
Gresham, OR 97230
503-252-1529
888-292-1137
www.nwffo@europa.com

Hines
Kiger Creek Fly Shop
120 Northwest Circle Drive
Hines, OR 97738
541-573-1329

Hood River
Gorge Fly Shop
201 Oak Street
Hood River, OR 97031
541-386-6977

Idleyld
Blue Heron
109 Hargis Lane
Idleyld, OR 97447
541-496-0448

Joseph
Joseph Fly Shoppe
203 North Main
Joseph, OR 97846
541-432-4343
www.eoni.com/~flyshop

Klamath Falls
Trophy Waters Flyfishing Shop
800 Klamath Avenue
Klamath Falls, OR 97601
541-850-0717

LaGrande
Four Seasons Fly Shoppe
10210 Wallowa Lake Highway
LaGrande, OR 97850
541-963-8420

Maupin
Deschutes Canyon Fly Shop
599 South Hwy 97
Maupin, OR 97037
541-395-2565

Medford
McKenzie Outfitters
1340 Biddle Road
Medford, OR 97504
54-1773-5145

Merlin
Silver Sedge Fly Shoppe
325 Galice Road
Merlin, OR 97532-9703
541-476-2456

Oregon City
Fisherman's Marine Supply
1900 Southeast McLoughlin #60
Oregon City Shopping Center
Oregon City, OR 97545
503-557-3313

Portland
Countrysport
126 Southwest 1st Avenue
Portland, OR 97205
503-221-4545
www.csport.com

Fisherman's Marine Supply
1120 North Hayden Meadows Drive
Portland, OR 97217
503-283-0044

Prineville
Fin N Feather Fly Shop
785 West 3rd
Prineville, OR 97754
541-447-8691

Salem
Creekside Fly Shop
345 High Street Southeast
Salem, OR 97301
503-588-1768
www.viser/~flyfish

Fly Country Outfitters
3400 State Street, Suite G704
Salem, OR 97301
503-585-4898
www.flycountry.com

Valley Fly Fisher
153 Alice Avenue South
Salem, OR 97302
503-375-3721
www.valfly@open.org

Sisters
The Fly Fisher's Place
151 West Main
Sisters, OR 97759
541-549-3474

Sunriver
The Hook
Sunriver Village Mall, Bldg 21
Sunriver, OR 97707
541-593-2358
www.hookfish.com

Sunriver Fly Shop
#1 Venture Lane
Sunriver Business Park
Sunriver, OR 97707
541-593-8814
www.transport.com/~flyshop

Tigard
Kaufmann's Streamborn
8861 Southwest Commercial
Tigard, OR 97223
503-639-7004
www.kman.com

Welches
The Fly Fishing Shop
68248 East Hwy 26
Hoodland Park Plaza
Welches, OR 97067
503-622-4607
www.teleport.com/~flyfish

Troutdale
Stewart's Fly Shop
23830 Northest Halsey
Troutdale, OR 97060
503-666-2471

Yachats
Dublin House
251 West 7th Avenue
Yachats, OR 97498
541-547-3200

Index

S

T

U

V

W

Z